THE

LONG

WAR

AGAINST

GOD

This book is lovingly dedicated

to my youngest son,

Dr. Andrew H. Morris,

(1949–1989),

a faithful soldier

and casualty

in the long war.

Acknowledgments

I wish to especially thank Dr. David Jeremiah, president of Christian Heritage College, pastor of Scott Memorial Baptist Church (El Cajon, California), and well-known radio and conference speaker, for reading the manuscript and writing the foreword.

In addition, a number of key creationist scholars have reviewed the manuscript and made many helpful suggestions, which I appreciate very much. These include the following:

L. Russell Bush III, Th.D., Vice President for Academic Affairs, Southeastern Baptist Theological Seminary, Wake Forest, North Carolina

Kenneth B. Cumming, Ph.D., Dean of the Graduate School, Institute for Creation Research

John D. Morris, Ph.D., Administrative Vice President, Institute for Creation Research

Ker C. Thompson, Ph.D., Head of Science Division, Bryan College, Dayton, Tennessee

Richard B. Bliss, Ed.D., Head of Curriculum Division, Institute for Creation Research

John R. Meyer, Ph.D., Head of Science Division, Baptist Bible College, Clarks Summit, Pennsylvania

Finally, I thank Mrs. Mary Ruth Smith, who typed the manuscript.

Contents

Foreword

In my college and seminary days, I had seen the name Henry Morris on a number of books that were assigned for collateral reading, but I did not meet him until I moved to San Diego in the fall of 1981 to become the senior pastor of the Scott Memorial Baptist Church and the president of Christian Heritage College. At that time, the Institute for Creation Research shared an administrative office building with the church and the college, and my office was just a few doors from his.

Henry Morris was one of the first to invite me to lunch after my arrival. My initial impression of him was twofold: listening to him pray led me to believe that he was a godly man; listening to him talk convinced me that he was passionately committed to biblical and scientific creationism. Dr. Morris loved all of God's Word, but he has made a special study of the vital importance of the early chapters of Genesis, as well as other Scriptures dealing with creation. I had always been a thoroughgoing creationist, but I had never placed that truth at the center of the Christian message. I knew that Henry was sincere in his crusade, but I wondered if perhaps his perspective had been clouded by a narrow focus of study over the years.

Today I know better! My mind has been changed by the influence of Dr. Morris's books. I am now convinced that all significant problems of society are the children of an ignorant or indifferent attitude toward creationism.

And if there were any remaining doubts, this book has put them finally and emphatically to rest.

The Long War Against God is the most comprehensive treatment of a single important subject that I have ever seen. To read this book carefully is to receive a uniquely significant, in-depth perspective on the origin and operation of our world.

Many layers of error have been built on the faulty foundation of evolutionism. Humanism is the natural result. If God is not central in all our thinking, then man must be. Atheism is humanism's twin brother, and consistent evolutionists cannot logically believe in the personal God of the Bible, the God who is the Creator of all life. Abortion, infanticide, and euthanasia are logical behaviors for those who have so easily disposed of the image of God in the eternal soul of man. The concept of a resurrected body and eternal life is also a casualty of this evil philosophy.

The average person neither knows nor cares much about the error of evolution, and yet his or her life is constantly being influenced by it. Pornography, adultery, divorce, homosexuality, premarital sex, the destruction of the nuclear family — all are weeds that have grown from Satan's big lie about the universe. We are now on the verge of adopting full-fledged animalism in human practice — promiscuity, vandalism, hedonism, even incipient cannibalism. Even the Holocaust is "explained" by evolution. Hitler's extermination of the Jews grew out of his desire to speed up the evolutionary process.

When one views the carnage of the evolutionary dogma, it is hard to explain its wide acceptance and influence. How did belief in Darwinism become so widespread when it was developed mainly by an apostate divinity student (Darwin), a lawyer (Lyell), an agriculturist (Hutton), a journalist (Chambers), and other non-scientists? Dr. Morris documents the fact that the idea of evolution did not originate with Darwin. Evolutionism is basic in ancient and modern ethnic religions and in all forms of pantheism. Naturalist Alfred Russel Wallace admitted that he received the basic tenets of the Darwinian form of this heresy while in an occult trance in a Malaysian jungle. It does not take a theologian to figure out the identity of the revealer. Satan and his evolutionary gospel hate God as the Creator, Christ as the Savior, and the Bible as the Word of God. Modern evolutionism is simply the continuation of Satan's long war against God.

I believe that this volume ought to be read by every pastor and educator in our Christian schools, and all Christians serious about their faith and the problems of society. I pray that it will serve to slow the advance of the cancerous doctrine of evolution.

The result of a lifetime of dedicated study, *The Long War Against God* is a classic presentation by my friend and fellow warrior.

— David Jeremiah, BS, ThM, DD

Introduction

This book is bound to be controversial, but I believe its message is urgently needed by the rising generation. The many crises and deadly dangers of our time can only grow worse if we do not recognize their basic cause. I believe we can show that this is nothing less than the long-continued rebellion of men and women against God.

The denial of God — rejecting the reality of supernatural creation and the Creator's sovereign rule of the world — has always been the root cause of every human problem. This evolutionary, humanistic, pantheistic — even atheistic — worldview has taken many different forms over the ages, varying with the time and culture, but it has always been there in one guise or another, to turn the minds and hearts of people away from their Maker. There has indeed been an age-long war against God. It has been going on from the beginning of time and will increase in intensity in these last days.

I have tried to document this theme as thoroughly as possible in a book of this size. Evolutionists of all stripes will surely oppose and ridicule my presentation, but that is to be expected, considering the very nature of the controversy. Nevertheless, the facts speak for themselves, and I believe that open-minded, open-hearted readers will be convinced.

If the theme is valid, as I strongly believe the facts of history and true science demonstrate, nothing can be more important than for men and women of the new generation to repudiate the old, tired evolutionary humanism of their teachers and other opinion makers of the establishment. It is imperative that they return in faith to the God who created them — the personal, omnipotent, loving, saving God of the Bible. Therefore, I hope each reader will patiently and carefully follow with me through the pages of this book, which represents the considered and firm conviction of almost 50 years of active study and participation in the conflict.

In the first three chapters, I have tried to document the pervasively harmful influence of evolutionism in the thought and life of the world for the century since Darwin. Next I have devoted two chapters to tracing the history of this warfare through all the ages of the world before Darwin. Then, in the final chapter, I have outlined the history of the battle *for* God and His plan, including His sure and final victory in the age to come.

The history of this long, long war is intensely fascinating in itself. But it is also tremendously important for a true understanding of the present world situation, as we make preparation for the climactic future that is almost upon us.

1

The Evolutionary Basis of Modern Thought

An unprecedented confusion is now permeating the modern world. Everything has seemingly been turned upside-down, and the older standards of right and wrong have been almost completely interchanged. Observe the symptoms: huge nuclear arsenals in the great nations, developing nuclear capabilities in many smaller nations, the imminent AIDS pandemic, chemical and biological weapons ready to be unleashed, the unknown dangers of genetic engineering looming ahead, the terrors and conflicts generated by world communism (not to mention Nazism, racism, imperialism, and other evil systems), the wide resurgence of paganism and occultism, the inexorable spread of the cancerous drug culture, giant crime syndicates in the capitalist nations, pan-Arabic aggression in the Islamic nations, and a worldwide breakdown of personal and governmental morality. It is no wonder that there is everywhere "upon the earth distress of nations, with perplexity . . ." (Luke 21:25). Surely the world has gone mad!

Ideas and theories usually have visible consequences. Effects have causes. I propose to show in this book that there is an underlying idea behind these consequences and that this idea, though it goes by many names — naturalism, materialism, etc. — is basically nothing else than the almost sacrosanct doctrine of evolution. Furthermore, this situation is nothing new, but indeed has been the underlying cause of most of the major problems of the world throughout human history. If this statement seems extreme, I can only ask you to defer judgment until you see the evidence.

I am not speaking here only of Darwinism, nor even of biological evolution in general, but of evolution as a total philosophy that purports to explain the origin and development of all things by natural properties and processes in a closed universe, one with no involvement by any external supernatural Creator. In this sense, evolutionism is essentially synonymous with naturalism or materialism, with the space-time-matter cosmos regarded as the ultimate reality out of which everything, from elementary particles to complex human beings, has evolved.

In arguing that evolutionary thinking is the root cause of the major harmful systems and practices in the world, I am not suggesting that any particular person who believes in evolution is therefore "evil" or immoral. The only issue is the evolutionary philosophy itself, not the people who believe it. I realize that many kind, sensitive people believe in evolution. The fact is, regardless of whether or not evolution has been misunderstood or misapplied, it really *has* been made the pseudo-scientific rationale for all kinds of evil doctrines and influences in the world. And people need to know this!

Most people regard evolution as merely a biological theory of no great consequence in their lives, having no idea of its tremendous importance as the philosophy underlying all the evils of the world. Even many Christians regard evolution as nothing more than God's method of creation, utterly ignoring its completely anti-biblical and even anti-theistic character.

In this chapter, however, I only want to show that evolutionary theory does indeed dominate modern thought in virtually every field — every discipline of study, every level of education, and every area of practice. This fact in itself indicates the tremendous responsibility that evolutionism must assume for present world conditions.

Evolution — the World's View

The fact that this globalistic view of evolution is held by the leading evolutionists themselves — the ones who know the most about their theory and its implications — should be (though it is not) well known by now. For instance, Sir Julian Huxley, grandson of Thomas Huxley (Darwin's "bulldog") and brother of Aldous Huxley (leading atheist philosopher and patriarch of the modern drug culture) and arguably the leading evolutionist of the 20th century, stress the ubiquitous influence of evolutionism in the following words:

The concept of evolution was soon extended into other than biological fields. Inorganic subjects such as the life-history of stars and the formation of the chemical elements on the one hand, and on the other hand subjects like linguistics, social anthropology, and comparative law and religion, began to be studied from an evolutionary angle, until today we are enabled to see evolution as a universal and all-pervading process.[1]

When he wrote these words, Sir Julian had already served as UNESCO's first director-general and had established its basic tone and philosophy, which served also to guide the United Nations organization itself during its formative years. In that connection, he wrote:

It is essential for UNESCO to adopt an evolutionary approach. . . . The general philosophy of UNESCO should, it seems, be a scientific world humanism, global in extent and evolutionary in background. . . . Thus the struggle for existence that underlies natural selection is increasingly replaced by conscious selection, a struggle between ideas and values in consciousness.[2]

That is, evolution was not only the basis for all explanation in the sciences and in past history, but should now also be the guide for future, *controlled* developments in human societies.

Perhaps next in importance to Huxley among 20th-century evolutionists was the geneticist Theodosius Dobzhansky, originally from the USSR, then later on the faculties at Columbia University, Stanford, Rockefeller Institute, and the University of California at Davis. He also stressed evolution as the complete worldview:

Evolution comprises all the stages of the development of the universe: the cosmic, biological, and human or cultural developments. Attempts to restrict the concept of evolution to biology are gratuitous. Life is a product of the evolution of inorganic nature, and man is a product of the evolution of life.[3]

---

1. J.R. Newman, editor, *What Is Science?* "Evolution and Genetics," by Julian Huxley (New York: Simon and Schuster, 1955), p. 272.
2. Julian Huxley, "A New World Vision," *The Humanist* 39 (March/April 1979): p. 35–36. This paper was originally written as Huxley's proposed framework for UNESCO, but was not released publicly until many years later. UNESCO is the acronym for the United Nations Educational, Scientific and Cultural Organization.
3. Theodosius Dobzhansky, "Changing Man," *Science* 155 (Jan. 27, 1967): p. 409.

Of almost equal importance to Huxley and Dobzhansky in the modern evolutionary scene is the Harvard scientist Ernst Mayr. With relation to the worldview nature of evolution, Mayr has written:

> Man's worldview today is dominated by the knowledge that the universe, the stars, the earth, and all living things have evolved through a long history that was not foreordained or programmed.[4]

> I am taking a new look at the Darwinian revolution of 1859, perhaps the most fundamental of all intellectual revolutions in the history of mankind. It not only eliminated man's anthropocentrism, but affected every metaphysical and ethical concept, if consistently applied.[5]

These three men (Huxley, Dobzhansky, and Mayr) dominated modern evolutionary thought through at least the first two-thirds of the 20th century. Along with George Gaylord Simpson, G. Ledyard Stebbins, and others (all of whom agreed with them on the ubiquitous application of naturalistic evolution in every field of thought), they developed the system known as neo-Darwinism, emphasizing gradual evolutionary changes in populations by chance mutations and natural selection. Although this particular system is currently under challenge by "punctuationism" or "revolutionary evolution," it has exerted profound influence on almost everyone for three generations, and is still the dominant view in most textbooks and curricula.

If the leaders of evolutionary thought have regarded evolution as their complete worldview, it is not surprising that this is also the dogma taught by their followers. Typical is the following summary by one of the nation's top ecologists, in a national Sigma Xi lecture:

> Most enlightened persons now accept as a fact that everything in the cosmos — from heavenly bodies to human beings — has developed and continues to develop through evolutionary processes. The great religions of the West have come to accept a historical view of creation. Evolutionary concepts are applied also to social institutions and to the arts. Indeed, most political parties, as well as schools of theology, sociology, history, or arts, teach these concepts and make them the basis of their doctrines.[6]

---

4. Ernst Mayr, "Evolution," *Scientific American* 239 (Sept. 1978): p. 47.
5. Ernst Mayr, "The Nature of the Darwinian Revolution," *Science* 176 (June 2, 1972): p. 981.
6. Rene Dubos, "Humanistic Biology," *American Scientist* 53 (March 1965): p. 6.

That such ideas are not limited to biologists is made clear in the following statement from the former head of physics at MIT, also then president of the American Academy of Arts and Sciences:

> The evolutionary history of the world, from the "big bang" to the present universe, is a series of gradual steps from the simple to the complicated, from the unordered to the organized, from the formless gas of elementary particles to the morphic atoms and molecules and further to the still more structured liquids and solids, and finally to the sophisticated living organisms.[7]

George Wald, Nobel Prize winner at Harvard, specializing in bio-optics, stresses that evolution has occurred even among the most elementary particles of the cosmos:

> Back of the spontaneous generation of life under other conditions than now obtain upon this planet, there occurred a spontaneous generation of elements of the kind that still goes on in the stars; and back of that I suppose a spontaneous generation of elementary particles under circumstances still to be fathomed, that ended in giving them the properties that alone make possible the universe we know.[8]

Modern astrophysicists, in fact, are currently speculating that the universe itself spontaneously evolved out of nothing!

> In this picture, the universe came into existence as a fluctuation in the quantum-mechanical vacuum. Such a hypothesis leads to a view of creation in which the entire universe is an accident. In Tryon's words, "Our universe is simply one of those things which happen from time to time."[9]

There is obviously no need for God in any portion of this comprehensive modern evolutionary scenario. The evolutionists quoted above are all writing within either an atheistic or pantheistic frame of reference and apparently reflecting their own beliefs. If everything from the universe itself to man has evolved by natural processes from primeval chaos (or perhaps

---

7. Victor F. Weisskopf, "The Frontiers and Limits of Science," *American Scientist* 65 (July–Aug. 1977): p. 409.
8. George Wald, "Fitness in the Universe: Choices and Necessities," *Origins of Life* 5 (1974): p. 26.
9. James Trefil, "The Accidental Universe," *Science Digest* 92 (June 1984): p. 101.

nothingness!) into their present complex forms and relationships, God becomes quite redundant.

There are a number of evolutionists, of course, who are theists, rather than atheists or pantheists. Theistic evolutionists are almost always followers, rather than leaders, of evolutionary thought, but they also acknowledge evolution as basic in all fields. One of these is Stanley Beck, an entomologist at the University of Wisconsin, and faculty adviser to a religious group at that institution. He says:

> Twentieth century biology rests on a foundation of evolutionary concepts. . . . The evolutionary basis is also apparent in peripheral independent fields such as chemistry, geology, physics, and astronomy. No central scientific concept is more firmly established in our thinking, our methods, and our interpretations than that of evolution.[10]

Similarly, a professor of history at Calvin College (a denominational college sponsored by the Christian Reformed Church) and himself a witness for the evolution side at the 1981 Arkansas creation law trial, admits:

> In any case, creation scientists are correct in perceiving that in modern culture "evolution" often involves far more than biology. The basic ideologies of the civilization, including its entire moral structure, are at issue. Evolution is sometimes the key mythological element in a philosophy that functions as a virtual religion.[11]

Probably the most famous of all theistic evolutionists, an active paleontologist as well as a Roman Catholic priest, was Pierre Teilhard de Chardin. To him, evolution was not only a worldview; it was almost synonymous with God, as is evident from the following quotation:

> ✳ [Evolution] is a general postulate to which all theories, all hypotheses, all systems must henceforward bow and which they must satisfy in order to be thinkable and true. Evolution is a light which illuminates all facts, a trajectory which all lines of thought must follow.[12]

---

10. Stanley D. Beck, "Natural Science and Creationist Theology" *Bioscience* 32 (Oct. 1982): p. 738.

11. George M. Marsden, "Creation Versus Evolution: No Middle Ground," *Nature* 305 (Oct. 13, 1983): p. 574.

12. Pierre Teilhard de Chardin, as cited by Francisco Ayala in " 'Nothing in Biology Makes Sense Except in the Light of Evolution': Theodosius Dobzhansky, 1900–1975," *Journal of Heredity* 68, no. 3 (1977): p. 3. This eulogy to Dobzhansky (who himself was a pantheist even though a church member at his death) noted that spiritually he was a de Chardin disciple.

Teilhard's voluminous writings in this vein are important not so much for their quasi-scientific and philosophical content (he has even been implicated by a number of his fellow evolutionists as one of the perpetrators of the infamous Piltdown Man hoax!) as for the tremendous number of his followers, especially in the so-called New Age movement. He was on excellent terms with many leading evolutionary scientists during the first half of the 20th century and has exerted a profound influence on modern thought.

In fact, it would be hard to find any real leaders in modern evolutionary thought who did not and do not regard evolution as their worldview — indeed, to all intents and purposes, their "religion" and philosophy of life and meaning. It would easily be possible to produce much more documentation to this effect, but the above should suffice to establish the point beyond question. Evolution is not merely a biological theory of little significance. It is a worldview — *the* worldview diametrically opposing the Christian worldview. Therefore, Christians ignore it or compromise with it at great peril! ✳

Evolution and the Science of Life

The discussion in the foregoing section has necessarily been rather general. Let us now examine a little more fully the direct impact of evolutionary thinking in various major disciplines. Interestingly enough, the actual impact of evolutionary thinking has been felt more in the social sciences and humanities, but this is largely because of the widely promoted belief that evolution has been "proven" by the natural sciences. The fact is, however, that although the natural sciences are commonly interpreted in an evolutionary framework, no one has ever observed real evolution take place, not even in any of the life sciences, let alone the earth sciences or the physical sciences. True science is supposed to be observable, measurable, and repeatable. Evolution, however, even if it were true, is too slow to observe or measure and has consisted of unique, non-repeatable events of the past. It is therefore outside the scope of genuine science and has certainly not been *proven* by science.

Nevertheless, all of these sciences *assume* evolution and diligently seek to interpret all their data in an evolutionary context. This is especially the case in the biological sciences. Ever since Darwin, it has been argued that "nothing in biology makes sense except in the light of evolution," as Dobzhansky frequently was quoted as saying. It is almost funny to read and hear evolutionary biologists repeating their litany: "We know evolution is true, even though we don't know how it works, and have never seen it happen!"

Almost four decades ago, for example, the University of California geneticist Richard Goldschmidt, now recognized as a chief forerunner of modern punctuationism, was saying:

> Evolution of the animal and plant world is considered by all those entitled to judgment to be a fact for which no further proof is needed. But in spite of nearly a century of work and discussion there is still no unanimity in regard to the details of the means of evolution.[13]

The last sentence in this quote is a classic understatement. Now, with a new generation of biologists still researching evolutionary mechanisms, there is far less unanimity than at any time since Darwin on not just the details but the entire question of mechanism. One biologist observed, "Today we are less confident and the whole subject is in the most exciting ferment. Evolution is . . . nagged from within by the troubling complexities of genetic and developmental mechanisms and new questions about the central mystery — speciation itself."[14]

The above evaluation was written by a professor of biology and dean of the graduate school at Yale University. If the formation of new species is still the central mystery of biology 130 years after Darwin's famous book *The Origin of Species* supposedly had solved the problem, one wonders why evolutionary biologists still persist in believing in evolution at all. Where is the evidence?

Well, today's leading evolutionary spokesman, Dr. Stephen Jay Gould, of Harvard University, has given us the answer: "Indeed, to make the statement even stronger, imperfections are the primary proofs that evolution has occurred, since optimal designs erase all signposts of history."[15] This is an amazing admission. Dr. Gould is the chief advocate of "punctuated equilibrium," the modern form of evolutionary saltationism, the notion that new species form suddenly rather than gradually. Gould is bitterly resentful of creationists, frequently calling them "yahoos" and other choice terms of ridicule, insisting that evolution is a proven fact of science that no rational person should question.

Yet the best evidence he can offer is that of *imperfections*! The fact that there are some structures in animals that Gould considers "imperfect," such as the panda's thumb, is supposed to prove that God could not have designed

13. R.B. Goldschmidt, "Evolution, as Viewed by One Geneticist," *American Scientist* 40 (Jan. 1952): p. 84.

14. Keith S. Thomson, "The Meanings of Evolution," *American Scientist* 70 (Sept./Oct. 1982): p. 529.

15. Stephen J. Gould, "The Panda's Thumb of Technology," *Natural History* 96 (Jan. 1987): p. 14.

them — thus, there is no God, and evolution is true! This is arrogant, since Gould merely assumes he knows all about the purpose of these structures. It is almost irrelevant, since the fact that an originally perfect structure deteriorates with time says nothing at all about how it was produced in the first place.

Be that as it may, there is no doubt that the biological sciences today are almost everywhere interpreted and taught in an evolutionary context. There is no scientific proof that vertically upward evolution occurs today, has even occurred in the past, or is even possible at all, yet it is widely promoted as a proven fact.

The Origin and History of the Earth

The same is true in the earth sciences, especially those bearing on history (geology, archaeology, paleontology, etc.). In spite of the fact that real history, documented by written records, covers only the past few thousand years (since the first dynasty of Egypt, say, or the first king lists in Sumeria), evolutionists inevitably allege that the earth is several billion years old (the current "official" figure is 4.6 billion) and that the early hominids began to evolve from their nonhuman ancestors several million years ago. All such age estimates, of course, have to be based on a number of unprovable assumptions, since actual records have existed only since the invention of the calendar and some form of written language.

The assumptions that are necessary in formulating an earth history are nicely summarized in the following classical geology textbook treatment: "Lyell [that is, Charles Lyell, the father of historical geology] was imbued with a conviction that present causes solely have operated in the past. More than that, he insisted that they have always acted at the same rate."[16]

That is the famous Lyellian principle of *uniformitarianism* ("the present is the key to the past"). It is nothing but the old philosophy of naturalism, as applied to the study of earth history. Uniformitarianism by itself, however, does not provide a *history*, but only the naturalistic framework within which that history is assumed to have taken place. Since the types of rocks, minerals in the rocks, structural features of the rocks, and all other physical features are the same in every geological "age," uniformitarianism must be combined with some other principle if the earth sciences are to give a coherent record of chronology and development. For example: "Historic geology relies chiefly on paleontology, the study of fossil organisms. . . . The geologist utilizes knowledge of organic evolution, as preserved in the fossil record, to identify and correlate the lithic records of ancient time."[17]

---

16. O.D. von Engeln and K.E. Caster, *Geology* (New York: McGraw-Hill, 1952), p. 25.
17. Ibid., p. 423.

Thus, naturalistic evolution, or evolutionary uniformitarianism, provides the basic interpretive framework for the earth sciences as well as the life sciences. The key is the fossil record, which supposedly provides the means of identifying the geological ages when the sedimentary rocks containing them were first laid down. That this procedure has not changed since the above was written (or, for that matter, since the days of Lyell and Darwin) is confirmed by the following:

> No paleontologist worthy of the name would ever date his fossils by the strata in which they are found. . . . Ever since William Smith at the beginning of the 19th century, fossils have been and still are the best and most accurate method of dating and correlating the rocks in which they occur.[18]

Note also the following affirmation of this principle by two outstanding geologists, one in continental Europe, one in the United States:

> The only chronometric scale applicable in geologic history for the stratigraphic classification of rocks and for dating geologic events exactly is furnished by the fossils. Owing to the irreversibility of evolution, they offer an unambiguous time-scale for relative age determinations and for worldwide correlations of rocks.[19]

> Merely in their role as distinctive rock constituents, fossils have furnished, through their record of the evolution of life on this planet, an amazingly effective key to the relative positioning of strata in widely separated regions and from continent to continent.[20]

This is the fundamental principle upon which modern evolutionary geology still rests.

Such authorities have made it very clear that the supposed record of evolution in the fossil remains of plants and animals, all interpreted in terms of naturalistic formation by normal sedimentary processes of the rocks containing

---

18. Derek Ager, "Fossil Frustrations," *New Scientist* 100 (Nov. 10, 1983): p. 425. Dr. Ager, head of the geology department at Swansea University, Wales, is a past president of the British Geological Association.
19. O.H. Schindewolf, "Comments on Some Stratigraphic Terms," *American Journal of Science* 255 (June 1957): p. 394. Schindewolf, Europe's foremost paleontologist, long anticipated modern punctuationism in paleontology.
20. Hollis D. Hedberg, "The Stratigraphic Panorama," *Bulletin of the Geological Society of America* 72 (April 1961): p. 499. This was Dr. Hedberg's presidential address at the society's annual meeting.

them, is the basic premise in the study of the earth sciences, particularly in relation to earth history. Just as in biology, however, evolution and uniformity have simply been *assumed*, not proved! The only real evidences we have of the past go back only the few thousand years of so-called recorded history.

Furthermore, even though the fossil record is interpreted in terms of evolution, there is no evidence of evolution in the fossils themselves, for they all fit neatly into the families, orders, phyla, and other categories of the same classification system used for present-day plants and animals, and *these* are not evolving! Of course, there are many extinctions revealed in the fossils (e.g., the dinosaurs), but extinction is the polar opposite of evolution! In fact, there have been thousands of species' extinctions during human history, but no new species have evolved. Evolution seems to be going in the wrong direction!

The most significant feature about the fossil record is the utter absence of any true evolutionary transitional forms. Leading paleontologist S. M. Stanley, of John Hopkins, writes, "The known fossil record fails to document a single example of phyletic evolution accomplishing a major morphological transition."[21] He adds elsewhere: "Evolution happens rapidly in small, localized populations, so we're not likely to see it in the fossil record."[22]

Remember also, as Ager has pointed out, that the fossils are not "dated" by the rock strata where they are found. Instead, the rocks are dated by the fossils, on the basis of the stage of evolution that they supposedly represent. Thus, without the unproved assumption of evolution, there is not any objective basis for the whole system of geological ages.

In fact, the uniformitarian premise, which — along with evolution — has guided historical interpretations in the earth sciences ever since Lyell and Darwin, is itself now being rejected by modern geologists.

> Furthermore, much of Lyell's uniformitarianism, specifically his ideas on identity of ancient and modern causes, gradualism, and constancy of rate, has been explicitly refuted by the definitive modern sources as well as by an overwhelming preponderance of evidence that, as substantive theories, his ideas on these matters were simply wrong.[23]

---

21. Steven M. Stanley, *Macroevolution: Pattern and Process* (San Francisco, CA: W.M. Freeman, 1979), p. 39.
22. Steven M. Stanley, "Resetting the Evolutionary Timetable," Interview by Neil A. Campbell, *Bioscience* 36 (Dec. 1986): p. 725.
23. James H. Shea, "Twelve Fallacies of Uniformitarianism," *Geology* 10 (Sept. 1982): p. 456. Dr. Shea is editor of the *Journal of Geological Education.*

In fact, Derek Ager and many other "neo-catastrophist" geologists are now arguing that every geologic formation was produced rapidly and catastrophically, rather than gradually and uniformly. Ager observes, "In other words, the history of any one part of the earth, like the life of a soldier, consists of long periods of boredom and short periods of terror."[24]

In summary, the earth sciences no less than the life sciences are interpreted and taught everywhere today on the premise of evolution and uniformity. Nevertheless, the real scientific evidence in both domains of science is firmly opposed to evolution. The study of biology shows no evidence whatever of evolution occurring in the present, and the study of geology/paleontology shows no evidence that it ever occurred in the past. Yet most scientists in these fields continue their dogmatic faith in the alleged fact of evolution.

Evolution and the Physical Sciences

Not to be outdone, evolutionists in the physical sciences (especially physics, chemistry, and astronomy) have developed even more fantastic explanations for the evolution of the universe, the elements, the stellar heavens, complex molecules, and finally life. The actual evidences supporting these evolutionary speculations, however, are even more illusory than those supporting biological evolution, since they are based on the most indirect sorts of observations.

As noted in the previous section, the present consensus suggests that the entire cosmos suddenly evolved out of nothing, first as an infinitesimal particle of space/time, which proceeded rapidly through an inflationary stage, then through an incredibly hot "big bang," followed by universal expansion into its present form.

In the first moments of the big bang, so the story goes, all the elementary particles of matter evolved, then the simplest of the chemical elements, hydrogen. The energy of the primeval explosion was also able to develop helium, but the heavier elements had to await the evolution of the first stars and their disintegration into supernova explosions. In the meantime, many stars and galaxies somehow evolved from the expanding hydrogen, accumulating by unknown evolutionary pressure into galactic clusters.

The heavier elements generated from supernovas may evolve into planetary systems (although the planets of our own solar system are the only ones actually observed in the universe), and then the complex molecules evolving on some planets may somehow evolve into living cells (but no life forms have yet been observed anywhere in the universe except on earth).

---

24. Derek Ager, *The Nature of the Stratigraphical Record* (New York: John Wiley, 1981), p. 106–107.

This remarkable pre-biological evolutionary scenario is actually believed in varying degrees by great numbers of PhD astronomers, biochemists, mathematical physicists, and others in the physical sciences. Its "evidence," however, is entirely mathematical, since none of these evolutionary stages have ever been observed, nor could they ever be reproduced in the laboratory.

As far as the origin from non-living chemicals of the first form of life is concerned, the idea that this could have happened by natural processes is completely fanciful, even though schoolchildren everywhere are taught that this happened in the primeval oceanic soup about four billion years ago. The fascinating comments of Sir Fred Hoyle are relevant in this connection:

> I don't know how long it is going to be before astronomers generally recognize that the combinatorial arrangement of not even one among the many thousands of biopolymers on which life depends could have been arrived at by natural processes here on the earth. Astronomers will have a little difficulty at understanding this because they will be assured by biologists that it is not so, the biologists having been assured in their turn by others that it is not so. The "others" are a group of persons who believe, quite openly, in mathematical miracles. They advocate the belief that tucked away in nature, outside of normal physics, there is a law which performs miracles (provided the miracles are in the aid of biology). This curious situation sits oddly on a profession that for long has been dedicated to coming up with logical explanations of biblical miracles. . . . It is quite otherwise, however, with the modern mathematical miracle workers, who are always to be found living in the twilight fringes of thermodynamics.[25]

Sir Fred's reference to thermodynamics is very appropriate. Though every stage of the prebiotic evolutionary scenario goes squarely against the second law of thermodynamics, the assumption is that somehow a "naturalistic miracle" makes this all right. And if miracles are necessary to generate the biopolymers on which life depends, try to comprehend the mathematical marvels by which our modern generation of mathematical astrophysicists

---

25. Fred Hoyle, "The Big Bang in Astronomy," *New Scientist* 92 (Nov. 19, 1981): p. 526. Sir Fred has long been recognized as one of the world's top mathematical astrophysicists, author of many books and originator of the once-revered but now abandoned steady state theory of the origin of the universe. An original and unintimidated thinker, he has in recent years incurred the wrath of the scientific establishment because of an increasingly anti-evolutionary attitude.

can create a universe out of nothing, and then stars and galactic clusters and planets out of hydrogen.

As long as people have been observing the stars, no one has ever seen a star evolve from anything. The stars have always looked exactly as they do now, except for the occasional nova or supernova, which are stars disintegrating — not evolving. Yet these modern miracle workers have developed an extremely complex scheme of nuclear and cosmic evolution, comprehensible only to specialists but imposed on the intimidated public as "scientific fact."

In an important review article, Steven Wienberg, a leading astrophysicist, makes a number of important admissions to this effect:

> Among the most important relics are the structures we see in the sky: many stars are grouped into clusters, the clusters themselves along with loose stars like our sun are grouped into galaxies, and the galaxies themselves are grouped into clusters of galaxies. A second great disappointment of astrophysics has been that we still do not have a clear and detailed understanding of how these structures were formed. We do not even know whether the smaller structures formed first and then coalesced into the larger ones, or whether the larger structures formed first and then broke up into smaller ones. ... It is also a bit disturbing that all these estimates of the ages and compositions of the stars rest on elaborate calculations of what is going on inside them, but all that we observe is that light emitted from their surfaces.[26]

The contradiction between the concept of an evolving universe and the famous second law of thermodynamics — which, along with the first law (mass-energy conservation), constitute the best-proved and most universal laws of science — is summarized in these words by the famous British astronomer Paul Davies:

> For the past century, scientists have discussed the question of cosmological order in the context of the laws of thermodynamics. According to the second law, the Universe is inexorably degenerating, sliding irreversibly towards a state of maximum entropy, or chaos. Yet the facts flatly contradict this image of a dying Universe. Far from sliding *towards* a featureless state, the Universe is progressing *from* featurelessness to states of greater organization and complexity.

---

26. Steven Weinberg, "Origins," *Science* 230 (Oct. 4, 1985): p. 16.

This cosmic progress defines a global arrow of time that points the opposite way to the thermodynamic arrow.[27]

Apparently Davies himself does not believe in a personal God, but he has used the term *miracle* to describe the unknown factors that presumably have overcome the second law to produce increased complexity. He speaks of the " 'miracle' of life,"[28] for example, and the "miracle of the big bang."[29] His explanation of these phenomena is neither that of supernatural creation nor the standard equivocations of the scientific establishment. Like a number of other New Age scientists, he tries to think in terms of complex systems, networks, and non-linear periodicities that somehow might generate order out of chaos.

In recent years, in fact, a number of scientists in various fields have tried to develop theories that might explain how to overcome the second law of thermodynamics and bring higher complexity out of lower. These theories are highly speculative, however, and do not really solve any of the problems of evolution at all, either at the level of the primeval big bang or at that of forming more complex species out of lower. So far as all scientific *observations* go, the second law is still universal in its effects, and the only way a more complex system of any kind can be produced is by an input of specific creative intelligence and directed energy, never by mere chaotically pulsating fields, as modern "self-organization" theoreticians seem to think.

Davies suggests, for example, that a showpiece of self-organization is "the astonishing ability of an embryo to develop from a single strand of DNA, via an exquisitely well-orchestrated sequence of formative steps, into an exceedingly complex organism."[30]

How is it that such a brilliant scientist as Davies can believe that this marvelous process is an example of chaos generating order? Does he really think that the intricately complex genetic code, as well as the other complex energy-directing programs in the simplest living cell, somehow organized themselves in the primeval chaos of chemical elements to produce the first DNA molecule and all the necessary accessories for the first and simplest living system?

---

27. Paul Davies, "The Creative Cosmos," *New Scientist* 116 (Dec. 17, 1987): p. 41–42. Dr. Davies is professor of theoretical physics at the University of Newcastle upon Tyne.
28. Ibid., p. 44.
29. Paul Davies, "Universe in Reverse: Can Time Run Backwards?" *Second Look* (Sept. 1979): p. 27.
30. Davies, "The Creative Cosmos," p. 42.

The same types of questions apply to every other supposed evolutionary step in pre-biological evolution — and also in biological evolution, for that matter. The universe is *not* "progressing from featurelessness to states of greater organization and complexity," as Davies and other evolutionary mathematicians fantasize. It is running down — *at every observable level* — toward chaos, as stipulated by the scientific laws of thermodynamics. Local and temporary increases in complexity are only possible when driven by *designed* programs and *directed* energies, neither of which is possessed by the purely speculative notion of vertically upward evolution.

Yet cosmic evolution, stellar evolution, and chemical evolution are all taught as fact today in the physical sciences, and further speculation in these fields is continually being funded by massive grants of tax money. All the hard data in the earth sciences show it did not occur in the past, and all the genuine data in the physical sciences show it is not possible at all. Nevertheless, evolution is almost universally accepted as a fact in all the natural sciences.

Creationists do not reject the *actual, factual data* of any of these sciences. They are all legitimate sciences (the founding fathers of which, incidentally, were almost all creationists!), and they have contributed immeasurably to our knowledge about God's created world and our ability to use its resources for man's benefit. All of the real data of these sciences can be understood much better in the context of creationism. It is the evolutionary framework in which they are taught and the evolutionary premises upon which they are built that ought to be rejected by true Christians — in fact, by all genuine theists as well as true scientists.

Human Behavior in the Light of Evolution

There is probably no academic field of study and application more thoroughly saturated with evolutionary thinking than psychology and the other fields dealing with human behavior. Ever since Darwin — and especially since Freud — psychologists have assumed that man is merely an evolved animal and have evaluated his behavior problems on an animalistic basis. Experiments with monkeys or other animals (even with insects) are used for guidance in dealing with human problems.

This approach is wrong because man is *not* an "animal." He did not evolve from other life forms but was *created* in the image of God, with an eternal soul. Ironically, "psychology" means "study of the soul," but modern psychologists do not even believe in the soul.

Sigmund Freud is generally considered to be the founder of modern psychology. Although many of his ideas are no longer accepted by psychologists of the present day, he has surely exerted more influence over the theory and practice in this field than any other single individual. It has always been known that Freud was an ardent follower of Darwin, but this has been even more emphasized by the recent discovery of certain papers left by him. D. Goleman writes:

> In a 1915 paper, Freud demonstrates his preoccupation with evolution. Immersed in the theories of Darwin and of Lamarck, who believed acquired traits could be inherited, Freud concluded that mental disorders were the vestiges of behavior that had been appropriate in earlier stages of evolution.[31]

This latter notion is itself a vestige of the infamous "recapitulation theory" of the ardent Darwinian racist Ernst Haeckel, the philosophical forerunner of Adolf Hitler in Germany. Goleman continues, "The evolutionary idea that Freud relied on most heavily in the manuscript is the maxim that 'ontogeny recapitulates phylogeny,' that is, that the development of the individual recapitulates the evolution of the entire species."[32]

The bitter fruit of the recapitulation theory (long since discredited scientifically) continued to grow in many areas of society, and we shall return to it in other connections later. In this connection here, however, since Lamarckianism, Darwinism, and Haeckelism are all dead wrong scientifically, it cannot be surprising that Freudian methods of psychoanalysis and treatment of supposed mental disorders are not only wrong but commonly harmful as well.

In fact, most modern psychologists have now disavowed Freud, even though they have built on his foundation. They, of course, still operate completely within an evolutionary framework, regarding man as merely an evolved animal, with animal problems and animal solutions. A large majority are atheists or pantheists, whether J.B. Watson with his behaviorism, B.F. Skinner with his humanistic psychology (neo-behaviorism), Carl Rogers, Jung, Adler, or a host of other leaders in the counseling field.

In fact, so committed to evolutionism are most modern psychologists and philosophers (with whom they have a close kinship) that they now tend

---

31. Daniel Goleman, "Lost Paper Shows Freud's Effort to Link Analysis and Evolution," *New York Times*, Feb. 10, 1987, p. 19.
32. Ibid., p. 22.

to regard biblical Christianity itself — especially creationism — as a form of mental disorder. In fact, any form of religion is considered by many evolutionists to be unhealthy, a vestige of sociological pressures in the animal societies from which they claim humans developed. Dr. Edward Wilson of Harvard, a leader in this kind of study, has said:

> When we understand the evolutionary sources, the adaptive meaning, and the genetic history of the religious impulse, I suspect that fatal flow will have been dealt to religious dogmatism, and yet it will simultaneously disclose a human history and a set of mental phenomena so complex as to serve as a permanent source of wonder.[33]

It surely would be a cause of "wonder" that the complex human brain and its "mental phenomena" have somehow evolved out of the "socio-biological" relationships in animal societies, as Wilson believes. His attitude (as a one-time Southern Baptist turned evolutionary entomologist) toward biblical Christianity is as follows: "Bitter experience has taught us that fundamentalist religion . . . in its aggressive form is one of the unmitigated evils of the world."[34]

Wilson regrets that fundamentalism "cannot be quickly replaced by benign skepticism and a purely humanistic worldview, even among educated and well-meaning people" and would obviously be in favor of any measures that would eradicate this "unmitigated evil," a goal he believes is currently precluded by the strength of "dogmatic religions and religion-like political ideologies." But he does hold out hope and an effective weapon to his fellow atheists: "Liberal theology can serve as a buffer."[35]

It is not surprising that "liberal" churches and other religious institutions are more and more turning away from genuine biblical studies and theology, and becoming more and more enamored of psychology and counseling. This is even true of evangelical institutions. Increasing proportions of seminary students are majoring in counseling, and there are no doubt a number of excellent Christian counselors and psychologists today. The field as a whole, however, is saturated with evolutionary thinking.

---

33. Edward O. Wilson, "Toward a Humanistic Biology," *The Humanist* 42 (Sept./Oct. 1982): p. 56.
34. Edward O. Wilson, "The Relation of Science to Theology," *Zygon* (Sept./Dec. 1980). This paper was presented at a conference co-sponsored by the American Academy of Arts and Sciences and the Institute of Religion in an Age of Science.
35. Ibid.

The general attitude of leaders in the behavioral sciences toward Christianity is indicated still further by the following pronouncements (both emanating from Canada):

> That people in our age can believe that they have had a personal encounter with God, that they could believe that they have experienced conversion through a "mystical experience of God," so that they are born again in the Holy Spirit, is something that attests to human irrationality and a lack of a sense of reality.[36]

> I want you to entertain the hypothesis that Christian doctrine, the existential soother par excellence, is incompatible with the principles of sound mental health and contributes more to the genesis of human suffering than to its alleviation. . . . In my view, all religions are inhuman anachronisms, but here I am only dealing with Christianity and, more specifically, with the noxious nature of Christian doctrine at the personal and interpersonal levels.[37]

From the perspective of the Bible, of course, arrogant pseudo-intellectuals such as these are the ones who are mentally ill. "Professing themselves to be wise, they became fools" (Rom. 1:22). It surely does seem, at least to those who eschew counseling from unregenerate humanists, that psychologists, psychiatrists, and philosophers exhibit far more personal problems in their own lives than their numbers warrant. Some in their own profession have noted this phenomenon. One observer writes:

> The average psychiatrist has more power to do harm in the lives of individuals than most religious leaders on Earth. . . . Moreover, it would be hard to find a more unhappy lot than those clustered in the mental health field. Especially among psychiatrists, suicide, depression, drug addiction, and alcoholism are notoriously rife. Among non-medical mental health professionals, the situation doesn't seem much better. Not only are many mental health professionals unhappy but they do not live ethically inspired lives. Too many, for example, prostrate themselves before the psychiatric establishment.[38]

---

36. Kai Nielsen, "Religiosity and Powerlessness," *The Humanist* 37 (May/June 1977): p. 46. Nielsen is professor of philosophy at the University of Calgary.
37. Wendell W. Watters, "Christianity and Mental Health," *The Humanist* 47 (Nov./Dec. 1987): p. 5. Watters is clinical professor of psychiatry at McMaster University.
38. Peter R. Breggin, "Mental Health Versus Religion," *The Humanist* 47 (Nov./Dec. 1987): p. 13.

The author of this evaluation, Peter Breggin, is a practicing psychiatrist and is evidently a humanist himself, so his opinion carries special weight. If he is right, anyone who would go get psychological or psychiatric counseling, as the cliché puts it, "ought to have his head examined"!

The Bible, on the other hand, is filled with practical wisdom for daily living in every aspect of life. It has worked in the lives of uncounted millions for thousands of years. A truly *biblical* system of psychology and counseling is being developed and practiced by a few Christian specialists in these fields, and this holds great promise. On the whole, however, the whole area of the behavior sciences today is thoroughly dominated by evolutionary humanism, and this has resulted in incalculable harm.

Human behavior problems do not stem from an animal ancestry, as Freud and most others in these fields have alleged, but from *sin* — from rebellion against God and His Word. Men and women are not mere animalistic assemblages of biological components. Each person has an eternal soul, destined for heaven or hell, and this must be of primary consideration in any successful psychological formula.

There are evidently some personality disorders, however, that have a direct physical cause, genetic or chemical. These should be treated medically or physiologically, rather than psychologically. The field of Bible-based Christian psychiatry is important and promising in this connection.

Even here, however, a word of caution is in order. Although some notable specialists *do* believe in the soul, it is not necessarily the biblical doctrine. Sir John Eccles, for example, was an outstanding research psychiatrist, winner of a Nobel Prize in 1963, and he was strongly committed to the concept of immortality of the soul. "Eccles strongly defends the ancient religious belief that human beings consist of a mysterious compound of physical matter and intangible spirit."[39] Well and good, so far. But read further:

> Eccles is not the only world-famous scientist taking a controversial new look at the ancient mind-body conundrum. From Berkeley to Paris, and from London to Princeton, prominent scientists from fields as diverse as neurophysiology and quantum physics are coming out of the closet and admitting they believe in the possibility, at least, of such unscientific entities as the immortal human spirit and divine creation.[40]

---

39. John Gliedman, "Scientists in Search of the Soul," *Science Digest* 90 (July 1982): p. 77.
40. Ibid.

Eccles did believe in the "divine creation" of each "immortal spirit," but in a pantheistic context, not in the biblical sense. This "new look at the ancient mind-body conundrum" is not new at all. Sir John and certain scientists at Princeton, Berkeley, and other institutions are giving a scientific perspective to the so-called New Age movement, which is as active in the psychological professions as anywhere. But all of this, in essence, is a revival of ancient intellectual pantheism.

Breggin has also commented on this: "At annual and regional meetings of the Association for Humanistic Psychology, we are more likely to find yoga sessions and Sufi dancing than psychotherapy seminars. The latest fad is reducing the science of physics to metaphysics and spirituality."[41]

In summary, modern psychology and other behavioral sciences are firmly based in evolutionary humanism. A growing number of its practitioners are involved in New Age pantheism, although most are evidently still committed to old-fashioned evolutionary atheism. In either case, evolutionism provides the pseudo-scientific base and framework of interpretation.

Evolution and Society

The social sciences, no less than the behavioral sciences, are firmly committed to evolutionism as their intellectual rationale. For that matter, psychology itself is often considered a social science, since human societies are made up of human individuals. Sociology, therefore, is essentially the study of group psychology.

As noted previously, one of the current fads in evolutionary thinking is that of "sociobiology," as developed and promoted especially by the followers of Edward O. Wilson, professor of entomology at Harvard University. The results of Wilson's studies of the "social insects," in particular, have been applied to human societies. This is evolutionism with a vengeance! But let Wilson himself explain:

> From the viewpoint of the biological sciences, sociobiology is very orthodox, because it has been based cautiously on population genetics, ecology, and evolutionary theory and is a new amalgam or body of evolutionary theory. . . . Above all, sociobiology is the scientific discipline most congenial to humanism.[42]

It is worth nothing, incidentally, that the origin of these complex insect societies (ants, bees, etc.), which sociobiologists consider so instructive for

41. Breggin, "Mental Health Versus Religion," p. 12.
42. Wilson, "Toward a Humanistic Biology," 42, p. 41.

human sociology, is utterly mysterious. Pierre Grasse, certainly one of the most knowledgeable of all evolutionary biologists, frankly admits: "We are in the dark concerning the origin of insects."[43] Even if we could rationally attribute the structure of human societies to an origin in the insect world (which is absurd!), this would not help, since we have no idea how *these* arose. Yet most social scientists persist in trying to solve human societal problems by appeal to evolutionary theory. No wonder human societies are in such a mess!

Sociobiology represents one of the most recent applications of evolutionism to the social sciences. However, these disciplines (which include not only sociology as such but also such derivative fields as economics, social psychology, cultural anthropology, political science, and others) have been dominated by evolutionary thinking since their very beginnings. Most authorities identify the French positivist/atheist August Comte as the father of sociology in the modern sense.

Comte died in 1857 at the relatively young age of 59 and had been insane for a time, even attempting suicide on one occasion. He was profoundly egotistic, claiming not only to have invented the true science of society, which he instead followed the same kinds of laws as the "positive" sciences of physics and chemistry, but also to have formulated what he called the true religion of humanity. Comte's political system envisioned an all-powerful state enforcing these supposed laws, and his positivistic philosophy had great influence on both Karl Marx and Herbert Spencer. His scientific philosophy was structured around the pre-Darwinian evolutionary concept known as the Great Chain of Being.

Herbert Spencer is generally reputed as second in importance only to Comte in the founding of modern sociology. Both Marx and Spencer also became profoundly committed to Darwinism. It is ironic that these two bitterly anti-Christian philosophers, both followers of Comte and both promoters of Darwin, became the founders of two sociological systems that have been competing ever since. Marx was the father of the left-wing sociological system known as "communism," while Spencer became the main founder of the right-wing sociological system known ever since as "social Darwinism."

The sociological and political systems proposed by Comte and Spencer — not to mention Marx — have been profoundly influential all over the world and, of course, are thoroughly saturated with evolutionary philosophy. Herbert Spencer was almost as effective as Thomas Huxley

---

43. Pierre P. Grassè, *Evolution of Living Organisms* (New York: Academic, 1977), p. 30.

in promoting Darwinism in England and the United States. He was a doctrinaire evolutionist even before Darwin became one, in fact, and coined the phrase "survival of the fittest" as the famous watchword characterizing Darwinism. Spencer even wrote a biological treatise and could well have laid claim to anticipating Darwin on many points. As one observer commented:

> In his own day, which was that of Darwin, too, Spencer was regarded as a giant, and his *Principles of Biology* was adduced as one of the chief evidences for this high estimation. . . . Spencer's preliminary essays were published some time before *The Origin of Species*.[44]

In any case, Herbert Spencer has long been recognized as the father of modern sociology, especially as it was developed and taught for almost a century in England and America. It has been noted, "Undoubtedly the most potent influences contributing to the rise and development of truly historical sociology were Spencer's theory of cosmic evolution and the Darwinian doctrine of organic evolution and their reactions upon social science."[45] The author of this evaluation was one of the leading sociologists of the 20th century.

One of the major sociological emphases of the late 19th century, continuing on until about World War II, was the "science" of eugenics:

> Darwinism spawned many outshoots. One of these was launched by Darwin's first cousin, Francis Galton.
>
> Obsessed, as were many, by the implications of the "fittest," Galton set out in 1883 to study heredity from a mathematical viewpoint. He named his new science eugenics, from a Greek root meaning both "good in birth" and "noble in heredity." His stated goal was to improve the human race, by giving "the more suitable races or strains of blood a better chance of prevailing speedily over the less suitable." His unstated goal was to play God.[46]

The famous (but fallacious) stories of the dismal genetic heredity of the "Jukes and Kallikaks" were conveyed to generations of schoolchildren all across the country (including this writer) until the pseudo-science of

---

44. George Kimball Plochmann, "Darwin or Spencer?" *Science* 130 (Nov. 27, 1959): p. 1452.

45. Harry Elmer Barnes, *Historical Sociology* (New York: Philosophical Library, 1948), p. 13.

46. Otto Scott, "Playing God," *Chalcedon Report*, no. 247 (Feb. 1986): p. 1.

eugenics fell out of favor when Adolf Hitler applied it so viciously in Germany. "Scientific" racism was quite common, in fact, among practically all the leading sociologists and anthropologists of the West before Hitler gave it such a bad name with his programs for promoting Aryan/Teutonic racial supremacy.

The evolutionary basis of racism, however, as well as that of communism, Nazism, and laissez-faire capitalism, will be discussed and documented more fully in the next chapter. For the moment, simply be aware that the social sciences, from their very beginnings, have been polluted by evolutionism.

Even the Humanities!

Scholars dedicated to promoting what they call a true "liberal arts" education often decry any great emphasis on science and the technical professions in the nation's schools and colleges. They speak of a clash between the "two cultures," arguing that young people should be taught more of how to live than how to make a living, with the implication that this can be accomplished by more dedication to the humanities (literature, history, linguistics, philosophy, ethics, law, classics) and the fine arts (music, art, dance).

The fact is, however, that these disciplines are also permeated with evolutionary humanism and becoming more so all the time. In fact, the very term *humanities* is almost synonymous today with *humanism*, as popularly understood. Modern humanism is based squarely on evolutionism, of course, though not necessarily Darwinian evolution. Humanist Paul Kurtz writes: "Humanism is a philosophical, religious, and moral point of view as old as human civilization itself. It has its roots in classical China, Greece, and Rome; it is expressed in the Renaissance and the Enlightenment, in the scientific revolution, and in the twentieth century."[47]

It is significant that practically all the literature studied in high school and college classrooms today is humanistic in tone. For example, the supposedly exemplary literary collection known as "The Great Books of the Western World" could just as well be called "The Great Humanistic Books of the Western World." The listing contains almost none of the great Christian classics

---

47. Paul Kurtz, preface to the re-publication of Humanist Manifestos I and II; booklet distributed by the American Humanist Association, Buffalo, New York. Humanist Manifesto I, first issued in 1933, when the American Humanist Association was incorporated in Illinois, contains the famous "Tenets of Humanism," the first two of which are statements of faith in cosmic and human evolution, as the foundational premises of humanism. Humanist Manifesto II, published forty years later (1973), reaffirmed the completely naturalistic basis of humanism.

nor any of the great volumes of biblical exposition or Christian apologetics, but is replete with all the great classics of humanistic thought and purpose. The books that touch on religion at all tend to promote either paganism or deism or, at best, unitarianism and Christian liberalism. Many, of course, are overtly evolutionistic, including Darwin's *The Origin of Species.*

Many liberal arts scholars would contend that studies in the humanities and fine arts produce graduates who are "cultured" and "sensitive," but this is not necessarily so. In a key address given over 30 years ago by June Goodfield (a scholar working in both science and the humanities) to a combined meeting of the American Association for Advancement of Science and the Phi Beta Kappa Society (devoted to scholarship in the humanities), the following cogent observations were made:

> In the attempt to humanize ourselves, to enhance our ethical and moral sensibilities, people have often appealed to the humanities to do it for us, almost as to an ideology. The redemptive power of the humanities to produce an enlarged consciousness, to make us aware of the reality of the human predicament, and to enlarge our sympathies has been an important theme in Wordsworth, in Shelley, and in many twentieth-century writers. I am skeptical about this assumption. People can be extraordinarily sensitive to music and poetry and not necessarily apply this sensitivity to their daily lives. George Steiner . . . has reminded us that people returned from a day's work as guards in the concentration camps and then put Mozart on their gramophones. . . . We must not delude ourselves into believing that words and university courses are a substitute for human hearts and human actions.[48]

Dr. Goodfield also made the following rather plaintive plea in concluding her address: "Now is very much the right time — is it not? — when we may use old-fashioned words such as 'morality' and honor' without being sneered at."[49] Judging from the rapidly increasing decadence and amorality of modern literature in the last three decades — not to mention increasing commitments to atheism in the general intellectual establishments — her words produced little effect.

Not only in literature, but also in history and the other humanities — especially philosophy — evolutionary humanism reigns supreme today. The

---

48. June Goodfield, "Humanity in Science," *Key Reporter* (Phi Beta Kappa, Summer 1957): p. 3.
49. Ibid., p. 8.

increasingly radical, almost nihilistic character of modern art and music is of great concern everywhere.

Consider also the fields of ethics and law. These fields, relating so directly to the principles that ought to guide human attitudes and actions, were long governed primarily (at least in Western civilization) by biblical standards and precepts. The original colonies of the United States, in particular, were founded mainly by men and women seeking freedom to practice biblical religion as they understood it. These principles lie strongly in the background of the writing of the Declaration of Independence and the Constitution, especially the Bill of Rights. Our nation's original schools and colleges were founded for the very purpose of promulgating and transmitting to future generations these timeless moral, ethical, and spiritual guidelines for thought and action. Almost all historians and other scholars have agreed on these facts — until very recently, when revisionism in history has suddenly come in vogue. The Bible and its principles have certainly been the foundational framework for law and ethics in the past.

Not so today! Morals and ethics — and thus law as well — are considered to be products of evolution. Therefore, morality and ethics must continue to evolve in accord with the changing social environment, and so must the law and even the interpretation of the Constitution. With respect to the principles of ethics, here is the dictum of two leading thinkers, philosopher Michael Ruse and biologist Edward O. Wilson: "Attempts to link evolution and ethics first sprang up in the middle of the last century, as people turned to alternative foundations in response to what they perceived as the collapse of Christianity."[50]

These authors are certainly not the first to expound evolutionary theories of ethics. Thomas Huxley wrote a famous essay on this subject back in the early days of Darwin-mania.[51] So did John Dewey, the noted architect of American public education, at the turn of the century.[52] The eminent British anthropologist Sir Arthur Keith wrote an entire book on the subject just after World War II.[53] Many others have expounded the same theme, so that it is now commonly taught just about everywhere that man's moral nature, no

---

50. Michael Ruse and Edward O. Wilson, "Evolution and Ethics," *New Scientist* 208 (Oct. 17, 1985): p. 50. Dr. Ruse is professor of philosophy at a Canadian university, a very prolific writer and defender of neo-Darwinism. Dr. Wilson, the previously discussed founder of sociobiology, is at Harvard.

51. Thomas Henry Huxley, "Evolution and Ethics," 1894.

52. John Dewey, "Evolution and Ethics," *The Monist* 8 (1897–1901), later republished in *Scientific Monthly* (Feb. 1954): p. 66.

53. Arthur Keith, *Evolution and Ethics* (New York: Putnam, 1947).

less than his physiological structure, is the product of blind evolution. Ruse and Wilson comment:

> Morality, or more strictly our belief in morality, is merely an adaptation put in place to further our reproductive ends. . . . Ethics is seen to have a solid foundation, not in divine guidance, but in the shared qualities of human nature and the desperate need for reciprocity.[54]

Just how all this may have happened has been the object of some remarkable evolutionary fantasizing. Note the following just-so stories, invented by other atheistic scholars:

> This truly "old-time religion" developed at the end of the last Ice Age, when the tribe was the largest human grouping maintaining any degree of coherence. The religion of the Old Testament is a cultural fossil held over from the Pleistocene Epoch, and it reflects an atmosphere of intense intergroup competition. Petrified like the bones in a paleontologist's cabinet, the greatest ideas of the Ice Age still can be found on display between Genesis and Malachi.[55]

> For what religious man came eventually to think of as "conscience" is simply the faculty that enabled his hominid ancestors to inhibit their programmed responses to stimuli in the interests of some longer-term advantage. "Guilt" is the unease that accompanies and sometimes motivates that control, and "god" is the idealist projection of the conscience in moral terms.[56]

Perhaps the most distressing evidence of the dominance of modern life and thought by evolutionism, however, is the fact that modern institutional Christianity itself has largely accepted evolution and reinterpreted the Bible and theology to fit it. Departments of philosophy and religion in secular universities have largely become completely humanistic, either atheistic or pantheistic. In Christian colleges and seminaries, especially in the mainline denominations, theistic evolution is all but universally accepted, with the early chapters of Genesis dismissed as spiritual allegories. This undermining

---

54. Ruse and Wilson, "Evolution and Ethics," p. 51–52.
55. Frank R. Zindler, "Religion, Hypnosis and Music: An Evolutionary Perspective," *American Atheist* 26 (Oct. 1984): p. 22. Zindler is former chairman of the science division at the Fulton-Montgomery campus of the State University of New York.
56. John M. Allegro, "Divine Discontent," *American Atheist* 28 (Sept. 1986): p. 26. Allegro is best known as a member of the Dead Sea Scrolls editing team.

of Christianity's foundations in Genesis has inevitably led to "liberalization" of the rest of the Bible in many of these institutions, explaining away the miracles of the Bible and the traditional authorship of its 66 books.

> As far as Christianity was concerned, the advent of the theory of evolution and the elimination of traditional theological thinking was catastrophic. The suggestion that life and man are the result of chance is incompatible with the biblical assertion of their being the direct result of intelligent creative activity. Despite the attempt by liberal theology to disguise the point, the fact is that no biblically derived religion can really be compromised with the fundamental assertion of Darwinian theory. Chance and design are antithetical concepts, and the decline in religious belief can probably be attributed more to the propagation and advocacy by the intellectual and scientific community of the Darwinian version of evolution than to any other single factor.[57]

The general apostasy of institutional Christianity is further documented in chapter 3, and it could easily be shown that this is primarily because of the belief by theologians that science had "proved" evolution. Once the historicity of Genesis is abandoned in a church or school (and this is what evolution requires), it is inevitable that the whole structure of supernatural Christianity will eventually collapse in the teachings of that institution.

The seminaries and colleges of the major denominations (Catholic, Methodist, Baptist, Presbyterian, Episcopalian, Lutheran, Reformed, Congregations, Disciples, etc.) have almost all been committed to evolution for many, many years, some since soon after publication of Darwin's *Origin* in 1859. Nevertheless, in almost all of these denominations there are still significant numbers of creationists among their members; these have, in some cases, even started creationist schools of their own. The latter, however, are never recognized by the denominational hierarchies but are invariably opposed by them.

Today, many of the schools of the smaller, evangelical denominations, as well as many of the originally sound non-denominational schools, are again in the process of compromising with evolution, thus beginning again the oft-traveled slide down into apostasy. Some have descended into full-fledged theistic evolution; some are still at the day-age theory or gap theory stage;

---

57. Michael Denton, *Evolution — A Theory in Crisis* (London: Burnett Books, 1985), p. 66. Denton, an Australian researcher in molecular genetics, is not a creationist but has an incisively critical understanding of evolutionism.

others are trying to ignore the whole issue. But all are in real danger of eventual apostasy unless they return soon to true creationist convictions.

The sad truth is that all the humanities — including ethics and religion — are today saturated with evolutionary humanism, even in most ostensibly Christian schools. This is a truly amazing latter-day phenomenon, especially in view of the complete absence of any real scientific evidence for evolution. (There *is* an explanation for this situation, but it must be deferred until chapter 6.)

Evolutionary Education and the Schools

Not only is the content of modern education (natural sciences, social sciences, humanities) dominated by evolutionism, but so is its very philosophy and even its methodology. The absolute reign of evolution in America's public schools is one of the most remarkable phenomena of modern life. The socialist Jeremy Rifkin acknowledges this: "Evolutionary theory has been enshrined as the centerpiece of our educational system, and elaborate walls have been erected around it to protect it from unnecessary abuse."[58]

It was not always like this. It is well known that the original schools and colleges of this country were all church-related, firmly committed to the Bible as the Word of God. The very first school was in the Jamestown colony, taught by a pastor and ship chaplain. Similar church-controlled community schools were soon established in all the colonies.

The same was true of the nation's first colleges. Harvard, Yale, Brown, Princeton, Dartmouth, Pennsylvania, and others were established primarily to promote and transmit true education in the context of biblical Christianity to future generations. Gradually, however, deism and unitarianism infiltrated the colonies, especially in New England, undermining the supernatural aspects of Christianity, even though there was still a commitment to the concept of a personal transcendent God who had created all things in the beginning. Pre-Darwinian evolutionism also made its impact, especially the idea of "long ages." This belief of the ancient pagan religions was re-introduced into England by Hutton, Playfair, and Lyell and was soon being promoted in this country, even by such creationist geologists as Agassiz, Silliman, and Dana. Also, the famous "nebular hypothesis" for the evolutionary origin of the solar system, introduced in continental Europe by Kant and LaPlace, made numerous American converts, including the leading Christian biologist Asa Gray, who would soon become Darwin's main propagandist in the United States.

---

58. Jeremy Rifkin, *Algeny* (New York: Viking, 1983), p. 112.

In *Creation by Natural Law*, Ronald Numbers demonstrates that the scientific and religious establishments had accepted a naturalistic theory of the origin of the solar system decades before the *Origin of Species*.

Acceptance of the nebular hypothesis had become sufficiently entrenched that Asa Gray, appealing for Darwinian evolution in the 1860s, pointed to the hypothesis as an analogy in organic development for the organic development of species. . . .

The nebular hypothesis was one element in a growing scientific culture in which secular naturalism broadly prepared the way for Darwinism.[59]

Nevertheless, because of the strong Christian and biblical tradition in America, evolutionism did not capture the schools here as rapidly as it did in England. Horace Mann, a Unitarian legislator in Massachusetts, had been able to get the first public schools established in 1837, and other states quickly followed. However, these public schools themselves continued to teach creationism and other Christian truths for many years.

There is no need to discuss in detail the various steps by which our schools were all gradually taken over by evolutionary humanism. This has been done with compelling clarity by others.[60] The end result has been that — apart from miraculous divine intervention — the public schools, as well as all the secular colleges and universities, have been irretrievably lost.

The latter were the first to go. Perhaps the key event was the appointment of Charles W. Eliot as president of Harvard University in 1869, a post he retained for 40 years. Eliot not only was a prominent Unitarian but had spent several years in Europe studying science and educational philosophy, returning a convinced evolutionist. He appointed John Fiske, another prominent Unitarian, to teach science and history at Harvard, specifically to introduce and popularize evolutionism in the Harvard curriculum. This goal was also furthered by the evolutionary teachings of the aforementioned Asa Gray in botany, also at Harvard. Gray, a Presbyterian, made this transition easier by espousing theistic evolution as a valid option for Christians.

---

59. Ronald C. Tobey, "New Ideas in America" (review of *Creation by Natural Law* by Ronald L. Numbers, University of Washington Press, 1977), *Science* 197 (Sept. 2, 1977): p. 977. Dr. Numbers is professor of the history of science and medicine at the University of Wisconsin.

60. Particular reference might be made to two books by Samuel L. Blumenfeld, *Is Public Education Necessary?* (Greenwich, CN: Devin-Adair Co., 1981), 286 p.; and *NEA: Trojan Horse in American Education* (Boise, ID: Paradigm, 1984), 284 p.

As America's leading university, Harvard became the example to others, and almost the entire university world quickly followed her down the evolutionary trail. The extension of evolutionary dominance to the public schools, however, required first that the teachers in these schools also become committed to evolutionism, and this took much longer to accomplish.

During the period from 1838 to 1845, Horace Mann, with the aid of many powerful Unitarian colleagues in Massachusetts, was able to establish a number of "normal schools" for the training of that state's public school teachers. These were copied in other states, and it was not long before each state exercised much control over the education of virtually all its children, through its state university and its various teacher-training colleges.

It was not until the 20th century, however, that the educators really gained a high degree of control over curricular content and textbooks. Until then, American schools were mostly still rural establishments, with locally elected school boards and textbooks, especially famous McGuffey Readers, that were still fundamentally sound.

The formation of teachers' associations in the various states led in 1857 to the establishment of the National Education Association (NEA), which has now become probably the most powerful labor union in the country. Its membership includes not only teachers but also administrators, book publishers, suppliers, and, in fact, anyone interested in advancing the goals of the association, which are now at least as much political as educational.

The influence of Massachusetts — particularly Harvard University — has permeated public education ever since its beginnings. Mann and his fellow Unitarians, later followed by Eliot, Fiske, and others, were all profoundly influenced by the Prussian school system and Hegelian philosophy. The former was highly centralized and government controlled. The latter was pantheistic and humanistic, though still somewhat idealistic.

When Darwinism took over, beginning about 1870, the metaphysical idealism of Hegel was soon replaced by blatant materialism and even atheism in the colleges and universities and among the leadership in the teachers' colleges and educational hierarchies — even if not yet among the teachers and textbooks.

There were many key people involved in the eventual complete takeover by the evolutionary humanists, but the most important of all, undoubtedly, was John Dewey. Born in 1859 (the year Darwin published his *Origin*), Dewey had a long and profoundly influential career. Under the tutelage of ardent evolutionist James Hall at John Hopkins University, he also became profoundly committed to evolutionism — biologically, psychologically, and sociologically. Dewey's greatest influence was as head of the uniquely influential teachers' colleges at the University of Chicago and (especially) at Columbia University. From these and other institutions influenced by them have come many of the key leaders in the educational establishment throughout most of the 20th century.

John Dewey is generally conceded to be the chief founder and promulgator of the "progressive education movement," which has profoundly changed education not only in America but also in many other countries. One observer has commented:

> An absolute faith in science became the driving force behind the progressives. . . . The most important idea that would influence the educators was that of evolution — the notion that man, through a process of natural selection, had evolved to his present state from a common animal ancestry. Evolution was as sharp a break with the Biblical view of creation as anyone could make, and it was quickly picked up by those anxious to disprove the validity of orthodox religion.[61]

The underlying assumption of progressive education was that the child is simply an evolved animal and must be trained as such — not as an individual created in God's image with tremendous potential as an individual. A child was considered but one member in a group and therefore must be trained collectively to fit into his or her appropriate place in society. Dewey studied Russia's educational system extensively and was a socialist himself, as well as a materialistic pantheist.

To some degree the progressive-education philosophy espoused by Dewey — like the behavior psychology based on animal experimentation that he also espoused — has failed and is repudiated today. Nevertheless, its evolutionistic base is more strongly entrenched than ever in our public schools.

Although the progressive-education movement was being promoted and consolidated during the early 1900s, this was delayed by the interruption of World War I and then by the fundamentalists revival accompanying and following the war. It was then greatly encouraged in the aftermath of the Tennessee Scopes Trial of 1925, when the university world, the education hierarchy, and the thoroughly indoctrinated journalists of the day, in a scenario carefully orchestrated by the American Civil Liberties Union,

---

61. Samuel L. Blumenfeld, *NEA: Trojan Horse in American Education* (Boise, ID: Paradigm, 1984), p. 43.

managed to make the creationist fundamentalists and their spokesman, William Jennings Bryan, look ignorant and foolish.

The Great Depression that began in 1929 seemed to play into the hands of Dewey and his socialist colleagues, along with the Rooseveltian New Deal that followed. It was during some of these years (1925–1935) that I was attending the public schools of Texas. At the time, the Bible and prayer were still acceptable components of education; patriotism was stressed in history and literature; and there was strong emphasis on the basics of reading (including phonics and spelling), writing (including good penmanship), and mathematics. But there was also an implied general acceptance of evolution, an undercurrent of socialism in civics, and a mishmash of elective courses and option activities. At the time, no doubt, the Texas schools had not moved as far toward "progressive education" as those in more liberal states. Even there and then, however, evolutionism was assumed, either overtly or covertly, throughout the curriculum.

John Dewey and like-minded evolutionists founded the American Humanist Association in 1933, and he became its first president. The Tenets of Humanism — largely either written or approved by him — were published that same year and have since become the unofficial framework of teaching in just about all public schools. The already-mentioned Humanist Manifestos I and II (1933, 1973) both stress evolution as the basis of humanism and decry creationism and biblical fundamentalism. (See footnote 47 in this chapter.) Still a third manifesto, called a Secular Humanist Declaration, was drafted by Dr. Paul Kurtz, a professor at the State University of New York at Buffalo, and published in the first issue of *Free Inquiry*, edited by Dr. Kurtz, in October 1980. Signers included such prominent scholars as Isaac Asimov (probably the most prolific science writer of this century and current president of the American Humanist Association), behavioral psychologist B.F. Skinner, philosopher Kai Nielsen, situation-ethics theologian Joseph Fletcher, and Albert Ellis, Ernest Nagel, Sidney Hook, and numerous others of equal influence.

Drafted in response to the recent revival of creationism and biblical fundamentalism, the 1980 declaration fulminated against the "reappearance of dogmatic authoritarian religions." *The New York Times* summarized its tone as follows: "Reflecting elements of two earlier humanist manifestos, in 1933 and 1973, the declaration depicts supernatural religion and divine revelation as enemies of the rational process that leads to progress."[62]

---

62. Kenneth A. Briggs, "Secular Humanists Attack a Rise in Fundamentalism," *New York Times*, Oct. 1980.

To all intents and purposes, these humanistic-evolutionary tenets have become the state-supported religion of our public schools everywhere. Anything hinting at biblical and/or Christian values — especially the foundational doctrine of supernatural creation — is systematically excluded, under continuing pressure from the American Civil Liberties Union, the American Humanist Association, the Nation Educational Association, and the intellectual and educational establishments in general. This trend is firmly supported by the radical-liberal news media everywhere.

The humanists themselves acknowledge that their system is essentially "religious." The following statement was featured prominently on the back cover of a recent issue of the AHA magazine, *The Humanist*:

> Humanism does not include the idea of a God and as such is considered a philosophy rather than a religion. In a way it is an alternative to all religions. However, whether or not one looks to humanism as a religion or a philosophy to live by or a way of life is, we believe, largely a matter of personal temperament and preference. Those caught up by its religious aspects know that it provides a vibrant, satisfying faith. Those who think of it as a philosophy find it both reasonable and adequate.[63]

This "religious" system of secular humanism or evolutionary humanism is certainly unconstitutional (as a state-endorsed religion). Yet, by *excluding* other religions — especially the religion of creationism and biblical Christianity on which our nation and its schools were originally founded — and exclusively teaching the concepts in the Tenets of Humanism, this system has indeed become the legally enforced, *de facto* state religion. Humanism is promulgated throughout our public schools exactly as envisioned by Dewey and his predecessors, associates, and followers long ago.

The religious nature of evolution is evident not only from the complete lack of scientific evidence supporting its precepts, but also from the viciously emotional defenses that the modern creationist revival has engendered. Over 40 anti-creationist books and hundreds of anti-creationist articles have been published in recent years. Almost all are highly sarcastic and emotional, exhibiting a complete lack of understanding of the creationist arguments and evidences, and *never* citing any real evidence for evolution.

The crowning blow is that the courts have supported this evolutionary takeover of the public schools. This is not really too surprising, however, for

---

63. Lloyd Morain, "How Do Humanists Define Their Beliefs?" *The Humanist* 47 (Sept./Oct. 1987): back cover. The author was a former editor of *The Humanist*.

the law schools for over a generation have also taught evolution, including the evolution of the law and the Constitution. The trend of interpreting the United States Constitution, in accord with evolving social policy rather than the intentions of the "founding fathers" and the original states, either began or was accelerated by the widely read legal analyses and opinions of Oliver Wendell Holmes, who was an associate justice of the U.S. Supreme Court from 1902 until his death in 1935. According to the *Encyclopedia Britannica*, Holmes "uniformly favored a liberal interpretation of the constitution and his opinions have been conspicuous for their literary style and epigrammatic force." Like his father, the famous poet, Associate Justice Holmes was a so-called free thinker who was opposed to traditional biblical Christianity, and his influence on subsequent courts has undoubtedly been most significant.

In any case, whenever any attempt to get creationism back into the public schools — even on a strictly scientific, two-model basis — has reached the courts, it has invariably been rebuffed. This has happened in Tennessee, Indiana, California, New York, Arkansas, Florida, Arizona, Louisiana, and other states.

The Louisiana "creation law" itself finally reached the U.S. Supreme Court in 1987, and there the concept of supernatural creation has received an apparently conclusive and final rejection. Speaking for the 7-2 majority, Justice Brennan said, "The preeminent purpose for the Louisiana legislature was clearly to advance the religious viewpoint that a supernatural being created humankind." The law was thrown out primarily on this basis — that belief in a supernatural God is nothing but a "religious viewpoint" and, as such, is to be excluded from our public institutions. To all intents and purposes, the Court's decision officially designates the United States of America to be, like Communist Russia, an atheistic nation, at least as far as the education of the young in public schools is concerned. Evolution is now the law of the land!

But evolution is not even a testable scientific hypothesis, let alone a scientific *law*! This is truly an amazing development in a nation founded upon belief in the God of the Bible.

A British teacher of science, not a creationist, summarizes the situation in his country (and it would be an even more appropriate summary in America) as follows:

> For some time, it has seemed to me that our current methods of teaching Darwinism are suspiciously similar to indoctrination.[64]

---

64. G.H. Harper, "Darwinism and Indoctrination," *School Science Review* 59 (Dec. 1977): p. 258.

The Darwinist can always make a plausible reconstruction of what took place during the supposed evolution of a species. Any difficulties in reconciling a given kind of natural selection with a particular phase of evolution can be removed by the judicious choice of a correlated character.[65]

Looked at in this way, the teacher of Darwin's theory corresponds with the latter, since he undoubtedly is concerned to put across the conclusion that natural selection causes evolution, while *he cannot be concerned to any great extent with real evidence, because there isn't any.*[66]

The thesis of this chapter — namely, that evolutionism permeates and dominates modern thought in every field — could be expanded and further documented at great length if necessary, but most readers will agree that the point has been made quite compellingly already. That being the case, it inevitably follows that evolutionary thought is basically responsible for the lethally ominous political developments and the chaotic moral and social disintegrations that have been accelerating everywhere in recent decades. These cause-and-effect relationships will be demonstrated in the next two chapters.

---

65. Ibid., p. 265.
66. Ibid. Italics are mine.

2

Political Evolutionism — Right and Left

It would be a matter of great concern even if evolution were used *only* as the theoretical framework for all the various disciplines of study, as discussed in the preceding chapter. Unfortunately, it has also been made the pseudo-scientific rationale for just about every political, economic, and social system that capitalizes on human greed and lust for power, resulting in suffering and death for millions of people during the past century.

Many of the conflicts in modern society are formulated in oversimplified two-sided terms — left versus right, liberal versus conservative, East versus West, communism versus capitalism, and so on. The remarkable fact, however, is that the philosophers on both sides of such conflicts commonly maintain that their systems are firmly grounded in evolutionary science. In this chapter we shall consider some of the more important of these systems.

The Tragedy of Social Darwinism

Charles Darwin had barely published *The Origin of Species* in 1859 before the industrialists of England — and later, America — were using it to justify their monopolistic practices, their exploitation of labor, and laissez-faire capitalism in general. The terms "struggle for existence," followed by "natural selection" and "survival of the fittest," which were intended by the evolutionary biologists as slogans to apply to organic evolution, were catch phrases that caught on quickly in industrial economics. The resulting system, which came to be known as "social Darwinism," was tremendously significant in the business, industrial, and political life of Europe and the United States for almost a century. This fact is an embarrassment to most modern evolutionists, who excuse it by saying it was due to a misunderstanding of evolution. If so, the leading evolutionists of the day, as well as their popularizers, all misunderstood evolution.

To some considerable degree, in fact, Darwinism was actually developed to justify the socio-economic-military beliefs and practices prevalent at the time. It came in the midst of an age of expansion and technological progress in the Western democracies, and sociologists found it easy to apply the Darwinian scheme to the perpetuation and extension of the existing system, thereby giving it a persuasive and supposedly scientific rationalization. The socialist Jeremy Rifkin makes the following incisive evaluation:

> Darwin borrowed heavily from the popular economic thinking of the day. While by Darwin's own admission, Malthus's economic writings were a key influence in the development of his theory, Darwin was equally influenced by one of the other great economic philosophers of the eighteenth century, Adam Smith. An examination of Smith's and Darwin's writings shows how deeply indebted the latter was to the thoughts Smith penned in *The Wealth of Nations*, published in 1776.[1]

A key component of Darwin's theory was the idea of the "struggle for existence" in nature, with animal populations growing more rapidly than the food supply, resulting in the reign of tooth and claw, and only the strongest surviving to reproduce. The very phrase "struggle for existence" was borrowed from Thomas Malthus's *Essay on the Principles of Population*.

Malthus argued that any proposed measures to improve the lot of the laboring classes would only encourage them to reproduce more and thus make the struggle for existence more severe than ever. Since populations always tend to grow faster than the food supply, there would always be too many people unless population growth could somehow be discouraged. Darwin — as well as A.R. Wallace, Herbert Spencer, and others before them — then interpreted this as leading to the survival of only the "fittest," and thus eventually to progressive evolution.

---

1. Jeremy Rifkin, *Algeny* (New York: Viking, 1983), p. 86.

Spencer applied the doctrine to human societies with a vengeance: "If they are sufficiently complete to live, they *do* live, and it is well they should live. If they are not sufficiently complete to live, they die, and it is best they should die."[2]

It was Spencer who coined the phrase "survival of the fittest," and his sociology soon enjoyed a great vogue among laissez-faire capitalists, especially in America. R. Hoftstadter, in his definitive work on social Darwinism, observes:

> Spencer deplored not only poor laws, but also state-supported education, sanitary supervision other than the suppression of nuisances, regulation of housing conditions, and even state protection of the ignorant from medical quacks. He likewise opposed tariffs, state banking, and government postal systems.[3]

It is true that Spencer's evolutionary philosophy did envision the ultimate transformation of society for the good of all, but this would be accomplished by the very slow Darwinian process of small variations optimized by natural selection. Hoftstadter elaborates:

> A science of sociology, by teaching men to think of social causation scientifically, would awaken them to the enormous complexity of the social organism, and put an end to hasty legislative panaceas. Fortified by the Darwinian conception of gradual modification over long stretches of time, Spencer ridiculed schemes for quick social transformation.[4]

To considerable extent, this Darwinian concept of struggle and survival seemed to support the Calvinistic (and biblical) work ethic that had played such an important role in the founding and development of the original American colonies and then the United States. Consequently, especially in an age of progress and the American Dream, it seemed to fit right in with the old virtues and quickly obtained a great following, especially among those who were its greatest beneficiaries.

---

2. Herbert Spencer, *Social Status,* 1850, p. 414-415.
3. Richard Hofstadter, *Social Darwinism in American Thought,* revised edition (Boston, MA: Beacon Press, 1955), p. 41. Hofstadter's definitive study of social Darwinism was first published in 1944 by the University of Pennsylvania Press. It has been drawn on extensively by most later writers on these subjects.
4. Ibid., p. 45.

According to Hofstadter, the 19th-century railroad magnate Chauncey Depew asserted that the men who attained fame, fortune, and power in New York City represented the survival of the fittest, through "superior ability, foresight, and adaptability."[5] Another railroad baron, James J. Hill, alleged that "the fortunes of railroad companies are determined by the law of the survival of the fittest."[6]

Likewise, the legendary John D. Rockefeller, ruthless developer of one of America's greatest oil empires, and a staunch evolutionist, said, "This is not an evil tendency in business. It is merely the working-out of a law of nature and a law of God."[7]

The equally legendary Andrew Carnegie, honored today for his philanthropies and devotion to culture, but cruel and heartless in his own day to competitors and laborers alike, commented in his autobiography, "I remember that light came in as a flood and all was clear. Not only had I got rid of theology and the supernatural but I had found the truth of evolution."[8] Elsewhere he wrote, "[The law of competition] is here; we cannot evade it; no substitutes for it have been found; and while the law may sometimes be hard for the individual, it is best for the race, because it insures the survival of the fittest in every department."[9]

Such beliefs were common among the industrialists and businessmen of the post-Darwin century:

> Darwin's theory offered a resolution to humanity's perennial crisis of guilt. By proposing that each organism's drive for self-containment actually benefited the species as a whole, Darwin found a convenient formula for expiating the accumulating guilt of an age when self-interest and personal aggrandizement ruled supreme.[10]

The bourgeoisie was in need of a "proper" justification for the new factory system with its dehumanizing process of division of

5. Chauncey Depew, *My Memories of Eighty Years* (New York: 1922), p. 383–384. Cited in Hofstadter, *Social Darwinism*, p. 45.

6. James J. Hill, *Highways of Progress* (New York: 1910), p. 126, 137. Cited in Hofstadter, *Social Darwinism*, p. 45.

7. John D. Rockefeller, quoted in William J. Ghent, *Our Benevolent Feudalism* (New York: Macmillan, 1902), p. 29. See Hofstadter, *Social Darwinism*, p. 45.

8. Andrew Carnegie, *Autobiography* (Boston, MA: Houghton Mifflin Co., 1920), p. 327. See Hofstadter, *Social Darwinism*, p. 45.

9. Andrew Carnegie, "Wealth," *North American Review* 148 (1889): p. 655–657. Cited in Hofstadter, *Social Darwinism*, p. 46.

10. Rifkin, *Algeny*, p. 95.

labor. By claiming that a similar process was at work in nature, Darwin provided an ideal rationale for those capitalists hell-bent on holding the line against any fundamental challenge to the economic hierarchy they managed and profited from.[11]

The most influential American social Darwinist was William Graham Sumner, professor of political and social science at Yale University from 1872 to 1909. It is interesting that he was converted to evolutionism by the fossil finds of a colleague, Professor Othniel Marsh, who had arranged these into the so-called family tree of the horses. It is even more interesting that many evolutionists still regard this artificial "tree" (long since acknowledged by modern evolutionists to be, at best, a "bush," with no clear sequence of evolution at all) as the best "proof" of evolution.

Sumner exerted a profound influence on vast numbers of students and others in his generation. His Darwinian view contradicted many basic American ideals. Hofstadter comments, "Sumner concluded that these principles of social evaluation negated the traditional American ideology of equality and natural rights."[12]

We do not need to document that particular fruit of evolutionism much further. Rifkin summarizes it as follows:

> Darwin's cosmology sanctioned an entire age of history. Convinced that their own behavior was in consort with the workings of nature, industrial man and woman were armed with the ultimate justification they needed to continue their relentless exploitation of the environment and their fellow human beings without ever having to stop for even a moment to reflect on the consequences of their actions.[13]

Other fruits of evolutionism closely related to social Darwinism (racism, militarism, imperialism) will be considered below. First, however, it should be noted that this system is not only contrary to the true principles

---

11. Ibid., p. 89. As a modern socialist, Rifkin is devastating in his attack on Darwinism and the social Darwinism that is generated.
12. Hofstadter, *Social Darwinism*, p. 59.
13. Rifkin, *Algeny*, p. 108. Kenneth Hsu, chairman of earth sciences at the Swiss Federal Institute of Technology, says that "we were victims of a cruel social ideology that assumes that competition among individuals, classes, nations, or races is the natural condition of life, and that it is also natural for the superior to dispossess the inferior. . . . The law of natural selection is not, I will maintain, science. It is an ideology, and a wicked one" (*Earthwatch* (March 1989): p. 17).

of American democracy, as expressed especially in the Declaration of Independence and the Bill of Rights, but also directly in conflict with biblical Christianity and Christian ethics.

The idea that a loving, wise, and powerful God used evolution — with its "struggle for existence" and "survival of the fittest" — as His method of creation is grotesque! Evolution is the cruelest, most wasteful, and most irrational method of "creation" that could ever be imagined, not even to mention the fact that it is scientifically untenable. The postulated suffering and death of multiplied billions of animals in the course of evolutionary "progress" from amoeba to man is a libel against the character of the Creator — who must certainly have been capable of creating each organism complete, with its own perfectly designed structure for its own unique function, *right from the start*. Evolution may make some sense in the context of atheism, but it certainly does not fit Christian theism! As the atheistic biologist Jacques Monod expressed it:

> And why would God have to have chosen this extremely complex and difficult mechanism? When, I would say by definition, He was at liberty to choose other mechanisms, why would He have to start with simple molecules? Why not create man right away, as of course classical religions believed.[14]

Monod was an outstanding biologist, winner of a Nobel Prize, and thoroughly convinced of evolutionism, but he could see no way it could be compatible with theism:

> [Natural] selection is the blindest, and most cruel way of evolving new species. . . . The struggle for life and elimination of the weakest is a horrible process, against which our whole modern ethics revolts. . . . I am surprised that a Christian would defend the idea that this is the process which God more or less set up in order to have evolution.[15]

Bertrand Russell, another atheistic scientist/philosopher, put it this way:

> Religion, in our day, has accommodated itself to the doctrine of evolution. . . . We are told that . . . evolution is the unfolding of an idea which has been in the mind of God throughout. It appears that during those ages . . . when animals were torturing each other

---

14. Jacques Monod, "The Secret of Life," Interview with Laurie John, Australian Broadcasting Co., June 10, 1976.
15. Ibid. Monod gave this interview shortly before his death.

with ferocious horns and agonizing stings, Omnipotence was quietly waiting for the ultimate emergence of man, with his still more widely diffused cruelty. Why the Creator should have preferred to reach His goal by a process, instead of going straight to it, these modern theologians do not tell us.[16]

Now it does seem that if these leading atheistic scientists are offended by the thought of God's creating man by such a wastefully cruel process as evolution, the Christian believer, taught to follow Christ's sacrificial example (neither selfish nor belligerently competitive), should be able to understand that the very concept of evolution diametrically opposes everything that Christianity is supposed to teach.

It is not surprising, therefore, in view of its excesses of the past, that this older style of social Darwinism has been largely displaced today by evolutionism of the left (socialism, communism, various forms of collectivism) instead of individualism (evolution of the right). Occasionally it surfaces again, however, as in the modern libertarian movement.

It is a mistake to assume, as many do, that political "conservatism" is necessarily compatible with biblical Christianity. For example, Robert Welch, founder of the rightist John Birch Society, was a strong evolutionist, as were many of its other early leaders.

Similarly, many leaders in the present-day Republican Party (e.g., the Rockefellers and other leaders in Wall Street and the interlocking directorates of the giant corporations) are really the spiritual heirs of the 19th-century social Darwinists. Most of them are firmly committed to evolutionism and the amassing of great fortunes by whatever methods will succeed in the economic struggle for existence. The recent betrayal of the "religious right" is a painful reminder of this fact to disillusioned Christians. This group joined forces with the ostensibly conservative Republican establishment in order to help restore traditional "Americanism" (family values, prayer and creationism in schools, sexual morality in society, etc.) and to elect Ronald Reagan president. Its members then saw their own concerns ignored in favor of concentration on economic measures designed to restore a greater degree of Darwinist laissez-faire capitalism. Bible-believing Christians must not forget that most political "conservatives" today are still evolutionists (especially those in prominent positions), just as are most political and religious "liberals," and as such have their own agenda.

---

16. Bertrand Russell, *Religion and Science* (New York: Oxford University Press, 1961), p. 73.

The Preservation of Favored Races

Racism existed long before Darwin, just as did selfish human aggression. Darwinism, however, gave racism scientific respectability and apparent justification, just as social Darwinism was rationalized as a pseudo-scientific extension of a law of nature ("self-preservation is the first law of nature," so they say).

Darwin's book *The Origin of Species by Natural Selection* had as its subtitle *The Preservation of Favored Races in the Struggle for Life.* Modern apologists for Darwin stress that he had reference mainly to animal "races," or subspecies, but there is really no doubt that he meant it to include human races as well. In his later book, *The Descent of Man,* Darwin wrote:

> At some future period, not very distant as measured by centuries, the civilized races of man will almost certainly exterminate and replace the savage races throughout the world. At the same time the anthropomorphous apes . . . will no doubt be exterminated. The break between man and his nearest allies will then be wider, for it will intervene between man in a more civilized state, as we may hope, even than the Caucasian, and some ape as low as a baboon, instead of as now between the negro or Australian and the gorilla.[17]

Darwin's motion that the various races were at different evolutionary distances from the apes, with Negroes at the bottom and Caucasians at the top, was not unique to him, but rather was almost universal among the evolutionary scientists of the 19th century.

Thomas Huxley, whose ardent advocacy of Darwinism was the single factor most responsible for its rapid acceptance, said:

> No rational man, cognizant of the facts, believes that the average negro is the equal, still less the superior, of the white man. And if this be true, it is simply incredible that, when all his disabilities are removed, and our prognathous relative has a fair field and no favor, as well as no oppressor, he will be able to compete successfully with his bigger-brained and smaller-jawed rival, in a contest which is to be carried on by thoughts and not by bites.[18]

---

17. Charles Darwin, *The Descent of Man,* second edition (New York: A.L. Burt Co., 1874), p. 178.
18. Thomas H. Huxley, *Lay Sermons, Addresses and Reviews* (New York: Appleton, 1871), p. 20. Huxley was arguing that blacks could not compete intellectually with Caucasians, even under equal and fair conditions.

It was not only Darwin and Huxley, the two top evolutionists, who were racists. *All* of them were! This fact has been documented thoroughly in a key book by John Haller,[19] appropriately entitled *Outcasts from Evolution*. One reviewer of this book said:

> This is an extremely important book, documenting as it does what has long been suspected, the ingrained, firm, and almost universal racism of North American men of science during the nineteenth (and into the twentieth) century. . . . *Ab initio*, Afro-Americans were viewed by these intellectuals as being in certain ways unredeemably, unchangeably, irrevocably inferior.[20]

Another reviewer, convinced by Haller's massive documentation, said, "That generation of scientists believed that no artificial process of education or forced evolution would ever enable the blacks to catch up."[21]

Haller was concerned primarily with racism among American scientists, but these concepts were, if anything, even more strongly indoctrinated in European evolutionists. For example: "In nineteenth-century Europe the concept of race was a preoccupation for the growing human sciences. . . . These first physical anthropologists helped to develop the concept of Aryan supremacy, which later fueled the institutional racism of Germany in the 1930s, and of South Africa today."[22]

This evolutionary racism was a natural inference from the slow-and-gradual chance evolutionary process envisioned by Darwin and his followers. On that basis, "race" is simply a "subspecies," which, if left to struggle for its existence in competition with other subspecies, may eventually triumph and become a distinct species. Each of the various human "races" had thus developed from some ancient primate stock, and some had progressed more than others.

A very common model for this concept was Ernst Haeckel's famous (or "infamous" and long-since refuted) "biogenetic law," or "recapitulation theory." Let modern evolutionist — and *anti*-racist — Stephen Jay Gould, explain:

---

19. John S. Haller Jr., *Outcasts from Evolution: Scientific Attitudes of Racial Inferiority, 1859–1900* (Urbana, IL: University of Illinois press, 1971), 228 p.
20. Sidney W. Mintz, *American Scientist* 60 (May/June 1972): p. 387. Prof. Mintz was on the anthropology faculty at Yale University.
21. Book review section, *Science* 175 (Feb. 1972): p. 506.
22. James Ferguson, "The Laboratory of Racism," *New Scientist* 103 (Sept. 27, 1984): p. 18.

In Down's day, the theory of recapitulation embodied a biologist's best guide for the organization of life into sequences of higher and lower forms. (Both the theory and "ladder approach" to classification that it encouraged are, or should be, defunct today.) This theory, often expressed by the mouthful "ontogeny recapitulates phylogeny," held that higher animals, in their embryonic development, pass through a series of stages representing, in proper sequence, the adult forms of ancestral, lower creatures. Thus, the human embryo first develops gills slits, like a fish; later a three-chambered heart, like a reptile; still later a mammalian tail. Recapitulation provides a convenient focus to the activities of their own children for comparison with normal, adult behavior in lower races.[23]

Assuming that all the races had gone through a mammalian stage shortly before birth, the various stages of the Caucasian childhood are said to represent the various lower races and their attainments — with the blacks at the bottom, then the yellow races, and the whites at the top:

> The Negroid stock is even more ancient than the Caucasian and Mongolian, as may be proved by an examination not only of the brain, of the hair, of the bodily characters, such as teeth, the genitalia, the sense organs, but of the insects, the intelligence. The standard of intelligence of the average adult Negro is similar to that of the eleven-year-old youth of the species Homo sapiens.[24]

The author of the above extreme racist opinion, H.F. Osborn, was not a backwoods bigot, but rather the most prominent American anthropologist of the first half of the 20th century, director of the American Museum of Natural History, and a leading evolutionist. His opinion was not based on innate prejudice or on some strained biblical interpretation, for he was a highly educated scientist and did not believe the Bible at all. Osborn honestly felt his racism was based on evolutionary *science*! So did most other anthropologists, before Adolf Hitler gave racism such a bad name.

Russell H. Tuttle, a prominent modern anthropologist at the University of Chicago, reviewing an article by C. Loring Brace of the University of Michigan, notes this fact:

---

23. Stephen Jay Gould, "Dr. Down's Syndrome," *Natural History* 89 (April 1980): p. 144. The title refers to the popular identification of the Down's Syndrome as "mongolism," so named by Dr. Down in the belief that people with this handicap corresponded to the stage of evolution achieved by the yellow races.
24. Henry Fairfield Osborn, "The Evolution of Human Races," *Natural History,* Jan/Feb 1926. Reprinted in *Natural History* 89 (April 1980): p. 129.

Brace squarely confronts racist influences on the two chief founders of institutional physical anthropology in the United States — [Ales] Hrdlicka, based at the American Museum of Natural History, and E.A. Hooton, with whom most of the second generation of physical anthropologists studied at Harvard.[25]

Osborn, Hooton, Hrdlicka, Huxley, Darwin, Haeckel — a veritable "Who's Who" of leading evolutionists and anthropologists — all committed to evolutionary racism. Many, many other names could be added. As Hofstadter has pointed out in his incisive and authoritative review of social Darwinism: "Common among men of learning was the conception, taken over from Haeckel's Biogenetic Law, that, since the development of the individual is a recapitulation of the development of the race, primitives must be considered as being in the arrested stages of childhood or adolescence."[26]

Of all the so-called scientific evidences of evolution, the most disreputable is surely this pseudo-science of paleoanthropology, which parades one "missing link" after another to try to prove human evolution, only to see them denied by other anthropologists, if not eventually rejected altogether in great embarrassment (e.g., Piltdown Man, Nebraska Man). And all of it was intricately involved in this race business:

> We cannot understand much of the history of late nineteenth century and early twentieth century anthropology, with its plethora of taxonomic names proposed for nearly every scrap of fossil bone, unless we appreciate its obsession with the identification and ranking of races.[27]

Authors varied in their opinion of the number of human races, from Cuvier's three to as many as thirty or more in the 20th century, but with a few exceptions they agreed that the concept of race was sound.[28]

As previously noted, we are not suggesting that racism *began* with Darwin and the other 19th-century evolutionists. Racism seems to be as old as the nations. Almost every tribe and nation has, in one way or another and

25. Russell H. Tuttle, "Five Decades of Anthropology," reviewing *A History of American Physical Anthropology*, Frank Spencer, editor (New York: Academic, 1982), in *Science* 220 (1983): p. 832. Brace's article was titled "The Roots of the Race Concept in American Physical Anthropology."

26. Hofstadter, *Social Darwinism*, p. 193.

27. Stephen Jay Gould, "Human Equality Is a Contingent Fact of History," *Natural History* 93 (Nov. 1984): p. 28.

28. R.W. Wrangham, book review section of *American Scientist* 72 (Jan./Feb. 1984): p. 75.

at one time or another, held the belief that it was superior to others. Whatever the original source of such beliefs may have been, it was not the Bible! The modern slanderous fallacy that racism — especially the notion of white supremacy — is a biblical doctrine could not be further from the truth. The Scriptures teach plainly that God "hath made of one blood all nations of men" (Acts 17:26) and that all men have "one father" (Mal. 2:10). The fact that some have distorted certain biblical passages to teach racism (e.g., the Hamitic curse) does not by any means involve the Bible itself in racism, for it is clearly opposed to it.

Although racism is an ancient fallacy, it was Darwinian evolutionism that first seemed to give it scientific plausibility. For many decades after Darwin, the idea of different origins for the different human races seemed to have displaced the biblical doctrine of just one race.

> The new anthropology soon became a theoretical battleground between two opposed schools of thought on the origin of humans. The older and more established of these was "monogenism," the belief that all humankind, irrespective of color or other characteristics, was directly descended from Adam and from the single and original act of God's creation. Monogenism was promulgated by the Church and universally accepted until the 18th century, when opposition to theological authority began to fuel the rival theory of "polygenism," which held that different racial communities had different origins.[29]

In recent years, however, especially after World War II, racism has fallen into disfavor among evolutionary scientists, and so have most other aspects of social Darwinism. Gould observes:

> This theory of ancient separation had its last prominent defense in 1962, when Carletoun Coon published his *Origin of Races*. Coon divided humanity into five major races — caucasoids, mongoloids, australoids, and, among African blacks, congoids and capoids. He claimed that these five groups were already distinct subspecies during the reign of our ancestor *homo erectus*.[30]

All anthropologists now seem to agree that all the different human races have a common origin. In fact, they now seem to have (unintentionally) returned to the biblical doctrine that there are *no* races except the human race:

---

29. Ferguson, "The Laboratory of Racism," p. 18.
30. Gould, "Human Equality Is a Contingent Fact of History," p. 28.

We recognize only one formal category for divisions within species — the subspecies. Races, if formally defined, are therefore subspecies. . . . Human variation exists; the formal designation of races is passé.[31]

Brace's closing comments are upbeat. He reiterates the modern view that we should abandon the concept of race altogether and instead record the gene frequencies and traits of populations that are identified simply by their geographic localities. This genotypic and phenotypic information is to be interpreted in terms of historical and proximate selective forces.[32]

The fact that evolutionists now agree with the biblical doctrine of one race, however, does not mean that they agree with the biblical doctrine of creation. As strongly committed to evolutionism as ever, they are merely casting about for different possible mechanisms and sequences of evolution.

Even with this concession, however, the very chronology of evolution still lends itself to racism. L.L. Cavalli-Sforza, a professor of genetics at Stanford, says:

When we look at the main divisions of mankind, we find many differences that are visible to the unaided eye. It is not hard to assess the origin of an individual with respect to the major racial subdivisions: the straight-haired, tan Orientals, the wiry-haired, dark Africans, and the lank-haired pale Caucasians. If we analyze our impression in detail, we find that they come down to a few highly visible characteristics: the color of the skin, the color and form of the hair, and the gross morphology of the face, the eye folds, the nose, and the lips, it is highly likely that all these differences are determined genetically, but they are not determined in any simple ways. For example, where skin color is concerned, there are at least four gene differences that contribute to variations in pigmentation.[33]

The problem is that, in the context of slow-and-gradual evolution, it would take a very long time to develop these different characteristics by

---

31. Ibid., p. 30.
32. Tuttle, "Five Decades of Anthropology," p. 832.
33. L.L. Cavalli-Sforza, "The Genetics of Human Populations, *Scientific American* 231 (Sept. 1974): p. 85.

chance mutation and natural selection, from an original common source. Cavalli-Sforza elaborates:

> The simplest interpretation of these conclusions today would envision a relatively small group starting to spread not long after modern man appeared. With the spreading, groups became separated and isolated. Racial differentiation followed. Fifty thousand years or so is a short time in evolutionary terms, and this may help to explain why, genetically speaking, human races show relatively small differences.[34]

The very idea of calling "fifty thousand years or so" a "short time" is a testimony to the esoteric nature of evolutionary thought. This is ten times longer than all recorded history! If this great span of time produced physical variations, it would certainly also produce mental variations, and some "races" surely would have evolved to higher levels of intellect and ability than others under the impact of segregation into different environments during all those years. Evolutionary gradualism thus clearly tends to generate racial distinctives and therefore naturally tends to justify racism. The same is true of the "punctuational" model of evolution. Stephen Jay Gould, the chief advocate of this system, has said that "the division of humans into modern 'racial' groups is a product of our recent history. It does not predate the origin of our own species, *Homo sapiens*, and probably occurred during the last few tens (or at most hundreds) of thousands of years."[35]

At any rate, there was ample time to produce distinctive racial differences by *any* model of chance evolution, and thus ample "scientific" basis for racism. Therefore, modern-day racists (as in South Africa) still quite reasonably justify their racism by appeal to evolutionary theory. So do modern advocates of so-called genetic engineering, who think they can produce a super-race. However:

> The public is already suspicious of genetics. It recognizes that earlier, pseudoscientific extrapolations from genetics to society were used to rationalize racism, with tragic consequences, and it has developed much anxiety over the allegedly imminent prospect of genetic manipulation in man.[36]

Those of the so-called lower races have every right to resent this particular fruit of Darwinism. One noted Chinese scientist has recently written:

---

34. Ibid., p. 89.
35. Gould, "Human Equality Is a Contingent Fact of History," p. 31.
36. Bernard D. Davis, "Social Determinism and Behavioral Genetics," *Science* 189 (Sept. 26, 1975): p. 1049.

My abhorrence of Darwinism is understandable, for what member of the "lower races" could remain indifferent to the statement attributed to the great master (Darwin, 1881, in a letter to W. Graham) that "at no very distant date, what an endless number of the lower races will have been eliminated by the higher civilized races throughout the world." . . . Charles Darwin was not a prophet, not a messiah, not a demigod. He was a gentleman scientist of the Victorian Era, and an establishment member of a society that sent gunboats to forcibly import opium into China, all in the name of competition (in free trade) and survival of the fittest.[37]

This evolutionary author quite rightly castigates Darwinism for its implied racism, but he apparently fails to see that any other form of evolution lends itself equally well to this evil system.

In sharp contrast to the history of this depressing aspect of human society, the biblical record is far nobler and more realistic. Neither the concept of "race" nor the word itself is ever found in the Bible. All present nations and tribes are descendants of Noah, after the great Flood (note Gen. 9:17–19, 10:32), with their actual dispersion into distinct linguistic (therefore, tribal) units dating only from the miraculous confusion of tongues at Babel (Gen. 11:8–9). This event cannot be dated earlier than perhaps 7,000 years ago at the outside, but more likely less than 5,000 years ago, and this corresponds well with all confirmed (by written records, that is) dates of the world's most ancient kingdoms (Egypt, Sumeria, Syria, China, etc.). This amount of time certainly would not suffice to generate different "races" of mankind by any process of chance evolution. However, it would be quite adequate to develop the different tribes and nations with their distinctive physiological characteristics, by the *known* and *observed* biological processes of recombination (of *created* genetic factors present in Noah's family to begin with), followed by isolation of small founder populations in different environments. In very similar fashion (that is, genetic isolation of small groups), all the different varieties of dogs have been developed in just a few thousand years of selective breeding. The point is that all the genetic potential for variation must be present to begin with.

There is really only one race of human beings, and this is the human race. Our primeval parents did not evolve from one or more populations of ancient primates, but were directly created by God, in His own image. God

---

37. Kenneth J. Hsu, letter to the editor in *Geology* 15 (April 1987): p. 377. Dr. Hsu is an outstanding Chinese geologist, currently in Switzerland. Although an evolutionist, he is an advocate of neo-catastrophism in geology and punctuationism in biology.

did establish at Babel distinct nations corresponding to the various languages He also established at that time, with a purpose for each nation and tribe. In that sense there is divine justification for national patriotism in a nation, but only in consistency with God's purpose for *that* nation in the context of his overall purpose for *all* nations. There is no basis whatever — theological or scientific — for notions of "racial" superiority. These ideas have led to great suffering, as will be discussed in the following sections.

Militarism, Imperialism, and the White Man's Burden

Social Darwinism, when extended beyond individual and corporate struggle-and-survival practices, can easily become militaristic nationalism. Similarly, racism, when extended beyond national boundaries, can become imperialism. Just as was true with racism and what is now called social Darwinism, militarism and imperialism have frequently surfaced throughout the ages. However, for the first time in history, modern evolutionism has provided them a pseudo-scientific justification, and many have taken advantage of it.

Social Darwinism has often been understood in this sense: as a philosophy, exalting competition, power, and violence over convention, ethics, and religion. Thus it has become a portmanteau of nationalism, imperialism, militarism, and dictatorship, of the cults of the hero, the superman, and the master race.[38]

The implication of Darwinism for national policy was believed to be ". . . the nation is the instrument that will raise civilization to a more sublime state. And as [the hero] made his way by struggle and force, so the nation must make its way in the world by war and conquest."[39] It was more than coincidence that the century after Darwin was the great age of European and even North American imperialism.

A widely read article in the United States, published just 30 years after the *Origin*, said, "The greatest authority of all the advocates of war is Darwin. Since the theory of evolution has been promulgated, they can cover their natural barbarism with the name of Darwin and proclaim the sanguinary instincts of their inmost hearts as the last word of science."[40]

---

38. Gertrude Himmelfarb, *Darwin and the Darwinian Evolution* (London: Chatto & Windus, 1959), p. 343–344.
39. Ibid., p. 344.
40. Max Nordau, "The Philosophy and Morals of War," *North American Review* 169 (1889): p. 794. Cited in Hofstadter, *Social Darwinism*, p. 171.

Similarly, the article on "Imperialism" in the *Encyclopaedia Britannica* (1949 edition, as written by Hans Kohn, professor of history at Smith College) acknowledges this influence:

> The new period of imperialism at the end of the 19th century found its spiritual support in Bismarckism and social Darwinism, in all the theories glorifying power and success, which had swept over Europe with the German victory over France in 1870. Racial theories seemed to give to this attitude, which was in opposition to all the traditional theories of morality, a justification of "science" and "nature," the belief in which was almost becoming the dominant faith of the period.

In the Franco-Prussian War of 1870, both sides had invoked Darwinism in expounding the conflict's rationale, and this theme became increasingly significant in European commentary as time went on, culminating finally in the extreme evolutionism of Hitler and the Nazis. But more of this later.

Evolutionary philosophy also contributed significantly to the development of the so-called "white man's burden" idea, with its motivating conviction of Anglo-Saxon superiority, and the resulting imperialistic expansion of the British Empire and, to a lesser extent, the United States' sphere of influence. As already noted, almost all 19th-century evolutionists, especially the anthropologists, considered the Caucasian "race" to be at the top of the evolutionary ladder. It was easy enough for some Englishmen and North Americans, riding the crest of industrial supremacy, to focus on Anglo-Saxonism.

The idea of racial superiority was certainly not confined to England and North America. Darwin's books were quickly translated, not only into German and French, but also into Spanish, Russian, Czech, Polish, Hebrew, and Japanese, exerting profound influence on the leadership in many nations. The eminent historian Jacques Barzun commented in 1958:

> War became the symbol, the image, the inducement, the reason, and the language of all human doings on the planet. No one who has not waded through some sizable part of the literature of the period 1870–1914 has any conception of the extent to which it is one long call for blood, nor of the variety of parties, classes, nations, and races whose blood was separately and contradictorily clamored for by the enlightened citizens of the ancient civilization of Europe. . . .
>
> The militarists of the second half of the century poeticized war and luxuriated in the prospect of it. With relative impunity for themselves,

they took it for granted that all struggles in life must be struggles for life, and the death of the loser its "natural" goal.[41]

Barzun was for many years professor of history and dean of the graduate faculties at Columbia University. His remarkable book *Darwin, Marx, Wagner* is a uniquely incisive evaluation of the scientific, sociological, and cultural causes of the terrible moral breakdown of the modern world. In it he noted:

> In every European country between 1870 and 1914 there was a war party demanding armaments, an individualist party demanding ruthless competition, an imperialist party demanding a free hand over backward peoples, a socialist party demanding the conquest of power, and a racialist party demanding internal purges against aliens — all of them, when appeals to greed and glory failed, or even before, invoked Spencer and Darwin, which was to say, science incarnate. . . . Race was biological, it was sociological; it was Darwinian.[42]

This ubiquitous racism and militarism played a large role in the imperialist expansionism of the European nation. The conviction of Anglo-Saxon supremacy was dominant in the thinking of Cecil Rhodes, for example, in his South African colonialist adventures, as well as in the slaughter of the natives of the Congo forest by the Belgians. His will, which established the famous Rhodes Scholarships, indicated the purpose of Cecil Rhodes to be that of uniting the English-speaking peoples for greater racial development. The same mood prevailed in the United States: "The Darwinian mood sustained the belief in Anglo-Saxon racial superiority which obsessed many American thinkers in the latter half of the nineteenth century. The measures of world dominion already achieved by the 'race' seemed to prove it the fittest."[43]

One of the most influential Americans of this era was Theodore Roosevelt, soon to be president. He was a strong advocate of what he called, in a famous speech, "the strenuous life." During the years 1889 to 1896, Roosevelt wrote a four-volume work entitled *The Winning of the West*, which maintained that a racial war to the finish with the Indians was inevitable

---

41. Jacques Barzun, *Darwin, Marx, Wagner* (Garden City, NY: Doubleday, 1958), p. 92–93.
42. Ibid., p. 94–95.
43. Hofstadter, *Social Darwinism*, p. 172–173.

and represented the culminating achievement of the spread of the English-speaking people over the world. He also urged on his countrymen in the international struggle for existence in Cuba, Puerto Rico, Hawaii, and the Philippines, regarding the taking of these islands as part of our "manifest destiny."

Harvard evolutionist John Fiske, President R.B. Hayes, General W.T. Sherman, John Hay, Henry Cabot Lodge, and the Rev. Josiah Strong were among many other prominent American promoters of Anglo-Saxonism and militant expansionism in the late 19th century. Surprisingly enough, one of the strongest and most influential books in this vein was written by the latter, who was the executive secretary of the Evangelical Society of the United States. In this book, written to raise money for missions, Strong said:

> Then will the world enter upon a new stage of history — the final competition of races for which the world is being schooled. If I do not read amiss, this powerful race will move down upon Mexico, down upon Central and South America, out upon the islands of the sea, over upon Africa, and beyond. And can anyone doubt that the result of this competition of races will be the "survival of the fittest"?[44]

Unfortunately, in common with many other "evangelicals" of this period, Josiah Strong was both a theistic evolutionist and a strong advocate of the so-called social gospel, as well as an Anglo-Saxon racist.

Many believed that Anglo-Saxon world domination would be brought about peacefully, by virtue of the innate superiority of Anglo-American democratic and capitalist ideals. The evolutionary poet Alfred, Lord Tennyson, who had written of the "reign of tooth and claw" in nature, now also wrote glowingly of a future "Parliament of Man, the Federation of the World."

Toward the end of the 19th century, however, many of these ideas began to encounter serious opposition, especially the goal of American imperialistic expansionism, as well as the tenets of social Darwinism in general. Evolutionism was not generally opposed, of course, but was increasingly brought into service in the interests of peaceful cooperation as a major factor of evolutionary progress.[45] Finally, even this country's entry into World War I was justified publicly, not by Darwinist slogans, but by the goal of bringing in world peace and "making the world safe for democracy."

---

44. Josiah P. Strong, *Our Country: Its Possible Future and Its Present Crisis* (c. 1885), p. 174. Cited in Hofstadter, *Social Darwinism*, p. 179.

45. An influential book in this vein, still often cited by defensive evolutionists, was *Mutual Aid*, by Prince Peter Kropotkin, published in London in 1902.

In Germany as well as in some other European nations, it was a different story. Darwinism was applied with a vengeance, increasing from the Franco-Prussian War up to World War I and then even more with Hitler and the Nazi movement.

The German philosopher Friedrich Nietzsche was a younger contemporary of Darwin and was profoundly influenced by his evolutionism, especially its racist implications. Nietzsche is especially remembered today for his "God is dead" pronouncements (based on his conviction that Darwin had proved atheism) and his promotion of the myth of the coming "superman" or "super-race." He disagreed with Darwin, however, on the method by which the latter would be obtained — not, he insisted, by random variation and natural selection, but by warfare and eugenics, with merciless extinction of inferior peoples and races. Conway Zirkle explains:

> Both Nietzschean ethics and social Darwinism emphasized the value of the superior individual but they also recognized the value of superior groups. Nietzsche even extended his ethical standards to master and slave races. It was necessary only to mix his ethics with Machiavellian statecraft, to *bouleversé* his individualism into Marxian collectivism, to add the Hegelian worship of the State, and the witches' brew of totalitarianism would be complete. Thus do our notions afflict us, and that which glows up in the brains of philosophers and theoreticians may ultimately have to be debated on the fields of battle.[46]

Nietzsche's philosophy had much influence everywhere, but especially in his native Germany, where it contributed significantly to the growth of German militarism and the myth of Teutonic racial supremacy. Nietzsche himself eventually went insane.

Of even greater influence than Nietzsche, however, was the German biologist Ernst Haeckel. George Stein, who is on the faculty of Miami University's School of Interdisciplinary studies, has observed:

> Ernst Haeckel (1834–1919) was the man who brought Darwinismus into German intellectual life. Not only did he succeed in establishing his interpretation of the strictly scientific aspects of Darwin as the correct view for a generation of scholars, but he went far beyond science to establish a unique form of social Darwinism. This

---

46. Conway Zirkle, *Evolution, Marxian Biology and the Social Scene* (Philadelphia, PA: University of Pennsylvania Press, 1959), p. 168–169.

social Darwinism combined an almost mystical, religious belief in the forces of nature (i.e., natural selection as the fundamental law of life) with a literal and not analogical transfer of the laws of biology to the social and political arena. It was, in essence, a romantic folkism synthesized with scientific evolutionism. It included the standard Darwinian ideas of struggle (*Kampf*) and competition as the foundation for natural law, and therefore social law, with a curious "religion" of nature, which implied a small place for rationalism, the lack of free will, and happiness as submission to the eternal laws of nature.[47]

Haeckel was considered at the time to be a great evolutionary biologist, almost equal in stature to Darwin himself. However, his most famous contribution, the recapitulation theory, has long since been proved false. "Ontogeny" does *not* "recapitulate phylogeny," even though many generations of high school students (including the present one) have been taught that it does. Furthermore, Haeckel advocated Lamarckianism as well as Darwinism. Worst of all, he was forced to admit that he had "schematized" (or, better, "fabricated") the famous series of sketches supposedly showing that the embryos of all mammals (including man) are essentially identical to each other for some time after conception. These fallacious drawings have been reproduced in text after text since they were first developed by Haeckel as part of his atheistic propaganda. Even today, they are still being use as one of the key evidences for evolution.

Although Haeckel's scientific contributions have long since been proved to be minimal at best, his political and sociological influence has been enormous: "Along with his social Darwinist followers, he set about to demonstrate the 'aristocratic' and non-democratic character of the laws of nature. . . . He became one of Germany's major ideologists for racism, nationalism, and imperialism."[48]

George Stein has summarized Haeckel's sociological ideas, developed more fully in the publications of the Monist League, which he founded, as follows:

The basic outline of German social Darwinism as developed by Haeckel and his colleagues is clear. It was argued that, on scientific

---

47. George J. Stein, "Biological Sciences and the Roots of Nazism," *American Scientist* 76 (Jan/Feb 1988): p 53–54.

48. Daniel Gasman, *The Scientific Origins of National Socialism: Social Darwinism in Ernest Haeckel and the German Monist League* (New York: American Elsevier, 1971), p. xvi–xvii.

grounds, man was merely a part of nature with no special transcendent qualities of special humanness. On the other hand, the Germans were members of a biologically superior community. German social Darwinism, contrary to Anglo-American social Darwinism, rejected the liberal individualistic state in favor of a natural, organic, folkish state of blood and soil. It attacked the alienation and atomization of individualistic modern civilization in the name of a psychological fulfillment resulting from union with the natural processes of evolution seen as a collective struggle for existence. And, of course, it argued that politics was merely the straightforward application of the laws of biology.[49]

Darwin, Nietzsche, and Haeckel thus laid the foundations for the intense German militarism that eventually led to the Great War of 1914–1918. There were others who participated in the development, of course, including many of the German generals and political leaders, all very much under the spell of the German variety of social Darwinism. General Friedrich von Bernhardi said, "War gives a biologically just decision, since its decisions rest on the very nature of things. . . . It is not only a biological law, but a moral obligation, and, as such, an indispensable factor in civilization."[50]

The historian William Thayer interpreted Germany's aggression, including the Kaiser's motivation, in strictly Darwinian terms. Writing during the conflict, he said:

> This widely quoted assertion [that is, of General von Bernhardi] was used to help stimulate America's entry into the war against Germany.
>
> In all directions, the Germans saw proof that they were the Chosen People. They interpreted the doctrine of evolution so as to draw from it a warrant for their aspirations. Evolution taught that "the fittest survived."
>
> The champions of supermania lean heavily on biology to support their creed. . . . You might infer, to hear them buzz, that . . . the fact that you survive is proof that you are the "fittest."[51]

In a strong sense, therefore, World War I could be regarded as a Darwinian struggle between two "favored races" for "survival of the fittest"

---

49. Stein, "Biological Science," p. 56.
50. Friedrich von Bernhardi, *Germany and the Next War* (c. 1912), cited in Hofstadter, *Social Darwinism*, p. 197.
51. William Roscoe Thayer, *Germany Versus Civilization* (New York: Houghton Mifflin, 1916), p. 80–81. Cited in Hofstadter, *Social Darwinism*, pp. 197-198.

— British Anglo-Saxonism versus German Teutonism. Other nations were drawn into the conflict, but its evolutionary implications were widely discussed both before and after the war years. In fact, it is well known that America's most vocal post–World War I anti-evolutionist, William Jennings Bryan, was drawn into this role not because of either scientific or biblical considerations, but because of the tremendous harm caused by evolutionary thinking, both in terms of German militarism and also because of its increasingly demoralizing effect on America's young people. In terms of both of these effects, however, there was much worse yet to come, as we shall see.

Hitler — Evolution in Full Flower

Social Darwinism, racism, militarism, and imperialism finally reached their zenith in Nazi Germany under the unspeakable Adolf Hitler. As we have shown, all these systems, even though basically rooted in sinful human nature, are logical extensions of the evolutionary philosophy. Consequently, they all flowered more abundantly than ever after Darwin, whom their practitioners could cite now for their scientific justification. Hitler himself became the supreme evolutionist, and Nazism the ultimate fruit of the evolutionary tree.

As a result, the traumatic experience of the West with Hitler in World War II effectively ended its open infatuation with racism, imperialism, and social Darwinism in general.

> The military collapse of Germany and the unveiling of the death camps promoted a universal revulsion of the intelligentsia against the intellectual traditions that had contributed to Nazi ideology, foremost among them the motion of a hierarchical subordination of human populations. That notion, which had underlain most earlier thinking about human evolution, was extirpated from anthropological thought after World War II and replaced with a firm faith in the unity, continuity, and equality of the Family of Man.[52]

However, though these "intellectual traditions that had contributed to Nazi ideology" were largely abandoned by modern intellectuals, the evolutionary philosophy that had energized them is, unfortunately, still alive and well. In fact, whereas every public school student is now well instructed in the evils of Hitler and his National Socialism, they are almost never taught that it

---

52. Matt Carmill, David Pilbeam, and Glynn Isaac, "One Hundred Years of Paleoanthropology," *American Scientist* (74 July/Aug 1986): p. 418.

was all founded on evolutionism. This has been an amazing cover-up, even a rewriting of history. Modern evolutionists react angrily when reminded that evolution provided the rationale for Nazism, but it is true nonetheless.

Sir Arthur Keith, the leading British evolutionary anthropologist of the first half of the 20th century, wrote a remarkable book right after World War I, titled *Evolution and Ethics*. Having endured with other Londoners the terrible bombing of Britain by Hitler's Luftwaffe, Keith certainly had no affection for Hitler. Nevertheless, in consistency with his own evolutionary commitments, he honored Hitler as a thoroughgoing evolutionist, in practice as well as theory:

> To see evolutionary measures and tribal morality being applied rigorously to the affairs of a great modern nation, we must turn again to Germany of 1942. We see Hitler devoutly convinced that evolution produces the only real basis for a national policy.[53]

> The German Fuhrer, as I have consistently maintained, is an evolutionist; he has consciously sought to make the practices of Germany conform to the theory of evolution.[54]

Adolf Hitler and his Nazi philosophy did not appear suddenly out of nowhere, of course. We have already reviewed the preparations for Hitler through the long century preceding him, as social Darwinism and racist imperialism grew stronger and stronger in German thought and practice. Stein comments:

> There really was very little left for national socialism to invent. The foundations of a biopolicy of ethnocentrism, racism, and xenophobic nationalism had already been established within German life and culture by many of the leading scientists of Germany well before World War I. . . .
> It is simply true historically that German academics and scientists did, in fact, contribute to the development and eventual success of national socialism, both directly through their efforts as scientists and indirectly through the popularization or vulgarization of their scientific work.[55]

Of all the forerunners of Hitler in Germany — Hegel, Comte, Nietzsche, Bernhardi and others — the most significant was certainly Ernst Haeckel, the

---

53. Arthur Keith, *Evolution and Ethics* (New York: Putnam, 1947), p. 18.
54. Ibid., p. 230.
55. Stein, "Biological Science," p. 57.

atheistic founder of the Monist League and the most vigorous promoter of both biological Darwinism and social Darwinism in continental Europe in the late 19th and early 20th centuries.

> Along with his social Darwinist followers, [Haeckel] set about to demonstrate the "aristocratic" and non-democratic character of the laws of nature. . . . Up to his death in 1919, Haeckel contributed to that special variety of German thought which served as the seed-bed for National Socialism. He became one of Germany's major ideologists for racism, nationalism, and imperialism.[56]

The Monist League was influential in turning many German scientists and other intellectuals to materialistic monism (the philosophy that bases all reality on matter alone) or atheism. Haeckel was also a strong racist. That Hitler was profoundly influenced by him is confirmed by Kenneth J. Hsu, a leading Chinese geologist now in Switzerland:

> Haeckelian Darwinism found its terroristic expression in national socialism. For Hitler, evolution was the hallmark of modern science and his "views of history, politics, religion, Christianity, nature, eugenics, science, art, and evolution . . . coincide for the most part with those of Haeckel" (Gasman, 1971, p. 161). In the biological theory of Darwin, Hitler found his most powerful weapon against traditional values.[57]

But let Hitler speak for himself. The very title of his famous book *Mein Kampf* means literally "My Struggle," the concept directly reflecting the Darwin-Spencer-Haeckel emphasis on the "struggle for existence" and "survival of the fittest," a concept that governed all his thinking. R.E.D. Clark observes:

> Adolf Hitler's mind was captivated by evolutionary thinking — probably since the time he was a boy. Evolutionary ideas — quite undisguised — lie at the basis of all that is worst in *Mein Kampf*. A few quotations, taken at random, will show how Hitler reasoned. . . . "He who would live must fight, he who does not wish to fight in this world where permanent struggle is the law of life, has not the right to exist."[58]

---

56. Gasman, *The Scientific Origins of National Socialism*, p. xvi–xvii.
57. Kenneth J. Hsu, "Sedimentary Petrology and Biologic Evolution," *Journal of Sedimentary Petrology* 56 (Sept. 1986): p. 730.
58. Robert E.D. Clark, *Darwin: Before and After* (London: Paternoster Press, 1948), p. 115.

The strongest theme in Hitler's writing and speaking, other than this repeated emphasis on the necessity of struggle, was the theme of Nordic race
supremacy:

> *Mein Kampf* became the "Bible" of National Socialism, and one
> of the most widely read books in German history, having sold more
> than 11,000,000 copies in 1944. According to *Mein Kampf*, the es-
> sence of history lay in interminable struggle between races. Politics
> was war by other means, and war man's highest destiny. The noblest
> of all human stocks was the Nordic race. The Jews formed a sub-
> human counter race, predestined by their biological heritage to evil,
> just as the Nordic race was designated for nobility. . . . A radiant
> future would beckon to a world redeemed by the Aryan spirit, liber-
> ated from the "Jewish World Poisoners," and also from the shackles
> of Judaic-descended Christianity. History would culminate in a new
> millennial empire of unparalleled splendor, based on a new racial
> hierarchy ordained by nature herself.[59]

Yes, ideas *do* have unforeseen consequences. Darwin's idea that evolution means "the preservation of favored races in the struggle for life" eventually led to Nazism and the Jewish holocaust — even though Darwin himself would have been appalled at the thought. There is nothing in Darwin's
Origin or even in the writings of Haeckel that would directly encourage the
genocide eventually attempted by Hitler, but the Nazi leaders certainly used
evolutionary theory to provide scientific justification for their barbaric actions. Dr. Edward Simon, professor of biology at Purdue University, although
an evolutionist himself, has said, "I don't claim that Darwin and his theory
of evolution brought on the holocaust; but I cannot deny that the theory of
evolution, and the atheism it engendered, led to the moral climate that made
a holocaust possible."[60]

Adolf Hitler was not alone among the Nazi leaders in his idolatrous worship of evolution. Heinrich Himmler, head of the Gestapo, "stated that the
law of nature must take its course in the survival of the fittest."[61] In fact, all
of the Nazi leaders were committed to both evolution and Germanic racism,
as were most German scientists and industrialists during those dark years.

59. L.H. Gann, "Adolf Hitler: The Complete Totalitarian," *the Intercollegiate Review*
    (Fall 1985): p. 24.
60. Edward Simon, "Another Side to the Evolution Problem," *Jewish Press* (Jan. 7, 1983):
    p. 24B.
61. Cited in *How Shall We then Live?* by Francis Schaeffer (Old Tappan, NJ: Revell,
    1976), p. 151.

Typical of the latter was the "angel of death," Joseph Mengele, noted for his gruesome experiments on humans at Auschwitz. Though he was diligently sought after as a German war criminal, he was never captured, and is believed to have drowned in 1979. His biographers say:

> In Munich, meanwhile, Joseph was taking courses in anthropology and paleontology, as well as medicine. . . . Precisely it was a combination of the political climate and that his real interest in genetics and evolution happened to coincide with the developing concept that some human beings afflicted by disorders were unfit to reproduce, even to live. . . . His consummate ambition was to succeed in this fashionable new field of evolutionary research.[62]

The most committed evolutionist of all, however, was Adolf Hitler himself. Although he intensely believed in German race supremacy, he was even more convinced of the infallibility of the evolutionary principle of survival.

> Hitler believed in struggle as a Darwinian principle of human life that forced every people to try to dominate all others; without struggle they would rot and perish. . . . Even in his own defeat in April 1945 Hitler expressed his faith in the survival of the stronger and declared the Slavic peoples to have proved themselves the stronger.[63]

> As Hitler saw it, Germany would be forever lost if the war were lost. Germany, having shown herself too weak for her historical mission, must therefore abdicate to the stronger nation from the East.[64]

Thus, Hitler yielded to the great god Evolution, even though he found he had been mistaken in his belief that Germans constituted Evolution's supreme race in the human struggle. There is no question that evolutionism was basic in all Nazi thought, from beginning to end. Yet it is a remarkable phenomenon how few are aware of this fact today. Though Hitler and his Nazis are today considered the prime villains of modern history, their evolutionary

---

62. G.L. Posner and J. Ware, *Mengele* (New York: McGraw-Hill, 1986) p. 9. See also Benno Muller-Hill, *Murderous Science: Elimination by Scientific Selection of Jews, Gypsies and Others, Germany, 1933–1945* (New York: Oxford University Press, 1988), 208 p., for thorough documentation of the role played by German evolutionary scientists in Nazi racial policies.
63. P. Hoffman, *Hitler's Personal Security* (London: Pergamon, 1979), p. 264.
64. Gann, "Adolf Hitler: The Complete Totalitarian," p. 27.

foundations are generally unrecognized, and evolutionism is more firmly entrenched in our world educational systems than ever. As R.E.D. Clark notes:

> Volume after volume has poured from the publishing houses describing every phase of the Hitler regime, but their writers are so timidly afraid of being classed as anti-evolutionary "fundamentalists" that one may search through their books by the score (this is *not* an exaggeration) and scarcely find a mention of evolution or Charles Darwin. Numerous books on race and racism have also appeared in which evolution is, once again, either not mentioned at all or severely kept in the background.[65]

A portion of this evolutionary defensiveness, even cover-up, has also been expressed in certain attempts to depict Hitler as a right-winger, or even as a Christian. Even though he was an anti-Communist (except when it suited his devious thinking to unite with Russia in the pact that precipitated World War II!), Hitler was certainly not a Christian, in any sense whatever. He opposed and persecuted Christians — both Catholic and Protestant — as well as Jews, blacks, gypsies, and other "inferiors." And, again, evolutionary philosophy provided his rationale. Gasman says:

> [Hitler] stressed and singled out the idea of biological evolution as the most forceful weapon against traditional religion and he repeatedly condemned Christianity for its opposition to the teaching of evolution. . . . For Hitler, evolution was the hallmark of modern science and culture, and he defended its veracity as tenaciously as Haeckel.[66]

Whether or not Hitler ever had some nominal connection with the Catholic Church as a boy may not be clear, but he was bitterly anti-Christian and anti-God all his adult life. He was perhaps more a pantheist than an atheist, dabbling in spiritism, astrology, and other forms of occultism — even promoting a return to the ancient Germanic idolatrous pantheon of gods and goddesses, in symbol if not in reality. But, above all, he was an evolutionist in every fiber of his being. Modern evolutionists may be embarrassed about this, but it is true nonetheless.

Nazism was an overripe fruit of the evolutionary tree. So was fascism! And so have been all the other varieties of totalitarianism that have plagued the world since Darwin. For example:

---

65. Clark, *Darwin: Before and After*, p. 117.
66. Gasman, *Scientific Origins*, p. 168.

Mussolini's attitude was completely dominated by evolution. In public utterances, he repeatedly used the Darwinian catchwords while he mocked at perpetual peace, lest it should hinder the evolutionary process. For him, the reluctance of England to engage in war only proved the evolutionary decadence of the British Empire.[67]

Modern American evolutionists may protest vehemently (and they do!) that creationists have no right to mention such things now. These evolutionists are *not* in favor of social Darwinism or imperialism. They are not Nazis and are very much opposed to racism. Those systems are all decried as aspects of right-wing capitalism — and they certainly don't want to be identified with that!

Nevertheless, evolutionism was indeed the rationale used by scientists of the post-Darwin century to support and promote these now-deplored beliefs and practices. If their scientific predecessors were all guilty of misunderstanding evolution in promoting these supposedly right-wing causes of the past, how can we really trust present-day scientists when they use "science" to promote their "liberal," left-wing causes today? Stein comments:

> If it is true that there can be no scientific base for racist policies, must it not be true that there can be no scientific base for advocating nuclear disarmament? Or must we not admit that the scientific finding of the natural science of sociobiology or the social sciences of biopolitics are as likely to be appropriated by interested parties, even scientists, to serve political ends as were the scientific finding of the German social Darwinists, racial anthropologists, and eugenicists? The history of scientific racism, ethnocentrism, and nationalist xenophobia suggests that this is no mere academic question.[68]

As a matter of fact, as we shall see in the next section, the so-called left-wing philosophies (e.g., socialism, communism) are also squarely based on evolutionism, and their scientific advocates are every bit as dogmatic in using "science" to promote *their* ideologies as the right-wing social Darwinists ever were.

J. Rifkin observes:

> As Geoffrey West notes: "Darwinism has been seized upon by all parties as a strong bulwark in defense of their contradictory preconceptions. On the one hand Nietzsche, on the other Marx, and between

---

67. Clark, *Darwin: Before and After*, p. 115.
68. Stein, "Biological Sciences," p. 58.

them most shades of Aristocracy, Democracy, Individualism, Socialism, Capitalism, Militarism, Materialism, and even Religion."[69]

We have seen that evolution dominates not only all disciplines of modern
thought, but all modern political systems and philosophies as well. It cannot
escape responsibility, therefore, for the tumultuous and turbulent condition
of the modern world!

The Evolutionary Morass of Communism

Modern evolutionists often try to disavow the evolutionism of the right
simply by dissociating themselves from social Darwinism, racism, imperialism, and Nazism. They attribute these mainly 19th-century phenomena to a
misunderstanding of evolution's meaning by the scientists of an earlier era.
When creationists remind them that these systems all seemed at the time
(and still do, to some) to be legitimate applications of evolutionary theory
and were so viewed by most evolutionary scientists then, they angrily dismiss
all this as irrelevant today.

When we turn our attention to the left wing, on the other hand, socialism
and communism are intensely relevant today, and these are believed by their
own scientists to be grounded even more firmly in evolution. Socialistic and
communistic governments currently reign over most of the world's nations,
and Marxist theory is widely taught as the wave of the future in the schools
and colleges of even the democratic nations. To a large extent the "liberal"
elements in the democracies (e.g., the Democratic Party in the United States,
the Labor Party in England) promote Marxist policies in their social and
educational programs.

Marxism is a current problem in every sense of the word! In its imperialistic form, as in Russian Communism, with its effective control over many
other nations beyond its Iron Curtain, it is every bit as militaristic, totalitarian, and xenophobic (with "class" substituted for "race" as the struggling
evolutionary unit) as Hitler and his Nazis were at their worst. The millions of
people slaughtered in promoting this class struggle in communistic nations
far exceed — by a factor of ten or more — the victims of Hitler's genocidal
aggressions.

All of this is well known to most readers of this book. What may *not* be
so well known, however, is the fact that Marxism, socialism, and communism, no less than Nazism, are squarely based on evolutionism. Relatively
speaking, there is more emphasis on the effect of environment and culture

---

69. Geoffrey West, *Charles Darwin: A Portrait* (New Haven, CT: Yale University Press,
    1938), p. 324. Cited in Rifkin, *Algeny,* p. 105.

than on genetics and heredity, and the competing evolutionary units are social classes (at least in human and cultural evolution) rather than individuals or nations or races. But it is all evolution, just the same.

Karl Marx and his associate Friedrich Engels were already evolutionists and atheists before they encountered Darwin's *Origin of Species*, but it was the latter with which they quickly became enamored, once it was published. Note the following testimonies and evaluations from various later historians and biographers.

Marx and Engels accepted evolution almost immediately after Darwin published *The Origin of Species*. Within a month, Engels wrote to Marx (Dec. 12, 1859): "Darwin, whom I am now reading, is splendid." Evolution, of course, was just what the founders of communism needed to explain how mankind could have come into being without the intervention of any supernatural force, and consequently it could be used to bolster the foundations of their materialistic philosophy. In addition, Darwin's interpretation of evolution — that evolution had come about through the operation of natural selection — gave them an alternative hypothesis to the prevailing teleological explanation of the observed fact that all forms of life are adapted to their conditions.[70]

It is a commonplace that Marx felt his own work to be the exact parallel of Darwin's. He even wished to dedicate a portion of *Das Kapital* to the author of *The Origin of Species*.[71]

Like Darwin, Marx thought he had discovered the law of development. He saw history in stages, as the Darwinists saw geological strata and successive forms of life. . . . In keeping with the feeling of the age, both Marx and Darwin made struggle the means of development.[72]

There was truth in Engel's eulogy on Marx: "Just as Darwin discovered the law of evolution in organic nature, so Marx discovered the law of evolution in human history." What they both celebrated was the internal rhythm and course of life, the one the life of nature, the other of society, that proceeded by fixed laws, undistracted by the will of God or men. . . . God was as powerless as individual man

---

70. Zirkle, *Evolution, Marxian Biology and the Social Scene,* p. 85–86.
71. Barzun, *Darwin, Marx, Wagner,* p. 8.
72. Ibid., p. 170.

to interfere with the internal, self-adjusting dialect of change and development.[73]

More significantly, Marx and Engels were convinced that Darwin had "delivered the mortal blow" to teleology in natural science by providing a rational explanation of functional adaptation in living things, and by proving his explanation empirically on the most general level, they welcomed Darwin's theory, and complementary theories of geological and cosmic evolution, as confirmation of their belief that throughout nature (the human variety included) present reality continually "negates" itself, continually gives rise to a different reality in accordance with natural laws that can be established scientifically. These were presumably the reasons for their repeated statements to the effect that Darwin's work "contains the basis in natural history for our view [of human history]." Indeed, Marx wanted to dedicate parts of *Capital* to Darwin, but Darwin "declined the honor" because, he wrote to Marx, he did not know the work, he did not believe that direct attacks on religion advanced the cause of free thought, and finally because he did not want to upset "some members of my family."[74]

Defending Darwinism is nothing new for socialists. The socialist movement recognized Darwinism as an important element in its general world outlook right from the start.... And of all those eminent researchers of the nineteenth century who have left us such a rich heritage of knowledge, we are especially grateful to Charles Darwin for opening our way to an evolutionary dialectical understanding of nature.[75]

It is clear, therefore, that Marx and Engels based their communistic philosophy squarely on the foundation of evolutionism. Their brand of evolution, however, was not pure Darwinism. With communism's emphasis on environmental influences, there has also been a long-continued mixture of Lamarckianism (inheritance of acquired characteristics) and saltationism (sudden evolution instead of the slow-and-gradual process postulated by Darwinism and neo-Darwinism). The Marxist "dialectic," taken from Hegel,

---

73. Gertrude Himmelfarb, *Darwin and the Darwinian Revolution* (London: Chatto & Windus, 1959), p. 348.
74. David Jorafsky, *Soviet Marxism and Natural Science* (New York: Columbia University Press, 1961), p. 12.
75. Cliff Conner, "Evolution Versus Creationism: In Defense of Scientific Thinking," *International Socialist Review: Monthly Magazine Supplement to the Militant* (November 1980).

maintains that progress — both in thought and in society — going from the-sis and antithesis to synthesis, lends itself to rapid qualitative evolutionary changes as well as slow quantitative changes.

Whatever differences in details of evolution are involved, it is still evolu-tion. These differences may express themselves sociologically in the differences between right-wing social Darwinism and left-wing socialistic Darwinism, but both types of socioeconomic systems are fundamentally based on evolutionism.

Marx and Engels were doctrinaire evolutionists, and so have all Com-munists been ever since. Since atheism is a basic tenet of Marxism in general, and Soviet Communism in particular, it is obvious that evolution must be the number-one tenet of communism. Lenin and Trotsky and Stalin were all atheistic evolutionists, and so are today's Communist leaders. In fact, they *have* to be in order to ever get to be Communist leaders!

> In spite of the disestablishment of the Russian Orthodox Church in 1918, there is in fact an official state religion in the Soviet Union. Originally, it was called "The Science of Marxism" or "Dialectical Materialism," the philosophy of Marxism. But since 1954, the year after the death of Stalin, by decree of the Central Committee of the CPSU, it has officially been dubbed "Scientific Atheism." This reli-gion — or counter-religion — is spearheaded by a think tank of some forty scholars comprising the Institute for Scientific Atheism, head-quartered in Moscow, a division of the Academy of Social Sciences, founded in 1963. . . . One of the most important tasks of the parent institute is to design the curricula for the required university one-se-mester course on scientific atheism, which was introduced in 1964.[76]

The continuing commitment of modern communism to atheistic evolu-tionism is evident in communistic publications all over the world. The fol-lowing is from the "theoretical and discussion journal" of London's Com-munist Party.

> The explanation of the origins of humankind and of mind by purely natural forces was, and remains, as welcome to Marxists as to any other secularists. The sources of value and responsibility are not to be found in a separate mental realm or in an immortal soul, much less in the inspired words of the Bible.[77]

---

76. Robert M. Homstreet, "Religious Humanism Meets Scientific Atheism," *The Hu-manist* 47 (Jan/Feb 1987): p. 6.

77. Robert M. Young, "The Darwin Debate," *Marxism Today* 26 (April 1982): p. 21.

On the other side of the world is Communist China. One might at first suppose that an ancient nation such as China, with its various pantheistic religions (Taoism, Confucianism, Buddhism) would not be easily converted to a system identified with a British capitalistic evolutionist like Charles Darwin. But not so! In reviewing the recent book *China and Charles Darwin*, by James R. Pusey, the Canadian philosopher Michael Ruse, an ardent modern Darwinist, says, concerning early 20th-century China:

> Thus, there was a turning to Western ideas, and with it came fertile ground for the scientific theory of Darwin: the gradual evolution of all forms from humble beginnings, by the process of natural selection. These ideas took root at once, for China did not have the innate intellectual and religious barriers to evolution that often existed in the West. Indeed, in some respects, Darwin seemed almost Chinese! . . . Taoist and Neo-Confucian thought had always stressed the "thingness" of humans. Our being at one with the animals was no great shock. . . . Today, the official philosophy is Marxist-Leninism (of a kind). But without the secular materialist approach of Darwinism (meaning now the broad social philosophy), the ground would not have been tilled for Mao and his revolutionaries to sow their seed and reap their crop.[78]

The same social evolution has taken place, and is still taking place, in many other countries. The concept of biological evolution was rapidly welcomed almost everywhere. Initially, however, its main sociological impact, especially in the West, took the form of social Darwinism and racism. Eventually, the excesses of these systems — child labor, anti-union violence, the imperialistic slaughter of the natives of the "lower races" in Central Africa, Tasmania, and elsewhere, and finally the Great War of 1914–1918 — generated a worldwide revulsion against social Darwinism, with is associated laissez-faire capitalism and imperialism. This reaction would finally culminate in the spread of international communism.

It was only in Russia, however, that communism was able to gain control by the time of World War I. The systems associated with "right-wing evolutionism" continued to dominate the Western nations and their colonies, and even the emerging Eastern nations such as China and Japan until the trauma of World War II. Then reaction against the racist imperialism of Germany, Italy, and Japan, as well as the still-arrogant colonialism of Europe and Amer-

---

78. Michael Ruse: "The Long March of Darwin," *New Scientist* 103 (Aug. 16, 1984): p. 35.

ica, provided fertile soil for the explosive spread of "left-wing evolutionism," or international communism, all over the world.

Many other factors contributed, of course, including the Great Depression, the progressive-education movement, and the student riots of the sixties. We need not discuss these here, but it is most significant that with all the great changes taking place — in geography, economics, politics, law, and in society generally — the underlying assumption of evolution remained almost unchallenged everywhere. Evolutionary mechanisms were being revised to better accommodate class struggle and environmentalism instead of nationalism and heredity, along with rapid changes instead of gradual changes, but evolution itself was even more basic in socialism and communism than in laissez-faire capitalism. C. Zirkle wrote in 1959: "Something would have to take the place of social Darwinism when it was finally rejected, something of about the same complexity and on the same intellectual level. Marxian biology was ready and waiting to fill the vacuum left by the discarded doctrine. . . ."[79]

"Marxian biology," as this writer called it, included the idea that evolution could be accelerated and guided by controlling the environment. Lamarckianism, or evolution through inheritance of acquired characteristics, was promoted not only by Marx and Engels, but also by Lenin and Stalin. All of these men wrote extensively on biology, and two generations of Russian biologists were essentially forced to follow this official Communist Party position.

When it finally became evident that controlled environmental evolution would not work, Communist evolutionists began to promote the idea of saltational evolution — that is, evolution in big spurts, brought about presumably by chaotic and uncontrolled changes in environment (such as revolutions). Though this idea has even less evidence to support it than Lamarckianism, it has nevertheless become quite popular in recent years — not only in Russia but even in the United States, where it is identified now by such euphemisms as "punctuated equilibrium," "dissipative structures," or "order through chaos."

It is significant that large numbers of university professors in this country today are Marxist in philosophy, though not many are actually members of the Communist Party. One of the most important is Stephen Jay Gould, who teaches biology, paleontology, and geology at Harvard University, and who is almost certainly the most articulate and influential evolutionist in America today. He and Niles Eldredge of the American Museum of Natural History have popularized the idea of "punctuated equilibrium." In their definitive treatment of this subject, they wrote:

---

79. Zirkle, *Evolution, Marxian Biology and the Social Scene,* p. 166.

Hegel's dialectical laws, translated into a materialist context, have become the official "state philosophy" of many socialist nations. These laws of change are explicitly punctuational, as befits a theory of revolutionary transformation in human society. . . .

In the light of this official philosophy, it is not at all surprising that a punctuational view of speciation, much like our own . . . has long been favored by many Russian paleontologists. It may also not be irrelevant to our personal preferences that one of us learned his Marxism, literally at his daddy's knee.[80]

A very substantial number of other Harvard evolutionary scientists are also actively Marxist in philosophy. Among these are Richard Lewontin, a professor of population genetics; Jonathan King, associate professor of biology; Noam Chomsky, professor of linguistics; and others. All of these are recognized as top scientists, and there are many others around the country, all committed to Marx-style evolution. Many are members of a radical organization called Science for the People, which grew out of the campus rebellions and anti-war protests of the 1960s.

Gould and other "punctuationists" are bitterly anti-creationist, of course, but they are also bitterly opposed to what they call "biological determinism," or traditional Darwinism and neo-Darwinism. As one writer sees it, "The group sees this approach as an apologia for the status quo and an excuse for avoiding social, economic, or political changes because, according to biological determinists, any rocking of the boat would be going against human nature.[81]

These scientists especially oppose sociobiology, which they consider to be a reversion to social Darwinism and racism. Edward O. Wilson, also at Harvard, is the nation's chief exponent of sociobiology, and he has had a number of abrasive confrontations with his colleagues Gould and Lewontin. Speaking of Gould, Wilson says:

He's willing to denigrate his own field of evolutionary biology in order to downgrade the enemy, sociobiology, which is a small but important branch of evolutionary biology. When Darwin conflicts with Marx, Darwin goes.[82]

---

80. Stephen Jay Gould and Miles Eldredge, "Punctuated Equilibria: the Tempo and Mode of Evolution Reconsidered," *Paleobiology* 3 (Spring 1977): p. 145–146.
81. Robin Hennig, "Science for the People: Revolution's Evolution," *Bioscience* 29 (June 1979): p. 342.
82. Ibid., p. 343.

Wilson here is accusing Gould of what many scientists consider sacrilegious: to sacrifice Darwin, a symbol of scientific knowledge, at the altar of Marx, who symbolizes pure politics.

The fact that Gould, the most influential modern spokesman for evolution, does indeed allow his Marxism to influence his scientific beliefs is confirmed by fellow evolutionist Michael Ruse:

> Quite openly, one of the leading punctuated equilibrists, Stephen Jay Gould, admits to his Marxism, and lauds the way in which his science is informed by his beliefs, and how conversely his beliefs are bolstered by his science. . . .
>
> In short, what I argue is that through and through Gould produces and endorses a view of paleontology which is molded by, and conversely supports and proclaims a view of, the world he holds dear. We are offered the fossil record as seen through the lens of Marxism.[83]

Of course, Ruse is defending his own preference, that of neo-Darwinism, so this is a case of pots and kettles calling each other black. "Of the essential jerk theory, one can say as Gould did of sociobiology, that it brings no new insights, and can cite on its behalf not a single unambiguous fact."[84] In other words, there is no real evidence for either slow evolution or rapid evolution! All the *real* facts support special creation. Nevertheless, both punctuationists and gradualists stand united against creationism. Darwinists Ruse and Wilson are atheists, but so are Gould and Lewontin.

In any case, their united stand against creationism does not mitigate their mutual hostility to each other. A Harvard group, including Gould, "denounced Wilson's work as being in the intellectual tradition of Adolf Hitler."[85] On the other hand, socio-biologists, as well as other neo-Darwinists, call their opponents "reds" and "revolutionaries."

Lewontin and Levins co-authored a book on Marxist biology.[86] As one reviewer said, their book is clearly both scientific and political:

> Richard Levins and Richard Lewontin are two of the most knowledgeable and innovative evolutionary biologists working today. They

---

83. E. Geisler and W. Scheler, editors, *Darwin Today*, "The Ideology of Darwinism," by Michael Ruse (Berlin: Akademie-Verlag, 1983), p. 246.
84. John Turner, "Why We Need Evolution by Jerks," *New Scientist* 101 (Feb. 9, 1984): p. 35.
85. Ibid., p. 34.
86. Richard Levins and Richard Lewontin, *The Dialectical Biologist* (Cambridge, MA: Harvard University Press, 1986), 303 p.

also view themselves as Marxist revolutionaries. As Marxists, Levins and Lewontin insist that the economic substructure of a society strongly influences its ideational superstructure, including science.[87]

The most significant aspect of this conflict between left-wing and right-wing evolutionists is the fact that both groups are motivated, not by scientific evidence, but by religious or political considerations. In other words, "As the Harvard radicals so cogently argued in the case of race and IQ, when an essentially meretricious scientific theory causes such a fuss, we must look to non-scientific causes."[88]

Speaking of the conflict between Edward Wilson (an apostate Southern Baptist fundamentalist) and his Harvard colleague Richard Lewontin, an anthropologist at nearby Smith College concludes:

> For Wilson, the "reductionist program" represented the tool which would help him combat metaphysical holism and irrational religious dogma, while Lewontin felt compelled by his more recent Marxist ambitions to criticize reductionism and especially reductionist claims about humans as both scientifically incorrect and politically suspect.[89]

The fiction that evolution has been proved scientifically to be true is false! It is simply a belief system, devised for political or religious reasons. Basically formulated as a means of escaping God, its so-called supporting data can be manipulated to fit the politics of either left or right, depending on one's preference. In either case, it is *not* derived from the scientific data. The data are selected and interpreted in accord with the preconceived belief.

> The natural world is, after all, filled with billions of "facts"; only a tiny fraction in any given period are observed and classified by scientists. And it seems that the facts that *are* picked out tend to recommend themselves precisely because they are to some degree aligned with political expectations. A good example increasingly under discussion is Darwin's theory of evolution. . . . As with genetic theories of race, this has been found to have implications contrary to the egalitarian spirit of the times, hence in need of revision. As one would expect, the recent attack on Darwinism has come from the left.[90]

87. David L. Hull, "Darwin and Dialectics," *Nature* 320 (March 6, 1985): p. 23.
88. Turner, "Why We Need Evolution by Jerks," p. 35.
89. Ullica Segerstrale, "Colleagues in Conflict: An 'In Vivo' Analysis of the Sociobiology Controversy," *Biology and Philosophy* 1, no. 1 (1986): p. 79.
90. Tom Bethell, "Burning Darwin to Save Marx," *Harper's* (Dec. 1978): p. 36.

No longer is unrestrained competition, once perceived as beneficial to business production and animal production alike, considered acceptable. We now live in a time when lip service, at least, is paid to notions of collective effort and collective security. One can see why Darwinism would upset the Left. . . . Evolution was nature's eugenics program. How do you think our Marxist biologists like that idea? They don't like it at all.[91]

In spite of its scientific deficiencies, evolution's alleged scientific character has been used, as we have seen, to justify all kinds of ungodly systems and practices. The most successful of all of these, thus far, seems to be communism, and its adherents all over the world have been deluded into thinking that communism must be true because it is based on the science of evolution. "An historian can hardly fail to agree that Marx's claim to give scientific guidance to those who would transform society has been one of the chief reasons for his doctrine's enormous influence."[92]

A prominent British Marxist theoretician, Dr. Robert M. Young, has commented incisively on the "social" (as distinct from "scientific") implications of Darwinism:

Darwinism is social because science is. And of all science the theory that links humanity to the history of nature is likely to be most so. . . . The scientific left celebrates science and tries to show that socialism is scientific. The right attempts to defend science and its autonomy in a way that guarantees that ruling ideas of the prevailing ruling class are scientific. The history of science is, of course, one battleground in this struggle.[93]

Young is here assuming that evolution ("the theory that links humanity to the history of nature") is science. He is wrong about this, of course, for evolution is quite false and is utterly devoid of any scientific evidence. Nevertheless, he does see clearly that both Marxism and capitalism ("social Darwinism," he would call it) defend their views as being based on evolution. He thinks, with good reason, that social Darwinism is evil, but seems to ignore the far greater evils of Marxist communism.

We would stress again that, even though a given evolutionist is neither Marxist nor fascist, racist nor imperialist, or a proponent of any of the other

91. Ibid., p. 38.
92. Jorafsky, *Soviet Marxism and Natural Science*, p. 4.
93. David Kohn, editor, *The Darwinian Heritage*, "Darwinism Is Social," by Robert M. Young (Princeton, NJ: Princeton University Press, 1985), p. 637.

evil systems discussed in this chapter, he or she cannot escape the truth that those who *are* (or *were*) any of these things have believed that evolution is the scientific basis and justification for their faith in them.

There is in this world a law called cause-and-effect, which is basic in science and in all human experience. Effects are invariably assimilated to their causes. As Jesus said: "Wherefore by their fruits ye shall know them" (see Matt. 7:16–20). A good tree will produce good fruits; a bad tree produces bad fruits.

The evolutionary tree has, to date, produced nothing but bad fruits.

3

Evolutionist Religion
and Morals

By far the most serious indictment against evolution is its destructive effects upon true theology and Christianity. It is bad enough to be the victim of evolution-encouraged racism or evolution-incited warfare, but it is far worse to lose one's eternal soul because of evolution-distorted theology. Evolutionism is diametrically opposed to both Christian faith and Christian practice, and its casualties in the Christian world have been legion. In this chapter, the impact of evolution on Christian doctrine in general and the worldwide crisis in all human standards of morality in particular will be discussed and documented. The creation-evolution issue is not merely an academic question in biology or geology; it is nothing less than the touchstone of human belief and behavior. Choose your religion. Will it be God-centered or man-centered, theistic creationism or evolutionary humanism?

Evolution and the Christian Church

Unfortunately, even among evangelicals who accept biblical inerrancy, there are still many people who profess Christianity yet think that the question of evolution is a matter of indifference or else (in some cases) that evolution was actually God's method of creation. Historically, however, the practice of either ignoring or accommodating evolution in either one's own mind or in a church or other Christian institution has often been the first step in a long descent into Christian liberalism or even pantheism or atheism.

Charles Darwin himself can be considered an example of this. It is well known that he started out as an orthodox — if somewhat indifferent — creationist and nominal Christian. After an abortive attempt to study medicine at the University of Edinburgh, he transferred to Cambridge to prepare for the ministry, and a divinity degree was the only degree he ever earned. Almost immediately, however, Darwin's aristocratic friends procured for him his famous five-year appointment on HMS *Beagle* as companion to the ship's captain and naturalist (despite his lack of training in this field and the presence of a more qualified naturalist on board). It was during the voyage of the *Beagle* that Darwin read his first edition of Charles Lyell's *Principles of Geology* and was converted to uniformitarianism and the concept of geological ages.

Darwin would later acknowledge his great debt to Lyell for justifying the vast time spans needed to make evolution by random variation and natural selection appear rational, as an alternative to the strong evidence for creative design in nature. For a while he became a "progressive creationist," still believing in God and occasional acts of creation, as well as intermittent catastrophes in an overall context of uniformity and gradualism.

As a result of his observations in and around South America while on the *Beagle*, however, plus the reading of Malthus shortly after his return to England, Darwin very quickly became a theistic evolutionist. This phase did not last long either, and he soon was a thoroughgoing materialist or at least an agnostic, long before he published his *Origin*. In his autobiography he testified: "I had gradually come, by this time [that is, by about 1837, just after his experience on the *Beagle*] to see that the Old Testament, from its manifestly fake history of the world . . . was no more to be trusted than the sacred books of the Hindus, or the beliefs of any barbarian."[1]

Darwin soon gave up the New Testament also, for the Old and New Testaments comprise a great unity, and they stand or fall together. He elaborated: "I can indeed hardly see how anyone ought to wish Christianity to be true, for if so the plain language of the text seems to show that the men who do not believe, and this would include my father, my brother, and almost all my best friends, will be everlastingly punished. And this is a damnable doctrine."[2]

In place of the Bible, with its grand revelation of creation and redemption, Darwin substituted materialistic evolutionism, and he himself soon

---

1. Charles Darwin, *The Autobiography of Charles Darwin, with Original Omissions Restored*, Nora Barlow, editor (New York: Norton, 1969), p. 87. The editor was Darwin's granddaughter.
2. Ibid.

became, to all intents and purposes, an atheist. As Harvard's Stephen Jay Gould (himself an atheist) has said:

> He knew that the primary feature distinguishing his theory from all other evolutionary doctrines was its uncompromising philosophical materialism. Other evolutionists spoke of vital forces, directed history, organic striving, and the essential irreducibility of mind — a panoply of concepts that traditional Christianity could accept in compromise, for they permitted a Christian God to work by evolution instead of creation. Darwin spoke only of random variation and natural selection.[3]

Reports have circulated over many years that Darwin renounced his evolutionary teachings and returned to the Christian faith shortly before his death in 1882. The evidence for this, however, is doubtful, and none of his family (including his wife, who was a professing Christian) ever acknowledged any such conversion. One of Darwin's most recent biographers says: "Upon word of his death, his detractors circulated a rumor that he had repented on his deathbed, and asked God's forgiveness for his blasphemies. There was not an iota of truth to the charge, yet it still surfaces today, presented as fact by those who would like to believe it."[4]

So far as most evidence goes, Charles Darwin started his professional career as a creationist and professing Christian, soon changed to uniformitarianism and progressive creationism, then to theistic evolutionism, and eventually to materialistic evolutionism and probably atheism, in which unhappy condition he died. This tragic sequence has since been repeated in the lives of countless individuals.

Ever since the beginning, the compromising and defeatist attitude of the Christian community on this issue has been especially distressing. Even when the *Origin* was first published, the main opposition was from scientists on scientific grounds, not from the theologians, who were quite ready to compromise.

> Darwin expected that his book would arouse violent criticism from the scientific world, and it certainly came from that quarter.

---

3. Stephen Jay Gould, *Ever Since Darwin* (New York: Norton, 1977), p. 24–25.
4. Jeremy Cherfas, editor, *Darwin Up to Date,* "The Death of Darwin," by Irving Stone (London: *New Scientist Guide,* IPC Magazines, 1982), p. 69–70. However, for a recent study supporting the story of Darwin's conversion, see *The Life and Death of Charles Darwin* by L.R. Croft, professor of biology at Salford University (Durham, England: Evangelical Press, 1989).

According to his own account, most of the leading scientists of the day believed in the immutability of species. . . .

On the other hand, many Christian leaders took a very different line, even from the early stages. . . .

Owen Chadwick, Regius professor of modern history at Cambridge, wrote after extensive research: "At first much of the opposition to Darwin's theory came from the scientists on grounds of evidence, not from theologians on grounds of Scripture. . . ."

Despite abundant evidence to the contrary, it is widely believed that the Church was a bitter opponent of evolution.[5]

In fact, if the Christian church had taken a stronger stand, especially in England and North America, it is doubtful if Darwinism would ever have triumphed as it has, even among scientists. As it was, Darwinism evolution quickly became the worldview of Western leaders everywhere, with all of the deplorable results in social Darwinism and international socialism/communism already discussed in chapter 2.

The theologians, with a few such notable exceptions as Charles Hodge in America, tried to either work out a compromise with evolution or else ignore it in favor of "just preaching the gospel." As a result, evolutionary philosophy very soon attained worldwide dominance. F. Gregory, a leading modern specialist in the history of science, elaborates:

> The theological reconcilers appeared in at least three guises. Some believed that importing evolution into theology, while it would change some things, would not so alter orthodox thought that it would become unrecognizable. Others felt less concern about conserving the traditional expressions of Christianity than about reformulating Christian doctrine in a manner in tune with the times. Still others made evolution the very cornerstone of their theological perspective. All three adjusted Biblical chronology as needed and preserved some form of an argument from design; but where the first faction gave the appearance of being forced into such reconciliation, the latter two reveled in the newfound opportunity to revitalize doctrines that were beginning to tax the loyalty of modern Christians.[6]

---

5. Francis Glasson, "Darwin and the Church," *New Scientist* 99 (Sept. 1983): p. 638–639.
6. David C. Lindberg and Ronald L. Numbers, editors, *God and Nature: Historical Essays on the Encounter between Christianity and Science*, "The Impact of Darwinian Evolution on Protestant Theology in the Nineteenth Century," by Frederick Gregory (Berkeley, CA: University of California Press, 1986), p. 379.

While these "reconcilers" tried to accommodate evolution and the geological ages to Christianity, and a few stalwarts like Hodge (whose famous 1874 book *What Is Darwinism?* showed conclusively that evolution was fundamentally atheistic) tried to stem the tide, probably most Bible-believing Christians — even such great evangelists and preachers as Moody and Spurgeon — tended to ignore the whole question.

Whatever the motives or methods of these professedly Christian leaders in the post-Darwin era may have been, the end result was the almost complete triumph of evolution in Christendom, especially in the mainline Christian schools and churches:

> By the turn of the century, liberal theologians had reached a consensus that the gospel had to be reinterpreted in terms of evolutionary thought.[7]

> At the turn of the twentieth century, liberalism dominated the theological scene. Liberals saw the Bible as one of many religious writings, Jesus as one of many religious teachers; they viewed progress as inevitable, human nature as essentially good, and morality as the heart of religion.[8]

Religious liberalism (or "modernism," as it was also called) continued to dominate institutionalized Christianity throughout most of the first half of the 20th century, and it was based squarely on evolutionism. It not only accepted naturalistic evolution instead of supernatural creation in science and history, but it also embraced the idea that evolution had produced religion itself. Their "higher criticism" of the Bible was based on this completely invalid notion.

> Sometimes people talk as though the "higher criticism" of texts in recent times has had more influence upon the human mind than the higher criticism of nature. This seems to me to be nonsense. The higher criticism has been simply an application of an awakened critical faculty to a particular kind of material, and was encouraged by the achievement of this faculty to form its bold conclusions. If the biologists, the geologists, the astronomers, the anthropologists had not been at work, I venture to think that the higher critics

---

7. Ibid., p. 383.
8. Lindberg and Numbers, *God and Nature: Historical Essays on the Encounter between Christianity and Science*, "Protestant Theology and Natural Science in the Twentieth Century," by Keith E. Yandell, p. 448.

would have been either non-existent or a tiny minority in a world of fundamentalists.[9]

If the written Word was considered to be the product of evolution, so was the living Word. Jesus Christ was no longer accepted as the unique Son of God but simply as a highly evolved human being, perhaps the pinnacle of the evolutionary process. His Resurrection became a "spiritual" resurrection and the virgin birth was rejected altogether. His miracles were explained naturalistically, and His death on the Cross was like that of any other martyr, with no particular saving efficacy except as an example.

Thus, biblical Christianity was all but destroyed by evolutionism. The great universities that were originally founded to promote biblical Christianity (e.g., Harvard, Yale, Princeton, Brown, Dartmouth, and many others) are citadels of humanism today. Even more significantly, the large Christian denominations (Roman Catholic, Methodist, Episcopalian, Presbyterian, Baptist, Disciples, Lutheran, Congregational, and essentially all denominations represented in the National and World Councils of Churches) were thoroughly permeated with evolutionary philosophy in both faith and practice.

A system called neo-orthodoxy eventually became prominent in European and American Protestantism as a reaction against the cult of inevitable evolutionary progress — a reaction engendered by the two World Wars, which were themselves largely caused by the complex of movements associated with social Darwinism. Neo-orthodoxy was ostensibly an anti-liberal theology, but it still was firmly committed to evolutionism and biblical criticism. It did not accept creation and the other great events of biblical history as *real* history, but only as theological history, or supra-history. It rejected the idea of approaching God through either science or human reason, stressing only some kind of existentialist encounter as the means of attaining theological truth and salvation. All the neo-orthodox theologians rejected creation, most rejected a literal Adam and Eve, and many even rejected a personal God. With such strong emphasis on existentialism, each person in effect became his or her own god.

A considerable proportion of modern church and seminary teachings, at least among those institutions that formerly were committed to either liberalism or neo-orthodoxy, seem now to be occupied largely with social activism and "liberation theology," sympathetic with Marxism and the goals of socialistic and communistic movements wherever they develop. As far as doctrine

---

9. F.M. Powicke, *Modern Historians and the Study of History: Essays and Papers* (London: 1955), p. 228.

is concerned, modern teachings are a variable mix of liberalism, existentialism, and Christian orthodoxy, in all cases strongly humanistic. All, of course, are firmly committed to evolutionism, and everything is predicated on the supposed fact of the geological ages that provide its necessary framework.

A brief discussion of the role of uniformitarianism (the assumption that only the gradual processes of the present have operated throughout the past) is in order at this point. A major reason for the rapid capitulation of institutional Christianity to evolutionism in the 19th century was its prior acceptance of uniformitarianism and the geological ages. As we have seen, Darwin himself first had to be convinced that the biblical chronology could be rejected and the authority of the Old Testament discredited before he was able to develop a credible naturalistic theory of evolution. Charles Lyell, generally considered to be the father of geological uniformitarianism, was a friend of Darwin's. Even though Lyell professed to believe in creation (in the form of "progressive creationism" over the geological ages), he was the one who strongly urged Darwin to publish his *Origin of Species* before Alfred R. Wallace could publish his own similar theory. It was also Lyell who persuaded a publisher to publish the *Origin* for Darwin.

All of the above events of history are well known, but it is not so well known that Lyell's motives were more complex than those of pure scientific progress. Both he and Darwin were aristocrats, men of independent means, so their scientific pursuits were not for the purpose of making a living. Darwin was an apostate divinity student who became a biologist by avocation, ending up world-famous as the popularizer of materialistic evolutionism. Lyell was trained as a lawyer but then devoted his life to the avocation of geology, becoming known as the father of uniformitarianism. Just as Darwin had, in the minds of the world, destroyed the biblical account of creation, so Lyell earlier had seemingly destroyed the biblical record of the worldwide Flood. This two-pronged demolition of the foundational chapters of Scripture would inevitably undermine the whole edifice of Christianity. The end result, with effects seen everywhere around us today, is what has been euphemistically called "the post-Christian era."

That Lyell was motivated primarily by hatred of the Bible can easily be inferred from his associations and his letters, if not by his more cautiously worded textbook. In his textbook, the first four chapters are largely given over to discrediting his predecessors in the study of geology for holding to the authority of what he called "the Mosaic systems" and thus to Flood geology. Indications are strong that Lyell was a believer in LaPlace's evolutionary hypothesis for the origin of the solar system, as well as in the evolutionary theories of Jean Lamarck, the French botanist who was bitterly anti-Christian. Nevertheless, Lyell long maintained a superficial adherence to progressive creationism for fear of unnecessarily alienating the Christian clergy and laity in England.[10]

Lyell, though never trained in geology, became a leading figure in the London Geological Society, which had been formed in 1807 by 13 amateur geologists. The professionally trained geologists of the day were committed to "diluvialism" or "catastrophism," but Lyell and his associates apparently desired to promote the uniformitarian ideas of a then recently deceased amateur geologist named James Hutton, who had been the first to suggest abandoning the Mosaic chronology in favor of endless ages and uniform processes.

An interesting hypothesis suggests another ulterior motive for discrediting Genesis and its record of the universal deluge: "Liberalism was moving, and its method was to go after Biblical geology (specifically the Flood) in order to disarm the Monarchists."[11] This was all in the immediate aftermath of the French Revolution, and the winds of revolutionary thought were blowing all over Europe at the time, including England:

> Paley's doctrine was required study in the universities, and was the received wisdom in society. There was only one way to reform Parliament, and that was to destroy Paley's Natural Theology — and the only way to do that was to discredit the catastrophists notions of its religious defenders who sought to reconcile the geological evidence with the story of Genesis. . . . If the scientific evidence denied the truth of the Bible, then it also denied any connection between God and the Monarchy, thus freeing Parliament and the people to redefine the political equations.[12]

Thus uniformitarianism, with its slogan ("the present is the key to the past") was not deduced from the scientific evidence (which has always favored catastrophism), but was politically motivated, promoted by a handful of amateur geologists and liberal clergymen.

There may well have been other behind-the-scenes activities involved in the triumph of evolutionism, but we must reserve further discussion of the

---

10. A fascinating book with Malcolm Bowden, a British engineer who has studied the history of Darwinism at firsthand for many years, should be consulted for much documentation of this topic. See *The Rise of the Evolution Fraud* (San Diego, CA: Creation-Life, 1982), 227 p..

11. Alex Marton, "What Is Uniformitarianism, and How Did It Get Here?" *Horus* 1, no. 2 (1985): p. 12.

12. Ibid., p. 13.

history of evolutionism to the following chapter. At this point our purpose has been simply to demonstrate the terrible impact of evolutionary thought on institutional Christianity. The churches and schools of the mainline denominations had actually been involved in compromise on evolution even before Darwin, especially yielding on the matter of uniformitarianism and the geological ages. Then Darwin triggered an almost immediate and large-scale capitulation to evolutionism, liberalism, and humanism in the churches — a trend that has continued in various forms right up to the present day. This has surely been the worst of all the global damage wrought by evolutionism during the past two centuries.

Evangelical Compromise

Many orthodox, Bible-believing Christians might note at this point that the mainline churches and seminaries, controlled as they are by liberals, are filled with significant numbers of "unsaved" members, people who profess to be Christians but have never truly been "born again" through personal faith in the saving work of Christ. It is hardly surprising if such people, with only a veneer of the Christian religion, reject the doctrine of special creation and the other supernatural aspects of biblical Christianity.

This is all quite true, but it does not give a complete picture. The sad fact is that evolutionism has also deeply affected evangelical schools and churches. After all, even modern ultra-liberal theological schools (e.g., Harvard, Yale) and denominations (e.g., Methodist, Episcopalian) were once orthodox and zealous for the Scriptures. These institutions have traveled down the road of compromise with evolutionary humanism farther than most, but many evangelicals today seem to have embarked on the same icy road, unaware of the danger ahead and impatient with those who would warn them.

Evangelicals (meaning those who accept the inerrant authority of the Bible and believe in the deity of Christ and His substitutionary death and bodily Resurrection) generally "dare not call it compromise" and perhaps are not even aware of it. But compromise they have, in many, many instances. Some have accepted full-blown theistic evolution, but many more believe in either "progressive creation" or "reconstructive creation" (i.e., the so-called gap theory). With respect to the biblical Flood, those who advocate any of the above views (all of which accept the modern system of geological ages) must logically adopt either the local flood theory or the idea of a "tranquil flood." This is necessary because a worldwide cataclysmic deluge would have completely reworked and re-deposited all the geologic strata, which supposedly were formed during the vast ages when evolution was taking place. If there ever was such a global cataclysm, the present geologic formations must have been the end result thereof, recording the stages of the Flood rather than the geological ages required by evolution.

It was because of this vital role of the Flood in earth history that belief in flood geology and global catastrophism had to be destroyed before a credible system of vast geological ages, so essential for an acceptable system of organic and human evolution, could ever be established as the reigning paradigm in the historical sciences. This, in turn, was necessary before the true operation sciences could be captured for full-blown materialism and humanism. Lyell had to precede and promote Darwin, and Darwin had to adopt and use Lyell, before the resulting system of evolutionary uniformitarianism could then serve as the foundation for the host of evil systems and practices discussed in this book.

That these systems (theistic evolution, etc.) are actually dangerous compromises rather than legitimate interpretations of Scripture should be obvious for anyone committed to the proposition that the Bible really is the inerrant Word of God and that God is able to say what He means. Such a proposition does not preclude the use of symbolic language when the context and purpose so warrant, but it does assume that the reader should take the meaning literally otherwise.

The Wheaton College faculty (Wheaton, Illinois) is notorious among creationists for its compromising stand on these issues, but even one of its leading "progressive creationist" spokesmen, Pattle P.T. Pun, acknowledges that a recent six-day creation and worldwide Flood are the obvious teachings of Genesis:

> It is apparent that the most straightforward understanding of the Genesis record, without regard to all the hermeneutical considerations suggested by science, is that God created heaven and earth in six solar days, that man was created in the sixth day, that death and chaos entered the world after the Fall of Adam and Eve, that all of the fossils were the result of the catastrophic universal deluge which spared only Noah's family and the animals therewith. . . .
>
> However, the Recent Creationist position has two serious flaws. First it has denied and belittled the vast amount of scientific evidence amassed to support the theory of natural selection and the antiquity of the earth. Secondly, much Creationist writing has "deistic" implications. . . . The stipulation that the varieties we see today in the biological world were present in the initial creation

implies that the Creator is no longer involved in His creation in a dynamic way.[13]

This is strange reasoning for one who claims to believe the Bible. Dr. Pun suggests that biblical creationism is "deistic" because all the varieties of plants and animals are claimed to have been present at the initial creation, with God therefore no longer dynamically active in His creation. In the first place, no creationist has ever said that all the "varieties" were present in the initial creation, but only the basic "kinds" — which is exactly what Genesis says, no less than ten times in its very first chapter. Furthermore, God is certainly still dynamically active in His creation, though He is no longer *creating* it! The creation account in Genesis ends with the clear announcement that "on the seventh day God ended his work which he had made. . . . In it he had rested from all his work which God created and made" (Gen. 2:2–3).

The real reason why Dr. Pun rejects what he admits to be "the most straightforward understanding of the Genesis record" is that it "belittled" what he thinks is "the vast amount of scientific evidence amassed to support the theory of natural selection and the antiquity of the earth." He therefore concludes that what God meant to say in His inspired Word must be determined by the "hermeneutical considerations suggested by science" — that is, by 20th-century evolutionary biologists and geologists.

The same motivation constrains other evangelical compromisers, whether or not they admit it or are even aware of it. One of the most articulate and influential of these is Dr. Davis Young, professor of geology at Calvin College, another professedly evangelical college that has become notorious for its compromising position on evolution and related issues. In one of his books, Dr. Young frankly acknowledges that the literal-day interpretation of Genesis is "the obvious view" and that the Bible teaches a universal Flood.[14] Nevertheless, he rejects these plain teachings on the basis that "geology" (meaning geology as interpreted by the geological establishment) has disproved them.

There are thousands of scientists today, including a good number of geologists, who would sharply disagree with his assessment, but that is not the point. Regardless of the majority opinion of geologists, which undoubtedly favors evolution, the sad truth is that many evangelical leaders, who *profess*

---

13. Pattle P.T. Pun, "A Theory of Progressive Creationism," *Journal of the American Scientific Affiliation* 39 (March 1987): p. 14. Dr. Pun is professor of biology at Wheaton College.

14. Davis A. Young, *Creation and the Flood* (Grand Rapids, MI: Baker, 1977), p. 44, 172.

to believe in biblical inerrancy and authority, have also compromised with evolution. This is true not only at Wheaton College and Calvin College, but at many other prestigious evangelical colleges.

Knowing that many of their financial supporters are creationists and also realizing that their doctrinal statements usually include reference to a real Adam and Eve as created in God's image, most such colleges are reluctant to admit to such compromise in any official sort of way. They nevertheless allow their faculty to teach these compromise theories and seek to downplay any creationist ideas when being evaluated by accrediting agencies or other secular groups. The full-orbed theistic evolution position is promoted by only a minority of such schools, but a great many teach either progressive creation or the gap theory, accompanied usually by the local flood theory. Practically *all* accept the geological ages and the concept of a very old universe.

In 1973 an unofficial survey was conducted among the science teachers in the Christian College Consortium, an association of a dozen or so prestigious evangelical colleges (Wheaton, Gordon, Westmont, etc.). The report of the survey included the following summary: "Efforts to characterize and identify with the departmental positions result in all respondents calling themselves 'theistic evolutionists,' 'progressive creationists,' or infrequently 'fiat creationists.' "[15]

The great majority of these teachers thus teach either theistic evolution or progressive creation — that is, when they do not bypass the subject altogether. "Relatively few colleges emphasize the creationist-evolutionist dialogue at all. . . . The students are encouraged to make up their own minds regarding personal position."[16] This latter attitude — that of sheer indifference to the most basic of all truths — is even more deplorable than promoting a compromise view.

Unfortunately, even a great many fundamentalist schools and churches have taken this same hands-off attitude. (Perhaps a better illustration would be that of the ostrich!) They may justify this on the grounds that evangelism and godly living are more important than creationism, but they fail to recognize that a sound understanding of creation is itself the basis of true evangelism and godliness. This foundational importance of creationism to all Christian faith and practice will be demonstrated more fully in a later chapter.

---

15. Albert J. Smith, "Creationism and Evolutionism as Viewed in Consortium Colleges," *Universitas* (March 1974), special report.
16. Ibid.

The fact is, however, that the failure of Bible-believing Christian churches and schools to aggressively defend and promote true biblical creationism is a major cause of the takeover by evolutionary humanism of our entire society — its schools, news media, courts, and all other aspects thereof. Especially tragic is the all-but-total defection of our mainline Christian denominations to evolutionism, as well as the widespread compromise with evolution now prevalent in evangelicalism and fundamentalism.

We do recognize that the creationist revival of the last two decades has encouraged many schools and churches to take a more biblical and aggressive stand on true creationism. The overall situation has improved significantly over what it was prior to the infamous Darwinian centennial celebrations in 1959. At least one unofficial survey of evangelical and fundamentalist colleges in 1980, for example, indicated much more positive results than the 1973 Consortium survey discussed above. Of the 69 schools receiving questionnaires, 52 responded. Of these, 48 replied that they do consider the subject of origins very important, and 38 indicated that Genesis is interpreted literally. That means, however, that 31 of the 69 schools contacted were unwilling to be counted as teaching literal creation! Furthermore, only 24 of the schools said they teach that all things were created in six literal days out of nothing. This is less than half of even the schools that responded, so a compromising position on the supposed evolutionary ages of earth history is still a very real problem, even among schools that hold to biblical inerrancy.

In 1980 an association of colleges and seminaries was formed for the specific purpose of recognizing and accrediting schools committed to strict creationism and biblical inerrant authority. This is the Trans-National Association of Christian Schools (TRACS). To date, only about 15 schools have formally affiliated with TRACS, but about 75 others have indicated significant agreement and interest.

The number of churches adhering to strict creationism is undoubtedly large and growing, but no statistical data exist on this, so far as I know. The hierarchies in the large denominations are almost completely evolutionist-controlled, but many individual congregations (especially among Baptists, Lutherans, and Presbyterians) show growing concern for creation. Some individual pastors and priests, even among the Catholics and the more liberal Protestant denominations, are creationists. The charismatic churches (Assemblies of God, Pentecostal, etc.) are an enigma. Most have held to the gap theory, and a significant number of their colleges (e.g., Oral Roberts University, Evangel College, CBN University) have a mixture on their faculties, with a goodly number teaching progressive creation or even theistic evolution. This uncertain sound has also gone forth from many of their colorful television evangelists (e.g., Oral Roberts, Jimmy Swaggart). More and more of these churches and schools, however, are indeed turning back to true creationism.

Independent churches, especially the so-called Bible churches and independent Baptist churches, are almost all at least nominally creationist, though some still hold to the gap theory and probably even more tend to downplay the creation issue as relatively unimportant.

The Southern Baptists and Missouri Synod Lutherans are partial exceptions to the general trend of compromise and eventual apostasy in the mainline denominations. These also had been capitulating more and more to the evolutionary worldview, but in recent years both denominations have been recaptured by conservatives, at least in the elective offices. It is a slow and painful process, however, to reclaim schools, publishing houses, and official hierarchies, and the ultimate outcome of the struggle is still uncertain in these two key denominations.

A number of key trans-denominational organizations have played significant roles during the past two decades in stimulating a significant revival of genuine creationism among evangelicals. The Creation Research Society (CRS), a membership association of more than 600 creationist scientists, and the Bible-Science Association (primarily a lay society) — both organized in 1963 — deserve special mention in this connection, but there are at least 100 other such associations now active around the world. The Institution for Creation Research (ICR) with a full-time staff of scientists and a graduate school offering MS degree programs in the various key sciences, has been active since 1970, sponsoring about 70 book publications, over 200 major creation-evolution debates on university campuses, and thousands of lectures all over the world. It has had probably the greatest impact in stemming the tide of evolutionary advance among evangelicals, fundamentalists, and conservatives generally. A key result has been the conversion of many scientists and great numbers of students away from evolutionism to creationism.

An organization known as the American Scientific Affiliation, on the other hand, has had a major impact in the opposite direction. The ASA has been promoting the theistic-evolution and progressive-creation compromises for over 40 years. Its supposedly "intellectual" approach has undoubtedly been significantly responsible for the widespread defections of evangelical colleges and seminaries as noted above. It started out in 1941 as a creationist association but soon was taken over by the compromising Christian intellectuals in the secular universities, as well as those in Wheaton College, Calvin College, and similar prestigious Christian institutions. It has now been dominated by theistic evolutionists for many years. The Inter-Varsity Christian Fellowship, with which ASA has maintained fraternal ties, has undergone a similar deterioration from its once-sound creationist beginnings. So have many other interdenominational organizations, Christian journals, missionary organizations, and other evangelical institutions.

These negative trends are never viewed as "compromise" by the institutions involved, of course. Ever since Darwin, and even before, such changes have been justified on the basis of keeping up with science, maintaining a dialogue with secular intellectuals, or some similar and apparently worthy motive. The sad thing about all this is not only that sound biblical Christianity is perpetually being undermined in this way, but also that it never satisfies the evolutionists anyway! *They* do not compromise; such dialogue as they maintain with evangelicals is only for the purpose of inducing further compromise on the latter's part.

A good case in point is the recent liberal reaction to the latest American Scientific Affiliation compromise, a widely distributed booklet[17] designed to appease the secular evolutionists in their fight against modern creationism, by offering theistic evolution or progressive creation as a mediating position for classroom use.

The reaction of the scientific establishment, however, was insultingly negative. Evolutionists considered this as merely another creationist ploy to get God back into the schools and would have none of it! Biologist William Bennetta has edited a collection of essays[18] "from leading evolutionists" reviewing the ASA publication. These scientists all attack the compromise as viciously as they do the strict creationism of the ICR or CRS. Stephen Gould, Niles Eldredge, Douglas Futuyma, Michael Ghiselin, and others contribute bitterly negative critiques to this collection of reviews. A typical comment is that of biologist Lynn Margulis (a proponent of New Age pantheistic evolutionism): "The result is treacherous. Authentic scientific and didactic principles have been put to nefarious use, for the writers' ultimate purpose is to coax us to believe in the ASA's particular creation myth."[19]

---

17. Walter Hearn, editor, *Teaching Science in a Climate of Controversy* (Ipswich, MA: American Scientific Affiliation, 1987), 48 p.

18. William J. Bennetta, "Scientists Decry a Slick New Packaging of Creationism," *The Science Teacher* (May 1987): p. 36–43.

19. Ibid., p. 40.

In the *Creation-Evolution Newsletter,* the anti-creationist Committees of Correspondence also have come down hard on the booklet,[20] followed by a rather plaintive response by Walter Hearn,[21] one of the booklet's coauthors, complaining in effect that the ASA was merely trying to defend evolutionism against the creationists. Subsequent issues of the aforementioned newsletter continue to be filled with attacks on the ASA and its "creationist pseudo-science."

The previously mentioned Davis Young, professor of geology at Calvin College, has over the years been following the same path traveled by Charles Darwin over a hundred years ago. That is, starting out as a strict creationist, he converted to progressive creationism in graduate school, then to theistic evolution. Now, finding that no such compromise really works or is acceptable to the secular evolutionists he longs for approval from, Young proposes to give up Genesis altogether, so far as any actual scientific relevance is concerned. He wrote in 1987: "I suggest that we will be on the right track if we stop treating Genesis 1 and the flood story as scientific and historic reports."[22] This type of approach is the same old compromise attempted a century ago by those schools and churches that have long since capitulated completely to religious liberalism and total evolution. If Dr. Young's "suggestion" is followed by other evangelical institutions, they may well end up in total apostasy like many others before.

No amount of compromise ever satisfies the evolutionists or persuades them to meet Christians halfway. According to their viewpoint, evolution is sufficient to explain everything, so there is no need for religion at all, except possibly as an emotional crutch or intellectual opiate.

> Science and religion are dramatically opposed at their deepest philosophical levels. And because the two world views make claims to the same intellectual territory — that of the origin of the universe and humankind's relation to it — conflict is inevitable.[23]

> Despite the attempts by liberal theology to disguise the point, the fact is that no biblically derived religion can really be compromised

20. *Creation-Evolution Newsletter* 6, no. 6 (1986): p. 3–9, reviews by Robert Schadewald, William Bennetta, and Karl Fezer.

21. *Creation Evolution Newsletter* 7, no. 1 (1987): p. 16–19. The Committees of Correspondence comprise a nationwide network of anti-creationist activists, also called the National Center for Science Education.

22. Davis B. Young, "Scripture in the Hands of Geologists," Part II, *Westminster Theological Journal* 49 (1987): p. 303.

23. Norman K. Hall and Lucia K.B. Hall, "Is the War between Science and Religion Over?" *The Humanist* 46 (May/June 1986): p. 26.

with the fundamental assertion of Darwinian theory. Chance and design are antithetical concepts.[24]

The greatest tragedy involved in trying to compromise Scripture with evolution, of course, is that evangelicals thereby are denying the very Word of God. Even the secularists can see this.

> Cheer Number One goes to the creationists for serving rational religion by demonstrating beautifully that we must take the creation stories of Genesis at face value. . . . Many Christians have taken the dishonest way of lengthening the days into millions of years, but the creationists make it clear that such an approach is nothing but a makeshift that is unacceptable Biblically and scientifically. . . . Creationists deserve Cheer Number Two for serving rational religion by effectively eliminating "theistic evolution". . . . Creationists rightly insist that evolution is inconsistent with a God of love. . . . Three cheers, then, for the creationists, for they have cleared the air of all dodges, escapes, and evasions made by Christians who adopt non-literal interpretations of Genesis and who hold that evolution is God's method of creation.[25]

This road of compromise with evolution, taken already by such multitudes of Christian people, is actually a one-way street, ending in a precipice beyond which lies the awful void of so-called rational religion (meaning *atheism*). How much better and more satisfying — as well as really more scientific — to stay on the straight and narrow road of the pure Word of God!

Evolution would be the most wasteful, inefficient, and cruel process that could ever be conceived by which to "create" human beings. It is absurd to suggest that the omnipotent, omniscient, loving, and saving God of the Bible could ever be guilty of such a thing!

The Religion of Atheism/Humanism

The logical and almost inevitable end result of evolutionism is atheism. Soon after the Darwinian bombshell burst on the world, the Presbyterian scholar Charles Hodge published his famous critique of Darwinism, lucidly and compellingly answering the question, *What is Darwinism?* (1874). This

---

24. Michael Denton, *Evolution — A Theory in Crisis* (London: Burnett Books, 1985), p. 66.
25. A.J. Mattell Jr., "Three Cheers for the Creationists," *Free Inquiry* 2 (Spring 1982): p. 17–18.

was the title of his book, and the answer, given plainly and without compromise, was "Darwinism is atheism." Hodge made it plain that he was not
saying that evolutionists are atheists. In fact, Hodge's book was written to try
to stop his clerical colleagues in their all-too-rapid acceptance of evolution,
under the delusion that it could be viewed as God's method of creation. Not
all evolutionists are atheists, but evolution itself is atheistic, for the simple
reason that its very purpose is to explain things without God. Sir Julian Huxley made it clear as crystal when he said in his famous keynote address at the
1959 Darwinian Centennial:

> Darwin pointed out that no supernatural designer was needed;
> since natural selection could account for any known form of life,
> there was no room for a supernatural agency in its evolution. . . . We
> can dismiss entirely all idea of a supernatural overriding mind being
> responsible for the evolutionary process.[26]

It would be utterly redundant to impose any kind of "god" upon the evolutionary process if it is sufficient to explain everything just by itself. More
recently, W.B. Provine, Cornell University professor of history and biological
sciences, has emphasized again that there is no need for God for a consistent
evolutionist:

> Evolutionists still disagree about the precise mechanisms of
> evolution in nature, but they have nevertheless given overwhelming
> support to Darwin's belief that design in nature results from pure-
> ly mechanistic causes. As Jacques Monod, E.O. Wilson, and many
> other biologists have pointed out, modern evolutionary biology has
> shattered the hope that some kind of designing or purposive force
> guided human evolution and established the basis of moral rules. In-
> stead, biology leads to a wholly mechanistic view of life. . . . There are
> no gods and no designing forces. The frequently made assertion that
> modern biology and the assumptions of the Judeo-Christian tradi-
> tion are fully compatible is false.[27]

Jacques Monod, the Nobel Prize–winning biologist mentioned in the
above reference, said near the close of his very influential book on this theme,
"The ancient covenant is in pieces; man knows at last that he is alone in the

---

26. Sol Tax, editor, *Issues in Evolution* (Chicago, IL: University of Chicago Press, 1960),
    p. 45.
27. William B. Provine, "Influences of Darwin's Ideas on the Study of Evolution," *Bio-
    science* 32 (June 1982): p. 506.

universe's unfeeling immensity, out of which he emerged only by chance. His destiny is nowhere spelled out, nor is his duty."[28]

Similar assertions by modern scientific spokesmen could be cited at great length if necessary. There is no doubt that, to the modern establishment in science, God is considered unnecessary, since evolution is accepted as adequate to explain it all. There are some scientists who say that, even though God is an encumbrance in the actual "doing" of science, one can still believe in God if one wishes, but that one's science and his religion must be kept rigidly separated. Stephen Jay Gould, for example, says, "There is no place for God in evolution because there isn't a place for God in that sense in empirical science. That doesn't mean that there isn't a God or that one shouldn't believe in one."[29] As a Marxist, Gould himself sees no need for God. Nevertheless, he will allow others to believe, provided their particular "god" has nothing to do with the physical world!

On the other hand, many think even this allowance is too much:

> Relevant also in this context is the 1981 resolution by the National Academy of Sciences Council, mentioned in the preface of their brochure,[30] stating that "religion and science are separate and mutually exclusive realms of thought whose presentation in the same context leads to misunderstanding of both scientific and religious belief." A very courageous resolution! However, the corollary of it is that religious scientists have to entertain "mutually exclusive realms of human thought," that is, to practice doublethink. I generally put it to my religious colleagues more bluntly: "You can't have your cake and eat it."[31]

Materialistic evolutionists are confident that evolution can even account for moral and spiritual attributes in mankind. Edward O. Wilson, the Harvard sociobiologist, and neo-Darwinist philosopher Michael Ruse have written a remarkable comment to this effect:

> In an important sense, ethics as we understand it is an illusion fobbed off on us by our genes to get us to cooperate. . . . Ethical codes work because they drive us to go against our selfish day to day

---

28. Jacques Monod, *Chance and Necessity* (New York: Alfred A. Knopf, 1971), p. 180.
29. S.J. Gould, interview in *Unitarian Universalist World*, reported in *Context* (June 15, 1982): p. 5.
30. National Academy of Sciences, *Science and Creationism* (Washington, DC: National Academy Press, 1984), 28 p.
31. Gerrit J. Vander Lingen, "Creationism," letter to the editor, *Geotimes* 29 (Oct. 1984): p. 4.

impulses in favor of long-term group survival and harmony. . . . Furthermore, the way our biology forces its ends is by making us think that there is an objective higher code, to which we are all subject.[32]

It is amazing what scholars can manage to believe in order not to have to believe in God! They imply that evolution evolves our brains to believe in God, even though there is no God, in order to subject us to a moral code, which is necessary for our survival despite its non-existence! For example, one scientist writes:

> Whether we like it or not, there was a long time ago when religion was actually a "good" thing. That is to say, religion increased group fitness.[33]

> Although religion was a force accelerating human evolution during the Ice Age, it is now an atavism of negative value.[34]

The author of this strange evolutionary myth, for which there is not the slightest scientific evidence, is currently a columnist for *American Atheist* and was formerly chairman of the science division at the State University of New York at Fulton.

Evolution is believed by the scientific establishment to account for everything. As Huxley said, "Our present knowledge indeed forces us to the view that the whole of reality *is* evolution — a single process of self-transformation."[35]

Cornell's Professor William Provine puts it this way: "The implications of modern science, however, are clearly inconsistent with most religious traditions. . . . No inherent moral or ethical laws exist, nor are there absolute guiding principles for human society. The universe cares nothing for us and we have no ultimate meaning in life."[36]

An even more compelling reason for equating evolutionism with atheism, however, is its essential inconsistency with the character of God and His incarnate Son, the Lord Jesus Christ. God, as revealed in the Bible and

32. Michael Ruse and Edward O. Wilson, "Evolution and Ethics," *New Scientist* 208 (Oct. 17, 1985): p. 51–52.

33. Frank R. Zindler, "Religion, Hypnosis and Music: An Evolutionary Perspective," *American Atheist* 26 (Oct. 1984): p. 22.

34. Ibid., p. 24.

35. J.R. Newman, editor, *What Is Science?* "Evolution and Genetics," by Julian Huxley (New York: Simon & Schuster, 1955), p. 278.

36. William Provine, "Scientists, Face It! Science and Religion Are Incompatible," *The Scientist* (Sept. 5, 1988): p. 10.

in His Son, is omnipotent and is also a God of perfect love and great grace. The evolutionary scenario, with its billion-year spectacle of random variation, evolutionary meandering, struggle for existence, suffering and death, and extinction, utterly contradicts not only the plain teaching of Scripture but also the very nature of God. Evolution is the most cruel and inefficient process that could be devised for populating a world and creating man — and God should not be held responsible for any such system!

Most scientific evolutionists see this problem clearly, even though compromising religionists may try to explain it away and soon become atheists or pantheists as a result. The atheistic essence of evolution was pointed up in the concluding sentence of Darwin's *Origin*: "Thus, from the war of nature, from famine and death, the most exalted object which we are capable of conceiving, namely, the production of the higher animals, directly follows."[37] This famous statement could well be summarized by the cogent motto: "By struggle, suffering and death, came man!" But this directly contradicts the biblical revelation: "By man came death" (1 Cor. 15:21).

It is certainly true that there is an abundance of suffering and death in the world, and this has been true all through history. But evolution claims this is the very essence of things, the process that has "created" the world and man. The Bible stresses, on the other hand, that everything in the beginning was completed perfect from the start and was all "very good" (Gen. 1:31).

As we have seen, evolutionism consistently applied completely undermines biblical Christianity in particular and any form of monotheism in general. In its place is substituted the religion of humanism. As the name implies, humanism is centered in "humanity" as the pinnacle of evolution and as the measure of all meaning, rejecting altogether the concept of a transcendent Creator.

> Humanism does not include the idea of a God and as such is considered a philosophy rather than a religion. In a way, it is an alternative to all religions. However, whether or not one looks to humanism as a religion or as a philosophy to live by or as a way of life is, we believe, largely a matter of personal temperament and preference. Those caught up by its religious aspects know that it provides a vibrant, satisfying faith. Those who think of it as a philosophy find it both reasonable and adequate.[38]

---

37. Charles Darwin, *The Origin of Species*, last page (see, for example, p. 463 in Everyman's Library Ed., London, 1928, reprinted 1967).

38. Lloyd Morain, "How Do Humanists Define Their Beliefs?" *The Humanist* 47 (Sept/Oct 1987): back cover.

The above definition and discussion by Lloyd Morain is repeated from chapter 1 because of its clarity and importance. It was written by the former editor of *The Humanist*, which is the quasi-official journal of the American Humanist Association, and was featured on its back cover. This leading humanist official thus makes it very clear that humanism is a religion or a religious philosophy, and that its essential feature is rejection of the idea of God.

That humanism is merely a more genteel term for atheism is confirmed by the current president of the American Humanist Association, Dr. Isaac Asimov, who is also probably the most prolific writer in the whole world of science, having authored approximately 300 books, covering every scientific field. He says:

> I am an atheist, out and out. It took me a long time to say it. I've been an atheist for years and years, but somehow I felt it was intellectually unrespectable to say one was an atheist, because it assumed knowledge that one didn't have. Somehow it was better to say one was a humanist or an agnostic. I finally decided that I'm a creature of emotion as well as of reason. Emotionally, I am an atheist. I don't have the evidence to prove that God doesn't exist, but I so strongly suspect he doesn't that I don't want to waste my time.[39]

One very significant admission appears in this statement of atheistic faith by Asimov. Not only does he acknowledge that humanism is essentially the same as atheism, but also that atheism is nothing but an emotional belief. In spite of the fact that he is one of the most knowledgeable scientists in the world, having written books on just about every branch of science in existence, he recognizes that he has no "evidence to prove that God doesn't exist."

If Asimov has no evidence against God, we can be sure *nobody* does! He believes in humanism/atheism simply because that is what he *wants* to believe! The same is true for every other devotee of this man-centered religion. Yet they commonly deride creationism because it requires religious faith! One naturally thinks of Psalm 14:1: "The fool hath said in his heart, There is no God."

In any case, while atheism may be somewhat more blatant in its opposition to God, it is essentially synonymous with secular humanism, and both are firmly grounded in evolutionism. Furthermore, the system of humanism/

---

39. Paul Kurtz, editor, "An Interview with Isaac Asimov on Science and the Bible," *Free Inquiry* 2 (Spring 1982): p. 9.

atheism is clearly a religious system, despite any claims to the contrary. D.R. Oldroyd writes:

> So a metaphysical system, although naturalistic and secular, has been built up by modern humanists around the nucleus of biological evolutionism. Such a system may be seen to the best advantage in the writing of the well-known biologist Julian Huxley (1887–1975), grandson of Darwin's "bulldog," Thomas Henry Huxley. Really Julian Huxley espoused a new religion, rather than a mere metaphysical system. Accepting with enthusiasm the doctrine of evolutionism, he maintained that the future evolutionary process on Earth is to be carried out almost exclusively by man. Thus, man's destiny has become that of realizing his evolutionary potentialities and furthering the evolutionary process, which for Huxley is a notion that may be contemplated with a kind of religious enthusiasm.[40]

Sir Julian Huxley was not only the first director-general of UNESCO (as noted in chapter 1), but was also one of the founders (in 1933) and chief propagandists of the American Humanist Association. The well-known Tenets of Humanism, also formulated and published in 1933, make it crystal clear that humanism is directly based on evolutionism. The first two of these tenets are as follows:

> *First.* Religious humanists regard the universe as self-existing and not created.
> *Second.* Humanism believes that man is a part of nature and that he has emerged as the result of a continuous process.[41]

Similarly, the prominent humanist spokesman Corliss Lamont says the first two tenets of the humanistic faith are

1. naturalism;
2. the idea that man is an evolutionary product of nature.[42]

Julian Huxley himself defined humanism as follows:

---

40. D.R. Oldroyd, *Darwinian Impacts* (Atlantic Highlands, NJ: Humanities Press, 1983), p. 254. Professor Oldroyd is senior lecturer in the School of History and Philosophy of Science at the University of New South Wales in Sydney, Australia.
41. American Humanist Association, "Humanist Manifesto I," *The New Humanist* 6 (May/June 1933).
42. Corliss Lamont, *The Philosophy of Humanism* (London: Vision, 1962), p. 10.

I use the word "humanist" to mean someone who believes that man is just as much a natural phenomenon as an animal or plant; that his body, mind, and soul were not supernaturally created but are products of evolution, and that he is not under the control or guidance of any supernatural being or beings, but has to rely on himself and his own powers.[43]

Lest anyone think that humanism is the faith of only an insignificant minority of intellectuals, it should be stressed that its tenets are, to all intents and purposes, the unofficial state religion of this nation, taught in the schools to the exclusion of all other religions and enforced by the courts whenever challenged. Humanism may not be officially identified as the state religion, but it might as well be, and it is becoming more powerfully entrenched all the time. John Dewey, the chief architect of "progressive education," which has dominated our public schools throughout the 20th century, was one of the founders and main promoters of the American Humanist Association, along with Julian Huxley and others. As Oldroyd recognizes:

Although most Western men and women may not choose to identify themselves explicitly as philosophical humanists or spend their time at humanist society meetings, these ten points do encapsulate many of the basic assumptions of educated, Western, liberal society. Clearly the humanist creed represents a major component of the thinking of many of us.[44]

The "ten points" mentioned by Oldroyd are those listed by Corliss Lamont as his tenets of humanism, all based on evolution as its first tenets, as noted previously. Oldroyd summarizes the influence of evolutionary humanism as follows:

The tenets of the humanist movement mesh well with the generality of beliefs in the contemporary liberal West even though the number of people specially calling themselves humanists is quite small. In other words, in one direction at least, the evolutionary doctrines of Darwinism have merged as a point of wide consensus in the secular world of the twentieth century.[45]

---

43. Julian Huxley, quoted in promotional brochure distributed by American Humanist Association.
44. Oldroyd, *Darwinian Impacts*, p. 254.
45. Ibid., p. 255.

In summary, humanism is atheism — and both are squarely and with perfect logic based on evolutionism. This is the system of thought permeating our nation's schools and colleges, as well as our whole society. The same is true in other nations. And, sad to say, it is increasingly dominating even our religious schools and churches, not in its overtly atheistic form, but in the form of various compromise systems (e.g., theistic evolution, progressive creation).

Not all evolutionists are humanists or atheists, by any means, but all humanists and atheists are evolutionists! True theism — centered in the concept of a loving, merciful, omniscient, omnipotent, personal God — directly contradicts the whole evolutionary system, with its inordinately cruel and wasteful process of producing mankind. Evolution fits naturally and easily with atheism, even as it confronts and negates true theism.

> The balance sheet of evolution has so closely written a debit column of all the blood and pain that goes into the natural process that not even the smoothest accountancy can make the transaction seem morally solvent according to any standards of morals that human beings are accustomed to.[46]

The authors of the above analysis were not using this anti-theistic message of evolution to attack evolution because of its incompatibility with theism, but rather to attack theism because of its incompatibility with evolution. Furthermore, they were among the most highly respected biologists and scientific philosophers in England. It is a sad commentary on the state of modern Christianity that so many of its leaders are anxious to compromise with such an ungodly system as evolutionary humanism.

Atheism and humanism incorporate within their value systems the whole sphere of human thought and life. Although founded on evolutionism and anti-creationism, they build many other tenets in their statement of faith, and practically all of them are antithetical to true Christianity. For example, Humanist Manifesto II, written and published in 1973, 40 years after Humanist Manifesto I, discusses 17 broad categories of life on which it takes a definite position. The first of these has to do with religion and includes the following assertions:

> As non-theists, we begin with humans, not God, nature, not duty. . . . But we can discover no divine purpose or providence for the human species.

---

46. Peter B. Medawar and J.S. Medawar, *The Life Science: Current Ideas of Biology* (New York: Harper & Row, 1977), p. 169.

While there is much that we do not know, humans are responsible for what we are or will become. No deity will save us; we must save ourselves.[47]

Then the second of these broad tenets includes the following affirmations:

Promises of immortal salvation or eternal damnation are both illusory and harmful. . . . Rather science affirms that human species is an emergence from natural evolutionary forces. As far as we know, the total personality is a function of the biological organisms transacting in a social and cultural context. There is no credible evidence that life survives the death of the body.[48]

This second Manifesto was signed by 114 endorsers (the first had 34), later augmented by 148 others, all of whom held influential positions in education, government, industry, or religion.

Having rejected creation, it is natural that evolutionary humanism would also reject divine revelation and personal salvation, as well as all other basic Christian doctrines. As the very negation of Christianity, it is the ultimate goal toward which all Christian compromise with evolution leads. To these humanistic intellectuals, biblical Christianity ("fundamentalism," they call it), is utterly irrational. *They* do not intend to compromise! One spokesman elaborates:

But perhaps the best example of group irrationality is Christian fundamentalism. . . . The most visible conflict between fundamentalism and science is caused by fundamentalists' literal interpretation of Genesis.[49]

Fundamentalism is part of a fantasy world that many people believe or wish to be true. These people wish that the reason for human existence is an afterlife and that their lives are guided by a benevolent deity. In actuality, events in the universe may be based upon chance and physical laws that have always existed, and human existence has no other meaning than that we exist.[50]

Not only are Christians "irrational," they are "cowardly," according to the viewpoint fostered by the doctrinaire atheists:

---

47. American Humanist Association, "Humanist Manifesto II," *The Humanist* 33 (Sept/Oct 1973).
48. Ibid.
49. John R. Baker, "Fundamentalism as Anti-Intellectualism," *The Humanist* 86 (March/April 1986): p. 26.
50. Ibid., p. 34.

When the theory of evolution was advanced, that was the date that the Judeo-Christian religion began the decline in which it now finds itself in the West. The two theories are point-blank in contradiction one to the other.

Any scientists, any educators, any religious persons who state to you that there is no conflict simply want to hang on to both worlds because they have not been able to divest themselves of the infantile belief system which was programmed into them when they were children. They want a foot in each camp. Religion is their emotional security blanket. Science is facing a world of reality which — in the final analysis — they cannot face. They are too cowardly to see religion should be abandoned so they stand there one foot in and one foot out.[51]

In the perspective of the evolutionary establishments (those who control the schools, write and publish the books, program the media, and ultimately run the country), biblical Christians — especially creationists — are irrational fanatics, anti-intellectual rednecks, and fearful children. Christians urgently need to face the fact that compromise with such doctrinaire evolutionists and their beliefs is impossible. Even if God and His Word would allow it, the evolutionists themselves will not!

Christianity has fought, still fights, and will fight science to the desperate end over evolution, because evolution destroys utterly and finally the very reason Jesus' earthly life was supposedly made necessary. . . . If Jesus was not the redeemer who died for our sins, and this is what evolution means, then Christianity is nothing!

What all this means is that Christianity cannot lose the Genesis account of creation like it could lose the doctrine of geocentrism and get along. The battle must be waged, for Christianity is fighting for its very life.[52]

The tragedy is that the great majority of professing Christians — even evangelicals and fundamentalists — do not seem to understand this fact as well as the atheists do. We are engaged in a cosmic conflict, while many Christians are busy making daisy chains!

---

51. Genesis and Evolution," answer by editor to a question posed by O. Hambling in *American Atheist* 30 (Jan. 1988): p. 7.
52. G. Richard Bozarth, "The Meaning of Evolution," *American Atheist* 20 (Feb. 1978): p. 30.

One perceptive Syracuse University philosopher, Huston Smith, clearly sees the folly of trying to compromise with evolution:

> Darwin saw his discovery as strongly resistant to admixture with belief in God, while Jacques Monod goes further. "The mechanism of evolution as now understood," he tells us, "rules out any claim that there are final causes, or purposes being realized. [This] disposes of any philosophy or religion that believes in cosmic . . . purpose." Realizing that this conclusion could be colored by Monod's personal philosophy, I turn to the entry on "Evolution" in *The New Encyclopedia Britannica* for a statement that might reflect, as well as any, consensus in the field. It tells me that "Darwin showed that evolution's cause, natural selection, was automatic with no room for divine guidance or design."[53]

Humanism involves more than evolution, of course. As noted previously, the two Humanist Manifestos contain tenets advocating a number of others beliefs and practices that are explicitly contrary to biblical teachings. Humanist Manifesto I says that our "existing acquisitive and profit-motivated society has shown itself to be inadequate" and therefore that "a socialized and cooperative economic order must be established." It also says that "humanists demand a shared life in a shared world." This sounds like world communism but is ambiguous enough to let people read different meanings into it.

The second Manifesto makes quite explicit its goal of a "world community in which all sectors of the human family can participate. Thus we look to the development of a system of world law and a world order based upon transnational federal government."

As far as individual behavior is concerned, Manifesto II insists that any idea of divine law be renounced. "Ethics is autonomous and situational, needing no theological or ideological sanction." Since there is no heaven or hell, "we strive for the good life here and now." Among other things, this good life means that "the right to birth control, abortion, and divorce should be recognized." It is wrong to "prohibit, by law or social sanction, sexual behavior between consenting adults." As a general rule, tolerance of all sorts of behavior once considered immoral or even illegal is demanded. Manifesto II declares that "individuals should be permitted to express their sexual proclivities and pursue their lifestyles as they declare." Premarital sex, extramarital sex, easy

---

53. LeRoy S. Rounder, *On Nature*, "Two Evolutions," by Huston Smith, Vol. 6, Boston University Studies in Philosophy and Religion (South Bend, IN: University of Notre Dame Press, 1984), p. 48.

divorce, homosexuality — anything goes. In addition, not only is abortion promoted, but so are "euthanasia, and the right to suicide." Humanists are also aggressive feminists, "critical of sexism or sexual chauvinism."

Many portions of both Manifestos deal with various aspects of religious belief or practice, repeatedly repudiating any supernatural dimension of Christianity. Both of them, of course, base everything on the premise of evolution, as clearly stipulated in the opening tenets of each. These various derivative aspects of humanism and their relation to evolutionism will each be discussed later in this chapter. All seem to be meeting with great success these days, not only in the teaching of the schools but also in decisions of the courts and the attitudes and practices of the people.

A fund-raising letter written by Dr. Isaac Asimov, former president of the American Humanist Association, gloats over this fact:

> *We're on a roll and you can keep us there.* The fundamentalists can't stop us now. Only a lack of support from you can bring our growth to a halt. But I'm confident you're with me. I'm sure you think it's high time the AHA realized its full potential. So let's go for it! Please make out a check right now, while this is in front of you.[54]

There is no doubt that humanism is "on a roll," with all the political muscle of the American Civil Liberties Union, the full coffers of People for the American Way, and a host of other influential organizations promoting it. The United States was founded as a nation on the principles of biblical Christianity, but evolutionary humanism is rapidly becoming its quasi-official national religion — and relatively few American Christians seem to know or care.

Pantheism and the New Age

We have noted in the previous section that modern secular humanism, with its denial of the supernatural, is essentially identical with atheism. However, humanism over the ages has taken many different forms, and some of these ancient faiths are making a remarkable resurgence today in a modern pseudo-scientific garb. Many people, including a fair number of scientists, are perceptive enough to see that random processes in a chance universe could never generate the multitude of highly complex systems that now exist in the universe. However, being unwilling to attribute these systems to the personal Creator God of the Bible, they assume that the cosmos itself has creative powers, or even that it is alive and consciously directing its own evolution.

---

54. Isaac Asimov (emphasis his). Asimov's entire letter sounds much like a fund-appeal letter from a political party or television evangelist!

There are many such ideas floating around today, each with its own devotees and degree of sophistication. Since many of these people like to think
they are the vanguard of a new age of enlightenment for the world, this complex of systems is often called the New Age movement. As a matter of fact,
there is little that is "new" in any of this. The ancient religion of pantheism
has dominated the non-monotheistic nations in all ages and places since the
beginning of time. The New Age movement is actually nothing but a revival of this old "nature religion," in reaction against the strong monotheistic,
Christian, biblical awakening of the Western world following the Protestant
Reformation.

Pantheism is nothing but evolutionary humanism in a different guise.
The history of these earlier evolutionary systems will be outlined in a later
chapter, but here I wish to take a brief look at some of the modern systems
that are involved in the so-called New Age movement.

There are a host of different cults, fads, philosophies, and psychologies
floating around today in this milieu. Many of the older pseudo-Christian cults
fit this characterization — cults such as Christian Science, Unity, Spiritualism, Swedenborgianism, for example. There are many recently established
cults of similar type, including Divine Science, New Thought, Scientology,
Inner Light, Religious Science, Science of Mind, Unification Church, and a
great host of others. We might add to these the variant offshoots of Buddhism, Theosophy, Hinduism, Taoism, and other Eastern religions that have
proliferated in recent years, as well as various ancient cults that are experiencing revival today, such as astrology, Rosicrucianism, Illuminism, witchcraft, and even Satanism. There is also some evidence of revived worship of
the gods and goddesses of Greece, Babylon, and other ancient nations. The
number of cults is legion!

Pantheism is also experiencing a resurgence in various movements cen-
tering on the environment, holistic health, meditation, physical fitness, and
the like. The consciousness-raising seminars, group-encounter sessions, per-
sonal-development programs, and other retreat activities sponsored by many
businesses and industries, as well as government and the military, focus on
the same types of activities.

Many of the more liberal churches in the mainline Christian denominations have been profoundly influenced by New Age thinking, as have many
of the peripheral groups in the charismatic orbit. The "prosperity gospel," as
well as the "health gospel" and the "positive thought gospel" taught by many
quasi-evangelical preachers, are basically New Age concepts that are deceiv-
ing many.

The above listings only scratch the surface. Perhaps most remarkable is the fact that many scientists are being caught up in some aspects of New Age-ism. In fact, the various sub-groups and sub-movements such as those mentioned above generally claim to be "scientific" just because the wide New Age spectrum *does* include such scientists, even though the latter may decry some of the extreme groups associated with it. The discussion in this section will concentrate on these scientific aspects.

The "Gaia principle" (Gaia being the name of the ancient Earth goddess, essentially the same as Mother Nature) views the planet Earth as an actual living organism. The "anthropic principle" goes even further, citing many cosmic arguments to show that the entire universe is in the process of evolving itself for man's benefit. Both concepts are wholly pantheistic yet are now being promoted by a surprising number of humanistic scientists.

The leading proponents of the Gaia (or "Terra") concept have been James Lovelock, Fellow of the Royal Society and former professor of cybernetics at Reading University, who had also taught at Yale and Harvard; and Lynn Margulis, professor of biology at Boston University. Both are strong evolutionary humanists, but their concept of evolution is pantheistic. Lovelock says:

> Our interpretation of Darwin's great vision is altered. Gaia draws attention to the fallibility of the concept of adaptation. It is no longer sufficient to say that organisms better adapted than others are more likely to leave offspring! It is necessary to add that the growth of an organism affects its physical and chemical environment and that, therefore, the evolution of the species and the evolution of the rocks are tightly coupled as a simple indivisible process.[55]

The increasing influence of the Gaia hypothesis in the scientific community is evidenced by the full-blown scientific conference on Gaia sponsored by such a hard-nosed scientific society as the American Geophysical Union, held in San Diego on March 7–11, 1988. The main result of the five days of papers and discussions was that there was *no* result.

> Despite strenuous efforts, it became clear that no scientific question arising out of any study of the history or present state of life on

---

55. James Lovelock, "Gaia: The World as Living Organism," *New Scientist* 112 (Dec. 18, 1986). Dr. Lovelock recognizes that this idea is merely a revival of ancient paganism. "As far back as the earliest artifacts can be found, it seems that the Earth was worshipped as a goddess and believed to be alive. The myth of the great Mother is part of most early religions." *The Ages of Gaia* (New York: Norton, 1988), p. 208.

earth could be made to yield an answer that would distinguish the Gaia hypothesis from more conventional interpretations.[56]

Identifying testable Gaian hypotheses, which have been in painfully short supply, was the primary purpose of the meeting. Now that Gaia has been cloaked in more fashionable garb, there should be more testable links between the living and the nonliving worlds.[57]

In any case, whether or not the scientists eventually shift their philosophies from atheism to pantheism, *both* systems are firmly based on evolution. New Age humanism is every bit as much tied to evolution as is secular humanism.

On the cosmic scale, the "anthropic principle," which suggests that the entire universe is conscious in some sense and is inseparably tied in with the existence of human life on earth, is also attracting many scientific supporters, especially among physicists. Such outstanding modern physicists as P.A.M. Dirac, Robert Dicke, Freeman Dyson, Stephen Hawking, John Wheeler, Richard Got, and Brandon Carter (who coined the term) have contributed to the evidence supporting the anthropic principle. In its strongest form, John A. Wheeler, now of the University of Texas, draws on the idea that reality is defined only by that which is observed. Thus comments G. Gale:

The observer contributes to reality by the very fact of observation. Wheeler adopts an extreme version of this idea by proposing that for a universe to be real it must evolve in such a way that observers come into existence. . . . Wheeler rejects the common view that life and observership are only accidents in a universe independent of observers and argues instead that "quantum mechanics had led us to take seriously and explore the directly opposite view that the observer is as essential to the creation of the universe as the universe is to the creation of the observer."[58]

In actuality, as the above quotation implies, much of the supposed evidence for the anthropic principle is based squarely on the arbitrary assumption of the great age and evolution of the cosmos. Another eminent physicist and advocate of the anthropic principle is Paul Davies of England. He summarizes the argument as follows: "For clearly the universe is a very special place. . . . In

---

56. David Lindley, "Is the Earth Alive or Dead?" *Nature* 332 (April 7, 1988): p. 484.

57. Richard A. Kerr, "No Longer Willful, Gaia Becomes Respectable," *Science* 240 (April 22, 1988): p. 395.

58. George Gale, "The Anthropic Principle," *Scientific American* 245 (Dec. 1981): p. 169.

this respect the strong anthropic principle is akin to the traditional religious explanation of the world: that God made the world for mankind to inhabit."[59]

Yet neither Davies nor Wheeler nor the others promoting the anthropic principles believe in creation or in the Creator God of the Bible. All of them believe in some form of cosmic evolution as the basis for eventual organic evolution, with the supposed coincidental relationships between the two to be understood only in a vague pantheistic sense. As Freeman Dyson of the Institute for Advanced Study at Princeton expressed it, "The universe in some sense must have known we were coming."[60] Similarly, George Wald, Nobelist in physiology and medicine at Harvard University, has said, "The universe wants to be known. Did the universe come about to play its role to empty benches?"[61]

It is remarkable that men of such keen intellect as these are perceptive enough to see that the universe could not have come about by chance and yet refuse to believe in a personal God! The reviewer of a recent book on the anthropic principle, while commending its scholarship, rejects its implicit teleology in the following revealing words:

> They bring to their cause an impressively broad knowledge of scientific exotica, but the factual content of the book is only their means to an end that (in my opinion) is threatening to the modern scientific enterprise. That end is nothing less than the fusion of matters of science with matters of individual faith and belief. . . . This is a fascinating and entertaining book, one to read and think about. But it is also one whose extra-scientific agenda most of us will, ultimately, wish to reject.[62]

Undoubtedly the most widely read scientist currently active in the New Age movement is Fritjof Capra, professor of physics at the University of California at Berkeley. Capra has stressed the application of modern, scientific analysis of systems and networking to New Age ideology, as well as the correlation of the concepts of modern physics with Taoism and other Eastern pantheistic religions. The relation of his thought to evolutionary pantheism

59. Paul Davies, *The Accidental Universe* (Cambridge, UK; New York, NY: Cambridge University Press, 1982), p. 111, 121.
60. Freeman Dyson, as quoted by Judith Hooper, "Perfect Timing," *New Age Journal* 2 (Dec. 1985): p. 18.
61. George Wald, as cited by Dietrick Thomsen, "A Knowing Universe Seeking to Be Known," *Science News* 123 (Feb. 19, 1983): p. 124.
62. William H. Press, "A Place for Teleology?" Review of *The Anthropic Cosmological Principle* by J.D. Barrow and F.J. Tipler (Clarendon, 1986, 706 p.) in *Nature* 320 (March 27, 1986): 316. Press is professor of astrophysics at Harvard.

is seen in the following statement: "The universe is no longer seen as a machine, made up of a multitude of objects, but has to be pictured as one indivisible, dynamic whole whose parts are essentially interrelated and can be understood only as patterns of a cosmic process."[63] That "cosmic process," of course, is the process of evolution.

The immense variety of organizations and sub-movements that are part of the New Age complex would almost defy analysis except for the fact that all are based on evolutionism, as viewed in a pantheistic context, with this evolutionary process now operating on the human level and aimed at an eventual world culture under a world government.

There is no need here for an extensive discussion of all the aspects of New Age-ism, nor of the scientists associated with it. However, it is important to understand a little of the movement's background and sources. Its roots go back into the 19th century or earlier. James Hutton, the progenitor of Charles Lyell (the father of uniformitarian geology), held ideas practically equivalent to those of the scientists who are advocating the Gaia hypothesis today.

The revival of "spiritualism" in the mid-19th century, followed soon after by Madame Helena Blavatsky's Theosophical Society and then by Rudolf Steiner's Anthroposophy, stimulated a significant resurgence of ancient occultism. At about the same time, Mary Baker Eddy was developing her "Christian Science," which in many respects was an esoteric form of Buddhism. All of these systems were very similar to many aspects of the modern New Age movement, and all of course adapted easily to evolutionism. Darwin's co-promoter of natural selection, Alfred Russell Wallace, became a convinced spiritist, and both Steiner and Blavatsky built their systems around an evolutionary framework. Eddy's religious system was clearly pantheistic.

There were many other similar 19th-century trends, including various theories of creative evolution, such as those of Henri Bergson, Lloyd Morgan, and other philosopher/scientists who promoted different concepts of vitalism and orthogenesis. Most of the features of modern New Age-ism can be traced in the writings and speculations of these earlier writers.

Undoubtedly the most influential progenitor of the present New Age movement, however, was the highly controversial Jesuit priest-paleontologist Teilhard de Chardin. Marilyn Ferguson, whose book *The Aquarian Conspiracy* has become almost a "Bible" of this movement, has named Teil-

---

63. Fritjof Capra, *The Turning Point* (Toronto: Bantam, 1982), p. 77–78. His book *The Tao of Physics* (New York: Bantam, 1977) is even more widely known.

hard as the one most often mentioned as their mentor by New-Agers polled in a survey.[64]

Pierre Teilhard de Chardin (1881–1955) held a doctorate in paleontology from the Sorbonne University in Paris and was involved in the controversial discoveries of both Peking Man and Piltdown Man. Although ordained in the Roman Catholic Church, he began to advocate heretical doctrines almost from the first, and his many books were opposed by the Catholic hierarchy until after his death. With the increasing liberalization of the Catholic Church in the last two generations, however, and the now almost-universal teaching of evolution in its colleges and seminaries, Teilhard's writings have become very popular among both Catholic clergy and laity, as well as among non-Catholics, especially those in the New Age orbit.

At the risk of oversimplifying in order to keep this discussion brief, it is nevertheless fair to say that de Chardin's religion was a sort of "Christian" pantheism. His concept of God was certainly not taken from the Bible or from Catholic theology. To all intents and purposes, Evolution — with a capital "E" — was deified by him. Note the following statement of faith:

> Is evolution a theory, a system, or a hypothesis? It is much more: it is a general condition to which all theories, all systems, all hypotheses must bow and which they must satisfy henceforward if they are to be thinkable and true. Evolution is a light illuminating all facts, a curve that all lines must follow.[65]

Teilhard would have vigorously denied that he was an atheist, of course. He even claimed to be a creationist, but he meant simply that God used evolution to create. In fact, he insisted that this was the only possible way of creation: "God cannot create, except evolutively."[66] To say such a thing is really saying that God is not omnipotent and therefore not really God. Then God is nothing but evolution, and evolution is the "creative" power of the cosmos, creating more and more complexity as time advances.

Teilhard admitted in many ways that his doctrine was pantheistic and that both God and the Creator and Christ the incarnate Word were either synonyms or products of evolution. Note the following remarkable

---

64. Marilyn Ferguson, *The Aquarian Conspiracy* (Los Angeles, CA: Tarcher, 1980), p. 50.
65. Pierre Teilhard de Chardin, *The Phenomenon of Man* (New York: Harper & Row, 1965), p. 219.
66. Teilhard de Chardin, *Christianity and Evolution* (New York: Harcourt, Brace and Jovanovich, 1971), p. 179.

admission: "The world (its value, its infallibility, and its goodness) . . . that, when all is said and done, is the first, the last, and the only thing in which I believe."[67]

As previously mentioned, Teilhard de Chardin is, in effect, the patron saint of the New Age movement, and it would be interesting to study his philosophy in detail. However, our main purpose here is to point out that he, as well as other leaders and savants of New Age-ism, were and are all committed evolutionists and pantheists. For those who desire a complete exposition and critique of de Chardin, a recent book by Wolfgang Smith[68] is strongly recommended. Dr. Smith, professor of mathematics at Oregon State University, has an outstanding background in both physics and philosophy.

One final quotation from de Chardin, as cited in Dr. Smith's book, points up his blasphemous attitude toward Jesus Christ: "It is Christ, in very truth, who saves . . . but should we not immediately add that at the same time it is Christ who is saved by Evolution?"[69] According to Smith, Teilhard wrote these words in an essay completed just a month before he died.

Three other men might be mentioned as possible forerunners of the current New Age movement. Perhaps surprisingly, these are George Gaylord Simpson, Theodosius Dobzhansky, and Sir Julian Huxley, the three scientists (paleontologist, geneticist, and biologist, respectively) who are universally acknowledged as the three chief developers and promoters of neo-Darwinism. None of the three believed in a personal God, yet each was quite "religious" and all were good friends and quasi-disciples of Teilhard. Their religion, of course, like that of Teilhard himself, was humanism.

These men may have been progenitors of the New Age movement, but the current generation of New Agers has largely abandoned the neo-Darwinian evolutionary mechanism that they advocated — that is, the slow-and-gradual increases in complexity brought about by random mutations and natural selection. Modern evolutionists have had to acknowledge the total lack of scientific evidence for any gradual increase in complexity. In his analysis of Teilhard's evolutionism, Smith comes to the same conclusion as that of modern scientific creationists: "And yet the fact remains that there exists to this day not a shred of *bona fide* scientific evidence in

---

67. Ibid., p. 99.
68. Wolfgang Smith, *Teilhardism and the New Religion* (Rockford, IL: Tan Books, 1988), 248 p. Dr. Smith writes from the traditional Catholic perspective.
69. Teilhard de Chardin, *The Heart of the Matter* (New York: Harcourt Brace Jovanovich, 1979), p. 92.

support of the thesis that macroevolutionary transformations have ever occurred."[70]

Consequently, more and more modern evolutionists (especially among the paleontologists, who are painfully aware of the complete absence of any true transitional forms in the fossil record) are becoming converts to the Gould-Eldredge thesis of "punctuated equilibrium," the idea that macroevolution occurs suddenly in a small population, leaving no intermediate forms to be preserved as fossils.

This idea of sudden increase in complexity fits nicely with the sociological ambitions of the New-Agers, and so has quickly become a key component of the movement. Marilyn Ferguson, an influential leader in the New Age movement, explains the relevance of punctuated equilibrium to her "Aquarian conspiracy":

> (1) It requires a mechanism for biological change more powerful than chance mutation, and (2) it opens us up to the possibility of rapid evolution in our own time, when the equilibrium of the species is punctuated by stress. Stress in modern society is experienced at the frontiers of our psychological rather than our geographical limits.[71]

It is remarkable to note the recent popularization of this unscientific notion that higher degrees of organized complexity can suddenly emerge out of a chaotic milieu. This notion is completely contradicted by the famous second law of thermodynamics, which stipulates that all real systems and processes tend naturally to *deteriorate* to greater randomness and higher probability — that is, to lower degrees of organization and complexity — regardless of whether the system is open or closed. Furthermore, the more chaotic the environment, the more rapidly does this disintegration occur.[72] Only under certain very special conditions, not available to

---

70. Smith, *Teilhardism*, p. 6.
71. Ferguson, *The Aquarian Conspiracy*, p. 159. Cited in "The New Myth" by Elliot Miller, *Forward* (Winter 1966): p. 14. Miller also cites other New Age leaders who believe a quantum leap in human evolution to a state of higher consciousness is imminent, via the imagined punctuational mechanism.
72. The scientific aspects of this subject have been discussed in some detail in several books by this writer. See, for example, *King of Creation* (1980), p. 99–107, 109–136; *Creation and the Modern Christian* (1985), p. 82–90, 148–174; *What is Creation Science?* (co-author Gary E. Parker, 2nd ed., 1987), p. 21–26, 187–222; *Scientific Creationism* (second edition, 1985), p. 37–69; *The Biblical Basis for Modern Science* (1984), p. 185–215. All were published by Master Books, Green Forest, AR.

"evolution" in random processes, can the complexity of open systems be driven upward.

Nevertheless, the idea is spreading rapidly — promoted by both Marxists and New Agers, who rather approve of the notion of chaotic revolutions in society — that conditions of great stress and disorder can somehow create a higher order, all of a sudden! Marilyn Ferguson quotes the Association for Humanistic Psychology as proclaiming that "the very chaos of contemporary existence provides the material for transformation. We will search [out] new myths, and world visions."[73]

The idea of punctuated equilibrium, or sudden upsurges to higher complexity, is supported not by evidence, but by *lack* of evidence. That is, since there is no evidence of slow-and-gradual evolution, therefore evolution must occur too quickly to leave any evidence! This obviously begs the basic question, since it arbitrarily assumes evolution to be a fact. Yet Teilhard de Chardin, the patron guru of New Age-ism, has the effrontery to assert that evolution is "above all verification, as well as being immune from any subsequent contradiction by experience."[74] That is, evolution is simply an assumption that we know intuitively to be a fact, even though it can be neither verified nor contradicted empirically or scientifically.

Proponents of punctuated equilibrium assert that the universal evolutionary process has proceeded jerkily from the sudden big bang (which produced the universe), to a sudden explosion of some star (which generated the solar system and the complex chemical elements therein), to a sudden appearance of living systems in some chaotic disturbance of the primeval soup — then on up the chain of complex life to human beings. The notion is that each advance is somehow achieved by a mysterious quantum leap in organization in the midst of some unknown geologic extinction event. Now that man has arrived, "conscious evolution" can take over, so that future advances can be in the psycho-social sphere, culminating ultimately in a unified global consciousness and a perfect world order. This is the remarkable scenario being promoted in one form or another by most New Agers today. This is not really new, however, but only a revival of ancient paganism. As New Age savant Fritjof Capra says:

> The idea of fluctuations as the basis of order, which Nobel laureate Ilya Prigogine introduced into modern science, is one of the major themes in all Taoist texts. The mutual interdependence of all

73. Ferguson, *The Aquarian Conspiracy*, p. 39. See also Miller, "The New Myth."
74. Teilhard de Chardin, *The Phenomenon of Man*, p. 140. Cited by Smith, *Teilhardism*, p. 2.

aspects of reality and the non-linear nature of its interconnections are emphasized throughout Eastern mysticism.[75]

The Belgian scientist mentioned here by Cara, Ilya Prigogine, has become unduly famous for his mathematical studies suggesting the possibility of "dissipative structures" in certain chemical processes — that is, the formation of small ordered structures in larger fields of great disorder and energy dissipation. The minimal physical evidences of such a phenomenon (e.g., the formation of small vortices in a coffee cup by heat flow) has been extrapolated beyond all reason into a generalized concept of "order through chaos."

One commentator observes:

> Prigogine's work has long been of interest to systems theorists seeking to apply the logic of their fields to global problems. One such scientist is Ervin Laszlo of the United Nations. "What I see Prigogine doing," says Laszlo, "is giving legitimization to the process of evolution — self-organization under conditions of change. . . . Its analogy to social systems and evolution could be very fruitful."[76]

This is not the place to discuss the scientific basis for such notions as punctuated equilibrium and dissipative structures, which is extremely weak at best. It is important to note here, however, that these ideas are being applied enthusiastically in New Age philosophy as both a justification and a mechanism for attaining the globalistic goals of its leaders. Despite the utter lack of scientific evidence that such phenomena occur in nature — in fact, despite the compelling *negative* evidence of the second law of thermodynamics that they even *could* occur in nature — modern evolutionists and those who use them blithely assert that evolution is "legitimized" by these "discoveries" of Stephen Gould and Ilya Prigogine.

The main point being made in this section has been simply to document the fact that New Age humanism, no less than secular humanism, is based squarely on the premise of evolution. One system may be pantheistic evolutionism, in contrast to the atheistic evolutionism of the other, but they are both the same under the surface, continuing the age-long anti-creationist rebellion of the ancient Tower-builders at Babel against their Creator. Their

---

75. Fritjof Capra, "The Dance of Life," *Science Digest* 90 (April 1982): p. 33. Capra, a physicist, has tried to apply "systems theory" to biology.

76. Will Lepkowski, "The Social Thermodynamics of Ilya Prigogine," *Chemical and Engineering News* (April 16, 1979): p. 30. Ervin Laszlo, like Capra, is a leader in the scientific wing of the New Age movement.

whole foundation is evolutionism, for there is no other way to reject the Creator. Said another New Age globalist at the United Nations, Assistant Secretary-General Robert Muller: "I believe the most fundamental thing we can do today is to believe in evolution."[77] By the same token, the most fundamental thing that can be done by those who oppose the New Age movement is to believe aggressively in creation.

The Demise of Christian Morality

Evolutionary teaching has not only thoroughly undermined Christian doctrine in the churches and schools, it has also practically eliminated the semblance of Bible-based behavior from American life. Morality has been turned upside-down. Until this present generation, premarital sex, adultery, divorce, and homosexuality were considered wrong and often even illegal. Now, however, those who oppose these practices are considered "immoral" in seeking to restrain personal freedoms and the right to privacy. Unrestrained pornography prevails in literature, motion pictures, and to a large extent, television. Prostitution, both male and female, is at an all-time high, as is its attendant criminal activity. Even among Bible-believing Christians and their leaders, moral standards are much lower than they were a generation ago.

Hardly anyone would question these facts, but it might not be immediately obvious that evolutionary teaching is the basic cause of all such changes. Concerned citizens have mounted drives against pornography, homosexual proselytizing, and anti-Bible immorality in general, but they have largely compromised with the evolutionary concepts that are behind it all, not realizing that it does little good to chop away at the weeds in a garden while leaving their seeds in the ground.

All of these sexual sins are in reality sins against the divinely established institution of the family. God created man and woman, commanding them to have children in a God-centered home environment, and this primeval commandment was affirmed later by Christ. When questioned about easy divorce, Jesus replied by quoting from the two creation chapters in Genesis, juxtaposing them in one harmonious doctrine of the intended permanence of the husband/wife relation:

Have ye not read, that he which made them at the beginning made them male and female, and said, For this cause shall a man leave father and mother, and shall cleave to his wife: and they twain

---

77. Kristin Murphy, "United Nations' Robert Muller — A Vision of Global Spirituality," *The Movement Newspaper*, Sept. 1983, p. 10. Cited in Miller, "The New Myth," p. 1.

shall be one flesh? Wherefore they are no more twain, but one flesh. What therefore God hath joined together, let not man put asunder (Matt. 19:4–6).[78]

In this commandment, the Lord Jesus was merely quoting and applying parts of Genesis 1:27 and Genesis 2:24. These passages also instructed them to "be fruitful and multiply" (Genesis 1:28), that the children were not to leave their father and mother until ready for marriage themselves, and that the woman was to be "an help meet for" the man and therefore "was taken out of man" (Genesis 2:18, 23). The New Testament apostles quite properly also applied this passage to teach that "the husband is the head of the wife" and that he should "so love his wife even as himself" (Ephesians 5:23, 33). In view of this relationship, wives were instructed to "submit yourselves unto your own husbands, as unto the Lord," with each told to "see that she reverence her husband" (Ephesians 5:22, 33).

This primeval commandment — the first ever given by the Creator — clearly established what we call today the "nuclear family" (husband, wife, children) as the fundamental institution of human society, around which all human activities were to be centered. Immediately following this basic commandment, God ordained their "dominion mandate" when He said, "Be fruitful, and multiply, and replenish the earth, and subdue it: and have dominion over the fish of the sea, and over the fowl of the air, and over every living thing that moveth upon the earth" (Genesis 1:28). He had already said that their dominion was to be "over all the earth" (v. 26). This primeval mandate has never been withdrawn, and it essentially legitimizes every honorable human vocation, if exercised for man's good and God's glory. And it is structured around the foundational framework of the God-fearing home and family.

Furthermore, this is reinforced in the Ten Commandments, wherein one commandment prescribes that children should honor their parents, another forbids adultery, and another prohibits even coveting another man's wife. The fourth commandment, that of remembering the Sabbath, is based on the fact of a completed six-day creation, as outlined in the Bible's first chapter. The first two commandments prohibit pantheism/polytheism/humanism in any form. Thus, six of God's basic commandments look back to the creation account. The other four (prohibiting lying, stealing, murder, and taking God's name in vain) also presuppose God's sovereignty and the created image of God in man (Gen. 1:27), though the latter doctrine is not explicitly repeated here.

---

78. See also Mark 10:6–9.

With these facts in mind, it is obvious that the modern widespread rebellion against God's commandments related to the family is conditioned upon the prior rejection of His creation activity and the record thereof. Schools, colleges, and the media have been promoting evolution and ridiculing Genesis for at least two generations, and finally many in the modern generation have come to reject it as nothing but myth and fable.

The real history of the human race, such people maintain, is one of hominid populations evolving from lower animals. Consequently, though the Mosaic Decalogue may have served a purpose for a wandering tribe of Hebrews for a time, it has no particular relevance today. They teach that society continues to evolve and so must our ethics and system of morality. "Furthermore," they ask, "since evolution [whether by struggle and selection or by chaotic revolution] has brought us this far, why not continue on the same course?" If animalistic morality and violent upheaval worked in the past, why not now?

Appeals to maintain chaste moral standards on the basis of biblical commandments are now considered by many to be quaint and irrelevant. Their assertion is that these standards are squarely based on biblical creationism, so they can hardly be valid if the Genesis record is false. This, in turn, would mean that even Jesus Christ was merely a mistaken child of His times.

Evolutionism, on the other hand, warrants full sexual freedom, especially since even marriage and the nuclear family may no longer be "useful." Recall that the Tenets of Humanism explicitly call for complete freedom in sex matters, and that all the tenets of the Humanist Manifestos are based on the first two tenets, which lay down the premise of both cosmic and human evolution.[79]

Although most Christians seem not to recognize that modern sexual immorality in its various manifestations is causally related to the abandonment of creationism in favor of evolutionism, the evolutionary humanists understand this quite well. In a review article decrying the resurgence of creationism, anthropologist Bruce Grindal uses such rhetoric as the following:

> The doctrine of creationism and the attendant values involving rigid adherence to moral purity are impervious to arguments of reason.[80]

> The populist heart of the Christian fundamentalist mentality, demonstrating how the issue of creationism and its mythological

---

79. See discussion earlier in this chapter.
80. Bruce T. Grindal, "Creationism, Sexual Purity, and the Religious Right," *The Humanist* 43 (March/April 1983): p. 19.

view of world order is intimately related to the issues of sexual morality and to the deep corners of a people who see their way of life under
attack.[81]

> The thesis here is that sexuality is intimately tied to fundamental
> conceptions of world order, the foundation of which is the Christian
> family. Upon this foundation rests the proper nature of society, one
> in which men are men and women are women.[82]

Dr. Grindal, like other evolutionary anthropologists and humanists in
general, is a strong advocate of full sexual permissiveness. He sees the recent revival of creationism as the greatest threat to modern "advances" in sex
freedoms. Although he is opposed to creationism and biblical Christianity,
he does make a strong case for our current thesis — namely that the breakdown in society's moral standards is directly related to its abandonment of
creationism.

The divinely created relationship between men and women has also been
badly distorted in recent years by the liberal feminist movement. We do need
to realize, however, that this has largely been in reaction to the unbiblical
male chauvinism that has resulted, not from the clear roles set forth by God
for man and woman, but from a gross distortion of that doctrine based on
Darwinian evolutionary ideas.

> Darwin's concept of sexual selection and his associated inter-
> pretations of human evolution were . . . in some degree taken over
> from his socially derived perceptions of feminine characteristics and
> abilities. . . . Wilma George, in her recent book *Darwin* . . . pointed
> out that the origin of man by natural law rather than divine creation
> was made more palatable for its Victorian audience by Darwinian
> concepts of male superiority.[83]

Long before Darwin, earlier "evolutionists" had likewise relegated wom-
en to a role of subjugation and inferiority in both atheistic and pantheistic
religious cultures (consider the common image of the "caveman" dragging
his mate by the hair, as well as the subservient role of women in practically
all pagan and ethnic religions). Bible-based Christianity elevated women

---

81. Ibid., p. 20. Dr. Grindal is a professor of anthropology at Florida State University
    (Tallahassee) and is editor of *Anthropology and Humanism Quarterly*, published by
    the Society for Humanistic Anthropology.
82. Ibid., p. 21.
83. Eveleen Richards, "Will the Real Charles Darwin Please Stand Up," *New Scientist*
    100 (Dec. 22/29, 1983): p. 887.

against to the divine role intended for them, as "heirs together of the grace of life" with their husbands (1 Pet. 3:7). Not so in evolutionism!

> Perhaps it would be more appropriate to reserve the label ["sexist"] for those who insist on perpetuating the Darwinian tradition of legitimating our current sexual inequalities on the basis of an evolutionary reconstruction that centers on the aggressive, territorial, hunting male and relegates the female to submissive domesticity and the periphery of the evolutionary process.[84]

The Bible teaches that sexual relations of any kind are sinful except between husband and wife, united in a marriage dissolved only by death. It reserves its strongest condemnation, however, for the sin of homosexuality, since this practice repudiates the very nature of man and women as created by God. Some "Christian" homosexuals have made abortive attempts to reinterpret those biblical passages that condemn homosexuality, but this is like interpreting black as white. For the most part, any justification of this practice must be based on evolutionary concept. The editor of a magazine for "gays" expresses this argument as follows:

> Homosexuality is seldom discussed as a component in evolution, but it undoubtedly plays a role. Homosexual behavior has been observed in most animal species studied, and the higher we climb on the taxonomic tree toward mammals, the more apparent homosexual behavior we see.[85]

And just *how* has homosexuality contributed to evolution? Here are some suggestions:

> R.H. Dennison, professor of zoology at the University of Wyoming, has concluded that in evolution homosexuality acts as a tension-lowering device, satisfying the mating practices of more dominant males. . . . Homosexuality also serves evolutionary processes by acting as a form of population control.[86]

The author of the above two statements concludes his article with the following remarkable plea and forecast:

---

84. Ibid.
85. Jacob Smit, "In the Beginning — Homosexuality and Evolution," *Intl. N.W. Guide Magazine* (Issue 19, Aug. 1987): p. 6.
86. Ibid.

The removal of restrictive ranges of behavior and boundaries that interfere with the intimacy and learning of gay people, as well as assuring a better world for all mankind [sic]. Without question, this would represent a considerable evolutionary jump. It may well turn out to be that God does have room for an Adam and Steve.[87]

Christian morality involves much more than refraining from sexual sins, of course. The Ten Commandments have long been regarded as the basis of civil morality in this country, as well as the minimum measure of Christian righteousness. Honesty, truthfulness, industry, unselfishness, respect for others, and willingness to forgive others are all implied in these commandments, as is integrity toward God and family.

Today, however, these virtues have largely been displaced by the "numero uno" syndrome in human relationships, as well as ungodliness and infidelity in daily life. When lying or stealing gains some personal benefit and can be carried out without penalty, no outmoded Bible teaching is going to interfere — or so too many people think today! Even murder has been legalized, in the case of the unborn. Killers are almost never executed anymore (despite God's clear commands to this effect), and even the most flagrant criminals may spend little time in prison.

Though most scholars recognize that biblical laws, especially the Ten Commandments, originally formed the basis of our common-law system and even our federal constitution, the courts have now banned mention of the Ten Commandments in our schools and indirectly removed their controlling guidelines from our lives.

The Devaluation of Life

As night follows day, the explosion of sexual promiscuity in recent decades has triggered an explosion of unwanted pregnancies and then the legalization and popularization of abortion as a preferred means of dealing with them. In the Christian world, as well as in most other religions, abortion had long been essentially considered to be murder, on the assumption that the embryo in the womb was a baby — a true human being from the moment of conception. Accordingly, abortion had been a criminal offense carrying severe penalties.

To justify this rapid change in abortionism from criminality to respectability, it was essential for its proponents to argue that the embryo was not really a human being and therefore that abortion was not really murder but

---

87. Ibid., p. 8.

merely legitimate expression of "freedom of choice" on the part of the woman. Columnist Joseph Sobran explains, noting that the abortionizer imagines

> . . . that the human embryo undergoes something like the whole process of evolution, as in the old adage that "ontogeny recapitulates phylogeny." The adage has been discredited, of course, but this does not mean it has lost its power over the imagination of many modern people. They still suppose that the fetus is in the early stages of development a "lower" form of life, and this is probably what they mean when they say it isn't "fully human."[88]

The defense for abortion described above is saying that, in repeating the evolutionary history of its non-human ancestors, the fetus does not actually evolve into the human stage until very late in its prenatal development. It is not "murder," of course, to kill a fish or a monkey, so abortion is no great problem, so they say.

That this absurd notion is being promoted by modern evolutionary scientists is confirmed by the following rationalization for abortion, written by the director of the Biosystems Research Institute in La Jolla, California, also chairman of the Southern California Skeptics, a Pacific affiliate of the American Association for Advancement of Science:

> *Ontogeny recapitulates phylogeny.* This is a fundamental tenet of modern biology that derives from evolutionary theory, and is thus anathema to creationism as well as to those opposed to freedom of choice. Ontogeny is the name for the process of development of a fertilized egg into a fully formed and mature living organism. Phylogeny, on the other hand, is the history of the evolution of a species, in this case human being. During development, the fertilized egg progresses over 38 weeks through what is, in fact, a rapid passage through evolutionary history: From a single primordial cell, the conceptus progresses through being something of a protozoan, a fish, a reptile, a bird, a primate, and ultimately a human being. There is a difference of opinion among scientists about the time during a pregnancy when a human being can be said to emerge. But there is general agreement that this does not happen until after the end of the first trimester.[89]

---

88. Joseph Sobran, "The Averted Gaze: Liberalism and Fetal Pain," *Human Life Review* 9 (Spring 1984): p. 6.
89. Elie A. Schneour, "Life Doesn't Begin, It Continues," *Los Angeles Times*, Jan. 29, 1989, Part V.

It is bad enough that this recapitulation nonsense is still taught to gullible students as a "proof" of evolution, but it becomes a crime against God and humanity when it is used as the supposed scientific justification of abortion!

The fact is, however, that the "fetus" is a true human being from the very beginning. The old recapitulation theory of Ernst Haeckel is utterly false, as even such a doctrinaire evolutionist as Stephen Jay Gould admits: "In Down's day, the theory of recapitulation embodied a biologist's best guide for the organization of life into sequences of higher and lower forms. (Both the theory and 'ladder approach' to classification that it encouraged are, or should be, defunct today.)"[90]

We can justifiably charge this evolutionary nonsense of recapitulation-ism with responsibility for the slaughter of millions of helpless, prenatal children — or at least for giving it a pseudo-scientific rationale.

> So the abortion debate has its roots in two alternative ways of imagining the unborn. Our civilization, until recently, agreed in imagining the unborn child on the pattern of the Incarnation, which maximizes his dignity; but many people now imagine him on the pattern of evolution, as popularly understood, which minimizes his dignity.[91]

Even worse than the idea that the fetus is a not-yet-human animal is the attitude of many of the doctors associated with Planned Parenthood, the organization especially sanctioning abortion as a "choice."

> For the majority of medical authorities associated with Planned Parenthood actually seem to regard pregnancy as a disease or even a plague. For example, Dr. Warren Hern, writing in the January 1971 issue of Planned Parenthood's *Family Planning Perspectives*, describes pregnancy as "an episodic, moderately extended, chronic condition . . . an illness [to be treated] by evacuation of the uterine contents." That, of course, means abortion.[92]

---

90. Stephen Jay Gould, "Dr. Down's Syndrome," *Natural History* 89 (April 1980): p. 144. Gould, in this article, decries the recapitulation theory as responsible for the strong racism of the post-Darwin era. He also noted in passing that it was used as "the best guide for the organization of life into sequences of higher and lower forms" — that is, of developing a model for establishing the time sequence of fossils in the geo-logic column. Abortion, racism, the standard geologic column — quite a record of accomplishment for such a totally false construct of evolutionary philosophy!

91. Sobran, "The Averted Gaze," p. 6.

92. Kirk Kidwell, "Planned Parenthood Has Plans," *The New American* 2 (Jan. 20, 1986): p. 9

In either case, whether the embryonic child is viewed as an animal or as a disease, it is a naturalistic evolutionary philosophy that governs and motivates such apologists for abortion, a fact that adds yet another item in our indictment against evolution.

The question now is: If abortion is so widely accepted and practiced, can infanticide be far behind? The same evolutionary rationalization used to justify abortion might also be used to justify the murder of unwanted children, especially those with birth defects or illnesses that will prevent their contributing to society later on. Some of this is already being done in this country and more elsewhere. If populations continue to grow, especially in overcrowded, underdeveloped countries, pressure toward infanticide will surely also continue to grow, as one writer observes:

> Among some animal species, then, infant killing appears to be a natural practice. Could it be natural for humans, too, a trait inherited from our primate ancestors? . . . Charles Darwin noted in *The Descent of Man* that infanticide has been "probably the most important of all checks" on population growth throughout most of human history.[93]

Along with the upsurge in abortionism, there has also been increasing promotion of euthanasia, a practice already legalized in the Netherlands. For example, there has recently (1988) been a very strong drive to get a euthanasia initiative on the California ballot. This practice is promoted as "humane," giving those who are terminally ill or suffering intolerably the right to "death with dignity" (*euthanasia* means "easy death") — but this would be merely giving another name to "suicide" or even "murder," especially if the right to make the decision eventually passes (as it surely would, sooner or later) from the patient to his or her relatives or to doctors or to some government agency.

Once euthanasia is accepted as a viable option, one can easily foresee that it will soon come to be applied to anyone who is not capable of contributing to the social process. Euthanasia for the terminally ill, the hopelessly senile, and those who request release from great pain can perhaps be semi-justified, and these situations will make it easier to get the practice started. But already there is pressure to apply it to others. For example, one proponent said recently, "Mental defectives do not have a right to life, and therefore might be killed for food — if we should develop a taste for human flesh — or for the

---

93. Barbara Burke, "Infanticide," *Science* 84 (May 1984): p. 29.

purpose of scientific experimentation."[94] According to that extremist view, such people are mere animals whose evolutionary recapitulation was somehow arrested before they reach what the author of this statement calls "moral personhood."

Similarly, another observes:

> Humans without some minimum of intelligence or mental capacity are not persons, no matter how many of their organs are active, no matter how spontaneous their living processes are. . . . [Idiots] are not, never were, and never will be in any degree responsible. Idiots, that is to say, are not human.[95]

The author of this latter statement, strange to say, is a well-known theologian, though a thorough-going humanist. He is also famous for his advocacy of situation ethics and the "God is dead" idea, as well as being a pioneer in the "right to die" movement. He is also dead wrong in what he is saying here. According to the Bible and orthodox Christianity, not only "idiots" but also infants and even human embryos are human beings with eternal souls implanted by God at conception.

The modern world has already seen, in Nazi Germany, what can happen when this type of evolution thinking is applied to a whole group of people who are considered by the elite to be undeserving of existence. The fruit of two generations of evolutionary racism and Haeckelian recapitulationism was the unspeakable Holocaust and the attempted genocide of the Jewish people.

> Hitler, in his infamous *Mein Kampf*, whipped up an infinitely more diabolical creed, drawing facile analogies from the world of animals in his diatribe against the Jews. Each animal, he said, mates only with animals of its own species. Then, using the erroneous theory of blending inheritance, and the ideas of struggle for existence and survival of the fittest, he was able to give a *quasi*-scientific argument for the need of racial purity, the fundamental philosophical underpinning of Nazi movement.[96]

---

94. Peter Singer, as quoted in "Death Act Dies in California" by Martin Mawyer in *Fundamentalist Journal* 7 (June 1988): p. 61. Professor Singer calls himself a "moral ethicist." He was featured at the 1988 San Francisco Conference of the World Federation of Right-to-Die Societies.

95. Joseph Fletcher, also featured at the above-mentioned conference, as cited by Mawyer, "Death Act," p. 61.

96. Oldroyd, *Darwinian Impacts*, p. 217. Lest anyone misunderstand, Professor Oldroyd is an evolutionist, but he recognizes the deadly practices spawned by evolution.

On the basis of such pseudo-biological arguments, Hitler could call for the preservation of the purity of the so-called Aryan race, and ultimately for the attempted extermination of the Jews.[97]

The evolutionary delusion that certain groups should be exterminated in order to speed the evolutionary process, as exemplified by both the eugenics movement and the Nazi "final solution," may not be entirely a phenomenon of the past. Certain ominous rumblings among leaders in the New Age movement seem to suggest such a prospective fate for Christians in the future, when the New Age goal of world federalism, world government, and world religion is finally achieved.

The possibility of using the bodies of expendable or unfit people for scientific experimentation or even for food was noted above by Professor Peter Singer. It is not too surprising that some evolutionist writers today are beginning to even mention cannibalism, not as the unspeakably degenerate act that it is, but as a defensible social practice under certain conditions, especially in its supposed contribution to human evolution. A leading paleoanthropologist, Philip Tobias, is one example cited, as below:

> But research now suggests that [cannibalism] is far more widespread in nature than previously supposed, and that it was widely and actively practiced both by early humans and by the first civilizations. Speaking recently at the University of Alberta, Philip Tobias, a leading expert on human evolution, described the overwhelming evidence for cannibalism among early human ancestors.
>
> An exhaustive survey by biologist Gary Polis showed cannibalism in more than 1,300 species, including some human societies where human flesh was the single great source of protein.
>
> Among the experts, cannibalism is a hotly debated and emotion-charged issue. Still, given its obvious advantages plus our own history of cannibalism and its prevalence in nature, the wonder seems to be that modern humans have developed a repugnance for eating each other and have largely discontinued the practice.[98]

The reasoning would apparently be that since cannibalism is so common in the animal world, thus presumably contributing to evolution, and because of its probable nutritional value, perhaps it could contribute today to

97. Ibid., p. 218.
98. Paul Tisdall, "Cannibalistic Taboos a Recent Development," *Edmonton Journal,* Jan. 2, 1983.

still further evolution. A Columbia University anthropology professor notes that Aztecs and other peoples of antiquity ate the flesh of enemy soldiers as a means of overcoming protein deficiency:

> Surely there can be no special pride in the practice of letting millions of soldiers rot on the battlefield because of a taboo against cannibalism. One can even argue that, nutritionally, the best source of protein for human beings is human flesh because the balance of amino acids is precisely that which the body requires for its own proper functioning.[99]

As a matter of fact, cannibalism may never have been systematically practiced at all, according to an anthropologist at the State University of New York, in a scholarly survey[100] of all the hearsay reports of cannibalism, none of which apparently have ever been confirmed by reliable eyewitnesses. There has been quite a debate on this subject in recent years among anthropologists. Whether or not cannibalism has ever been consistently practiced for either religious or nutritional reasons, the significant point to note is that many evolutionists have tried to rationalize or justify it on the basis of its supposed evolutionary contribution. Even if ancient man never descended this low, it seems not too farfetched for modern men to seriously contemplate its possible advantages.

A rather bizarre practice tending in this direction is the recent rise — especially among the New Age people who are making almost a fetish out of both "natural" foods and "natural" home childbirth — of *placentophagia*, that is, eating a newborn baby's placenta. Writes one commentator, "In short, since they believe many other mammals and members of some human societies eat placenta, they assume it must make good sense nutritionally and medically and that the reason most Americans do not normally do so is because we are over-civilized."[101]

Those who endorse placentophagia seem to consider it both natural and nutritious, and the practice seems to increase as the percentage of home births increases. But there is also a strong religious aspect to it, in the pantheistic vein of New Age-ism: "The words *ritual, ceremony, spiritual, sacred,* and *reverence* are frequently used by such placenta eaters when describing their feelings and actions."[102] Whatever they may call it, most people would surely view it as a form of cannibalism, even though it is associated with birth instead of death.

99. Marvin Harris, "Our Pound of Flesh," *Natural History* 88 (Aug/Sept 1979): p. 36.
100. William Arens, *The Man-Eating Myth: Anthropology and Anthropophagy* (Oxford, UK; New York: Oxford University Press, 1979).
101. Karen Janszen, "Meat of Life," *Science Digest* 88 (Nov/Dec 1980): p. 78.
102. Ibid., p. 81.

Cannibalism and *placentophagia* are among the most bizarre and extreme products of evolutionism, though not the most important and deadly — not yet at least. When the very essence of evolutionism is struggle and survival, as Darwin and most of his followers have viewed it for over a century, then individual life and even group life easily become expendable, if such would serve the evolutionary cause.

Drugs, Crime, and Evolutionism

The modern drug culture and the parallel rise in criminal behavior of all kinds cannot be attributed directly to Darwinism, of course, for drugs and crime have been present in human society throughout history. But, for that matter, so has evolutionism in one form or another. Evolutionism is man's attempt to explain the world without God; crime is man's disobedience to God's law for human life; and drugs represent man's attempt to find a substitute for God in spiritual experience. All are therefore clearly related to man's rebellion against his Creator.

The connection of *modern* increases in crime and drug use to evolutionism is that, apparently for the first time in history, these phenomena are being rationalized and justified "scientifically" on the basis of their presumed evolutionary connections. The discussion in this section will therefore deal only with this current aspect. This is bad enough, of course, as drug use and violent crime — often causally connected today — have rapidly become problems of enormous proportion.

The modern drug culture had its initial rise largely through its popularization during the student rebellions of the sixties, especially following the example and teachings of Timothy Leary, then a Harvard University professor of psychology and a typical evolutionary pantheist. Leary ardently promoted the use of psychedelic drugs, taking them himself with the fervor of a religious devotee — which indeed he was as he sought union with the "infinite" through negating the mind and then "expanding" it with the drug experience. He even regarded his drugs as the "sacraments" in his religion of non-reason and mystical experience.

Even more influential than Leary in laying the foundation for the modern drug culture was Aldous Huxley. This English writer/philosopher was the brother of Sir Julian Huxley (whose writings and influence we have encountered frequently in these pages) and grandson of Thomas Huxley, long known as "Darwin's bulldog." All were atheists (though Grandfather Thomas preferred — and even coined — the term *agnostic*), and all were bitter in their hatred of Christianity.

Aldous was apparently the first distinguished intellectual to advocate hallucinogenic drugs as a means to experience "reality" in a world that science supposedly had proved to be irrational. In three influential books,[103] he promoted the use of supposed mind-expanding drugs for the Far East.

By the time these books had permeated the university world (beginning with Leary at Harvard and then, especially, at Berkeley), where evolutionism and existentialism had thoroughly prepared the ground, the student world of the "baby boom" generation was eagerly receptive to something that promised meaning in their spiritually barren lives. A.E. Wilder-Smith, a recognized scientific authority on the drug problem, writes:

> Aldous Huxley . . . brought to the notice of a wider public how he, following the example of some orientals, had obtained his transcendent ASC [meaning "altered state of consciousness"] ecstatic experience by means of psychedelic drugs. Such experiences are just what the younger generation has long been looking for — as indeed Huxley himself admits — starved as they have been of transcendent joy by having known little but the rat-race run by their fathers and mothers before them. Their purely materialistic upbringings in homes, schools, and universities had taken care of this for generations. . . . Huxley's experiences undoubtedly helped to touch off the psychedelic drug epidemic in the West, for the circumstances — scientific materialism for a century — were just ripe. A transcendentally deprived generation was, quite unconsciously, just ready for the psychedelic drug to give him the "religious" experience of which he and two or three generations before him had been starved.[104]

Evolutionism and its corollary teachings in the schools have so undermined the Bible by discrediting its record of creation and divine purpose that

---

103. Aldous Huxley, *Brave New World* (1932); *The Doors of Perception* (1954); *Heaven and Hell* (1956). All three books were published by Harper & Row, New York. Summarizing his siren song, Huxley said (*Scientific Monthly*, July 1957, p. 9): "The pharmacologists will give us something that most human beings have never had before. . . . If our desire is for life everlasting, they will give us the next best thing — eons of blissful experience miraculously telescoped into a single hour. . . . Many of our traditional notions about ethics and religion . . . will have to be reconsidered and reevaluated in the context of the pharmacological revolution. It will be extremely disturbing, but it will also be enormous fun."

104. A.E. Wilder-Smith, *The Causes and Cure of the Drug Epidemic* (Neuhausen-Stuttgart, West Germany: Telos International, 1974), p. 24. Dr. Wilder-Smith is an organic chemist and pharmacologist. With two doctorates, he has taught at universities in Switzerland, Norway, Turkey, and the United States.

the whole "Christian experience" has likewise been completely discredited in the minds of young people — despite the concentration of the evangelicals of the last two generations on Christian experience rather than doctrine. Wilder-Smith observes:

> The younger generation, being the heir of the older generation, is, of course, deprived too. Its science has robbed it of any belief in the transcendent or divine at all — Darwinism and Neo-Darwinism have long since taken care of that. In the East, the official state religion is, in fact, atheism, based entirely on the Neo-Darwinism developed in the West. But even though our generation thinks it cannot believe in God, it is nostalgic after transcendence, eternity, meaning, and beauty.[105]

Many other factors have contributed to the modern drug crisis (rock music, peer pressure, organized crime, etc.), but the underlying roots lie in the evolutionary philosophy, which had seemingly destroyed biblical authority and its genuine spiritual experience, mediated by such influential evolutionary teachers as Huxley and Leary, who were promising substitute religious experiences through drugs.

Along with the rise in drug use, there has been a corresponding explosion in serious crimes, in part to support the habits of young drug users. Prisons are overflowing, and the streets of our nation are not safe after dark anymore. One important contributing factor to this increase is judicial leniency on crime. This, in turn, is at least partially related to the same general rejection of biblical authority.

Also partially to blame is the widespread idea that criminals are not really responsible for their actions. Either society as a whole is to blame because of its toleration of slum environments, or "nature" is responsible, through the wrongdoers' genetic inheritance. The latter idea, in one form or another, has been taught ever since Darwin's day. In fact, many acts that civilization now considers criminal — stealing, raping, killing — were presumably quite normal behavior in the ancient reign of tooth and claw that characterized the struggle for existence:

> Many aspects of human behavior which appear incomprehensible, or even irrational, became meaningful when interpreted as survivals of attributes which were useful when they first appeared during evolutionary development. . . . The urge to control property and to dominate one's peers are also ancient biological traits which

---

105. Ibid., p. 25.

can be recognized in the different forms of territoriality and dominance among most if not all animal societies.[106]

Evolution is a hard, inescapable mistress. There is just no room for compassion or good sportsmanship. Too many organisms are born, so, quite simply, a lot of them are going to have to die, because there isn't enough food and space to go around. You can be beautiful, fat, strong, but it might not matter. The only thing that does matter is whether you leave more children carrying your genes than the next person leaves.[107]

Unbridled self-indulgence on the part of one generation without regard to future ones is the modus operandi of biological evolution and may be regarded as rational behavior.[108]

Natural selection can favor egotism, hedonism, cowardice instead of bravery, cheating, and exploitation.[109]

As we have just seen, the ways of national evolution, both in the past and in the present, are cruel, brutal, ruthless, and without mercy. . . . The law of Christ is incompatible with the law of evolution.[110]

The above quotations, taken almost at random from the writings of leading evolutionists of the two most recent generations (much stronger statements to the same effect were widely published in the 19th century), give the typical flavor of evolutionary explanations of human selfishness, aggression, and cruelty — the factors that produce crime. The writers were not trying to *justify* criminal behavior — but only to *explain* it! The true biblical explanation, of course, is sin — rebellion against God and His Word.

Some evolutionists have sought to deduce how the evolutionary process might be channeled into less cruel methods in the future. This was the theme of Thomas Huxley's famous 19th-century essay on "Evolution and Ethics," suggesting that once human ethics has "evolved," further evolution could be accomplished in a more kindly fashion. More recently, famed geneticist H.J. Muller wrote in the following vein:

---

106. Rene Dubos, "Humanistic Biology," *American Scientist* 53 (March 1965): p. 10–11. These thoughts were from a Phi Beta Kappa-Sigma Xi lecture.
107. Lorraine Lee Larison Cudmore, "The Center of Life," *Science Digest* 82 (Nov. 1977): p. 46. This statement was excerpted from her book of that name.
108. W.H. Murdy, "Anthropocentrism, a Modern Version," *Science* 187 (March 28, 1975): p. 1169.
109. Theodosius Dobzhansky, "Ethics and Values in Biological and Cultural Evolution," *Zygon,* as reported in the *Los Angeles Times,* June 16, 1974, Part IV, p. 6.
110. Arthur Keith, *Evolution and Ethics* (New York: Putnam, 1947), p. 15.

It has rightly been said that biological evolution is multi-directional and cruel and that the vast majority of lines of descent end in pitiful anti-climaxes. . . . Through the unprecedented faculty of long-range foresight, jointly serviced and exercised by us, we can, in securing and advancing our position, increasingly avoid the missteps of blind nature, circumvent its cruelties, reform our own natures, and enhance our own values.[111]

Human developments since Darwin's day — or even in the 30-plus years since Muller wrote so optimistically — would scarcely support his predictions!

More recently, the famed sociobiologist Edward O. Wilson and the almost equally notorious Darwinian philosopher Michael Ruse — both atheistic humanists — have even argued that somehow the evolutionary process, with all its cruelty and randomness, managed to evolve a humane moral code. They write: "We need something to spur us against our usual selfish dispositions. Nature, therefore, has made us (via the rules) believe in a disinterested moral code, according to which we *ought* to help our fellows. . . . In an important sense, ethics as we know it is an illusion fobbed off on us by our genes to get us to cooperate."[112] This is wishful evolutionary speculation *ad absurdum*!

The tendency to blame antisocial and criminal behavior on genetic factors has also led to the systems of psychology known as determinism and behaviorism. These in turn have led many criminologists and many jurists to regard criminals as not really responsible for their crimes. After all, they are merely animals and their behaviors are genetically determined, so why should they be punished? It is rather obvious that the modern opposition to capital punishment for murder and the general tendency toward leniency in punishment for other serious crimes are directly related to the strong emphasis on evolutionary determinism that has characterized much of this century.

One of the most extreme theories based on the idea of biological determinism was published by an Italian psychiatrist and criminologist named Cesare Lombroso in 1876. Stephen Jay Gould comments as follows: "Biological theories of criminality were scarcely new, but Lombroso gave the argument a novel evolutionary twist. Born criminals are not simply deranged or diseased; they are literally throwbacks to a previous evolutionary stage."[113]

Lombroso is considered the father of modern scientific criminology, with its emphasis on both evolutionary inheritance and environmental influences as

111. H.J. Muller, "Human Values in Relation to Evolution," *Science* 127 (March 21, 1958): p. 629.
112. Ruse and Wilson, "Evolution and Ethics," p. 51.
113. Gould, *Ever Since Darwin*, p. 223.

the causes of crime. Before his time, criminals were assumed to be *volitionally* responsible for their crimes, in accord with biblical truth. Lombroso's theories proposed that many criminals could actually be recognized by their apelike physical and social characteristics. This idea is no longer accepted, but belief in evolutionary inheritance as conducive to crime is still widely believed. Gould observes that "Lombroso's brand of criminal anthropology is dead, but its basic postulate lives on in popular notions of criminal genes or chromosomes."[114]

It would probably be an oversimplification to attribute the tremendous modern upsurge in crime directly to the ubiquitous presence of evolutionary emphasis in the schools, the media, and the courts, but there is certainly a significant connection. At the very least, this widespread evolutionary and humanistic teaching has not *stemmed* the growth in crime! Even though criminal acts are not really caused by genes or evolutionary throwbacks, they are certainly not discouraged by widespread disbelief in God, biblical law, and ultimate divine retribution. As humanist philosopher Will Durant admitted:

> By offering evolution in place of God as a cause of history, Darwin moved the theological basis of the moral code of Christendom. And the moral code that has no fear of God is very shaky. That's the condition we are in. . . . I don't think man is capable yet of managing social order and individual decency without fear of some supernatural being overlooking him and able to punish him.[115]

It is interesting that Durant didn't think that *he* needed God, but that society did! He was right about the latter, at least.

I have tried to point out in this chapter the baleful influence of evolutionary thinking on all the more important aspects of Christian theology and morality. In the two preceding chapters I attempted to document the pervasive and controlling influence of evolutionism in all the various significant disciplines of modern thought — the natural sciences, the social sciences, the humanities, the fine arts — and then also its role as the pseudo-scientific rationale for all the harmful philosophies and social systems that have plagued the world since the so-called Enlightenment of the Renaissance, with its revival of the ancient pagan cultures.

In all this, I have barely been able to scratch the surface. The impact of evolutionism in all these areas could easily be traced and documented in much fuller detail. One could also show its influence in many other areas of

---

114. Ibid., p. 224.
115. Will Durant, "Are We in the Last Stage of a Pagan Period?" *Chicago Tribune,* Syndicate April 1980.

life and study that have barely been mentioned at all — modern environmentalism, or recreation, or the labor movement, or a host of other things. After all, evolutionism is the only alternative worldview to true theistic creationism, and both must embrace "the whole of reality," as Huxley put it.

I trust, however, that this point has been adequately made without the need of any further analysis or documentation. Evolutionism is uniquely and pervasively important! Christians in particular — and any others who still believe in a personal, transcendent, omnipotent God — urgently need to wake up to the deadly dangers that lie ahead. Evolutionary humanism is far more than a scientific theory. It is being vigorously and more and more successfully promoted as the coming world religion, world culture, and world government.

But how can it be that what most people thought was a mere biological hypothesis can have obtained so much power and influence in such a short time? The average person neither knows nor cares much about the evolution issue, yet he is unconsciously being increasingly influenced and intimidated by it.

The fact is that evolutionism did not reach this position in a short time at all. The creation-evolution conflict did not begin at the time of Charles Darwin but, rather, has been raging ever since the dawn of history. We need to understand a little of this history if we are really to understand the present and be prepared for the future. This will be the theme of the next chapter.

4

The Dark Nursery
of Darwinism

The common belief today is that Charles Darwin discovered the law of evolution. As a result, he is widely acclaimed as one of the greatest scientists of all time. The fact is, however, that he really only served as the catalyst for a revival of ancient paganism, coming at just the right time in history to bring to fruition a revolt against God for which many in Western Europe had been preparing for over a century.

There were many evolutionists before Darwin. In fact, he was not even the first to suggest natural selection as the mechanism of evolution, even though he commonly called the idea "my theory." The worldwide impact of evolution, as outlined in the three preceding chapters, is an effect requiring a much greater cause than a single book written by Charles Darwin.

In this chapter, therefore, we need to survey the historical background of the evolutionary (and revolutionary) movements and philosophies that finally culminated in the triumph of Darwinism in the 19th century. The roots go very deep, and the road that led to Darwin stretches back into remote antiquity. We shall see that evolution is not a modern scientific theory at all, but only the ancient rebellion of men against their Creator. It has been updated a bit and is more sophisticated in its pseudo-scientific modern garb, but underneath is the same old pagan warfare that unbelievers have waged against God in every age. In order to understand its real significance, therefore, we must trace it back to its source. First of all, however, we must look at the immediate background of Darwinism, including the contemporary movements that accompanied and preceded it.

The Unnatural Selection of Charles Darwin

The influence of Darwin on post-Darwinian world history is truly an amazing phenomenon, for he himself was hardly the model of a brilliant scientist his modern disciples believe him to have been. A pampered timewaster in college, chronically ill most of his life with an uncertain malaise, and with his only college degree one in theology, Charles Darwin is still something of an enigma. Most of his "contributions" to experimental or observational science were quite mundane. His theories were not original and he consistently failed to give credit to his predecessors. Documentation in his books was almost nonexistent.

> Darwin was slippery . . . [using] a flexible strategy which is not to be reconciled with even average intellectual integrity. . . . He began more and more to grudge praise to those who had in fact paved the way for him. . . . Darwin damned Lamarck and also his grandfather for being very ill-dressed fellows at the same moment he was stealing their clothes.[1]

The above evaluation was published in the Darwinian Centennial Year (1959) by a leading British evolutionary biologist and science historian at a time when most of the news media and the scientific establishmentarians, with their camp followers, were heaping adulation on him. Another top evolutionist who did not go with the crowd in that fulsome year was Jacques Barzun, Columbia University's outstanding historian:

> Darwin was not a thinker and he did not originate the ideas that he used. He vacillated, added, retracted, and confused his own traces. As soon as he crossed the dividing line between the realm of events and the realm of theory, he became "metaphysical" in a bad sense. His power of drawing out the implications of his theories was at no time very remarkable, but when it came to the moral order it disappeared altogether, as that penetrating evolutionist, Nietzsche, observed with some disdain.[2]

---

1. Cyril D. Darlington, *Darwin's Place in History* (London, 1959), p. 60, 62. Darlington was professor of botany at Oxford.
2. Jacques Barzun, *Darwin, Marx, Wagner* (Garden City, NY: Doubleday, 1958), p. 84.

Darwin did, however, have a keen interest in nature and in reading, as well as the patience to devote much time to plodding observations and compilations. In addition, he had independent wealth from his father, so did not have to work elsewhere to support his large family. His mysterious illness, which started soon after his marriage, also kept him free from social entanglements. All of this contributed to his prodigious output of correspondence, as well as his study, books, and articles.

The one book for which Darwin is best remembered, however, is *The Origin of Species by Natural Selection*, first published in 1859, when he was 50 years old. It is probably safe to say that no other book since the Bible has so influenced the world. Even though most people today have never read it, the entire educational establishment looks to the *Origin* as the intellectual watershed from which all modern thought descends. Barzun comments: "Clearly, both believers and unbelievers in Natural Selection agreed that Darwinism had succeeded as an orthodoxy, as a rallying point for innumerable scientific, philosophical, and social movements. Darwin had been the oracle and the *Origin of Species* the 'fixed point with which evolution moves the world.' "[3]

Despite much evolutionist criticism of Darwin's theories in recent years, adulation of Darwin still persists. The man acknowledged as the top paleontologist of the neo-Darwinian school of thought said in 1959, "No other single human production has had so great an impact on science or on learning and thought in general as *The Origin of Species*."[4] Similarly, Harvard's great zoologist-systematist Ernst Mayr said that Darwin's work led to "perhaps the most fundamental of all intellectual revolutions in the history of mankind."[5]

Yet this same authority and evolutionary elder statesman, who was both a leader of neo-Darwinism and a forerunner of modern punctuational evolutionism (to which he has adjusted quite well), has also pointed out that the very title of Darwin's *Origin of Species* was badly misleading.

Niles Eldredge, co-founder of the "punctuated equilibrium" school of thought, comments, "As Ernst Mayr, one of the founders of the modern synthetic theory of evolution, pointed out in his *Systematics and the Origin of Species* (1942), Darwin never really did discuss the origin of species in his *On the Origin of Species*."[6]

---

3. Ibid., p. 69.
4. George Gaylord Simpson, "Charles Darwin in Search of Himself," *Scientific American* 199 (August 1959): p. 117.
5. Ernst Mayr, "The Nature of the Darwinian Evolution," *Science* 176 (June 2, 1972): p. 981.
6. Niles Eldredge, *Time Frames* (New York: Simon & Schuster, 1985), p. 33.

But if Darwin did not finally solve the mystery of the evolutionary origin of new species, as millions of students have been taught by their learned professors, exactly what *did* he write about? What did he discover or expound of such epochal importance as to warrant such expressions of awe? Why is Darwin so frequently called the Newton of biology?

A quick survey of the 15 chapters in his *Origin of Species* might be informative in this connection. Chapter 1 deals with the variations in domestic animals and plants, especially pigeons, and with the processes of artificial selection employed by breeders on such variants. Chapter 2 deals with similar varieties observed as occurring in nature. Neither one of the chapters deals with *macroevolution*, which is the only point at issue. No creationist, past or present, has ever questioned the reality of variation within species, so the discussion in these two chapters is essentially pointless, as far as the real origin of species is concerned.

The third chapter discusses the assumed "struggle for existence" in nature. This term had already been used by Herbert Spencer, and the idea had been derived from the fallacious theories on human populations popularized by Thomas Malthus. Darwin always considered this a key component of "his" theory, though there is actually much more cooperation in nature than competition. Darwin assumed that favorable varieties would be preserved in this imaginary struggle, but he was not able to show how such favorable varieties could ever arise in the first place.

Darwin's fourth chapter is entitled "Natural Selection: or the Survival of the Fittest." This is the heart of the book, and the preferred mechanism of natural selection was received by Darwin's followers as his great contribution to science. The fact is, however, that many evolutionists before Darwin had written about natural selection, and many after him have acknowledged that natural selection is a hypothesized process incapable in itself of generating new species. It is only a tautology — the "fittest" being simply the survivors, not recognizable as such until *after* they have survived.

The fifth chapter of the *Origin* was called "Laws of Variation," but no such laws were revealed therein. In his summary of this chapter, Darwin admits: "Our ignorance of the laws of variation is profound." He does propose sexual selection and acquired characteristics as two likely explanations for many cases of variation, but these are now universally acknowledged to be wrong.

Chapters 6 and 7 discuss difficulties in the theory of evolution and natural selection, respectively. Darwin tries, by various *ad hoc* and untestable speculations, to explain why there are no transitional species if all species have descended from a common ancestor, and also how natural selection might develop incipient structures into useful structures. He discusses many different animals and speculates how their distinctive structures might have arisen gradually, all without an iota of proof in any one case. He specifically repudiates what we today call punctuated equilibrium or quantum speciation, on the ground that such sudden changes would constitute miracles.

In his chapter 8 on instincts, Darwin tries to imagine how natural selection might have wrought various changes in the remarkable instinctive behavior of animals, though he frankly acknowledges complete ignorance of the *origin* of instincts. His treatment of hybrids and hybrid sterility in chapter 9 relates essentially to problems in "microevolution," which is essentially irrelevant to the larger issue.

Darwin next has two chapters on the imperfections of the geological record, acknowledging that the ubiquitous absence of transitional fossils constituted a major problem to the whole theory of evolution. He "solves" the problem by stressing the incompleteness of the geological record, in hopes that the missing links would eventually be found. The fact is, however, that today — 130 years after *The Origin of Species* first offered this solution and with the number of known fossils now multiplied a hundred-fold — the "links" are all still missing!

Chapters 12 and 13 both deal with the evidence from geographical distribution, stressing the related varieties and species that are found in now-separated geographical regions. Again, however, this type of argument relates essentially only to microevolution at best.

In chapter 14, Darwin reviews the standard arguments for evolution based on classification, comparative morphology, embryology, and vestigial organs — all of them already well known and used before his time. These arguments have either long since been discredited (e.g., vestigial organs, embryological recapitulation) or else shown to argue more effectively for creation by a common Designer than for evolution from a common ancestor (e.g., comparative embryology and morphology). Yet they are still often put forth by evolutionists as "evidence," thus illustrating the static and impotent state of the whole theory.

Darwin's final chapter in *The Origin of Species* is a recapitulation of the arguments for evolution and natural selection in the earlier chapters, together with certain philosophical and religious defenses thereof and brief predictions concerning their future impact on science. No new scientific evidences or arguments are given in this chapter.

In fact, one can search the whole book in vain for any real scientific evidences of evolution — evidences that have been empirically verified and have stood the test of time. No proof is given anywhere — no examples are cited of new species known to have been produced by natural selection, no transitional forms are shown, no evolutionary mechanisms are documented. Actually, the whole book is most notable for its complete lack of documentation. It is all speculation, special pleading, *ad hoc* assumptions. None of the *Origin*'s evidences or arguments have stood up under modern critical analysis, even by other evolutionists. One can only marvel that such a book could have had so profound an influence on the subsequent history of human life and thought. There is bound to be something more here than meets the eye!

As far as the main thesis of the book — natural selection — is concerned, the idea was by no means original with Charles Darwin, though he took credit for it. Gould comments:

> All scholars know that several prominent scientists — Lamarck in particular — developed elaborate systems of evolutionary thought before Darwin. Many, however, suppose that Darwin was the true originator of his own particular theory about *how* evolution occurred — natural selection. Yet, by his own belated admission (in the historical preface added to latter editions of the *Origin of Species*), Darwin allowed that two authors had preceded him in formulating the principle of natural selection.[7]

The two men referred to were William C. Wells, a prominent Scottish scientist whose paper dealing with natural selection was published in 1813, and Patrick Matthew, a Scottish botanist who published his in 1831. But there were also James C. Prichard and William Lawrence. Like Wells, these men were physicians and members of the Royal Society, and all three published papers on natural selection in 1813. "All three men advanced explicitly and in detail the alternative theory of natural selection foreshadowed by Erasmus Darwin," wrote one commentator in the *Origin*'s Centennial Year.[8]

Erasmus Darwin was Charles's grandfather, a very prominent scientific figure for many years before Charles was born. In fact, the term "Darwinian" was applied to Erasmus's *own* theories about evolution — which included

---

7. Stephen Jay Gould, *The Flamingo's Smile* (New York: Norton, 1985), p. 335.
8. Cyril D. Darlington, "The Origin of Darwinism," *Scientific American* 201 (May 1959): p. 62.

natural selection — as expressed especially in his widely read and translated *Zoonomia*. "A catalogue of evolutionary suggestions, anticipating not only Lamarckism but even the theory of natural selection, may be culled from the *Zoonomia* and the notes to the *Botanic Garden*,"[9] observes one writer. The book *Zoonomia* was first published in 1794, 65 years before *The Origin of Species*. To some considerable degree it inspired both Malthus and Lamarck in the development of their own theories. They in turn contributed much to Charles Darwin, though he never adequately acknowledged his debt to either Lamarck or his grandfather.

There were still other writers on natural selection before Charles Darwin's supposed great discovery. These included the British creationist scientist Edward Blyth,[10] American phrenologist J. Stanley Grimes,[11] and Lamarck himself, as well as Robert Chambers, in his *Vestiges of the Natural History of Creation*.

Perhaps surprisingly, even William Paley, the great theologian who wrote so convincingly on natural theology and the evidences of Christianity, wrote on natural selection. Stephen Jay Gould has commented on this:

> Darwinians cannot simply claim that natural selection operates since everyone, including Paley and the natural theologians, advocated selection as a device for removing unfit individuals at both extremes and preserving, intact and forever, the created type.[12]

> Failure to recognize that all creationists accepted selection in this negative role led Eiseley to conclude falsely that Darwin had "borrowed" the principle of natural selection from his predecessor E. Blyth. The Reverend William Paley's classic work *Natural Theology*, published in 1803, also contains many references to selective elimination.[13]

It is worth noting that Charles Darwin was tremendously impressed by reading Paley when he was a student at Cambridge. He was also acquainted

---

9. Gertrude Himmelfarb, *Darwin and the Darwinian Revolution* (London: Chatto & Windus, 1959), p. 143. See also p. 143–145 for various relevant excerpts from Erasmus Darwin's writings.
10. Loren Eiseley, "Charles Darwin, Edward Blyth and the Theory of Natural Selection," *Proceedings, American Philosophical Society* 103 (1959): p. 94–158.
11. Loren Eiseley, *Darwin's Century* (Garden City, NY: Anchor Books, 1961), p. 314–315.
12. Stephen Jay Gould, "Darwinism and the Expansion of Evolutionary Theory," *Science* 216 (April 23, 1982): p. 380.
13. Ibid., p. 386.

with Edward Blyth, citing many of his zoological observations of biological changes in both the *Origin* and *Descent of man*. Although he was bound to know of the natural-selection writings of both Paley and Blyth, Darwin gave them no credit for their contribution to his own misuse of their perfectly appropriate use of natural selection. Creationists have always recognized the validity of selection as a *conservative* mechanism, serving to prevent the establishment of unfit mutants as dominants in a population, but Darwinians still misuse this principle by assigning to it the power to develop higher, more complex species.

There were still other writers on natural selection before Darwin, including the French scientists Charles Naudin[14] and even Benjamin Franklin in America. Franklin, in fact, developed the population theories later appropriated by Malthus in his infamous *Essay on Population*, which in turn gave both Darwin and Alfred Russel Wallace the key they thought they needed for their theories of the struggle for existence, natural selection, and the survival of the fittest.

> Indeed, in an essay which predated Malthus' (1798) classic exposition by almost a half century, Franklin (1751) had already noted the inherent growth potential of human populations. . . . In fact, his statement on intra-specific competition and population growth may be viewed as a precocious synthesis of Malthusian and Darwinian theories, predating them by almost a half-century and full century, respectively.[15]

The most important "co-discoverer" of natural selection was Alfred Russel Wallace, credited even by Darwin with this accomplishment. Wallace was 18 years younger than Darwin but had made extensive explorations in the Amazon jungles and in the Malaysian archipelago. He was also, like Darwin, much influenced by Lyell and Malthus, as well as by the Chambers opus *Vestiges of the Natural History of Creation*. As a convinced evolutionist, he was researching the origin of species at least 12 years before Darwin's book was published. He and Darwin were acquainted with each other, at least by correspondence regarding their respective researches, although Darwin had kept his thoughts on Malthusian struggle and natural selection mostly to himself.

The story is well known. While ill in Malaysia, Wallace wrote and sent his own paper on natural selection to Darwin for his evaluation, at a time

---

14. Darlington, "The Origin of Darwinism," p. 63.
15. Ralph A. Otto, "Poor Richard's Population Biology," *Bioscience* 29 (April 1979): p. 242–243.

when Darwin was still procrastinating about writing up his own identical theory. Eiseley says, "It was Darwin's unpublished conception down to the last detail, independently duplicated by a man sitting in a hut at the world's end."[16]

Lyell persuaded Darwin to proceed immediately with his own book as a result. In the meantime, Wallace's paper was read at a meeting of the Linnaean Society in London in July 1858, along with an earlier letter by Darwin outlining his theory — thus establishing the latter's presumed priority in the "discovery." *The Origin of Species* was put together quickly and published a few months later, with all its impact on future world history strapped up in the implications of this remarkable coincidence.

Regardless of whether Darwin or Wallace or one of their many predecessors should be given credit for the invention of the natural-selection concept, the concept itself has proved to be utterly impotent as a scientific explanation of the origin of new species. Not only did Darwin fail to cite a single example of this phenomenon's actual occurrence, neither has anyone else ever since.

> No one has ever produced a species by mechanisms of natural selection. No one has ever gotten near it, and most of the current argument in neo-Darwinism is about this question: how a species originates, and it is there that natural selection seems to be fading out and chance mechanisms of one sort or another are being invoked.[17]

Many biologists have diligently *tried* to generate new species especially with the fruit fly, studying them for over 1,500 successive fruit-fly generations, and producing great numbers of radiation-induced mutations.

> All in all, scientists have been able to "catalyze the fruit fly evolutionary process such that what has been seen to occur in *Drosophila* (fruit fly) is the equivalent of many millions of years of normal

---

16. Loren C. Eiseley, "Alfred Russel Wallace," *Scientific American* 200 (Feb. 1959): p. 80.
17. Colin Patterson, "Cladistics," interview on BBC program (March 4, 1982) produced by Brian Leek; Peter Franz, interviewer. Dr. Patterson, senior paleontologist with the British Museum of Natural History, is a leading authority on evolution. Whether new "species" can be produced (e.g., by polyploidy) obviously depends on how one defines a species. Such processes as mutation, hybridization, recombination — even modern techniques of genetic engineering — obviously can produce new varieties, and some of these might be called species by some. At best, however, such processes are "horizontal" changes and are limited in potential scope.

mutations and evolution." Even with this tremendous speedup of mutations, scientists have never been able to come up with anything other than another fruit fly.[18]

Natural selection can hardly "select" a better variety if no better variety ever appears for it to work on. Yet evolutionists seem to think that the process can somehow "create" better organisms. Gould observes, "The essence of Darwinism lies in a single phrase: natural selection is the creative force of evolutionary change. No one denies that natural selection will play a negative role in eliminating the unfit. Darwinian theories require that it create the fit as well."[19]

Darwin simply *assumed* that normal variations would somehow include those that were more "fit" than the existing type, but this places faith in pure chance, with no known mechanism to generate any such higher degree of fitness. In retrospect, one can imagine how certain structures produced by chance would confer a selective advantage, but imagination is not evidence! Natural selection is a mere tautology if it is defined *after the fact* as the process that produced those organisms that happened to survive in the struggle for existence.

> Specifically, neo-Darwinists claim that natural selection working on chance mutations accounts for what has occurred. But "natural selection" turns out to be tautology, while the word "chance" denotes an occurrence that is inexplicable. A theory that claims to explain while standing with one foot on a tautology and the other in an explanatory void is in trouble.[20]

This discussion could be extended at length and copiously documented, but the above references suffice to justify the conclusion that Darwin's great contribution to science was really quite trivial, as well as false. He neither originated nor proved his claim that natural selection could generate even one new species, let alone all the plants and animals of past and present. Apart from the selection thesis, all his other "proofs" of evolution have since been shown to be either wrong or irrelevant. Says Wolfgang Smith, a highly qualified professor at Oregon State University:

---

18. Jeremy Rifkin, *Algeny* (New York: Viking, 1983), p. 134.
19. Stephen Jay Gould, "The Return of Hopeful Monsters," *Natural History* 76 (June/July 1977): p. 28.
20. Huston Smith, "Evolution and Evolutionism," *The Christian Century* 99 (July 7–14, 1982): p. 756. Smith is professor of philosophy and religion at Syracuse University.

And the salient fact is this: if by evolution we mean macroevolution . . . then it can be said with the utmost rigor that the doctrine is totally bereft of scientific sanction. . . . There exists to this day not a shred of bona fide scientific evidence in support of the thesis that macroevolutionary transformations have ever occurred.[21]

And the scientist who held the chair of evolution at Paris's great Sorbonne University for over 30 years, even though he was himself a confirmed evolutionist, ridiculed Darwinism and neo-Darwinism as follows: "Directed by all-powerful selection, chance becomes a sort of providence, which, under the cover of atheism, is not named but which is secretly worshipped."[22] Yet somehow this vaporous system of thought popularized by Charles Darwin has impacted the whole world more than any other scientific concept ever concocted, before or since! What goes on here?

The Mysterious Role of Charles Lyell

Charles Darwin was not the only actor in this strange scenario. Neither he nor his theories seemed very significant at the time, but their results were world-changing. We need to look more closely at the influence of certain of his predecessors and contemporaries to get a better understanding of this remarkable phenomenon. The influences bearing on the birth of modern Darwinism were a strange mix — liberal theology, humanistic philosophy, occultic mysticism, capitalistic jingoism, conspiratorial revolutionism — all presented in the revered name of science. This, however, was actually pseudo-science, which quickly evolved into a global system of scientism.

It is worth noting that almost none of the leaders of this evolutionary revival had been trained as scientists in the modern sense. None were educated as physicists or chemists or biologists or geologists or astronomers or other "natural" scientists. As already noted, Charles Darwin himself was an apostate divinity student whose only degree was in theology. Charles Lyell was a lawyer, William Smith a surveyor, James Hutton an agriculturalist, John Playfair a mathematician, Robert Chambers a journalist. Alfred Russel Wallace had little formal education of any kind, with only a brief apprenticeship in surveying. Thomas Huxley had an indifferent education in medicine. Herbert Spencer

---

21. Wolfgang Smith, *Teilhardism and the New Religion* (Rockford, IL: Tan Books, 1988), p. 5.
22. Pierre P. Grassè, *Evolution of Living Organisms* (New York: Academic, 1977), p. 107. Natural selection is a conservation mechanism rather than a creative process. It serves to hinder the spread of harmful mutations through a population, keeping the *status quo*.

received practically no formal education except some practical experience in railroad engineering. Thomas Malthus was a theologian and economist, while Erasmus Darwin was a medical doctor and poet. Of all the chief contributors to the revival of evolutionism commonly associated with Charles Darwin, only Jean Lamarck in France and Ernst Haeckel in Germany seemed to have had a bona fide education in the branch of evolutionary "science" that they pursued, and they had their own particular anti-Christian agendas to promote.

There were others involved in this odd scenario, of course, but these were the chief actors. Among them was hardly one genuine scientist, in the modern sense of having appropriate academic credentials. In fact, most of the genuine scientists of the day — men such as Faraday, Cuvier, Brewster, Pasteur, Maxwell, Joule, Sedgwick, and others — either opposed evolutionism or remained aloof from the conflict, at least for the first few years after the *Origin*. Eventually, with such leading theologians as Kingsley, Drummond, and Beecher capitulating quickly to evolution, almost the whole intellectual community soon jumped on the Darwinian bandwagon, and evolutionism has dominated the world ever since.

We need not consider the roles played by all these men, but a few are of special significance. Darwin gave special credit, for example, to Charles Lyell, so we also should give him some attention. It is generally acknowledged — and Darwin himself conceded — that his theory of evolution depended completely on long geological ages, which presumably had been confirmed by Lyell's arguments for uniformitarianism.

Lyell, however, was trained as a lawyer, not as a geologist. The leading geologists of his day — Cuvier, Buckland, for example — believed in catastrophism, and many of the geologists of our own day are now returning to the view. Lyell must have known that the actual data of geology predominantly favored catastrophism, not uniformitarianism. Yet he dogmatically insisted on long ages and uniformity, sarcastically rejecting the biblical chronology in the process.

Stephen Jay Gould, the leading modern evolutionist, has actually accused Lyell of deception in his promotion of this system:

> Charles Lyell was a lawyer by profession, and his book is one of the most brilliant briefs ever published by an advocate. . . . Lyell relied upon true bits of cunning to establish his uniformitarian view as the only true geology. . . . Lyell imposed his imagination upon the evidence.[23]

---

23. Stephen Jay Gould, *Ever Since Darwin* (New York: Norton, 1977), p. 149–150.

Assuming that Lyell knew better, which seems highly probable, the question then is *why* he would be so anxious to undermine the catastrophist geology that was held by the leading geologists and other scientists of the time. He was a creationist of sorts — or at least seemed to believe in the essential stability of the basic kinds of organisms — and did not become an open supporter of Darwin's evolutionary theory until several years after the *Origin* had been published and Darwinism had become widely accepted by the scientific and educational establishments.

Note that Lyell did not become an *open* evolutionist right away, but waited until it became the popular thing to do among the people of the scientific establishment. There is considerable evidence that he was a closet evolutionist all along, or at least was very sympathetic to naturalism and materialism. He was a thoroughgoing uniformitarian on questions of origins as well as history, and this would naturally incline him toward evolutionism.

One of the most thorough studies of the immediate background of Darwinism was that made by Gertrude Himmelfarb and published during the Darwinian Centennial Year. After a penetrating study of Lyell's seeming 30-year equivocation on evolution, Dr. Himmelfarb concluded that "Lyell was too shrewd a polemicist to be unaware of the ambiguous effect of his argument. And his letters written at the time confirm the suspicion that his basic sympathies were with the evolutionists."[24]

Sir Charles Lyell had read the evolutionary works of Lamarck and presented them very favorably, though equivocally, to the British public in his *Principles of Geology*, almost 30 years before Darwin's book was published. He also discussed the basic principles of later Darwinism in his *Principles*. Eiseley observes:

> Yet ironically enough, though Lyell failed to comprehend the creative importance of natural selection, he did not miss its existence. In fact, through a strange set of circumstances just discovered in the literature, it is likely that he was fundamentally instrumental in presenting Darwin with the key to the new biology.[25]

Although the question has been obscured by hazy difficulties of terminology, Sir Charles Lyell had already described before Dar-

---

24. Himmelfarb, *Darwin*, p. 157.
25. Loren Eiseley, "Charles Lyell," *Scientific American* 201 (Aug. 1959): p. 102. Eiseley, of the University of Pennsylvania, has written extensively on the history of Darwinism.

win the struggle for existence and, up to a certain point, natural selection.[26]

Despite all this, and despite his profound influence on Darwin, Lyell vacillated a long time before becoming an open disciple of Darwinism. Himmelfarb argues persuasively that this was for political reasons, Lyell wanting to retain favor with the theological, political, and scientific establishments, which were still committed at least nominally to creationism. It was safer, and in the long run more effective, to get uniformitarianism and the great age of the earth firmly established before openly endorsing evolutionism. Writes Himmelfarb:

> If Lyell is to be judged by his private rather than public sentiments he must be accounted among Darwin's predecessors. His misfortune, it may be hazarded, was that if his views of species were in advance of his age, his faith in tradition, and his notion of the philosopher as one who avoids unsettling establishment beliefs and institutions, were behind the times.[27]

In a private letter to one of his own disciples, George Scrope, Lyell said:

> If we don't irritate, which I fear that we may . . . we shall carry all with us. If you don't triumph over them, but compliment the liberality and candor of the present age, the bishops and enlightened saints will join us in despising both the ancient and modern physic-theologians. . . . I conceived the idea five or six years ago, that if ever the Mosaic geology could be set down without giving offence, it would be in an historical sketch. . . . Let them feel it, and point the moral.[28]

Lyell did indeed devote a great many pages in the opening section of his *Principles of Geology* to his "historical sketch" of the development of theology, thus giving him an opportunity to ridicule over and over against what he called the "Mosaic geology" of his predecessors — by which he meant the biblical chronology and especially the worldwide Flood of the Bible and its geological significance. He did this subtly, however, never referring to the Bible directly and never openly advocating evolution.

---

26. Ibid., p. 103.
27. Himmelfarb, *Darwin*, p. 159.
28. Letter written to George Poulette Scrope in 1830, then published in *Life, Letters and Journal of Charles Lyell*, Mrs. Charles Lyell, editor (London: John Murray, 1881), p. 270–271.

By this time it was safe to take that kind of position, as even the catastrophist geologists (Cuvier, Buckland, Sedgwick, etc.) had largely abandoned the biblical chronology in favor of a series of global catastrophes (of which the Noahic Flood was only the most recent). All Lyell needed to do was to so greatly increase the number of these catastrophes, while simultaneously minimizing their individual significance and extent, that eventually they would all become the typical catastrophes corresponding to present processes (volcanoes, earthquakes, and such). They would then fit nicely into an overall scenario of uniformitarianism spanning endless ages.

This is exactly what eventually happened, of course, thus confirming the subtle acumen of Lyell in planning it thus. Lyell's dominating motivation, though he was always careful not to express it publicly, was his desire to undermine the authority of the Bible. He could do this most effectively by first undercutting God's supernatural power (as in the doctrine of recent creation) and his judgment on sin (as in the Great Flood). People could still believe in a far-off creation, as did the deists and the freemasons, but this kind of god would have little relevance to their own life and times.

As to just *why* Charles Lyell was so anxious to get this deistic uniformitarianism established in place of biblical theism, one interesting theory has been advanced by certain modern non-biblical catastrophists, followers of Immanuel Velikovsky.

In the 18th century, the winds of democracy from America and the attacks of thinkers like Locke and Rousseau, among others, questioned the Monarchy as the natural form of government. Liberalism was moving and its method was to go after Biblical Geology (specifically the Flood) in order to disarm the Monarchists. . . . What the liberal middle class wanted was reform in Parliament, but traditional theological doctrine stood in the way. Paley's *Natural Theology* claimed that sovereignty descended from God to the King. . . . There was only one way to reform Parliament, and that was to destroy Paley's *Natural Theology* — and the only way to do that was to discredit the catastrophist notions of its religious defenders who sought to reconcile the geological evidence with the story of Genesis. . . . A young Whig lawyer named Charles Lyell decided to take a novel approach: in his *Principles of Geology*, he argued against the catastrophists by saying that the diluvial theory was, in effect, mythological, and that it stood in the way of progress in geology. . . . After some early skirmishes, Darwin's "theory of evolution" won the day — a mechanistic theory of evolution subservient to and dependent upon geological uniformitarianism.[29]

The above quotation is given at some length in order to convey this particular theory adequately. Whether or not it is valid is uncertain, but there may well be some truth to it. The days before and during Lyell's rapid rise to prominence were surely times when revolutionary movements were in the air. The French Revolution was just past, Karl Marx and other radicals were writing and plotting, and secret societies were active in many places.

In any case, Lyell personally had nothing more than a very nominal Christian commitment and was clearly determined to destroy the Old Testament cosmology and chronology. If not a secret evolutionist, he was at least very sympathetic to evolution. Furthermore, he undertook to become a friend and adviser to young Charles Darwin immediately upon his return to England from the *Beagle* voyage in the fall of 1836.

Darwin had read Lyell and had already become a convert to his uniformitarianism while on his five-year trip on the *Beagle*. In return, his observations and collections during this period were regularly sent back to England. These established his scientific reputation and, in particular, made a great impression on Lyell. The latter quickly introduced Darwin to other leading scientists around London and Cambridge. Himmelfarb writes that Darwin's "most intimate friend at this time was Lyell, whom he replied upon for information, advice, and a sympathetic hearing."[30]

It was also during this time that Darwin became a convinced evolutionist. A number of writers have argued that his discoveries while on the *Beagle* converted him to evolutionism, but he himself testified otherwise. After a thorough study of all his notes, diaries, and letters, Himmelfarb concluded:

> There is, in fact, no real continuity between the *Beagle* and the *Origin*. Between the two there intervened an idea. It was in the light of that idea that the experiences on the *Beagle* were reordered and reinterpreted by Darwin until they were ready to stand witness for the idea.[31]

Darwin's most intimate friend and adviser during the time he was converting to evolutionism was Lyell. Since it is known that Lyell encouraged him in his studies and eventually prodded him to publish them, it is difficult not to suspect that Lyell actually, though subtly, may have been persuading

29. Alex Marton, "What is Uniformitarianism, and How Did It Get Here?" *Horus* 1, no. 2 (1985): p. 12–13.
30. Himmelfarb, *Darwin*, p. 106.
31. Ibid., p. 103.

him toward evolution. It was apparently also about this time that Darwin abandoned even his nominal faith in Christianity.[32] And again, if Lyell's counsel was not directly responsible for this decision, it is at least obvious that he did nothing to discourage it.

It is almost certain that *The Origin of Species* would never have been published at all had it not been for Lyell. He became almost like a father to Darwin after the *Beagle* voyage, continually counseling and encouraging him in his research and his papers and finally his book. But Lyell's very system and framework of interpretation was essential for the development of Darwin' theory, as Darwin himself testified and as all his biographers have emphasized. Loren Eiseley, for example, says, "Lyell must be accorded the secure distinction, not alone of altering the course of geological thought, but of having been the single greatest influence in the life of Charles Darwin."[33] He also commented, "At almost every step of Darwin's youthful career Lyell was an indefatigable guide and counselor."[34]

Here is what Darwin himself said about Lyell's influence: "I always feel as if my books came half out of Lyell's brain, and that I never acknowledge this sufficiently."[35] With respect to Lyell's own motivation, Darwin said, "Lyell is most firmly convinced that he has shaken the faith in the Deluge far more efficiently by never having said a word against the Bible, than if he had acted otherwise."[36]

That Charles Lyell, in his fatherly guide of young Charles Darwin, was motivated at least as much by hatred of the Bible as concern for science is evident from both his devious approach to undermining Scripture and his insistence on total uniformitarianism in geology, despite all the abundant evidence to the contrary. His lawyer's training and attitude conditioned him well for such a role. As Harvard's neo-catastrophist Gould has said, "Lyell built his own edifice with the most brilliant brief ever written by a scientist. . . . Lyell constructed the self-serving history that has encumbered the study of earthly time ever since."[37]

---

32. See quotes cited from his autobiography in chapter 3 of this book.
33. Eiseley, *Darwin's Century*, p. 98.
34. Eiseley, "Charles Lyell," p. 106.
35. Letter explaining a dedication of one of his books to Lyell, as cited in Himmelfarb, *Darwin*, p. 81.
36. Unpublished manuscript at Cambridge, dated 1873, as cited in Himmelfarb, *Darwin*, p. 320. Lyell had expressed this purpose, it will be recalled, more than 40 years previously, and he held to it.
37. Stephen Jay Gould, *Time's Arrow, Time's Cycle* (Cambridge, MA: Harvard University Press, 1987), p. 104.

Gould, of course, had no objection to Lyell's anti-biblical polemics, but he did object to his unwarranted insistence on what Gould called "substantive uniformitarianism," or uniformity of process rates and complete denigration of all geological catastrophism. The conclusion seems inescapable that Lyell had his own hidden agenda and, whether intentional or not, that he used Charles Darwin to help implement it. The end result of the Lyell-Darwin one-two punch was exactly what the anti-Christian forces of the world must have ardently desired. Biblical creationism and catastrophism, which had been the interpretive framework for science throughout the scientific age ever since the days of Kepler and Galileo and Newton, had been effectively displaced by evolutionary uniformitarianism and all the social and political calamities that were soon to follow because of it.

Wallace and the Spirit World

With the latter-day burgeoning of the New Age movement, the idea of "spirit guides" is becoming almost commonplace, as is the idea that the universe itself is somehow conscious and intelligent, directing its own evolution. Such notions were almost endemic in the ancient pagan religions as part of the warp and woof of pantheism, but they were largely driven underground in the West by the two-pronged attack of both biblical Christianity (stemming especially from the Reformation) and modern science (which also developed largely out of the Reformation, though it soon became dominantly committed to naturalism and materialism).

Interestingly enough, the modern resurgence of pantheism and associated occultism — including spiritism — coincides with the rise and triumph of Darwinism. Just as it seemed that naturalism would prevail in even the life sciences and social sciences, suddenly there was a strong spiritist movement, influencing even many hard-nosed scientists. The idea of evolution was foundational in both, which meant that evolution could be embraced by either those of an atheistic inclination or those who preferred to allow a spiritual dimension as an integral component of nature ("Mother Nature," as it were).

Remarkably, these two aspects of evolutionary thought seem to have become personified in the two "co-discoverers" of natural selection as the agency of evolution. Charles Darwin, with his thoroughgoing commitment to complete naturalism, was balanced, so to speak, by Alfred Russel Wallace (1823–1913) and his well-known devotion to "spiritualism" (actually, a better term is "spiritism," because of the disembodied spirits involved in it).

Wallace, unlike Lyell and Darwin, was born and raised in genteel poverty. Whereas Lyell was educated in the law and Darwin in religion, Wallace had no formal higher education at all. Nevertheless, like Darwin, he acquired his knowledge of biology largely by extensive field observations in exotic lands, spending four years in the Amazon jungles and then eight years in the East Indies.

Although both Lyell and Darwin were raised in ostensibly Christian (though religiously liberal) homes, Wallace had no significant Christian background. He was from the beginning a skeptic in religion and was long enamored of socialism, Marxism, and even anarchism. A dedicated reader, Wallace read Tom Paine's *Age of Reason* while in his teens. In addition to books of exploration, which stimulated his own desire to travel and study the unknown flora and fauna of distant lands, he was greatly impressed by the theistic evolutionism of Chambers in his book *Vestiges of the Natural History of Creation* and also by *An Essay on the Principle of Population* by Thomas Malthus. The latter book was later to play a critical role in crystallizing the evolutionary ideas of both Darwin and Wallace, who also, in his field studies, continually referred to Lyell's *Principles of Geology*.

Wallace endured great hardships on his tropical journeys, but he did make valuable and extensive studies and collections, just as Darwin had on his *Beagle* voyage over 20 years earlier. He was intensely dominated also by evolutionary thinking, trying to understand how the many exotic species he was studying could have originated. Imbued with almost a missionary zeal, he wrote a paper on the origin of species, which was published in an English journal in 1855. It did not attract much attention, however, except by Darwin and Lyell, who realized suddenly how close Wallace was coming to Darwin's own researches, which he had been developing off and on for some 18 years.

Charles Darwin had indeed been collecting data and writing an extensive tome on evolution and natural selection, but he had been very cautious and hesitant to get it in shape for publication, despite Lyell's persistent prodding. Wallace had become acquainted with both Darwin and Lyell after returning to London from the Amazon. After reading his 1855 paper, Darwin wrote to tell him that he had been working on a large volume on the species problem, but he said nothing about his proposed mechanism. So Wallace continued to think about the origin of species, searching for a clue to its mechanism.

During all these years, Wallace apparently said little about his interest in the occult sciences. He had been introduced to them, however, when he was just 21 years old, about the same years he read Malthus and Darwin's *Journal*, as well as Lyell and Chambers. Says Himmelfarb:

> It was also in this eventful year that he was introduced to those other subjects that were, later in life, to compete with natural history for his affections: spiritualism, psychical research, and mesmerism; he had earlier been converted to phrenology.[38]

Although little has been written about Wallace's spiritistic interest during the following two decades, it is not likely that it was completely dormant. He later wrote of his admiration for the native people of the tropics, among whom he spent so many years, as Loren Eiseley points out:

> It is interesting to observe that Wallace reveals scarcely a trace of the racial superiority so frequently manifested in nineteenth-century scientific circles. "The more I see of uncivilized people, the better I think of human nature," he wrote to a friend in 1855, "and the essential differences between civilized and savage men seem to disappear." . . . So strongly did he differ from the major tendency to arrange natives on decreasing levels of intellect and to picture them as depraved in habits that Sir John Lubbock commented that Wallace's description of savage people differed greatly from that of earlier observers. Somewhere on the seas or in the forests, accompanied by his faithful Malay, Ali, he had ceased to be impressed by the typical conception of the native as a physical and mental fossil.[39]

In this opinion Wallace differed completely from Darwin and most other evolutionists of the day. In fact, he soon began to stress that all men — whether primitive or savage or civilized — were so different from animals in their mental capacities that there must be an intelligent Cause behind them. In all this, he was much closer to the biblical concept of man than was Darwin, and it eventually caused a partial break between them. However, Wallace's views were not derived from the Bible, which he rejected altogether, but from the pantheistic philosophy that had become a part of his thinking early on.

> Another paper by Wallace . . . appeared in 1869, and in this he drew for the first time a sharp distinction between men and animals, arguing that human intelligence and culture could only be accounted for by postulating some kind of "cosmic" intelligence. Darwin

---

38. Himmelfarb, *Darwin*, p. 201.
39. Eiseley, *Darwin's Century*, p. 303.

strongly objected to this, and he and Wallace thereafter gradually drifted apart on the question of the status of man in nature.[40]

This "cosmic" intelligence was not the Creator God of the Bible, of course, but the "all-god" of pantheism, the same as the "god" of the religions of the East, including the natives among whom Wallace had lived for eight years. These peoples were also animists, interacting regularly with the spirit world, and Wallace could hardly have failed to notice that the phenomena he was observing there were similar to those that were just then becoming widely noticed in the Western world, leading to the rapid rise of so-called spiritualism in Europe and America.

In any case, he eventually became not only a believer in spiritism and occultism, but a leader in the movement, investigating and promoting it with the same scientific thoroughness that he had devoted to biology and the species question. In 1876 Wallace published one of the definitive evidential textbooks on spiritism, a book entitled *Miracles and Modern Spiritualism*. Even before that, he had published a widely read two-part article, setting forth in considerable detail the physical phenomena attributable to the action of disembodied spirits (e.g., preserving from effects of fire, musical sounds, automatic writing, apparitions, clairvoyance, trance-speaking, healings, etc.). After citing numerous examples and experiments, with careful precautions against deception, Wallace concluded, "My position, therefore, is that the phenomena of Spiritualism in their entirety do not require further confirmation. They are proved quite as well as any facts are proved in other sciences."[41]

Lest anyone attribute this conviction to a senile aberration in his old age, Wallace published a monumental work, *Geographical Distribution of Animals*, still recognized as a classical scientific contribution, in the very same year! He wrote and published many other outstanding volumes after this, not only in biology but also in anthropology, economics, and other fields. He then brought out a new edition of his treatise on spiritualism in 1896. A. R. Wallace received England's Order of Merit in 1910, finally dying at age 90 in 1913.

---

40. D.R. Oldroyd, *Darwinian Impacts* (Atlantic Highlands, NJ: Humanities Press, 1983), p. 144. Wallace believed in the naturalistic evolution of the human body, but some kind of mystical evolution of mental and spiritual powers.

41. A.R. Wallace, "A Summary of the More Important Manifestations, Physical and Mental, of Spiritualism," *Fortnightly Review* (May and June, 1874). Wallace's classical treatise on natural selection, entitled *Darwinism*, was not written and published until 1889.

Wallace was never by any means an ignorant and emotional "religionist." The point to note is that his commitment to what we today would call occultic spiritism was an integral part of his brilliant scientific career throughout his long life. Based on what he considered to be incontrovertible evidence, he believed implicitly in the reality of the spirit world and the ability of the spirits to communicate with humans under certain conditions.

Wallace was not the only scientist of his day who became committed to spiritism. Others included Sir Oliver Lodge, the brilliant physicist; Camille Flammarion, the French astronomer; and Sir William Crookes, the famous chemist. In our day, of course, under the impetus of the New Age movement, there are many intellectuals who are committed to some form of occultism. It has become almost mundane to mention the idea of "spirit guides" and "spirit masters" — spiritual beings who convey truth and prophetic insights to men and women through an illumination process called "channeling."

However, the great majority of scientists, both in Darwin's day and our own, have rejected and continue to reject anything but a strictly naturalistic approach to scientific explanations. This is why Darwin eventually broke with Wallace, even though their respective theories of evolution by natural selection were practically identical.

All of which brings us back to Wallace's 1855 paper on species and the remarkable chain of events that quickly led thereafter to the publication of Darwin's *Origin* in 1859. Although the story is well known, it needs to be summarized here once again. Lyell had been urging Darwin to get his big book on the origin of species finished and published, but Darwin kept procrastinating, seeking more and more data and better evidence. When he and Lyell read Wallace's paper, they realized that the latter might well be about to solve the problem first. Lyell began pushing Darwin harder than ever, while Wallace, off in the Malayan jungles and quite unaware of any race for priority, continued collecting and thinking diligently about the problem of origins. Listen to his testimony, as pieced together from two of his books:

> I was then [February 1858] living at Ternate in the Moluccas, and was suffering from a rather severe attack of intermittent fever, which prostrated me every day during the cold and succeeding hot fits. During one of these fits, while again considering the problem of the origin of species, something led me to think of Malthus' Essay on Population. . . .[42]

---

42. Alfred Russel Wallace, *The Wonderful Century: Its Successes and Its Failures* (New York, 1898), p. 139.

The question arises as to what that "something" may have been. Wallace apparently then thought that the "struggle for existence," which Malthus had assumed in human populations, should apply also to animals:

> Then it suddenly flashed upon me that this self-acting process would necessarily *improve the race*, because in every generation the inferior would inevitably be killed off and the superior would remain — that is, the *fittest would survive*. Then at once I seemed to see the whole effect of this. . . .[43]

Again note the unusual language for a scientific paper: "Then it suddenly flashed upon me. . . . At once I seemed to see. . . ." Elsewhere Wallace added:

> The whole method of species modification became clear to me, and in the two hours of my fit I had thought out the main points of the theory. That same evening I sketched out the draft of a paper; and in the two succeeding evenings I wrote it out, and sent it by the next post to Mr. Darwin.[44]

Herein was a marvelous thing! A theory that Darwin had been developing for 20 years, in the midst of a world center of science and with the help and encouragement of many scientific friends, was suddenly revealed in full to a self-educated spiritist, halfway around the world, alone on a tropical island, and in the throes of a two-hour malarial fit. This is not the usual route to scientific discovery!

Loren Eiseley also marvels at these remarkable circumstances, expressing it as follows:

> Suddenly it occurred to the feverish naturalist in a lightning flash of insight that Malthus' checks to human increase . . . must, in similar or analogous ways, operate in the natural world as well. . . .
>
> It was Darwin's unpublished conception down to the last detail, independently duplicated by a man sitting in a hut at the world's end.[45]

Wallace hoped that Darwin would be as excited about his "discovery" as he was himself. Instead it filled him with despair:

> "All my originality, whatever it may amount to, will be smashed," Darwin wrote to Lyell on the same day. "I never saw a more striking

---

43. Alfred Russel Wallace, *My Life* (London: Chapman & Hall, Ltd., 1905), p. 362.
44. Wallace, *The Wonderful Century*, p. 140.
45. Eiseley, "Alfred Russel Wallace," p. 80.

coincidence. . . . Your words [here Darwin was referring to earlier warnings by Lyell that he might be anticipated] have come true with a vengeance."[46]

It was indeed a most "striking coincidence" that stimulated the sudden publication of what is arguably the most influential (and most harmful) book since the rise of modern science. It is altogether likely that, apart from this "coincidence," *The Origin of Species* would never have been written.

Lyell and other friends arranged to have a joint presentation of Wallace's paper and one quickly thrown together by Darwin (mainly to establish his priority to the theory) at a meeting of the Linnaean Society July 1858. Darwin hastily condensed his voluminous tome, scheduled to be called *Natural Selection*, into the popular-level *The Origin of Species*. It was quickly published the following year, and the rest is history. Wallace himself knew little of these developments in London. Eiseley comments, "A man pursuing birds of paradise in a remote jungle did not yet know that he had forced the word's most reluctant author to disgorge his hoarded volume, or that the whole of Western thought was about to be swung into a new channel because a man in a fever had felt a moment of strange radiance."[47]

What exactly was behind the "moment of strange radiance" that changed all subsequent Western thought? As one reads Wallace's testimony, knowing his intense subsequent commitment to spiritism, as well as his lifelong dedication to evolutionism and opposition to biblical Christianity, it is easy to sense that he believed that his thoughts were being directed by some intelligent entity or entities outside himself. Such an idea would surely be compatible with modern New Age concepts.

It would also be compatible with biblical concepts, though in a completely different sense. The Bible does indeed make it very clear that there is a spirit world and that spirits are able under certain circumstances to influence the thoughts and actions of human beings. These spirits are not, however, the ghosts of dead ancestors, as often taught by the practitioners of "spiritualism." Neither are they the "spirit guides" of the New Agers, or the gods and goddesses of the pagan religions. The Bible tells us that "we wrestle not against flesh and blood, but against principalities, against powers, against the rulers of the darkness of this world, against spiritual wickedness in high places" (Eph. 6:12).

The spirits inhabiting the earth's atmosphere (not the heaven of God's presence, but the heaven of the atmosphere, the "high places" or "heavenlies"

---

46. Ibid., p. 81.
47. Ibid.

of this verse) are actually *evil* spirits, or demons, who are opposing the purposes of the true God, the Creator and Redeemer of the world through Jesus Christ. This is the consistent teaching of Scripture, and these hosts of darkness are all under the dominion of God's great adversary, Satan, who is "the prince of the power of the air, the spirit that now worketh in the children of disobedience" (Eph. 2:2).

In this biblical frame of reference, it is not naïve fundamentalism but essential realism to recognize that Satan (same as the "Lucifer" of many secret societies and New Age cults) would somehow be very directly involved in this watershed development of 1858–1859 — when the book was published that would soon banish God from science and enthrone evolutionary uniformitarianism as the dominating premise of the intellectual world.

I shall return to this important consideration later, but there are still other aspects of the Darwinian genesis that first must be surveyed, and other key people who made significant contributions and need to be recognized.

Doctors of Revolution

At the birth of Darwinism, as we have seen, the two most important personages involved besides Darwin himself were Sir Charles Lyell and Alfred Russel Wallace. There were others whose roles were significant — men such as Herbert Spencer, Robert Chambers, and Joseph Hooker — and their stories are interesting and important. Furthermore, the men who actively promoted Darwinism after the *Origin* was published also played a vital part — especially Thomas Huxley and Ernst Haeckel, but also Asa Gray in America. Some of these men have already been discussed in our review of the effects of Darwinism, but it would make this volume inordinately long to attempt a more analytical survey of the background and motivations of all those who were involved in this key historical movement.

In order to trace the history of evolutionism back further, however, we do need to look more closely at some of the key historical antecedents of Lyell, Wallace, and Darwin. Although, ever since Darwin, many people have treated Darwin as if he were the actual originator of evolutionism, nothing could be further from the truth. Somehow he came at just the right time and was manipulated in just the right way to catalyze a sudden reaction against the creationist worldview that had dominated Christendom ever since the fall of Rome. Darwin became the watershed, and evolutionism has ruled Western thought ever since. But there had been certain very significant preparations before.

The two generations just before Darwin had been a period of political turmoil and revolution. First there was the American War of Independence, and then the French Revolution and its bloody aftermath. Following this, in Darwin's own generation, emerged the movement stimulated by Karl Marx and his followers, with their Communist Manifesto and general incitement to class warfare everywhere. Revolution was in the air all over Europe, not to mention various national conflicts (e.g., War of 1812). It is surely significant that the earlier leaders of evolutionary thought were often also involved, to one degree or another, with these political movements.

One of the most important of these was Darwin's own grandfather, Erasmus Darwin (1731–1802). As discussed previously, Erasmus anticipated his grandson on almost every point of evolutionary theory, especially in his book *Zoonomia*, published in 1794, 65 years in advance of *The Origin of Species*. However, Erasmus was best known as a medical doctor and poet, and his evolutionary views were too advanced for his times, only becoming widely known and appreciated after Charles resurrected them (without proper credit) in his own book.

The definitive biography of Erasmus Darwin was written relatively recently by Desmond King-Hele, a modern-day scientist and poet, and given the felicitous title *Doctor of Revolution*.[48] This is because, in his own day, it had been well known that many of Erasmus's friends and associates were sympathetic with the French revolutionaries. Darwin especially admired Rousseau, the chief philosopher of the Revolution. Reviewing King-Hele's book, Cambridge University zoologist Sydney Smith notes that Erasmus was

> . . . a founder member of the Lunar Society of Birmingham. He was a friend and collaborator of Josiah Wedgwood, Matthew Bolton, and James Watt, a lifelong friend of the chemist James Keir, correspondent with Rousseau and Franklin.[49]

All of these men were sympathizers with the French revolutionaries and were essentially deists in religion. Keir was also active in the Revolutionary Society, led by the radical Earl Stanhope. Another in this group was the chemist Joseph Priestley, whose revolutionary views became so unpopular

---

48. Desmond King-Hele, *Doctor of Revolution: The Life and Times of Erasmus Darwin* (London: Faber & Faber, 1977), 361 p. King-Hele is a mathematical physicist engaged in research by satellite, as well as a poet and authority on Shelley. He had written a shorter biography of Erasmus in 1963.
49. Sydney Smith, "Scientist, Versifier and Prophet," *Nature* 272 (April 27, 1978): p. 763.

that his home was eventually ransacked and burned by people in the community who resented his radicalism. Eiseley elaborates:

> The reaction, in England, to the French Revolution was destined to sweep Erasmus Darwin's ideas out of fashion, reinstitute religious orthodoxy, and lead to the derogation of Lamarck as a "French atheist" whose ideas were "morally reprehensible." In the end a conspiracy of silence surrounded his work. As has happened many times before in the history of thought, an idea had become the victim of social events and its re-emergence was to be delayed accordingly.[50]

King-Hele, Erasmus Darwin's biographer, expressed this in the following picturesque manner: "For the Lunar Society the wreck was total, or very nearly so; for Darwin, the Birmingham riots were a clear smoke signal. Britain's brief flirtation with the French Revolution was over. . . . From now onwards Darwin became much more cautious in publishing radical opinions."[51]

It may well be that Charles Darwin's notorious lack of acknowledgment of his grandfather's numerous contributions to his own theory was because of his reluctance to be identified with the older man's sociopolitical views. This was undoubtedly a cause of his well-known refusal to allow Karl Marx to dedicate *Das Kapital* to him. By mid-century, the age of progress was in full swing, and the Western world, looking for scientific support for its capitalist economy, was more than ready for social Darwinism, which followed so naturally from biological Darwinism.

There were other reasons for a proper Victorian capitalist household like that of Charles and Emma Darwin to eschew too much identification with Grandfather Erasmus:

> Where Charles was a model Victorian — trim, dignified, almost ascetic in feature — Erasmus was more typical of the eighteenth century, having the fat, bulbous, sensual, and dyspeptic appearance . . . deeply pitted pockmarks on his face, a corpulence of body (he was so fat that the dining table had to be cut out to accommodate his paunch) and clumsiness of gait . . . a pronounced stammer . . . the tongue habitually hanging out between his lips . . . false teeth which gave a peculiarly unpleasant contour to his jaws.[52]

---

50. Eiseley, *Darwin's Century*, p. 54
51. King-Hele, *Doctor of Revolution*, p. 212.
52. Himmelfarb, *Darwin*, p. 3.

Erasmus Darwin's morals were as unattractive as his appearance. Despite the latter, he courted and was courted by many women. In addition to his 12 legitimate children by two wives, he acknowledged at least two illegitimate children. He was also very miserly.

Nevertheless, Erasmus built a highly successful medical practice, published many books of science and poetry, and was later characterized by King-Hele as "the greatest Englishman of the eighteenth century."[53] In any case, he clearly anticipated practically all the basic arguments and mechanism of evolution later made famous (possibly plagiarized) by his grandson Charles. In addition, he was a deist and strong opponent of Christianity. This qualification, added to his radical political orientation and his profligate lifestyle, helped to equip Erasmus for his leading role in the conversion of Christendom from creationism to evolutionism.

Another preeminently important forerunner of Charles Darwin was Jean-Baptiste de Lamarck (1744–1829), who is justly famous for two major works in particular: *Philosophic Zoologique* (1809), and *Histoire Naturelle des Animaux sans Vertebres* (1815). In most modern biology textbooks, Lamarck is treated more or less as a foil for Darwin, having advocated the discredited theory of evolution by inheritance of acquired characteristics, through use and disuse. But his is a gross oversimplification, for Lamarck played a very important role in the development of modern evolutionism. As C.H. Waddington puts it:

> Lamarck is the only major figure in the history of biology whose name has become, to all intents and purposes, a term of abuse. Most scientists' contributions are fated to be outgrown, but very few authors have written works which, two centuries later, are still rejected with an indignation so intense that the skeptic can suspect something akin to an uneasy conscience.[54]

Lamarck, like A.R. Wallace, had no academic training. Nevertheless, he was able to teach himself botany by diligent reading and observation and become recognized as an authority in this field. After the French Revolution, he was appointed in charge of the invertebrate-zoology section of the Paris Museum of Natural History and proceeded to teach himself that science as well. Lamarck also wrote on geology (taking the uniformitarian position of Hutton), meteorology, and even psychology.

---

53. King-Hele, *Doctor of Revolution*, p. 323.
54. Sol Tax, editor, *The Evolution of Life*, "Evolution Adaptation," by C.H. Waddington (University of Chicago Press, 1960), Vol. 1, *Evolution after Darwin*, p. 383.

As noted previously, Lamarck was called a "French atheist" in England, probably because his appointment came through the French revolutionary government, but he was actually a deist, at least through most of his career. He was bitterly anti-Bible and anti-Christian, as noted by Sainte-Beauvè: "He was the mortal enemy of the chemists, of experimentalists and petty analysts, as he called them. No less severe was his philosophical hostility amounting to hatred for the tradition of the Deluge and the Biblical creation story, indeed for everything which recalled the Christian theory of nature."[55]

Lamarck's personal life was sad, to put it mildly. His first six children were illegitimate until he finally married their mother on her deathbed. He had two children by his second wife, none by a third. Two of his children died young; one was insane, one was deaf; two daughters were single and in poverty. He himself was ill for the last 20 years of his life and blind for the last 10. He died penniless and generally ridiculed by the scientists of his own generation.

Many of Lamarck's "explanations" were indeed laughable, including remarkable stories of how animals acquired their characteristics, such as how the giraffe got his long neck and how ruminants got their horns (fits of anger by the males, causing fluids of horny matter to flow to their heads). Nevertheless, it was — and still is — difficult to explain many supposed evolutionary developments without some such mechanism. In fact, Lamarck was neither the first nor the last evolutionary biologist to advocate it. Conway Zirkle of the University of Pennsylvania, who has made a special study of the history of Lamarckianism, has said, "At least fourteen of Lamarck's contemporaries endorsed the belief before he did, and some hundred descriptions of the notion have been collected from the earlier records."[56]

Furthermore, even though Charles Lyell in his *Principles of Geology* argued against Lamarck's explanations, he did credit him with originating the idea of evolution and persisted (to Darwin's dismay) in calling the theory of evolution Lamarckianism and Darwin's theory only an extension of Lamarckianism.

Darwin himself, though he called Lamarck's idea "rubbish" and "nonsense," still came to rely more and more on Lamarckist-type explanations

55. Charles A. Sainte-Beauvè, as cited in Charles C. Gillispie, "Lamarck and Darwin in the History of Science," *American Scientist* 46 (Dec. 1958): p. 397. Sainte-Beauvè was a prominent French critic during the Darwinian period.
56. Conway Zirkle, *Evolution, Marxian Biology and the Social Scene* (Philadelphia, PA: University of Pennsylvania Press, 1959), p. 74.

when he could not imagine a selectionist interpretation. Darwin's long-discarded theory of pangenesis was an attempt to explain how acquired characters could be transmitted through the body by small particles called gemmules.

Lamarck merits at least as much recognition (or, perhaps better, "blame") for developing the theory of evolution as does Darwin. Although the latter has been idolized and the former ridiculed by later generations of biologists, a recent authority says: "It cannot be disputed that of the two Lamarck was the one possessing the most extensive and systematic knowledge of biological facts."[57] In any case, Lamarck was one of the most important evolutionists before Darwin. He greatly influenced not only Lyell and Darwin but also Haeckel and Huxley and many other leading post-Darwin evolutionists. Like Erasmus Darwin, he was both a political radical and a bitter anti-Christian — and an important link in the long chain of evolutionary influence down through the ages.

Perhaps the most significant contribution of Lamarck, however, was his important role in the development of Marxism and communism in general. Many writers on the conspiracy theory of history have discussed the probable connection of the French Revolution with the world Communist conspiracy, through Karl Marx and Frederick Engels. Whether or not Lamarck had any direct connection with the secret leaders of this conspiracy during the French Revolution is irrelevant as well as unknown. Nevertheless, the fact is that Marx and Engels found Lamarckian evolutionism to be just what they needed as a supposed scientific base for their system, and Marxian biology was then developed along Lamarckian principles for a whole century or more.

As noted before, Marx wanted to dedicate *Das Kapital* to Darwin. Modern Communists continue to eulogize Darwin, but they have — until recent years — always tended to follow Lamarck more than Darwin in their biological theorizing. The obvious reason is that the idea of inheriting environmentally produced changes fits in better with the Marxists' ideas of social change. Marx and Engels appreciated Darwin because of his rejection of teleology but were strongly opposed to the influence of Malthus in the growing Darwinian movement.

The most thorough study of Marxist biology was made by Conway Zirkle and published in the Darwinian Centennial Year. He observed:

---

57. Soren Lovtrup, *Darwinism: The Refutation of a Myth* (London: Croom Helm, 1987), p. 60.

During its earliest period, when Marx and Engels were writing, Marxian biology was an easily recognizable deviant. . . . It always referred to Lamarck with respect and accepted completely the inheritance of acquired characters. At the time this was no real distinguishing characteristic, but later it became a major point of difference when scientific biology abandoned the inheritance of acquired characters and Marxian biology retained the belief.[58]

The well-known work of Weissman, Mendel, and Morgan, which finally disproved Lamarckianism and established modern genetics, was never really accepted by Marxist ideologists. Eventually, with the rise of I. V. Michurin and T.D. Lysenko as leaders of Soviet science under the regimes of Lenin and Stalin, Mendelian genetics was officially outlawed in Russia in 1948 and Lamarckianism established as Communist dogma.

Furthermore, this impact of official Marxist biology was felt not only in Russia. Because of the century-long international Communist movement, Lamarckianism infected evolutionary liberals everywhere, especially those in the literary and social-science fields. Writers such as Alfred Lord Tennyson, Jack London, and Bernard Shaw, as well as numerous others less well known, are examples of men who made effective propaganda for Lamarckian evolutionism.

Eventually, however, even Russian Communist leaders had to recognize that Lamarckianism had been disproved scientifically, and there are few Russian scientists or others who still cling to these doctrines today. They have not returned to neo-Darwinism, however (and certainly not to creationism!), but they have largely become proponents of some form of saltationism, or evolution by large jumps — what could well be called *revolutionary evolutionism*. This development has already been discussed, including its current American advocacy under men such as Harvard's Stephen Jay Gould, himself a Marxist.

It is at this point that another strange connection must be mentioned. The remarkable connection of evolutionism with occultism and spiritism has been peripherally explored in the case of Alfred Russel Wallace, the cofounder of Darwinian evolution. It was also noted that Wallace was very sympathetic with left-wing movements, even anarchism, as well as pantheism in religion. Wallace was definitely a Darwinian, rather than a Lamarckian — *except in the case of man*. For man's evolution, he postulated some mysterious spiritual cause.

---

58. Zirkle, *Evolution*, p. 112.

Note again that Karl Marx and later Communist leaders have followed the revolutionist Lamarck, rather than the capitalist Darwin, in their understanding of man and his nature. Most people today assume that Marx was an atheist who, in his youth, had once professed faith in Christ and later renounced Christianity for atheistic materialism. However, Marx was really a pantheist — like Erasmus Darwin and Jean Lamarck, and like Teilhard de Chardin and Julian Huxley and Theodosius Dobzhansky — among many modern evolutionists. In fact, like Wallace and many in the recent New Age movement, Marx was an occultist. Even more, it has recently been shown that he was actually a Satanist!

As we have seen, Karl Marx was a thoroughgoing evolutionist. As such, his tremendous influence, especially in Communist-controlled nations, has carried multitudes of his followers all over the world along with him into a God-denying evolutionary faith, offered in the disguise of concern for the world's downtrodden masses. (Communist leaders, of course, are nearly always well-fed intellectuals rather than starving proletariat.)

Karl Marx was born into a well-to-do family of Jewish Christians, but in later life he became strongly anti-Semitic and anti-black, as well as anti-Christian and anti-God. At first, however, and until his high school graduation, he gave every indication of being a knowledgeable and committed Christian. But then some unknown event occurred that changed his life's orientation drastically. The Rev. Richard Wurmbrand, an authority on the evils of communism, has observed, "Shortly after Marx received this certificate, something mysterious happened in his life: he became profoundly and passionately antireligious. A new Marx began to emerge. He writes in a poem, 'I wish to avenge myself against the One who rules above.' "[59]

That wish was fulfilled in ways far beyond what Marx could have envisaged as a young high school graduate, when one counts up the millions of souls lost and lives murdered as a direct result of the triumphs of communism during the past century. In view of Wurmbrand's recent well-documented research on Marx's Satanist commitments, one cannot help sensing some kind of occult cause-and-effect relation.

In addition to his economic and sociological writings, which were extensive, Marx wrote a number of poems and dramas, especially during his

---

59. Richard Wurmbrand, *Marx and Satan* (Westchester, IL: Crossway Books, 1986), p. 12. Wurmbrand, a former pastor, is an authority on the evils of communism, through both long study and experience, having spent 14 years in Communist prisons for his outspoken preaching and writing against communism.

college years. It is mainly in these that his dark religion is expressed. Just to give one example cited by Wurmbrand, consider one of his poems, called "The Player," written by Marx at about age 18 and evidently intended as a sort of personal testimony:

> The hellish vapors rise and fill the brains,
> Till I go mad and my heart is utterly changed.
> See this sword?
> The prince of darkness sold it to me.
> For me he beats the time and gives the signs
> Ever more boldly I play the dance of death.[60]

According to Wurmbrand, this is in reference to rites of initiation of the Satanist cult, in which an enchanted sword ensuring success in life is sold to the initiate for the price of a blood covenant with Satan for his soul at death.

We cannot produce Wurmbrand's book in its entirety, of course, but it all consists of well-documented evidence of the lifelong devotion of Marx — as well as many other Communist leaders — to Satan and his age-long war against God.

As we conclude this section, which has surveyed the leading actors in the great drama taking place when Christendom was being converted to pagan evolutionism, we note strong subversive political forces at work as well as mysterious occultic and even satanic influences. But the one common theme in all — Darwin, Lyell, Wallace, Erasmus Darwin, Lamarck, Marx, and indeed most all the rest — was hatred of God as Creator, Christ as Savior, and the Bible as God's Word.

The Great Chain of Being

As we continue to trace the history of evolutionary thought back before Darwin — and now even before Lamarck — we have to discern it behind the scenes, so to speak. In the Western world, biblical creationism had been generally accepted as representing the true history of the world ever since the fall of pagan Rome, and especially since the biblical reawakenings associated with the Reformation. Of course, the earlier forms of evolutionary pantheism, as expressed Buddhism and the other Oriental religions, continued to prevail in the East. Even in Christendom the old pagan evolutionary religions never really died out but persisted either underground (e.g., witchcraft) or in the pagan customs and Aristotelian philosophy amalgamated with Christianity

---

60. Ibid., p. 15.

in the medieval Catholic Church. This aspect of history will be surveyed in the next chapter.

In this section, however, we want to look briefly at the scientific atmosphere between the Renaissance and the period of Lamarck and Erasmus Darwin, when evolutionism came out into the open again. During the 18th century, there were a few cautious evolutionists among the scientists, but most competent scientists of the period were strong and convinced creationists — men such as Carolus Linnaeus, the father of taxonomy, for example.

Among the crypto-evolutionists, however, were Benoit de Maillet (1656–1738), Pierre de Maupertuis (1698–1759), and Comte de Buffon (1707–1788). All these, like Lamarck, were French, thus warranting the conclusion that modern evolutionism had its renaissance in Catholic France rather than in Protestant England.

De Maillet used the figure of a Hindu philosopher expounding the lore of India as a device to express his own views, in a posthumously published book called *Telliamed* (de Maillet spelled backward). These views included uniformitarian theories of both cosmic and geologic evolution, as well as total organic evolution. The world was said by de Maillet to be infinite in age, with all its systems products of chance. His works contain a number of occultic ideas and express antipathy to the biblical cosmology.

Maupertuis, primarily a physicist and mathematician, was a friend of the famous Voltaire, and both men were enemies of Christianity. Voltaire claimed to be a deist, but Maupertuis developed his own evolutionary theory (which included natural selection, survival of the fittest, mutations, and a good understanding of genetic heredity) primarily to argue against any form of theism. Much of this was originally published anonymously.

Comte de Buffon was an admirer of Maupertuis but was himself one of the greatest scientists of the 18th century. Serving as director of the Royal Botanical Gardens in Paris for over 50 years, Buffon authored the amazing 44-volume work *Histoire Naturelle*, dealing with just about every scientific or pseudo-scientific subject one could imagine. Scattered throughout these volumes can be found implications of most of the later teachings of both Lyell and Darwin. Writing before the French Revolution, however, he had to be careful in expressing his strong anti-Bible views. Loren Eiseley observes: "He wrote at times cryptically and ironically. . . . Buffon managed, albeit in a somewhat scattered fashion, to mention every significant ingredient which was to be incorporated into Darwin's great synthesis of 1859."[61]

Buffon, in common with most other scientists of his day, was still basically thinking in terms of the "Great Chain of Being," more or less equivalent to Aristotle's *Scala Naturae*. This concept can be traced back to Plato, but it was especially popular from the Renaissance on through the 18th century. It was a quasi-theological theory (though non-biblical) and exerted profound influence on the educated people of this period.[62] One of its most elaborate detailings was published by the Swiss naturalist Charles Bonnet (1720–1793) in 1769.[63]

According to this concept, living organisms can be arranged in a continuous linear scale, with man at the top and the simplest at the bottom. Below this are stones, metals, earth, water, air, and ether. Above man are higher worlds, angels, cherubim, and finally God. In this idea construct, there are no gaps, though many links may need yet to be discovered.

As this *Scala Naturae* was understood in the 16th, 17th, and 18th centuries, it was not an evolutionary series but a static system, representing the mind of the Eternal. However, in no sense was it ever a biblical system, for the Bible teaches plainly that each "kind" was quite distinct, clearly and permanently separated from all other kinds. Nevertheless, the idea of a "continuum" of systems, from inorganic to celestial, clearly lends itself easily to the concept of evolution, once it is set in motion and time values are imparted to the motion. As Eiseley elaborates:

> All that the Chain of Being actually needed to become a full-fledged evolutionary theory was the introduction into it of the conception of time in vast quantities added to mutability of form. It demanded, in other words, a universe not made but being made continuously. It is ironic and intriguing that the fixed hierarchical order in biology began to pass almost contemporaneously with the disappearance of the feudal social scale in the storms of the French Revolution. It was France, whose social system was dissolving, that produced the first modern evolutionists. As we look back upon the long reign of the Scale of Being, whose effects, as we shall see, persisted well into the nineteenth century, we may observe that the seed

---

61. Eiseley, *Darwin's Century*, p. 39.
62. The most thorough exposition is that by A.O. Lovejoy, *The Great Chain of Being* (New York: Harper & Row, 1960, first published 1936).
63. Charles Bonnet, *Contemplation de la Nature* (1769). Cited, with chart, in Oldroyd, *Darwinian Impacts*, p. 10–11

of evolution lay buried in this traditional metaphysic which indeed prepared the Western mind for its acceptance.[64]

Note that, according to Eiseley, who had a well-deserved reputation as an outstanding historian of evolutionary thought, the Great Chain of Being was a "traditional metaphysic," which was not really supported by the actual hierarchical array of living organisms as depicted by Linnaeus. Neither was it supported by the biblical system, which was Linnaeus's basic model in the first place. The question, then, is where the Great Chain of Being concept ever got started. It dominated Western thought for over three hundred years — especially in France, where it was most fully elaborated by Charles Bonnet. It formed the starting point for the evolutionary systems of Buffon and Lamarck, the pioneer modern evolutionists.

D.R. Oldroyd comments:

> In the first volume of the *Histoire Naturelle*, Buffon reveals himself as an exponent of the doctrine of the Great Chain of Being, with man being placed at the top of the chain.[65]

> As we have seen, Lamarck held a version of the ancient doctrine of the Great Chain of Being. Yet . . . it was not conceived as a rigid, static structure. By their struggle to meet the requirements of the environment, and with the help of the principle of the inheritance of acquired characteristics, organisms could supposedly work their way up the Chain — from microbe to man, so to speak. . . . Moreover, new creatures were constantly appearing at the bottom of the Chain, arising from inorganic matter through spontaneous generation. . . . Ascent of the Chain involved a continuous process of complexification, due to the so-called "power of life."[66]

Note that the Great Chain of Being, or the Scale of Nature, was described as not only a "traditional metaphysic" but also an "ancient doctrine." It was not supported by anything approaching an actual continuum of organisms in

---

64. Eiseley, *Darwin's Century*, p. 9–10. Similarly, a British scientist, G.H. Harper, notes that "the most intangible but far-reaching influence of evolution theory is to keep alive the notion of the *scala naturae*. . . . It was given a new lease on life by Darwinism, since the scale could now be seen as the sequence of stages through which the higher, complex and advanced species might have evolved from the lower, simple and primitive species" ("Darwinism and Indoctrination," *School Science Review* 59 [Dec. 1977]: p. 267).

65. Oldroyd, *Darwinian Impacts*, p. 23.

66. Ibid., p. 32.

the observable world — that is, by *science* — but it was tenaciously and widely believed anyway, having come down from great antiquity. Furthermore, it would play a most important role in the modern revival of evolutionism — which also, as we shall see, was a belief coming down from remote antiquity.

It is always possible, of course, to arrange any group of objects in some kind of sequence based on some arbitrary criterion, and it would be a more or less natural exercise for philosophers — whether ancient or modern — to try to organize living things in order of increasing complexity from microbes to men. This arbitrary sequence, with all its very real gaps, constitutes the only factual basis for the Great Chain of Being and for the evolutionary ladder that was based on it. In fact, the so-called evidences of evolution are to considerable extent simply corollaries of the assumed chain.

One such "evidence" is that from comparative anatomy and other measures of similarity. According to Oldroyd, "There can be little doubt that the rise of comparative anatomy is inextricably linked to the history of the Chain of Being concept with its gradations of complexity in living forms."[67] The same applies to the study of variations within existing types, fueled by the desire to find missing links in the chain: "Their zealous efforts to show that the apparent missing links in the scale could be found enormously stimulated the study of taxonomy and variation."[68]

Of course, none of the missing links were ever found. A greater appreciation of the stability of the basic kinds, with tremendous variations possible *within* the kinds, should have been the results of such studies. Instead, such philosophers continue to believe that the gaps somehow are bridgeable. Today they commonly assume that these variations, extended over vast ages of time, have somehow filled the gaps and completed the chain, through evolution.

Another very important application of the Great Chain of Being was made in the study of embryology. Since man was at the top of the scale, with one-celled organisms at the bottom, these "nature philosophers" began to teach that this sequence was also expressed in the embryonic development of human beings in the womb. This idea eventually became the recapitulation theory, but it was proposed initially not as an evolutionary concept, but as an illustration of the Chain of Being.

> The idea of ontogenetic recapitulation dates back to a speech given by Kidmayer in Tubingen, 1793. . . . The succession of organisms mentioned here may be taken to represent the "Chain of Being,"

---

67. Ibid., p. 7.
68. Ibid., p. 9.

and Kielmayer thus states that individual organisms during their development follow this sequence.[69]

Friedrich Kielmayer was one of the first in the series of German "nature philosophers" of the 18th and 19th centuries. They have also been called "transcendentalists" because of their somewhat mystical approach to the study of comparative morphology. Others who also used the recapitulation idea were Lorentz Oken (1779–1851) and Johann Meckel. The philosopher Johann Goethe (1749–1832) is today the best known of these German *Naturphilosophen*. Oldroyd notes that "Oken was able to show, by means of dissection of embryos at various stages of their development, that humans do, in fact, pass through stages that resemble different steps of the evolutionary history of the animal kingdom."[70] And Meckel wrote that "the higher animal, in its gradual evolution, passes through the permanent organic states which lie below it."[71]

When Darwinism came along, Charles Darwin made extensive use of recapitulationism as a "proof" of evolution; then Ernst Haeckel, calling it the "biogenetic law," made even greater use of it in Germany, where the idea had originated. "And the 'embryological argument' has for long been a powerful weapon in the dialectical armoury of the evolutionist," says Oldroyd.[72] As pointed out earlier, this hoary argument has long been discredited scientifically. Its empirical evidence is highly superficial, based solely on vague resemblances and parallels. It was really based on the Great Chain of Being, which itself has been abandoned by all scientists for 150 years.

Nevertheless, these two related concepts were long used to justify the deadly racist philosophies of the leading evolutionary scientists of the world prior to the anti-racist reaction engendered by Hitler's policies of racial genocide. Writes Eiseley:

> In making use of the living taxonomic ladder [Darwin] implies marked differences in the inherited mental faculties between the members of the different existing races. This point of view unconsciously reflects the old Scale of Nature and the tacit assumption that the races of today in some manner represent a sequence of time, a

69. Lovtrup, *Darwinism: The Refutation of a Myth*, p. 67
70. Oldroyd, *Darwinian Impacts*, p. 53.
71. E.S. Russell, *Form and Function* (London: John Murray, 1916), p. 93, cited in Oldroyd, *Darwinian Impacts*, p. 53.
72. Oldroyd, *Darwinian Impacts*, p. 53.

series of living fossils, with western European man standing biologically at the head of the procession.[73]

We have already noted the dreadful effects generated in Germany under the teachings of Haeckel, Nietzsche, and other social Darwinists who used recapitulationism as a basis for racist violence.

There is still another way in which the *Scala Naturae* became sublimated into an evolutionary history. When it was most popular (in the 17th and 18th centuries), very little was known about the fossil record of past life on the earth. The known fossils were generally attributed to the Noahic deluge. However, the old pagan beliefs in the great age of the earth began to be revived under the uniformitarian concepts of Buffon, Lamarck, and Hutton. Then William Smith (1769–1839) found that distinct strata in the rocks generally contained distinct sets of fossils. This led to the concept that, since the bottom strata must have been first deposited, there was a time sequence to the strata and therefore to the forms of life corresponding to them.

Since Smith himself was a practical civil engineer and a creationist, he did not impute any evolutionary significance to this discovery. The fossils he used in his system were all marine invertebrates, mostly mollusks, and there is certainly nothing much in these to speak of evolution. Very little was known as yet about the so-called fossiliferous geologic column. Furthermore, every local stratigraphic column has different fossil sequences from every other, so there is no obvious worldwide column that could be correlated with time.

How, then, could these fossil organisms be arranged in a time sequence? The answer was ready at hand — the Great Chain of Being!

More or less coincident with Smith's discovery with relation to the fossil marine invertebrates, the great vertebrate paleontologist Georges Cuvier (1769–1832) had been developing his theory of multiple catastrophes, with only the last being the Noahic Flood. Like Smith, Cuvier was a creationist, frequently debating with Lamarck about evolution. (Cuvier was professor of vertebrate zoology while Lamarck was professor of invertebrate zoology at the famous Paris Natural History Museum.) After each catastrophe, in Cuvier's system, a completely new assemblage of organisms was created (or, possibly, migrated from some other region), with each group being progressively more complex than the preceding. This system was therefore also called "progressionism."

When Lyell later began to promote Hutton's uniformitarianism, the main object of his attack (other than the Bible) was Cuvierian progressionism. In

---

73. Eiseley, *Darwin's Century*, p. 288.

the 18th and early 19th centuries, even the evolutionists, such as Buffon, thought more in terms of degenerative changes from man downward, in accord with the prevailing concept of the Great Chain, which always had been viewed in this fashion. Cuvier's progressionism/catastrophism was claimed by Cuvier and others to support the Bible's record, and Lyell therefore vigorously opposed it. This is basically why he also seemed to oppose Lamarckian and Darwinian evolution for a time. Both of these evolutionists appeared to support progressionism in biology, even though they accepted uniformitarianism in geology, and Lyell wanted to retain uniformitarianism in biology as well, with all forms of life present through all the ages.

In any case, the progressionist system had little support from the still largely unknown fossil record; it was essentially nothing but the Great Chain of Being taken in reverse, from the bottom up instead of starting from the top down. There was not enough known as yet about fossil sequences to choose. Buffon and Hutton, as well as Lyell for a long time, believed that the whole Scale of Nature was actually still represented in the living world. The phenomenon of extinction was not yet believed to be significant.

Here is how Soren Lovtrup, professor of biology for many years at the University of Umea in Sweden, summarizes this history:

> In order to understand Lyell's position in geology and his influence on Darwin, we must return to the *Scala Naturae*, this hypothetical ordering of all living beings in a descending scale of complexity. . . .
>
> In order to compromise between dogma and empirical evidence, the theory of Catastrophism was launched. According to this hypothesis the living world arose through a series of catastrophes causing multiple extinctions, the Noachian deluge being the last of these. Each catastrophe was followed by a creative contribution on the part of God, the succession of organisms thus arising being progressive with respect to organization and complexity. . . . The theory of Catastrophism was therefore also known as Progressionism."[74]

It must be remembered that the fossil record did not really support either progressionism or evolutionism. In the first place, there were no transitional forms, and there was also as yet no standard geological column with

---

74. Lovtrup, *Darwinism: The Refutation of a Myth*, p. 174. Lovtrup's book is highly critical of Darwinism, but Hobart M. Smith, in the key journal *Evolution*, says, "Lovtrup has given the world a truly epochal introspective analysis of inestimable potential value." 43: 3 (1989): p. 699.

its superficial appearance of progressionism. Nevertheless, scientists began to view the column in such a way, because of their sublimated commitment to the concept of the Great Chain.

The story of just how and when the standard geological column was established with its succession of geological "ages" is a fascinating tale, only part of which is commonly recited in textbooks. It is too long and involved to discuss here, except to note that the concept is essentially based on the Chain of Being rather than on the actual fossil record.

It is admitted, of course, that the two are similar, but not so generally acknowledged that the one is really based on the other. Eiseley comments: "As the progressive organic advancement in the rocks became better known and read, it was assumed that this stair of life, which was analogous with the Scale of Being in the living world, pointed on prophetically toward man who was assumed to be the goal of the process of creation."[75] We have already noted that embryological development was taken as illustrative of this Chain of Being, and also that comparative morphology was developed as a result of the incentive provided by the assumed Chain of Being. It was the study of the actual physical data provided by the study of these two new disciplines — comparative morphology and comparative embryology (especially as guided by the recapitulation theory) — that proved invaluable in helping the early paleontologists to build up the standard geologic column. Two current scientist leaders in evolutionary thought have (perhaps inadvertently) acknowledged this fact. Dr. Keith Stewart Thompson, dean of the graduate school and professor of biology at Yale University, in an article on the significance of the recapitulation theory, noted the following in passing:

> Another major factor keeping some sort of recapitulation alive was the need of comparative morphologists and especially paleontologists for a solid theoretical foundation for homology. They had long since come to rely on comparative ontogenetic information as a base.[76]

That is, ontogeny, which means embryonic growth, has long served as the "base" for the study of "phylogeny" by "paleontologists" in building up their fossil sequences and time scales. The reason why this could be done was their confidence that the ontogeny actually reproduced, on a reduced time scale, the actual evolutionary history of the organisms.

---

75. Eiseley, *Darwin's Century*, p. 67.
76. Keith S. Thompson, "Ontogeny and Phylogeny Recapitulated," *American Scientist* 76 (May/June 1988): p. 274.

Similarly, Stephen Jay Gould of Harvard University, in an article written to rebut the racism implicit in the recapitulation theory, also mentioned in passing the following: "In Down's day, the theory of recapitulation embodied a biologist's best guide for the organization of life into sequences of higher and lower forms."[77] Therefore, biologists could use the recapitulation theory (based on the *Scala Naturae*, as we have seen) to organize the time sequences of their fossils into earlier and later developments, and then fit these into the standard column that was being developed.

All of this indicates that, around the late 18th and early 19th centuries, when the standard fossil column was being developed, the Great Chain of Being (and especially the recapitulation theory that was based on it) provided the best key by which to organize the few fossils then available into a time sequence — first used to denote "progressionism," then later converted into "evolutionism." The geologic column eventually so constructed (and the fossil sequences corresponding to its different "ages") was soon to be considered as the best evidence for evolution. Yet it was really based, not on the actual vertical succession of fossils in the rock layers, but on the ancient concept of the Great Chain of Being.

This is why there are continually being encountered so many exceptions and contradictions between the standard column and the actual fossil sequences. Since the writer has discussed this topic in some detail in several other books,[78] the documented evidence for the inadequacy of the fossil record — either to prove evolution or to date the relative age of the rocks — will not be repeated here.

Our primary purpose here is not necessarily to refute evolution but to trace its history. As we have seen, it did not originate with Charles Darwin. There were many evolutionists before him, and many of their evolutionary ideas and supposed evidences were founded originally — whether intentionally or otherwise — on the Great Chain of Being. Even Darwin himself was influenced by this concept, as Eiseley notes:

> He reveals in occasional passages that he is unconsciously trans-
> ferring the concept of the eighteenth-century unilinear fixed scale

77. Stephen Jay Gould, "Dr. Down's Syndrome," *Natural History* 89 (April 1980): p. 144. The title of Gould's article referred to the physiologic infirmity known as mongolism, so named because of the notion that the Mongoloid "race" had not evolved as high as the Caucasians.

78. See, for example: *The Genesis Flood* (co-author John C. Whitcomb, 1961), p. 130–211; *Scientific Creationism* (1974), p. 75–122; *King of Creation* (1980), p. 137–168; *The Biblical Basis for Modern Science* (1984), p. 300–366. Any of these books can be ordered through the Institute for Creation Research (1806 Royal Lane, Dallas, TX 75229).

of being to, as Teggert puts it, a "concept of a unilinear and continuous series in time, parallel with the classificatory series." The classificatory series is, of course, the Scale of Being. Darwin speaks of the whole organic world as tending inevitably to "progress toward perfection."[79]

We can therefore conclude that this concept of the Great Chain of Being was very significant as the medium for transmitting evolutionary concepts into the era of modern science. The main arguments for evolution — comparative morphology, the recapitulation theory of embryology, the order of the fossils, the differences between the human "races" — were all based on it, as was the very idea of evolutionary "progression" with time. None of these arguments is supported by the actual data of science, but all were nevertheless effectively used in the 19th century to convince practically the whole intellectual world that evolution was valid.

The vital question, then, has to do with the *origin* of the Great Chain of Being concept. It did not come from empirical science, which it antedated. It obviously did not come from the Bible or the early Christians, because it clearly contradicts their teachings. As we have noted before, the Chain of Being — *Scala Naturae* — is a very ancient tradition, but that tradition is not Christian. In fact, it was associated closely with the evolutionism of the ancient pagan religions, which opposed Christianity.

In his brief historical review Lovtrup acknowledges this pagan origin as follows: "The *Scala Naturae, the Ladder of Nature, the Chain of Being, l'Echelle des Etres*, is a notion traceable back to Plato, Aristotle, and the Neo-Platonians, which experienced a resurgence in the eighteenth century."[80] Oldroyd goes into somewhat more detail on the origin of this imaginary chain. After reviewing its development by Plato, as modified by Aristotle and then by the Neo-Platonists, especially as codified by Macrobius about A.D. 400, Oldroyd says:

> Neo-Platonism has for long exerted a powerful influence on the Christian West, particularly in the Florentine period of the Renaissance. And it might be said that the doctrine of the Great Chain of Being formed part of the general mental furniture of most educated men from the Renaissance until almost the end of the eighteenth century.... References to the Great Chain of Being abound in Spenser, Henry More, and Milton. One finds it in the philosophical writings of Leibniz, Spinoza, and Locke in the seventeenth century, and

79. Eiseley, *Darwin's Century*, p. 283.
80. Lovtrup, *Darwinism: The Refutation of a Myth*, p. 45–46.

in the eighteenth century it was one of the standard ways of concep-
tualizing nature. . . .

The doctrine of the Great Chain of Being probably had its last
resting place (at least among biologists) among the German Nature
Philosophers of the nineteenth century, immediately before Darwin's time.[81]

As we have seen, this doctrine even influenced Darwin in certain ways,
as well as Lamarck, Lyell, and others in France and England. More recently
and under different terminology, it is currently experiencing a resurgence
in the so-called New Age movement. For those interested, the most detailed
study of the history of the Great Chain concept will be found in the classic
work of A.O. Lovejoy.[82]

Finally, one of the most influential works immediately preparing the
world for Darwin was the famous book by the journalist/publisher Robert
Chambers entitled *Vestiges of the Natural History of Creation*. Originally
published anonymously, the book was vigorously attacked by most scientists
of the time. As we have seen, however, it made a very favorable impression
on Alfred Russel Wallace, strongly moving him toward transcendental evolutionism. It also was widely read by the British public, thereby preparing
ordinary laymen to accept Darwinism when it came a few years later. It is
significant that Chambers was strongly motivated by the Germans and therefore by the Great Chain. Says Oldroyd: "Chambers' work was not based upon
the hypothesis of evolution by natural selection, but rather on the cosmic
evolutionism of the German Nature Philosophers."[83]

Chambers was much taken with the famous Nebular Hypothesis for the
evolution of the solar system, originally formulated by Kant and LaPlace.
This was incorporated into the cosmic aspects of the Great Chain and had
been widely accepted even before organic evolution was accepted.[84] Chambers also made effective use of two other concepts based on the Chain:

> Chambers had two most cogent arguments in favor of his evo-
> lution hypothesis: (a) the recapitulation argument from embryo-
> logical studies; . . . (b) the obvious structural similarities (or ho-
> mologies) that may be seen in most vertebrates. These Goethe and

81. Oldroyd, *Darwinian Impacts*, p. 9–11.
82. See note 62, this chapter, for publishing information.
83. Oldroyd, *Darwinian Impacts*, p. 54.
84. See Ronald Numbers, *Creation by Natural Law* (Seattle, WA: University of Wash-
    ington Press, 1977).

his followers had ascribed to the existence of a common archetypal plan, but Chambers referred the homologies to indications of common descent.[85]

Note again that the Great Chain of Being has been a profoundly influential concept in the development of the modern theory of evolution. It is obvious that it prepared the way for this so-called great discovery of modern science, as well as underlaid many of its arguments and concepts.

It has been my purpose in this chapter to trace the history of evolutionism back from Darwin to the Renaissance. Accordingly, I believe the evidence clearly establishes that evolutionism was a very active movement during this entire period, long before Charles Darwin appeared at just the right time to catalyze the simmering movement into the explosive reaction that quickly changed the world, reviving ancient paganism in the form of the ostensibly new science (falsely so-called) of Darwinism. The backward search continues in the next chapter.

---

85. Oldroyd, *Darwinian Impacts*, p. 55.

5

The Conflict of the Ages

Before we carry our history of evolutionary thought back into the so-called Dark Ages before the Renaissance, it will be good to pause for a brief review. There were many strange currents that converged on Charles Darwin, producing through this most unlikely confluence a surging flood of naturalistic and humanistic pollution that eventually inundated the whole world. Every discipline of modern thought is now contaminated and controlled by evolutionism. The schools and colleges are everywhere dominated not only by evolutionary thought but also by evolutionary methodology. Furthermore, all the devastating politico-economic movements of the past century, including the great wars, have been motivated by evolutionary philosophy. The moral decay and the widespread religious apostasy of these latter days are also founded squarely on evolutionary rationalizations.

Such a remarkable complex of baleful effects must somehow have an equally notable complex of causes. The very unremarkable studies and publications of Charles Darwin could not possibly be a sufficient explanation.

Those who specialize in conspiracy theories could no doubt make at least a circumstantial case here. We have already noted the semi-revolutionary Lunar Society founded by Erasmus Darwin and others who sympathized with the French revolutionaries, not to mention the closely associated Revolutionary Society itself, whose membership overlapped that of the Lunar Society. Both of these seem to have been involved to some degree with the Jacobin clubs in France, or even with the Illuminati. The latter society was founded in 1776, although there had already been other secret societies with similar

names in various places for two centuries or more. It was connected with certain Masonic lodges in France and is alleged by many students of such things
to have been the actual nerve center of the French Revolution, and then later
of the so-called League of the Just, under whose auspices Marx and Engels
published their original Communist Manifesto.

The Freemasons themselves have long constituted a notable complex of
secret societies whose influence has surely been profound, in the politics and
economies of many nations. Then there are the Jesuits, associated by many
writers, both Catholic and Protestant, with a wide range of conspiratorial activities. The founder of the Illuminati, Dr. Adam Weishaupt, was an ex-Jesuit,
with a number of notable friends in America and England, as well as France
and Germany.

All the above facts are well known, but how much they may have had
to do with the promotion of Darwin and Darwinism is not so clear. Many
of these secret societies were (and are) pantheistic in philosophy and thus
favorable to evolutionism in one form or another. Charles Darwin's own personal background was in this social environment. His father and grandfather
(Erasmus) were Freemasons, as well as anti-biblical; his wife and most of her
relatives were Unitarians.

There is also the enigmatic role of Charles Lyell, whose uniformitarianism was all-important to Darwin. Lyell seemed to oppose evolution for a
long while even while giving full support, advice, and encouragement to his
young protegé, Darwin, in developing and publishing his naturalistic evolutionary theories. Lyell's motivation was surely more than that of pure science.

The one thing that all of the influences brought to bear on Charles Darwin seemed to have in common, however, was their strong opposition to
biblical Christianity, both before and after publication of the *Origin*. If there
really was a conspiracy involved, therefore, it must have been *spiritual* rather
than political, directed by unseen spiritual forces opposing the Creator/Re-
deemer, Jesus Christ — not merely by some secret band of industrialists or
socialists out to use evolutionism to bolster their own causes.

There were also, as previously noted, certain occultic overtones to these
events — most notably the commitment of Alfred Russel Wallace to spiritism
and the strange device by which he was suddenly used to impel the reluctant
Darwin to publish his long-delayed book. On top of this, we may also note
the heavy presence of Satanism in the simultaneous development of Marxism and communism in general, as supported by Darwinism. Many writers
have also noted the possibility of occultic influences on Nietzsche and others
of this period.

This type of investigation could be pursued further, but the study thus far at least indicates the probability that the modern creation-evolution conflict is more than a mere scientific controversy, or even a battle between science and religion, as evolutionists pretend. It is nothing less than a new and critical phase in the age-long conflict between the only two basic worldviews. One is centered in the Creator of the world and His redemptive work on behalf of that lost world; the other is centered in the creatures of that world, not only man and his self-oriented goals, but also in the devil himself, who is ultimately behind all rebellion against God.

Evolution Underground

We have seen that evolutionism was in significant part carried into the modern world through the ancient tradition of the Great Chain of Being. The periods euphemistically designated as the Renaissance and the Enlightenment marked the transition from the Dark Ages (also a euphemism) to the modern age of science and Darwinism, when the Great Chain was gradually transmuted into a scenario of evolution over long geological "ages."

The millennium in Europe between the fall of Rome and the Renaissance (A.D. 400 to 1400) was dominated, of course, by the Catholic Church and therefore by nominal allegiance to the biblical/creationist worldview. Nevertheless, the evolutionism of the old pagan world had not died; it had merely gone underground, as it were. The original pagan form of the Great Chain, as described by Plato and Aristotle, had been semi-Christianized by Thomas Aquinas and others. Arthur Koestler describes these developments as follows:

> But in the hierarchy of values, which is attached to the hierarchy in space, the original simple division into sub-lunary and supra-lunary regions has now yielded to an infinite number of subdivisions. The original, basic difference between coarse earthly mutability and ethereal permanence is maintained; but both regions are subdivided in such a manner that the result is a continuous ladder, or graded scale, which stretches from God down to the lowest form of existence.[1]

The Scale of Being was considered to be static, with everything remaining fixed in its proper position on the scale. In its original Greek formulation,

---

1. Arthur Koestler, *The Sleepwalkers* (New York: The University Library, Grosset & Dunlap, 1963), p. 94. This book, by a prize-winning author of many important books, is a history of cosmological theories from antiquity to the present.

however, it had been an evolved series, proceeding downward from the eternal. Koestler explains:

> The One, the Most Perfect Being, "cannot remain shut up in itself; it must overflow" and create the World of Ideas, which in turn creates a copy or image of itself in the Universal Soul, which generates the "sentient" and "vegetative" creatures — and so on, in a descending series, to the "last dregs of things." It is still a process of degeneration by descent, the very opposite of the evolutionary idea; but since every created being is ultimately an emanation of God, partaking of His essence in a measure diminishing with distance, the soul will always strive upward, to its source.[2]

This concept of emanations, proceeding step-by-step downward from their primary source, is nothing but pantheism. The system is not evolution in the modern Darwinian sense of proceeding upward, but is evolution nonetheless, proceeding deterministically downward from primeval Oneness. Once everything had evolved (or "devolved"), the chain was thereafter considered permanently fixed.

The Scale of Being was, of course, not the only heritage of pagan pantheism that was transmitted through the Middle Ages, though it may well have been the most significant. In fact, the Renaissance (meaning "rebirth") has been so named for the very reason that the submerged pre-Christian culture of Greece and Rome was revived in this period.

The early Christian Church had to witness in a pagan world, and this meant interacting with Greek philosophy, among other temptations. Unfortunately, after the Apostolic age, many of its leaders began to equivocate and compromise on intellectual and philosophical issues. Like their counterparts in the modern Christian Church (as well as in every other generation), these men decided to "dialogue" with the Greek and Roman scientists/philosophers, especially in the matter of cosmology. The straightforward creation narrative of Genesis had to be allegorized in order to accommodate the long ages and evolutionary cosmogonies of the philosophers.

In the early part of the third century, this allegorization process became very strong, especially among the Christian community in Alexandria. David C. Lindberg, Evjue-Bascom Professor of the history of science at the University of Wisconsin, writes:

---

2. Ibid., p. 95.

There were varieties of opinion among the apologists of course, but all were familiar with Greek philosophy, esteemed portions of it . . . and put it to apologetic use whenever possible. Clement (d. between 211 and 215), a teacher in a catechetical school in Alexandria, regarded Greek philosophy as absolutely essential for the defense of the faith against heresy and skepticism and for the development of Christian doctrine.[3]

Since these early Christian apologists thought that certain aspects of Platonic philosophy, in particular, were compatible with monotheism and the doctrine of original creation, they felt free to adapt the other details of cosmology to Platonism, allegorizing Genesis as necessary. Says Lindberg:

> The attitude of Origen (c. 185–c. 254) toward Greek philosophy, particularly Platonic, was even more liberal than Clement's. Origen, also an Alexandrian teacher, possessed a thorough knowledge of Greek philosophy — Aristotelian, Platonic, Stoic, and Epicurean. He adopted the basic elements of Plato's theology, cosmology, and psychology, while borrowing his terminology and definitions from Aristotle.[4]

We shall look more closely at the cosmological and evolutionary aspects of these philosophies shortly, but it is important to note first that these were being transmitted, surreptitiously as it were, and perhaps with all good intentions, by some of the most influential Christian leaders of the early church. Origen was especially significant in this connection.

> This desire to find allegories in Scripture was carried to excess by Origen (185–256), who was likewise associated with Alexandrian thought, and he managed thereby to get rid of anything that could not be harmonized with pagan learning, such as the separation of the waters above the firmament from those below it, mentioned in Genesis, which he takes to mean that we should separate our spirits from the darkness of the abyss, where the adversary and his angels dwell.[5]

---

3. David C. Lindberg and Ronald L. Numbers, editors, *God and Nature: Historical Essays on the Encounter between Christianity and Science,* "Science and the Early Church," by David C. Lindberg (Berkeley, CA: University of California Press, 1986), p. 23–24.
4. Ibid., p. 24.
5. Multon K. Munitz, editor, *Theories of the Universe,* "Medieval Cosmology," by J.L.E. Dreyer (Glencoe, IL: The Free Press, 1957), p. 117.

There were, of course, a number of Christian leaders who opposed these compromises, such as Tatian, Tertullian, and others who insisted that the Bible — not Greek philosophy — was alone authoritative and sufficient. By and large, the "official" position of the Church throughout the Middle Ages, in fact, was based on the literal six-day creation account in Genesis. Evolutionism was present in the Church but was more or less underground.

There were other influential compromisers, of course, in addition to Clement and Origen:

> During this period it is significant that several of the church fathers expressed ideas of organic evolution even though the trend of ecclesiastical thought led more readily into other lines of reasoning. St. Gregory of Nyssa (A.D. 331–396), St. Basil (A.D. 331–379), St. Augustine (A.D. 353–430), and St. Thomas Aquinas (A.D. 1225–1274) expressed belief in the symbolical nature of the biblical story of creation and in their comments made statements clearly related to the concept of evolution.[6]

By far the most important theologians of the Church during the Middle Ages were Augustine and Thomas Aquinas, both of whom were thoroughly conversant with Greek philosophy, as well as the writings of the Church fathers. Both believed in the divine origin and authority of the Scriptures and therefore in the fact of creation by a transcendent Creator. Nevertheless, they also felt strongly the pressures of pantheistic philosophy to accommodate and allegorize Genesis.

Whether Augustine was a strict creationist or a theistic evolutionist has been debated by many modern writers. One of the most widely read historians of evolutionism was Henry Fairfield Osborn, longtime director of the American Museum of Natural History. Osborn said, concerning Augustine, "He thus sought a naturalistic interpretation of the Mosaic record, or potential rather than special creation, and taught that in the institution of Nature we should not look for miracles but for the laws of nature."[7]

Similarly, Lindberg, a more recent historian, says:

> According to Augustine, God created all things in the beginning, some actually and some potentially — the latter as seedlike principles, which later developed into mature creatures, much as a seed develops

---

6. Arthur Ward Lindsay, *Principles of Organic Evolution* (St. Louis, MO: C.V. Mosby, 1952), p. 21.
7. Henry Fairfield Osborn, *From the Greeks to Darwin* (New York: Scribner's, 1929), p. 72.

into a mature plant. Augustine thus uses Greek natural philosophy to resolve an exegetical problem — maintaining that God's creative activity is fully completed in the beginning, and yet taking full account of observational and commonsense notions regarding the development of natural things. It is noteworthy that Augustine applies the doctrine of seedlike principles even to the origin of Adam and Eve.[8]

Augustine thus sounds much like a modern theistic evolutionist when writing on creation! It is true that Augustine's writings are sometimes difficult to sort out, sometimes seemingly taking the six days of creation literally, at other times allegorically. Nevertheless, it is clear that he at least allows for a process of evolution in such passages as the following:

> It is one thing to build and to govern creatures from within and from the summit of the whole causal nexus — and only God, the Creator, does this; it is another thing to apply externally forces and capacities bestowed by him in order to bring forth at such and such a time, or in such and such a shape, what has been created. For all these things were created at the beginning, being primordially woven into the texture of the world, but they await the proper opportunity for their appearance.[9]

This is a clear exposition of what modern expositors would call theistic evolution (or "process creation," as some prefer). Lindberg therefore concludes that "Augustine, in his efforts to formulate a Christian worldview, put considerable portions of Greek natural philosophy (particularly Platonic) to work. Thus the church fathers used Greek natural science, and in using it they transmitted it. We must count this transmission as one of the major Christian contributions to science."[10]

To the extent that Greek "science" was framed around evolution, however, this so-called contribution should be deplored rather than praised. If Christians had built their worldview on the Bible — as Kepler, Newton, and others tried to do much later — the development of true science might have come much sooner.

Almost a millennium after Augustine, as the Dark Ages began to draw to a close, along came the "angelic doctor," Thomas Aquinas. Thomas made

---

8. Lindberg and Numbers, *God and Nature*, p. 36–37.
9. Augustine, *De Trinitate* 3.9.16, as quoted by Lindberg, "Science and the Early Church," p. 37.
10. Lindberg and Numbers, *God and Nature*, p. 40.

many significant contributions to Christian theology and apologetics, but he also helped in a critical way not only to bring on the Renaissance but also to reintroduce the Chain of Being and Greek evolutionism into European religious philosophy. Edward Grant comments:

> By the twelfth century, significant changes were under way that would eventually challenge theology's interpretation of the cosmos and the God who created it. The threat to theology and the church did not derive from astrology or witchcraft, which, though potentially dangerous, were successfully contained in the Middle Ages. It came from Greek natural philosophy and science, initially in its benign Platonic and Neoplatonic forms in the twelfth century and then in its powerful and truly menacing Aristotelian form in the thirteenth century.[11]

It was Thomas Aquinas who was most responsible for reviving Aristotle's philosophy, both in the Catholic Church and then in early Renaissance culture, and the effect was profound: "The impact of Aristotle's though on the late Middle Ages cannot be overestimated. . . . Aristotle's cosmic system . . . assumed a world without beginning or end and a deity who had no knowledge of that world."[12]

Koestler observes:

> The alliance, born of catastrophe and despair, between Christianity and Platonism, was replaced by a new alliance between Christianity and Aristotelianism, concluded under the auspices of the Angelic Doctor, Thomas Aquinas. Essentially, this meant a change of fronts from the negation to the affirmation of life, a new, positive attitude to Nature, and to man's striving to understand nature. Perhaps the greatest historical achievement of Albert the Great and Thomas Aquinas lies in their recognition of the "light of reason" as an independent source of knowledge beside the "light of grace."
>
> By using Aristotle as a mental catalyzer, Albert and Thomas taught men to think again.[13]

---

11. Lindberg and Numbers, *God and Nature*, "Science and Theology in the Middle Ages," by Edward Grant, p. 51. Dr. Grant is Distinguished Professor of History and Philosophy of Science at Indiana University.
12. Ibid., p. 52–53.
13. Koestler, *The Sleepwalkers*, p. 106. Koestler is evidently himself a pantheistic evolutionist of sorts. The man he calls "Albert the Great" is also known as Albertus Magnus (1193–1280), the teacher of Thomas Aquinas.

The emphasis of Platonism and Neo-Platonism, which had dominated Christian theology during the Dark Ages, was one that was built mostly on intuition and metaphysics, rather than scientific observation, to understand the workings of natural processes. Aristotle and other ancient scientists (Euclid, Archimedes, Ptolemy, Galen, etc.) were largely ignored in Western Europe during this period, although their works had been preserved by the Arabs. It was indeed a valuable service by Thomas to urge a restoration of empiricism and reason, but it was not good to do so in the context of Aristotelian pantheistic evolutionism. The so-called Enlightenment (or "Age of Reason"), which eventually followed this Renaissance, soon prostituted the new discoveries of true science to either ancient pantheism or deism.

There were several other questions about the relationship between science and the Bible that occupied the attention of the intellectuals of the late Middle Ages. In addition to the how and when of creation, there were controversies about the extent of the heavens, egocentricity, the shape of the earth, the long day of Joshua, the waters above the firmament, the possibility of other worlds, and related topics. The end result of the teachings of Augustine, Aquinas, and other well-intentioned theologians of the time was an undermining of biblical authority.

> Basic procedures for the application of science to the creation account had been laid down by Saint Augustine in his commentary on Genesis and were faithfully summarized by Saint Thomas Aquinas in the latter's own commentary on the six days of creation. . . . It is here that Augustine and Aquinas cautioned against a rigid adherence to any one interpretation lest it be shown subsequently untenable and thus prove detrimental to the faith.[14]

This freedom to interpret the creation record non-literally, if current science should so indicate, could obviously be applied anywhere else in the Bible if it became expedient to do so.

> Augustine admonished against the development of a special Christian science that would attempt to explain the literal meaning of difficult texts that conflicted with well-founded scientific truths. Such attempts would undermine the credibility of Christianity. Augustine's attitude was thus compatible with both literal and allegorical interpretations of Scripture.[15]

---

14. Grant, "Science and Theology," p. 63.
15. Ibid., p. 65.

The problem with this kind of biblical exegesis, however, is that it completely undermines the basic principle of biblical authority, since it enables the expositor to explain away any passage that seems to conflict with current scientific, philosophical, ecclesiastical, or ethical opinions. Grant writes, "During the late Middle Ages broad and liberal, rather than narrow and literal, interpretations were the rule in biblical exegesis involving physical phenomena."[16] He adds, "Indeed, the text of Holy Scripture was more often compelled to conform to the established truths of science than vice versa."[17]

It is appropriate, of course, when new scientific concepts are really established as facts rather than speculative opinions, to examine any contradictory biblical passages to see whether they have been misinterpreted. When this is done carefully and honestly, it will always be found that the *natural* interpretation (that is, the sense intended by the writer, in context) will conform to any demonstrated facts of true science. Many erroneous medieval interpretations of biblical texts (e.g., the idea of a flat earth) were wrong, not because the actual Scriptures were wrong, but because expositors had tried to explain them in terms of the then-accepted scientific idea. The Dark Ages were dark, not because Scripture discouraged scientific investigation (the "dominion mandate" of Genesis 1:26–28 actually *commands* scientific research), but because the Platonic philosophy with which the Church fathers tried to compromise did so.

In that connection, we have been using the terms *Dark Ages* and *Middle Ages* more or less synonymously, referring to the millennium from about A.D. 400 to about 1400. The terms are actually somewhat ambiguous, with various beginning and ending points, depending on different writers. Some would end the Dark Ages about A.D. 1000, extending the Middle Ages on up to as late as A.D. 1500. For our purposes here, the exact dates and names are irrelevant. The important point is that, even during the period when the biblical worldview (or, more exactly, the Catholic worldview) dominated the Christian world, evolutionism was still alive and well under the surface, in the form of certain theological compromises with earlier Greek philosophies. Evolutionism then came to the surface again in the humanistic emphases of the Renaissance and the Enlightenment periods, first in the revival of pantheism, then in deism, and finally in full-fledged atheism.

In addition, during these Dark Ages, another face of pagan pantheism was still very much present on the fringes of the institutional Christianity that dominated Western Europe. We refer here to such occultic beliefs

---

16. Ibid.
17. Ibid., p. 67.

and practices as astrology, witchcraft, magic, and even alchemy. Belief in ghosts was common, as well as in elves and fairies and such things, reflecting to some uncertain degree the reality of the same demonic powers that had been prominently active in the polytheistic aspects of ancient pantheism.

Another important component of evolutionary theory that was common all through the Middle Ages was belief in spontaneous generation. This was a prominent teaching of Aristotle, and strange to say, it continued to be promoted even by certain religious leaders (not all of course) throughout this period. Eventually disproved by Francisco Redi and Louis Pasteur, it continues to be believed — in the form of so-called abiogenesis — by practically all evolutionists today.

It may not yet be clear to the reader that these old Greek philosophies and ancient occult practices were actually manifestations of the evolutionary worldview. People today are so accustomed to identifying evolution with Darwinism that we need again to emphasize that evolutionism can take many forms. The essential attribute of an evolutionary concept is that it identifies ultimate reality with the universe of matter, space, and time, rather than with the transcendent Creator of that universe. Thus, Paul's great condemnation of the ancient pagan polytheists was that they had "worshipped and served the creature more than the Creator" (Rom. 1:25).

In the next section, we will look a little more closely at these pagan philosophies, in order to show conclusively that they were not theistic systems at all, but strictly evolutionary systems, sometimes pantheistic, sometimes atheistic. This will demonstrate again the fact that Darwin and the other 19th-century evolutionists made no great scientific discovery, but merely revived ancient paganism in a modern form.

Philosophy and Vain Deceit

It is significant that only once in the entire Bible is the word *philosophy* used. This is especially significant in view of the prominence of philosophy in the Graeco-Roman world of the New Testament and in the later theological developments of the Middle Ages, the Renaissance period, and even in modern Christianity. That one reference, of course, is Colossians 2:8: "Beware lest any man spoil you through philosophy and vain deceit, after the tradition of men, after the rudiments of the world, and not after Christ."

Many commentators have tried to skirt around the clear warning of this verse by applying it to some brand of philosophy other than the one they personally prefer. Nevertheless, the Apostle Paul was definitely concerned here with the very real doctrinal perils implicit in any form of philosophy that was man-centered ("tradition of men") or world-centered ("rudiments of the world"). The only true philosophy, if we call it that, must be Christ-centered — which means centered in the true God and Creator of all things. This would absolutely preclude any form of evolutionism or pantheism or humanism, as well as materialism or atheism. One of the great tragedies of Christian history is the perennial failure of Christian theologians and other leaders to heed the Apostle's warning here. Again and again as we have seen, Christians have been ready to compromise the biblical revelation of creation with the evolutionary philosophy then in vogue. This was especially true as the early Christians adapted to Platonism, then in the early Middle Ages to Neo-Platonism, and in the late Middle Ages to Aristotelianism, all of which were fundamentally pantheistic, humanistic, and evolutionistic.

It is not the purpose of this section to summarize the history of Graeco-Roman philosophy or to describe the distinctive features of the various philosophies that prevailed from time to time. All this is well known and is available from many other sources. What has not been done heretofore, however, is to point out the significance of the fact that *all* such philosophies have been founded on an evolutionary cosmogony — atheistic in some cases, pantheistic in others. Although certain philosophers (e.g., Plato, Aristotle) tried to combine these with the idea of a First Cause or a Prime Mover, the god that they sought to impose on the pantheism or materialism of the ancients was in no way comparable to the omnipotent, transcendent Creator revealed in the Bible. Consequently, when Christians attempted to accommodate biblical Christianity to one or another of these systems, the inevitable result was the subterranean retention and transmission of evolutionism to later generations.

The philosophy of Neo-Platonism was the system especially adapted by Augustine to Christianity. This system was mainly formulated by Plotinus (A.D. 205–270), who was born in Egypt but mostly lived in Rome. His system had high ideals but was almost pure mysticism and pantheism. Plotinus was primarily responsible for the form of the great Chain of Being as it was transmitted through the Dark Ages. In his philosophy, the whole world is the universal "soul" from which all things are "created" in a constantly descending stream. There is no true beginning and no ending, of either the cosmos or of individuals. Souls that have lived unrighteously are reincarnated in the bodies of lower animals, but there is an *eternal* striving upward toward the unattainable "Yonder."

It is a mystery how such a system could be partially equated with Christianity, as Augustine and later Catholic theologians sought to do. But that is what happened. Said the eminent Anglican theoloian W.R. Inge, who wrote a two-volume treatise on the life of Plotinus:

> It is no paradox to say with Eucken that the pagan Plotinus has left a deeper mark upon Christian thought than any other single man. In reading (his) *Enneads* we can realize the truth of Troeltsch's famous dictum, that the Catholic Church does not belong to the Middle Ages, but is rather the last creative effort of classical antiquity, which may be said to have died in giving birth to it.[18]

Before Augustine, the dominant form of Platonism that influenced such men as Clement and Origen, and which the Apostles themselves had to combat, was Gnosticism, a pseudo-Christian philosophy. After Augustine, the purely pagan Platonic philosophical religion was profoundly influential in all Christian intellectualism. A more modern scholar, D. Lindberg, agrees with Inge's assessment:

> Christianity was deeply influenced by Neoplatonic philosophy, and most Christian thinkers adopted some form of the Neoplatonic attitude. Gregory of Nyssa (c. 331–c. 396) believed deeply in the unreality and deceitfulness of the material world and yet recognized that it could provide signs and symbols that would lead mankind upward to God.[19]

Furthermore, Neoplatonism was replete with demons and other occult trappings of the animistic polytheism of ancient pantheism. Says Lindberg:

> Thus Neoplatonic authors such as Porphyry, Iamblichus, Proclus, and Damascius (third through sixth centuries) accepted the *Chaldean Oracles* (esoteric religious writings devoted to theurgy, demonology, and other forms of magic) as an authoritative source of revealed truth, beyond the reach of rational discussion and debate.[20]

As far as Gnosticism is concerned, its varied attributes were frequently critiqued by the New Testament writers. It was probably the "science falsely

---

18. W.R. Inge, "Plotinus," article in *Encyclopedia Britannica*, 1949 edition, p. 81.
19. Lindberg and Numbers, *God and Nature*, p. 31.
20. Ibid., p. 21.

so called" of Paul's sober warning (1 Tim. 6:20). The word for "science" was the Greek *gnosis*. Gnosticism was not exactly a philosophy, though it drew on many elements of Platonism. It was more of a complex of occultic religions. It originated at least a century or more before Christ and continued in various forms until into the fourth century after Christ. Many of its sects tried to incorporate Christianity into their systems, though none of them ever accepted the concepts of a transcendent Creator and the redemptive human incarnation of that Creator. Like most other Greek philosophies and religions, Gnosticism was fundamentally nothing but evolutionary pantheism, overlain with a great complex of spiritistic revelations, mystical communications with a hierarchy of angelic (actually demonic) gods, and rigid ascetic practices of its devotees (which, in some sects, however, degenerated into libertinism). In the Scale of Being, the Gnostics sought to ascend past seven hostile angel/gods to reach the divine Presence at the apex. The seventh and highest of these opposing "gods" was often equated by them with the angry Jehovah of the Hebrews, whom they must placate before they could reach the highest heaven.

> Gnosticism taught a radical discontinuity between salvation and creation, including in this latter term the present empirical world of matter. Consistently carried out, such a doctrine of discontinuity would have pushed the idea of creation so far back into history and so far down into matter that the spiritually minded Gnostic would not have to soil himself with creation at all.[21]

The early Christians opposed the Gnostics, of course, although some of them (e.g., Origen) tried to accommodate certain of their beliefs by allegorizing the Scriptures. Of greater significance in the intellectual world of the apostolic missionary movement, however, were the philosophies of the Stoics and the Epicureans.

The Roman Empire ruled the Mediterranean world during this period, but the Greek language and culture still dominated society, and the Stoic and Epicurean philosophies permeated both Greece and Rome. The Stoics were pantheists and were essentially the main heirs of Socrates, Plato, and Aristotle. The Epicureans, on the other hand, represented the tradition of the pre-Socratic philosophers and were atheistic materialists. Both systems, of course, denied special creation and were evolutionistic.

---

21. Sol Tax, editor, *Issues in Evolution*, "Creation and Causality in the History of Christian Thought," by Jaroslav Pelikan (Chicago, IL: University of Chicago Press, 1960), p. 35.

It is noteworthy that the only philosophers mentioned by name and called as such in the New Testament were these — when Paul encountered them at Athens. The account is as follows: "Then certain philosophers of the Epicureans, and of the Stoicks, encountered him. And some said, What will this babbler say? other some, He seemeth to be a setter forth of strange gods: because he preached unto them Jesus, and the resurrection" (Acts 17:18).

Obviously, the Stoics and Epicureans were opposed to Christian truth. Paul answered them by speaking first of the testimony of the created world to the omnipotence of its Creator and then of the identity of that Creator in the person of Jesus Christ, who alone could conquer man's great enemy: death. Their reaction was typical of evolutionists, even today. "And when they heard of the resurrection of the dead, some mocked: and others said, We will hear thee again of this matter. . . . Howbeit certain men clave unto him, and believed" (Acts 17:32–34). Just as today, when the whole gospel of creation/redemption/coming-judgment is preached, some will believe, many will delay, and others will mock and ridicule.

This is a dual message in which creation and Resurrection must always go together, for only the Creator *can* defeat sin and death, and the Creator *must* come to die and rise again if His purpose in creating men and women is to be accomplished. The message of creation is foundational to that of redemption but is incomplete without it. And only the omnipotent, transcendent, holy, yet gracious and loving God can be *either* Creator or Redeemer as well as coming Judge.

Our purpose here is merely to confirm that these two eminent systems of Graeco-Roman philosophy were evolutionary in essence. In an extensive historical review published about the time of the Scopes trial, Professor L.T. More, of the University of Cincinnati, gave the following evaluation:

> After Aristotle's death, Greek thought gradually divided into the two schools of the Stoics and the Epicureans. . . . As these two schools held the world of thought in allegiance well into the Roman Empire and exerted much influence on Christian writers, their ideas of science and evolution are very important.
>
> The Epicureans were materialistic monists without any reservations. . . . The Stoics were also materialistic monists but of a less thoroughgoing type.[22]

---

22. Louis Trenchard More, *The Dogma of Evolution* (Princeton, NJ: Princeton University Press, 1925), p. 67. This book was a series of lectures given by Dr. More at Princeton University in January 1925.

The "monist" appellation refers to those who believe only in the world of physical matter, with no nonmaterial entities existing of any kind that cannot in principle be incorporated into the realm of matter and its actions.

Epicurus (342–270 B.C.) to some extent was a follower of Aristotle, who died when Epicurus was still a young man. However, Epicurus denied that there was any purposive force in nature. He believed in an infinite number of worlds, but no gods. Everything on the earth had evolved directly from the earth material itself, according to Epicurus and his followers.

The most prominent Epicurean was not a Greek but a Roman, Titus Lucretius Carus (98–55 B.C.), known now simply as Lucretius. He was a Roman poet, author of *De Rerum Natura,* a six-volume work of great influence. His materialistic beliefs are expressed in the following:

> Certainly the atoms did not post themselves purposefully in due order by an act of intelligence, nor did they stipulate what movements each should perform. As they have been rushing everlastingly throughout all space in their myriads, undergoing myriad changes under the disturbing impact of collisions, they have experienced every variety of movement and conjunction till they have fallen into the particular pattern by which this world of ours is constituted. This world has persisted many a long year, having once been set going in the appropriate motions. From these everything else follows.[23]

This type of reasoning led Lucretius — just like modern evolutionary cosmogonists — to postulate an infinitude of worlds in various stages of growth and decay, all accomplished by this infinite field of randomly moving elementary particles. Even though he dedicated his poem to the goddess Venus and prayed her favor upon it, he apparently did not really believe that the gods and goddesses could do anything about creating or sustaining the universe: "Bear this well in mind and you will immediately perceive that *nature is free and uncontrolled by proud masters and runs the universe by herself without the aid of gods*"[24] (emphasis his).

Interestingly, Lucretius seemed to anticipate the two modern scientific laws of conservation and decay:

---

23. Lucretius, *The Nature of the Universe,* translated by R.E. Latham (New York: Penguin, 1951). Reprinted in *Theories of the Universe,* Milton K. Munitz, editor (Glencoe, IL: The Free Press, 1957), p. 53. Lucretius also believed in a purely naturalistic development of men and animals from the earth.

24. Ibid., p. 56.

I have taught you that things cannot be created out of nothing nor, once born, be summoned back to nothing.[25]

It is natural, therefore, that everything should perish when it is thinned out by the ebbing of matter and succumbs to blows from without. . . .

In this way the ramparts of the great world also will be breached and collapse in crumbling ruins about us. Already it is far past its prime. The earth, which generated every living species and once brought forth from its womb the bodies of huge beasts, has now scarcely strength to generate animalcules. For I assume that the races of mortal creatures were not let down into the fields from heaven by a golden cord, nor generated from the sea or the rock-bearing surf, but born of the same earth that now provides their nurture. . . . Everything is gradually decaying and nearing its end, worn out by old age.[26]

The Epicureans were also known for their belief that pleasure was the chief good of existence. Initially supporting high ethical ideals and moderation in lifestyle, they became more and more identified with a strong emphasis on materialistic accumulation of goods and pleasures.

Stoics, on the other hand, stressed the simple life and submission to whatever circumstances life might present. They believed in the beauty and orderliness of the world as an evidence of God, but their concept of God was purely pantheistic:

After endless and profitless circumlocutions the Stoics reconcile the two antinomies by identifying God with the active force. The result is a pure pantheism in which matter is vitalized because God has implanted in it from the beginning a *ratio seminalis,* or rational seed. Having once made a start the cosmos develops according to natural law in succession of time.[27]

Since these ancient philosophers knew very little about the fossil record, they did not try to develop the Lyell/Darwin system of step-by-step upward evolution over geological ages. They were true evolutionists nevertheless, believing in some form of natural generation of living creatures out of earth materials, possibly also as "emanations" from the cosmos.

The Stoics were essentially continuing the pantheistic systems of Plato and Aristotle and, even before them, Pythagoras. Lindberg explains:

25. Ibid., p. 46.
26. Ibid., p. 57.
27. More, *The Dogma of Evolution,* p. 68.

In antiquity there was a broad spectrum of attitudes toward the material world. At one end of the spectrum was pagan cosmic religion, constructed from a mixture of Pythagorean, Platonic, Aristotelian, and Stoic doctrines. This cosmic religion saw the material cosmos, or at least its upper heavenly part, as a perfect expression of divine creativity and providence "the supreme manifestation of divinity," and indeed itself a divine being.[28]

The most famous and influential philosophers of all were Plato (422–347 B.C.) and his student and successor, Aristotle (384–322 B.C.). Plato in turn had been a student of Socrates (469–399 B.C.). All three believed in a supreme God and in creation, and this belief provided the rationale used by so many Christians later to try to accommodate these philosophies within the framework of Christian theology.

Nevertheless, their concept of God was not at all the same as that of biblical revelation. Socrates left no written expositions, but Plato discussed his teachings and left voluminous writings. Plato's cosmology has been expressed in his famous dialogue, *Timaeus,* in which he combines both purpose and chance as his explanation of the cosmos. But that is not all.

> Plato also makes use of another analogical pattern of thought in describing the universe as an all-inclusive Living Creature, one whose body is perfectly spherical and whose soul animates the whole world. In addition to this World-Soul, the various individual heavenly bodies are regarded by Plato as divine beings.[29]

Such a view of creation is indistinguishable from pantheism. From this World-Soul "emanated" in descending fashion the entire Scale of Being. Explains Koestler:

> "Change" for Plato is virtually synonymous with degeneration; his history of creation is a story of the successive emergence of ever lower and less worthy forms of life — from God who is pure self-contained Goodness, to the World of Reality which consists only of perfect Forms or Ideas, to the World of Appearances, which is a shadow and copy of the former; and so down to man.[30]

---

28. Lindberg and Numbers, *God and Nature,* p. 30. Lindberg regarded Gnosticism, with its belief that the world was fully evil, as the other end of the spectrum.
29. Munitz, *Theories of the Universe,* p. 61.
30. Koestler, *The Sleepwalkers,* p. 55.

For Plato, the process of evolution was a combination of degeneration and reincarnation. He taught, for example, that cowardly and unjust men were reborn as women. Quoting from Plato's *Timaeus,* Koestler says, "After the women we come to the animals. 'Beasts who go on all fours came from men who were wholly unconversant with philosophy and had never gazed on the heavens.' It is a tale of the Fall in permanence: a theory of *descent* and *devolution* — as opposed to evolution by ascent"[31] (emphasis his).

Aristotle, as a young man, followed the teachings of Plato, his mentor. Later Aristotle became tutor to the young prince who would eventually become known as Alexander the Great. As Aristotle grew older, his philosophy became more materialistic and empirical than that of Plato, and his concept of God grew more and more impersonal. Instead of a divine Spirit, he began to think of God as an impersonal Prime Mover that had set the universe in motion. Aristotle did not believe in the transmutation of established species, but he continued to believe, like Plato, that they had all originally "devolved," one from the other, in a descending Scale of Being as emanations from the primal World-Soul, which increasingly became identified essentially as just the World.

> Aristotle believed in a complete gradation in Nature, a progressive development corresponding with the progressive life of the soul. . . . He put his facts together into an Evolution system which had the teaching of Plato and Socrates for its primary philosophical basis.[32]

In particular, Aristotle believed in an uncreated cosmos, as well as in the spontaneous generation of small organisms from nonorganic materials.

> Like his master Plato, Aristotle insists there is but one world, that is a central body like the earth surrounded by a finite number of planets and stars. This one world, of course, which makes up the entire universe, contains all existent matter. . . . Aristotle argues that the one world or universe we know is eternal, without beginning and without end.[33]

It was to Plato and Aristotle — not to the Bible — that the theologians and scientists of the Middle Ages owed their concept of a geocentric, three-storied universe. Although the Bible teaches no such thing, Aristotle did — and the scholasticism of this period was very largely derived from him. Copernicus and Galileo both believed the Bible, but their heliocentric system had to overcome Aristotelianism before it could be accepted.

---

31. Ibid.
32. Osborn, *From the Greeks to Darwin*, p. 48.
33. Munitz, *Theories of the Universe*, p. 63–64.

Plato and Aristotle also argued against the atomism of their predecessors, who had envisioned an infinitude of worlds evolving and deteriorating throughout the universe, all caused by nothing but the random collisions of the ubiquitous atoms. They correctly argued that the evidence of design in nature demonstrated a great intelligence behind it all, whereas the pre-Socratic atomists (as well as the later Epicureans) were atheistic materialists who believed in no real gods at all. Nevertheless, since they stopped far short of identifying this Intelligence, or World-Soul, as a transcendent Creator, their systems finally amount to little more than evolutionary pantheism.

As we proceed on back in time to the early Greek philosophers before Socrates, we find an even more modern-sounding evolutionary system. In the introduction to his history of evolutionism, anthropologist Henry Fairfield Osborn, longtime director of the American Museum of Natural History, said, "When I began the search for anticipations of the evolutionary theory . . . I was led back to the Greek natural philosophers and I was astonished to find how many of the pronounced and basic features of the Darwinian theory were anticipated even as far back as the seventh century B.C."[34]

These earlier philosophers arose in the city of Miletus in Ionia in Asia Minor, so their system is often called the Milesian, or Ionian, philosophy. Thales (640–546 B.C.) was the founder of this school and, in fact, is usually considered the father of Greek philosophy. His pupil Anaximander (611–547 B.C.) continued and elaborated his system, along with his own associate Anaximenes. Anaximander, in turn, taught the famous Pythagoras (580–495 B.C.).

Milton K. Munitz, professor of philosophy of science at New York University, summarized the Milesian teachings as follows:

> The type of thinking initiated by the Milesian school of pre-Socratic thinkers — Thales, Anaximander, and Anaximenes — in the sixth century B.C. was carried forward in many directions. One of the most remarkable outcomes of such speculations, representing a culmination of their materialistic thought, was to be found in the Atomist school. Originally worked out in its main features by Leucippus and Democritus in the fifth century B.C., the teachings of atomism were later adopted as a basis for the primarily ethical philosophy of Epicureanism. . . . It elaborates the conception of a

---

34. Osborn, *From the Greeks to Darwin*, p. xi.

universe whose order arises out of a blind interplay of atoms rather than as a product of deliberate design; of a universe boundless in spatial extent, infinite in its duration and containing innumerable worlds in various stages of development or decay. It was this concept of an infinite and, at bottom, irrational universe against which Plato, Aristotle, and the whole tradition of theologically oriented thought in Western culture set themselves in sharp and fundamental opposition. It was the same conception, however, which once more came into the foreground of attention at the dawn of modern thought and has remained up to the present time an inspiration for those modes of scientific thinking that renounce any appeal to teleology in the interpretation of physical phenomena.[35]

This materialistic philosophy, originating over 2,500 years ago, would have to be changed very little to conform to the basic ideas of modern evolutionary cosmogonists. The theory of evolution is not the epochal discovery of modern science that modern evolutionists like to proclaim it to be. It has been around a long, long time!

> The Milesian system pushed back to the very beginning of things the operation of processes as familiar and ordinary as a shower of rain. It made the formation of the world no longer a supernatural, but a natural event. Thanks to the Ionians, and to no one else, this has become the universal premise of all modern science.[36]

Many other philosophers contributed to this naturalistic philosophy in the two centuries between Thales and Plato. A partial list would include Xenophanes, Anaxagoras, Heraclitus, Empedocles, Democritus, and Leucippus. Thales and Anaximander taught that men evolved from animals, animals from plants, plants from inorganic elements, and all these from water. Xenophanes argued, on the basis of fossil shells on mountains, that land animals had evolved from marine animals. Both Heraclitus and Empedocles held that random changes led to development, which involved a form of struggle for existence and natural selection, long anticipating Darwin.

Democritus (460–362 B.C.) was of special significance in developing the "atomist school," teaching that all things were made of fundamental indivisible particles, which he called "atoms" (he coined the word, in fact). Wrote

---

35. Munitz, *Theories of the Universe*, p. 6.
36. F.M. Cornford, *Principium Sapientiae*, "Patterns of Ionian Cosmology" (Cambridge University Press, 1952), reprinted in Munitz, *Theories of the Universe*, p. 21.

L. T. More: "If evolutionists must find a cornerstone in Greek philosophy for their doctrine, they should give this honor to Democritus. His doctrine of mechanical and atomistic monism in which all phenomena are reduced to material particles moving according to natural law is, in the real sense of the word, modern science."[37]

All these ancient atheistic philosophers, as well as the ancient pantheistic philosophers (Pythagoras, Plato, Aristotle, etc.), were highly intelligent men and made many great contributions to science, mathematics, and general learning. Nevertheless, all rejected the true God of creation and promoted one or another evolutionist system of cosmogony and primeval life history.

The evolutionary philosophy that completely dominates the modern Western world has now been traced all the way back to ancient Greek philosophy, beginning about 2,500 years ago. We need to travel still further back, however, before we reach the ultimate source of this deadly system. Thales, the first of the Greek philosophers, did not invent his materialistic philosophy out of thin air. As we shall see later, Greek mythology and the mythologies of other nations all contributed to these philosophies.

At this point, however, we also need to look at other nations — those in the non-Christian world as well as those in so-called Christendom. Their religions and their histories are also of high importance in coming to a real understanding of both world history and the present world situation.

God and the Nations

The nations of the Western world (Europe, North and South America) have been nominally Christian and committed to the authority of the Bible for many centuries. Unfortunately, this commitment has been mostly superficial. As shown earlier, most educational systems in these nations are permeated with evolutionism. This is not a new development for, as we have also seen, evolutionism has actually been handed down, generation after generation, from the philosophers of ancient Greece. There has always been a conflict between true biblical creationism and some form of evolutionism in these ostensibly Christian nations.

But what about the other nations and religions of the world? What is their relation to the God of creation? If those nations that at least claimed to know Him, through His coming into the world and His written Word, have largely rejected Him in favor of evolution, how much further away from God must these other nations have fallen! Many of these countries are

---

37. More, *The Dogma of Evolution*, p. 48.

committed to such atheistic religions as Buddhism and Confucianism and now also Communism. Others follow pantheistic religions, such as Hinduism and animism. Some follow monotheistic religions, Judaism and Islam, for example. We will find that all of these have long ago rejected the true God of creation and redemption, even though their forefathers once knew Him, and even though He has always been accessible to any individuals in those nations who desired to find Him.

In this section, we shall look only at those aspects of the great national or international religions having to do with origins and primeval history, showing that these also are founded upon some form of evolution. We immediately note with some surprise that the sixth century B.C., the period of the founding philosophers of the Greek evolutionary systems, was also the century when many other religions were being established in other parts of the world. This was the time of Confucius (551–479 B.C.); of Lao-Tse, the founder of Taoism (about 604–517 B.C.); of Buddha (563–480 B.C.); of Mahavira, the founder of Jainism (599–527 B.C.); and of Zoroaster (around 600 B.C.). Although Hinduism is much older, its best-known school of thought, the Vedanta, also dates from the sixth century B.C. In terms of biblical history, this age was the time of Judah's Babylonian captivity and the last of the Old Testament Scriptures, just prior to the "400 silent years" that preceded the coming of Christ. It is significant that all of these new religious philosophies introduced during this period — whether in Greece or India or China — were more rationalistic than those they displaced. The older systems, based largely on mythologies, had been mainly animistic and polytheistic, but in most cases they did retain a dim tradition of a "high God" who was above all other gods and had created the world in the beginning. But the new religions of Thales and Confucius, of Buddha and Lao-Tse, tried to eliminate Him altogether.

Consider first the religions of China, the nation with the world's largest population. It is well known that Confucianism was strictly ethical, political, and pragmatic in its teachings. Confucius did not deal at all with "God," the supernatural, or life after death. A few passing references in his writings, however, indicate that he did accept at least nominally the traditional Chinese belief in a high God (Shang Ti) and heaven (T'ien), though these concepts often seem also to be associated merely with "Nature" and "the sky." Confucius strongly endorsed ancestor worship, which concept often became no different in practice from tribal animism.

A very definite and careful analysis of the Chinese idea of god, as found in all the classics, has even caused a number of investigators to declare the "deity" of the China of Confucius to consist in a mechanism of nature, living indeed and with a certain personality, but in reality a mere pantheistic machine. The Chang[Shang]-ti-Ti'en of Confucius is the highest, the driving force of nature, which embraces both the spiritual and the material and expresses itself in the eternal laws of being and activity.[38]

As far as the traditional religion that Confucius tacitly accepted is concerned, it was thoroughly evolutionist in its cosmology. At the time of the Darwinian Centennial in 1959, the definitive paper on evolutionism in the Far East was given by Ilza Veith, professor of the history of medicine at the University of Chicago. She said:

> In contrast to the Western world, the Far Eastern philosophers thought of creation in evolutionary terms. . . .
>
> The striking feature of the Chinese concept of cosmogony is the fact that creation was never associated with the design or activity of a supernatural being, but rather with the interaction of impersonal forces, the powers of which persist interminably.[39]

A more recent writer, David L. Johnson, chairman of the humanities division at Indiana State University, concurs: "From very early times the Chinese assumed views of the world that differ significantly from the thinkers of India or the thinkers of Western societies. The first of these is the presupposition that the universe originated by some natural process. . . . The universe is to be explained in terms of itself, its own ways of operating, and its own power or forces."[40]

This concept of evolution was not limited merely to the primeval cosmos but extended also to animals and humans. Dr. Veith writes:

> Though completely fanciful, this ladder of nature is noteworthy because it was conceived more than two millennia before the Western world began to re-examine its biblical chronology. But, beyond this, the above-quoted passage contains two highly important

---

38. P.E. Kretzman, *The God of the Bible and Other Gods* (St. Louis, MO: Concordia, 1943), p. 102.

39. Tax, *Issues in Evolution*, "Creation and Evolution in the Far East," by Ilza Veith, p. 2.

40. David L. Johnson, *A Reasoned Look at Asian Religions* (Minneapolis, MN: Bethany House, 1985), p. 27–28. The author holds a PhD in the history of religions from the University of Iowa.

points: first, a belief in an inherent continuity of all creation and, second, a reference to the merging of one specie into another — from primordial germ to man.[41]

Confucianism was rivaled for centuries in China by Taoism, a more pantheistic and often occultic religion developed around the writings of Lao-Tse, another sage of that period. It was also an evolutionary religion, built around the concept of "the Way," or *Tao*, which stressed the bipolar duality of the concept of Yin and Yang, as embracing everything in the universe.

> But the one organic whole which is the universe and its way carries polar forces called *Yin* and *Yang*. . . . *Yin* is characteristic in nature which expresses itself through femininity, passivity, coolness, darkness, wetness, earthiness. Water is almost a complete expression of *yin*. . . . *Yang*, on the other hand, exhibits characteristics of masculinity, activity, heat, light, dryness, and heavenliness (the bright blue sky, for example). Fire is almost a complete expression of *yang*.[42]

Note that this concept of cosmogony is not only pantheistic but also expresses its pantheism in terms of the two primordial elements: water and fire.

The great religion of Buddhism, established by Gautama, the Buddha ("the enlightened one"), also became very prominent in China, even though it originated in India. As a missionary religion, it became dominant not only in China but also — in various forms — in the various Indo-Chinese nations, Indonesia, Ceylon, Tibet, Nepal, and even Japan. It was eventually driven out of India, however. In China it more or less merged with Confucianism and Taoism, so that the religion of the typical Chinese citizen for centuries was a mixture of all three, along with a strong admixture of ancestor worship and animism thrown in — at least until the entrance of modern Darwinism and then Marxism in the 20th century.

Many writers have noted that the relatively easy entrance of Marxism and communism into Chinese thought and life was greatly facilitated by the prior entrance of Darwinism, which in turn had been smoothed by the long compatibility of the Chinese religions with evolutionary ways of thinking (refer, for example, to the previous discussions earlier in this chapter).

---

41. Tax, *Issues in Evolution*, p. 7. Dr. Veith was quoting from a Chinese mystic philosopher, Chuang-Tzu, writing about 300 B.C.
42. Johnson, *A Reasoned Look*, p. 51–52.

Some of the writings of Thomas Huxley had been translated into Chinese before the turn of the century and soon became widely read and believed. Veith observes: "But it was Darwinism, speaking through Huxley, and made to appear organically related to ancient Chinese thought on evolution, that furnished the intellectual basis for China's great upheaval beginning in 1911."[43] That upheaval, generated by the introduction of Darwinism, led ultimately to Mao Tse-tung and the slaughter of millions in China as communism became established there. Even before that development, World War I caused an outstanding Chinese scholar to raise doubts, back in 1920:

> This great European war has nearly wiped out human civilization; although its causes were very many, it must be said that the Darwinian theory had a very great influence. Even in China in recent years, where throughout a whole country men struggle for power, grasp for gain, and seem to have gone crazy, although they understand nothing of scholarship, yet the things they say to shield themselves from condemnations are regularly drawn from Yen Fu's translation of T.H. Huxley's *Principles of Evolution*. One can see that the influence of theory on men's minds is enormous.[44]

Buddhism is important not only because of its dominant influence in China and other Oriental nations, but also because of its increasing impact in the West in recent years. Our interest at this point, of course, has to do only with its concept of God and creation. Many of the Buddha's followers later made a "god" out of him, but neither Gautama nor his system had any place for God at all when he developed it.

> God in the objective, personal sense does not fit into the system. . . . Buddhism as taught by its founders is in no sense a system of faith and worship. He inculcated neither prayer nor praise, he offered neither redemption, nor forgiveness, nor heaven; he warned of no judgment and no hell. He refused to speculate on ultimate reality or the First Cause which originated the long, long chain of cause and effect, for that of which the universe is the outward form is far beyond human understanding.[45]

---

43. Tax, *Issues in Evolution*, p. 16.
44. Reported by Ssu-yii Teng and John K. Fairbank in *China's Response to the West* (Cambridge, MA: Harvard University Press, 1954), p. 267. Cited in Tax, *Issues in Evolution*, p. 16–17.
45. J.N.D. Anderson, editor, *The World's Religions*, "Buddhism," by David Bentley Taylor (London: Inter-Varsity Press, 1950), p. 126. The editor was a professor in the School of Oriental and African Studies, University of London.

Prominent in Buddhism is the doctrine of *karma,* a system of rigid cause-and-effect whereby one's deeds in any given incarnation are precisely reflected in his situation in his next incarnation. However, there is no mention by Gautama of how the whole process began. On the other hand, there have been many later sects in Buddhism, and some of these do speak of a beginning, but all in pantheistic terms exclusively. All modern varieties of Buddhism have easily adjusted to modern scientific evolutionism. It is possible that Gautama implicitly thought in terms of the Hindu cosmogony that he had been taught in his early life, even though he never mentioned it in his own writings.

> But where is the idea of god, of a supreme being, in the system? The answer, so far as Buddha's personal teaching is concerned, is that *his religion, theoretically at least,* is atheistic: there was no place in it for a god or gods. Yet the background of theological thought is evident in many precepts of Buddha's teaching, and in much of his later teaching mention is made of the sublime gods.[46]

Shinto, the state religion of Japan, is a conglomerate of Buddhism and the ancient polytheistic myths of the Japanese people, which taught that they were all descendants of the gods and were destined to rule the world. The emperor is supposed to be a direct descendant of the highest god, the sun-god. Even the small professing Christian population of Japan has been profoundly influenced by both Shintoism and religious liberalism. All of these belief systems have largely adapted to modern "scientific" evolutionism, which is now taught in all the schools. Statistics now show that much less than ten percent of the Japanese people believe in original special creation.

Whether Buddhism is atheistic or pantheistic, it is at least true that all of its many sects are one or the other. Therefore, whether or not they ever spell out an explicit cosmogony, they must be basically evolutionary: without a transcendent Creator, there is no alternative. It is noteworthy that Colonel H.S. Olcott, one of the founders of Theosophy, which is a modern quasi-Buddhist cult, undertook to codify what he called a "Buddhist Platform," upon which all Buddhists can agree. The second of these fundamental Buddhist beliefs was stated as follows: "The Universe was evolved, not created; and it functions according to law, not according to the caprice of any God."[47] The

---

46. Kretzman, *The God of the Bible and Other Gods*, p. 71, emphasis his.
47. Christmas Humphreys, *Buddhism* (London: Penguin, 1951), p. 71. Cited in *Handbook of Today's Religions* by Josh McDowell and Don Stewart (San Bernardino, CA: Here's Life Publishers, 1983), p. 311.

representatives of all or most of the different Buddhist sects of the world reviewed this "catechism" and approved it, so this could be considered as a quasi-official commitment to evolutionism by at least modern-day Buddhism.

Hinduism — until recent years, at least, when some of its sects have acquired significant followings in the West — has been confined to India throughout its long history. Because it is divided into a great number of sects, it almost defies description. Nevertheless, all of its sects are basically pantheistic and thus evolutionistic. The concept of essentially unending transmigration of souls is present in all its varieties, but the primeval beginning of this dismal *karma* system is not so clear.

> Hindu philosophy developed along two lines, known as the Sankhya and the Vedanta. The Sankhya is dualistic and in reality atheistic. It denies the existence of any beginning, or of a creator, but postulates two eternal realities, *atman* and *prakriti*. . . . The former is the complete abstraction, the ultimate soul of the universe, which neither produces nor is produced. The latter, through a series of developments, produces the world which we see and know. . . . At the end of each cosmic period all things are dissolved into their original elements, and so into prakriti, after which the whole evolutionary process begins again.[48]

The Vedanta system, on the other hand, is non-dualistic, assuming the *atman* to incorporate both soul and matter in one unity. It has been the most widely accepted school of thought in traditional Hinduism. In both the Vedanta and Sankhya systems, however, it is the *prakriti* "stuff" from which the universe evolves. D.L. Johnson elaborates:

> The whole of the universe as we know it (everything from shoes to ships) evolved out of the basic material stuff, *prakriti*. Prior to evolution into what things are evolving into today, matter was inert, undifferentiated, quiescent. It was simply a huge, globlike mass of material stuff. . . .
>
> Each individual human being is part of the cosmic process which began some time ago and which will continue as a process because the essential elements of matter became unbalanced. . . .
>
> The human being is tied to the world of evolving matter. Each person becomes a person as part of a determined evolutionary process.[49]

---

48. Anderson, *World's Religions*, "Hinduism," by G.T. Manley and A.S. Neech, p. 108.
49. Johnson, *A Reasoned Look at Asian Religions*, p. 87–88.

The variant modern offshoots of Hinduism, including those that have become popular in the West, will not be discussed here, but all are pantheistic and evolutionistic. These, along with the other Eastern religions that have experienced a Western resurgence (Buddhism, Taoism, etc.), have been incorporated into the New Age movement. As already noted, this complex of systems and organizations is completely dominated by evolutionary philosophy.

Jainism is a heretical offshoot of orthodox Hinduism. Its founder, Mahavira, so reacted against Hindu polytheism that he denied the existence of any gods at all. The later Jainists, however, in effect eventually deified their founder. Another Hindu heresy, Sikhism, was founded by Nanak about A.D. 1500, incorporating in it certain elements of Islam. Although the Sikhs profess to believe in one God, that God can take on so many manifestations that their nominal monotheism quickly takes on all the character of pantheism, just as in many other forms of Hinduism. Furthermore, the founder, Nanak, soon came to be worshiped essentially as a deity himself. Its message of salvation is likewise pantheistic.

"This method of obtaining salvation by a pantheistic merging of the individual self with the mystical world soul is identical with the method of salvation which had been taught in the Hindu Upanishads,"[50] writes R.E. Hume, who calls Sikhism a "monistic pantheism." Both Jainism and Sikhism, like Buddhism and Hinduism, teach the doctrines of *karma* and reincarnation, with "salvation" essentially nothing but *nirvana*, the deliverance from the endless chain of transmigrations and new existences into complete cessation of all individual consciousness.

What about animism? This is the very widespread worshipful belief in spirits (both human and demonic) as real entities distinct from the bodies they may or may not inhabit.

> As such, it is not only the religion of wild and savage tribes before contact with civilization, but the background of the religious philosophy of the Hindu, the Buddhist, the Shintoist, the Confucianist, and the Muslim, and is at the bottom of all the folklore of Christendom in Europe, as well as of the mythology of Egypt, Babylonia and Assyria, Greece, Rome and Scandinavia. In America, before the conquests by Spain and Portugal, we find Animism in a highly developed form as the religion of the Aztecs of Mexico and the Incas of Peru.[51]

---

50. Robert E. Hume, *The World's Living Religions* (New York: Scribner's 1959), p. 103.
51. Anderson, *World's Religions*, "Animism," by A.T. Houghton, p. 9. Spirit worship can include spirits of men and animals, especially the dead, as well as spirits of angels or demons influencing human activities or even natural phenomena.

The degree of sophistication of different groups of animists varies widely from place to place and time to time. In most all cases, however, the dominant motivation of animistic religions is that of fear. The animism of savage tribes is a simple form of polytheism, whereas that of pagan Greece and Rome was an elaborate pantheism, expressed on a high philosophical plane, involving both occult "mysteries" for the initiates and idol worship for the common people. The same is true in India and other Eastern nations today. There is often some form of personal communication with spirits, whether through the oracle in a temple, the ecstatic state in a dervish or witchdoctor, or the medium in a séance. An increasingly common experience today, even in Christian lands, is direct conversation with alleged spirits in a person possessed. This is much too complex a subject, however, to try to discuss in this connection.

Our concern here is only with the cosmogony of animism. Here again, the "primitive" tribes may put forth rather naive stories about how the world developed and how people were made — in contrast to those of the ancient Greeks and Hindus, who thought in terms of sophisticated cosmogonies centered around pantheistic emanations. Most of these are also evolutionary in essence, however, because they always start with pre-existing materials or creatures of some kind. This must always be true of religions that are pantheistic or polytheistic (which is really the same thing). The universe is itself the sum total of reality in such systems and so has either always existed or is "creating" itself.

Two prominent 19th-century anthropologists, Sir Edward Tylor and Sir James Frazer, popularized the notion that animism was merely the first stage in the evolution of religion by primitive man, to be followed by polytheism and eventually by monotheism. This evolutionary notion has since been displaced, however, by the ubiquitous evidence that even the most "savage" tribes today, as well as the very earliest traditions of the nations of the past (Egypt, Sumeria, India, China, Greece, etc.), manifest an original belief in a high God who originally made the world. In other words, within animistic tribes and cultures, their primitive monotheism had degenerated into pantheism, then polytheism, and finally into crude animism. One writer concludes, "But though every known tribe recognizes the existence of a Creator, with varying mythological views of His character and the story of creation, there seems to have been a universal departure from the worship of the Creator."[52]

The ancient creation-evolution conflict has thus been part of the age-long background of every animistic tribe or culture, and creationism has long

---

52. Ibid., p. 22.

been almost (but not quite) forgotten. A firsthand observer notes: "The Animism of today gives us the impression of a religion that carries the marks of a fall, of a worship no longer understood, and become an empty ceremony."[53] Evolutionary anthropologists have thus badly missed the mark in their attempt to understand the animistic religions of the "primitive" tribes. Such tribes are not primitive at all, but the result of many centuries of departure from the true God of creation, descending deeper and deeper into the morass of evolutionary pantheism.

Finally, of course, there are a few monotheistic religions that are committed at least theoretically to creationism. In addition to Christianity, which has already been discussed in detail, there are many nations that adhere to the religion of Islam. There is also Judaism, the religion of Israel and of the Jewish communities in a hundred other nations. A much smaller quasi-monotheistic religion is Zoroastrianism, once the religion of the great Medo-Persian Empire, but now of only a very small remnant in India, Iran, and Pakistan.

Zoroastrianism, though of little significance today, was the religion of the Persians (including the great kings Darius and Cyrus) while the Jews were their captives in the Medo-Persian Empire. It was probably also the religion of the Magi who came seeking the newborn Christ in Bethlehem. These all seemed to acknowledge the God of the Jews as the true God of heaven, with the Persians perhaps identifying Him with Ahura-Mazda, the God of Zoroaster. Nevertheless, though Zoroaster was supposed to have received his religion by special revelation, the new system was actually dualistic rather than monotheistic, with Satan (or Ahriman) equally eternal and powerful with God. Furthermore, the popular-level Zoroastrianism eventually disintegrated again into a practical polytheism, with Zoroaster himself being deified by later generations.

Of much greater importance is Islam, founded by Mohammed in A.D. 622. In a similar experience to that of Zoroaster long before, Mohammed wanted to replace the popular polytheism of Arabia with a strict monotheism, the essentials of which (also like Zoroaster) he claimed were revealed to him by angelic visitations. His system was much influenced by both Judaism and Christianity. For example, Mohammed accepted the biblical account of creation and Jesus as a true prophet sent from God. In one sense, Islam is a Judeo-Christian heretical offshoot — but it soon became, and has

---

53. Johann Warneck, *The Living Forces of the Gospel* (London: Oliphant, Anderson, and Ferrier, 1909), p. 99. The author of this book spent a lifetime of missionary work among primitive Indonesians, so he knew animism firsthand.

remained, one of the world's most powerful anti-Christian religio-political systems.

As far as cosmogony is concerned, there is no doubt that Mohammed's "divinely inspired" Koran accepts the Genesis account of creation. Mohammed even mentions with full endorsement the six days of creation, taking them literally. Like Judaism, Islam at least seems to be an authentic creationist religion, with the *Allah* of Islam being equivalent to the *Elohim* of the Old Testament.

There is a great deficiency, however, in both Judaism and Islam. They refuse to recognize that the Creator must also become the only Redeemer and Savior, a mission that can only be accomplished through a divine incarnation, sinless human life, substitutionary death, and bodily resurrection of the Creator Himself.

Furthermore, great numbers of nominal Muslims and Jews, like multitudes of nominal Christians throughout the centuries, have been quick to compromise with the humanistic philosophers around them, becoming theistic evolutionists or even pantheists. In the early days of Islamic expansion, for example, many of their philosophers tried to incorporate the teachings of Plato and Aristotle into their system. Sir Norman Anderson writes:

> These men seem for the most part to have started from the position of sincere Muslims; but they also wholeheartedly accepted Greek philosophy, with all its contradictory theories, as part of the very form of truth. . . . So to reconcile them they set out, with unconquerable spirit: and it was largely through these men that the philosophy and learning of ancient Greece was preserved and reintroduced into Europe.[54]

Even more influential than the Muslim philosophers have been the Muslim mystics, of which there has been a great variety through the centuries. Many of these seemed to exhibit a deep and sacrificial love for Allah, but mysticism easily leads to pantheism and occultism. Anderson continues:

> But mysticism soon began to develop along more speculative and philosophical lines. In this development it owed something to the Greek Church; a good deal to Persian and, ultimately, Indian

---

54. Sir Norman Anderson, *The World's Religions,* "Islam" (Grand Rapids, MI: Zondervan, 1975), p. 73.

influences; but most of all to Plotinus and the Neo-Platonists. It was only by refuge in mysticism that the Muslim philosopher could reconcile the crudities of the Qur'an with the abstractions of Greek philosophy.[55]

Others were not content to claim divine enlightenment, they claimed the very fusion and union of their beings with God. For them the Transcendental God of orthodox Islam was deposed, to be replaced by the Only Reality of the Pantheist.[56]

And from pantheism, one comes inevitably to evolutionism, or even atheism.

The great Princeton scholar B.B. Warfield compellingly argued almost a century ago that mysticism is easily transformed into rationalism, and vice versa. In effect, Muslim mysticism (as well as mysticism in other religions) is often a pseudo-spiritual form of rationalism, amounting eventually to humanism and self-worship as it replaces God's revelation with introspective feelings.

As Benjamin B. Warfield remarked: "Once turn away from revelation and little choice remains to you but the choice between mysticism and rationalism. . . . Warm up a rationalist and you find yourself with a mystic on your hands. The history of thought illustrates repeatedly the passage from one to the other. Each centers himself in himself, and the human self is not so big that it makes any large difference where within yourself you take your center."[57]

Mohammed himself, with his presumed visions and revelations, was something of a mystic, and there is legitimate reason to wonder whether or not his "angelic" visitations were really from God. Dr. Anderson observes:

It seems, however, that Mohammed himself was at first doubtful of the source of these revelations, fearing that he was possessed by one of the Jinns, or sprites, as was commonly believed to be the case with Arab poets and soothsayers. But Khadija [that is, his wife, fifteen years older than he] and others reassured him,

---

55. Ibid., p. 75.
56. Ibid., p. 76.
57. Samuel M. Zwemer, *Heirs of the Prophets* (Chicago, IL: Moody, 1946), p. 109. Dr. Warfield had been an older colleague of Dr. Zwemer at Princeton. Zwemer himself spent 38 years as a missionary to the Muslims of Arabia and Egypt and was professor of missions and history of religion at Princeton.

and he soon began to propound divine revelations with increasing frequency.[58]

Similarly, an authority on the history of Mohammed and Islam, Professor D.S. Margoliouth, argued that "there is reason to believe that his symptoms of revelation (the descriptions of which closely resemble epilepsy) were artificially produced and that certain accompanying effects were at times stage-managed."[59] Anderson goes on to note: "Alternatively, of course, the phenomena may be explained as symptoms of intermittent spirit-possession, as claimed by modern spiritist mediums."[60]

The "revelations" received by Mohammed from his visiting spiritual entities, while stressing the supremacy of Allah, presented a vastly different portrait of God's character and purposes than those inspired by the Holy Spirit through the prophets and Apostles of both Old and New Testaments. It is all but impossible that they could have been from the same source. Again, however, my purpose here is not to expound the characteristics of various religions, but to show that all have been infected with evolutionism, even those that profess to be monotheistic.

In addition to the centuries-old pantheistic dilution of Muslim monotheism by its philosophers and almost innumerable mystics of many varieties, the impact of modern scientism has taken its heavy toll of Muslim intellectuals, just as it has in Christianity and Judaism. Most universities in Islamic nations probably now teach evolution in some degree, just as do their counterparts in Christendom. This is being experienced in all Muslim nations, particularly those impacted most by Western science and technology and probably nowhere more so than in Turkey.

> The young people in Turkey are being weaned away from Mohammedanism. . . . The school books definitely say that there is nothing in the universe over and above nature. . . . The full force of official instruction is more subtly hostile to religion than if it were openly atheistic. Its attitude is one of condescending acceptance of religion as one of the vagaries of the human mind which society in the past has found useful, but which can be discarded when people become mature and educated.[61]

---

58. Anderson, *The World's Religions*, p. 55
59. Ibid., p. 58. Dr. Anderson is here referring to comments by Dr. Margoliouth in his book, *Muhammad* (London: Blackie, 1939), p. 81.
60. Ibid.
61. Samuel M. Zwemer, *The Cross Above the Crescent* (Grand Rapids, MI: Zondervan, 1951), p. 239.

This was the evaluation of the situation in Turkey by a Christian missionary in Turkey just before World War II, as reported by Dr. Samuel Zwemer, a longtime missionary himself and also a Princeton professor. Now, almost half a century later, there has been something of a revival of Muslim fundamentalism in Turkey as well as other once-Westernized Islamic nations, such as Iran and Lebanon. Nevertheless, evolutionism is still growing in strength throughout the Muslim world.

The same is true of Judaism, except in greater degree. Although nominally committed to the Old Testament and the Genesis record of creation, it is probable that only a small minority of the world's Jews, even those in Israel, still believe in special creation. The three main divisions of Jewry today are Orthodoxy, Conservative Judaism, and Reform Judaism. The latter two are products of the 19th century and retain very little of the doctrines and practices of the Old Testament Scriptures, having been profoundly influenced by Darwinism and other 19th-century radical movements. The Nazi-enacted Holocaust and the subsequent incorporation of multitudes of East European Jews behind the Iron Curtain of the Communist nations have also had a profound effect on Judaism. That is not all, says H.D. Luener:

> It is, however, not so much the deified materialism of Marx that claims most of those Jews who have given up their faith, but the fashionable pseudo-religious systems of humanitarianism, spiritism, Christian Science, Freemasonry, etc., or sheer indifference to anything that savors of human recognition of a power outside oneself.[62]

It is only in Orthodox Judaism that belief in the divine inspiration of Genesis still exists, and even here compromise is commonplace (e.g., the day-age theory of creation week, along with theistic evolution). The very idea of the Jewish Messiah, as the divine incarnation of the Creator for man's redemption, is largely abandoned. The authoritative *Jewish Encyclopedia* acknowledged this capitulation to evolutionism, even before World War II: "The doctrine of the Messiah is allied to that of physical evolution or Darwinism, and to that of political development, which looks forward to an omnipotent or just League of Nations that shall make peace universal."[63] The *Encyclopedia*

---

62. Anderson, *World's Religions,* "Judaism," by H.D. Luener, p. 46.
63. *Jewish Encyclopedia,* article on "Judaism" (London: Shapiro, Vallentine, 1938), p. 335.

said, further: "What is called the doctrine of the Messiah is, in reality, the belief in progress and hope."[64]

This drift of God's chosen people into evolutionary humanism did not begin with Darwinism, of course, any more than Christian compromise with evolution began with Darwin. The history of Israel, almost from the beginning, has been a tale of repeated apostasy into paganism and idolatry, as recorded in the historical books of the Old Testament. The situation finally culminated in captivity and exile, the ten tribes of the Northern Kingdom into Assyria and, later, Judah and Benjamin into Babylonia.

The post-Exilic kingdom was free of pagan idolatry but soon became encrusted with legalism and traditionalism, centered in the Talmud more than the Scriptures. And, of course, despite the overwhelming evidences that He provided for them, most Jews rejected the Creator when He came as their promised Messiah, with some arranging to have Him crucified by their Roman masters. Even after His Resurrection, attested by unimpeachable evidence, the Jewish people continue to reject Him.

Thus, even in the minds of most of those whom God long ago called to be His "peculiar people," to witness for Him to the pagan nations of the world, the very idea of the Messiah has been largely replaced by evolutionism. For too many, evolution has become not only their Creator but also their Savior!

This review of world religions has necessarily been brief, for men have made for themselves "gods many, and lords many" (1 Cor. 8:5), and all one can do here is make a sketchy survey of the cosmogonies of the world's major religions. Even this has been enough, however, to demonstrate the amazing ubiquity of evolutionary control over the minds of men and women of every nation — either in the form of blatant atheism or pantheistic humanism or polytheistic idolatry or occultic mysticism, or even truncated monotheism. The idea of God as personal, transcendent, omnipotent Creator and loving Redeemer is being rejected everywhere today.

Everywhere, that is, except by that small minority in every nation who believe the Bible as the inerrant, complete, authoritative Word of God! It is only in the Bible that the true account of origins has been revealed. When men reject God's Word, they cut themselves off from Him.

How misleading it is, therefore, for men to claim that evolutionism is science! Evolutionism, rather, is the basis of all the world's superficially diverse religions. In fact, evolution *is* the world's religion!

---

64. Ibid., article on "Messiah," p. 423.

Cunningly Devised Fables

The Apostle Peter testified in his final message: "For we have not followed cunningly devised fables, when we made known unto you the power and coming of our Lord Jesus Christ, but were eyewitnesses of his majesty" (2 Pet. 1:16). This would imply that all others — those who reject the omnipotent majesty of the incarnate Creator, the Lord Jesus Christ — have indeed "followed cunningly devised fables." The question is: who devised these cunning evolutionary fables that, age after age, have turned men and women away from the true God? As we have looked back generation after generation, we have seen that evolutionary cosmogonies have dominated most of the world since at least the sixth century before Christ. That century was the time of Thales and the other Greek atheist philosophers, as well as Buddha and the Vedanta, Confucius and Lao-Tze.

When we try to trace these histories further back than that, however, we find that history soon merges into myth. Even though there are earlier written records (e.g., Homer, Hesiod), the cosmogonies of those ages are clearly mythological rather than scientific or even philosophical. That does not mean that they have been fabricated out of pure (or, in many cases, impure) imagination, and so we shall now try to trace these evolutionary myths back to their source. Mythology has had more influence than most people realize in the development of modern evolutionary "science." Dr. Milton Munitz, professor of philosophy at New York University, has evaluated many of these ancient mythical cosmogonies in this light: "The fact is that primitive mythology lingers on in one form or another in the early career of science and, in the case of the efforts made in cosmologic speculation, determines the very pattern, in a broad sense, which these proto-scientific schemes exhibit."[65]

Dr. Munitz is here speaking particularly of the pre-Socratic philosophers of ancient Greece, whose schemes in turn clearly anticipated modern scientific cosmogonies, as we have already seen. He comments: "That the ordered world as we know it is not everlasting but arose in some fashion from an earlier primordial state is for Anaximander a belief which is not questioned but rather taken over from mythology."[66]

But the Greek myths appropriated by Thales and his disciple Anaximander had been in turn taken over from Babylonian mythology: "Anaximander reinterprets, while at the same time retaining, basically the same

---

65. Milton K. Munitz, *Space, Time and Creation* (Glencoe, IL, The Free Press, 1957), p. 8.
66. Ibid., p. 13.

pattern of cosmogonical development that is to be found in the Babylonian myth as this had already been partly transformed in the Greek version of Hesiod's *Theogony*."[67]

The reference here is to the Babylonian cosmogony known as *Enuma Elish*. This is a very important connection, to which we shall return later. First, however, we need to look more closely at the Graeco-Roman myths that are foundational to Western philosophy and evolutionary science.

Most of the Greek myths come from Homer and Hesiod, whose writings are dated at roughly 1000 B.C. and 800 B.C., respectively, though there is wide difference of opinion about both. Homer's famous works, including the *Iliad* and *Odyssey*, are the oldest extant Greek writings, but the history of Greece goes back at least another thousand years before Homer. The Greek myths that describe the exploits of Zeus and Aphrodite and Apollo and a plethora of other gods and goddesses are very earthy, though with supernatural trappings. It is possible that these tales, handed down orally to Homer from previous generations, are based to some degree on the blown-up histories of earlier peoples, mixed in with pantheism and polytheistic nature-worship, along with occultism and astrology. Some may also reflect distorted recollections of true biblical events. These ancient heroes finally became deified along with the spirits (angels and demons) with whom their priests and mystics seemed able to communicate, and the eventual result was the elaborate religious mythology of classical Greece and its equivalent in Rome.

It is chiefly Hesiod who has told us the cosmogony associated with the Greek myths: "Long before the gods appeared, in the dim past, uncounted ages ago, there was only the formless confusion of Chaos brooded over by unbroken darkness. At last, but how no one ever tried to explain, two children were born to this shapeless nothingness."[68]

Note again the evolutionary assumption. There is no real creation, only eternal matter. From this primeval "stuff," two beings somehow evolved. One of these was Night, the other Erebus, the deep. From these two was born Love, who created Light and Day.

> What took place next was the creation of the earth, but this, too, no one ever tried to explain. It just happened. . . . The poet Hesiod, the first Greek who tried to explain how things began, wrote, "Earth, the beautiful, rose up, Broad-bosomed, she that is the steadfast base of all things. And fair Earth first bore the starry Heaven, equal to

---

67. Ibid.
68. Edith Hamilton, *Mythology* (Boston, MA: Little, Brown, 1942), p. 77. Miss Hamilton is here paraphrasing Hesiod's great poem *Theogony*.

herself, to cover her on all sides and to be a home forever for the blessed gods."[69]

One can see in all this certain parallels to Genesis 1, except that the analogy begins with Genesis 1:2 — the formless deep — rather than Genesis 1:1, the creation itself. First there is darkness, then light, then earth rising up out of the watery chaos, then the starry heavens surrounding the spherical earth, where the angels would dwell. All of this speaks of a more or less quasi-naturalistic development of things, but with no concept of genuine creation by God.

Furthermore, this mythological cosmogony was not unique to Hesiod and the early Greeks. James Bailey writes:

> Hesiod's *Theogony,* the narrative of the birth of the gods and of the events which led to the order of things in Hesiod's day, is the only survivor among many Greek theogonies. Hesiod probably wrote before Homer. While we also know of theogonies from Finland, Estonia, India, Gaul, Germany, Scandinavia, Polynesia, and Japan, Hesiod's story is shown by M.L. West to be fairly similar in its details to Hittite, Hurrian, and Akkadian theogonies and the Phoenician theogony. Its source material is said to be very ancient indeed and was clearly known to all the Middle East and Mediterranean peoples of this period. They judged theogonies to be of the highest significance and they therefore recited them on important state occasions.
>
> The Phoenician theogony was said to have been recorded by one Sanchuniathon who wrote before the Trojan War and claimed to have derived his material from the pre-dynastic Egyptian culture hero named Thoth. His tale is very similar to Hesiod's.[70]

This remarkable similarity of the cosmogonies of many different nations of antiquity, as well as their respective pantheons of gods and goddesses, is obviously more than coincidence. The nations and their religious systems must have had a common origin. Discussion of all these different nations is not feasible here, but it will be well to look at a few of the more important ones that illustrate this point.

Consider the Pelasgians, for example, the seafaring peoples who apparently inhabited a part of Greece a thousand years earlier than the Greece of Homer and Hesiod. Archaeologist Robert Graves has been able to piece together a

---

69. Ibid., p. 78.
70. James Bailey, *The God-Kings and the Titans: The New World Ascendancy in Ancient Times* (New York: St. Martin's, 1973), p. 155–156.

portion of their cosmogony from monument evidence, even though none of
their writings have survived. Note the biblical parallels, as well as differences:

> In the beginning, Eurynome, the Goddess of All Things, rose
> naked from Chaos, but found nothing substantial for her feet to rest
> upon, and therefore divided the sea from the sky, dancing lonely
> upon its waves. She danced towards the south, and the wind set in
> motion behind her seemed something new and apart with which to
> begin a work of creation. Wheeling about, she caught hold of this
> north wind, rubbed it between her hands, and behold! the great ser-
> pent Ophion. . . . Next she assumed the form of a dove brooding on
> the waves and in due process of time, laid the Universal Egg. At her
> bidding, Ophion coiled seven times about this egg, until it hatched
> and split in two. Out tumbled all the things that exist, her children:
> sun, moon, planets, stars, the earth with its mountains and rivers, its
> trees, herbs, and living creatures.
>
> Eurynome and Ophion made their home upon Mount Olym-
> pus, where he vexed her by claiming to be the author of the Universe.
> Forthwith she bruised his head with her heel, kicked out his teeth,
> and banished him to the dark caves below the earth.[71]

Once again, despite any Genesis parallels, note that the cosmogony
starts, not with creation, but eternal, chaotic matter.

Let us turn now to India and the Indus valley, settled very early by people
related to the Greeks, as well as their Pelasgian and Mycenaean forerunners.
These people became the progenitors of the Asian Indians and the Hindu
religion, with all its sects and divisions.

As noted before, both Buddhism and Vedanta Hinduism were founded
about the same time as Thales and Anaximander were founding their own
rationalistic pre-Socratic philosophies in Greece. However, just as the Greek
mythology of Homer preceded Thales, so the Hindu mythology preceded
Buddha, and both may well have been derived from the same ultimate source,
in the Aryan peoples and the Sanskrit language. Barbara Sproul observed in
Primal Myths: Creating the World:

> The theology of the early "books" of the *Rig-Veda* [the first of the
> sacred books of Hinduism, meaning "Royal Knowledge"] is similar

---

71. Robert Graves, *Greek Myths*, vol. 1 (Baltimore, MD: Penguin, 1955), p. 27, cited in
    Barbara C. Sproul, *Primal Myths: Creating the World* (New York: Harper & Row,
    1979), p. 157. Note the parallel here with the prophesied bruising of the serpent's
    head by the heel of the coming seed of the woman (Gen. 3:15).

to that found in myths of other Indo-European people to the extent that it is fundamentally polytheistic and nature-oriented. There exists one major difference, however: while the polytheism of other Indo-European groups gradually evolved into a kind of modified monotheism with one deity heading the pantheon [e.g., Zeus], Vedism instead raised each deity (frequently credited with the attributes of the others) to a position of supremacy within the context of a given hymn. The individual identities of the gods thus became blurred, and in their place arose the concept of one divine principle expressed in many forms.[72]

It is believed that the most sophisticated of the several Vedic cosmogonies is the following , dated about 1200 B.C.:

> In the beginning was darkness swathed in darkness; all this was but unmanifested water. Whatever was, the One, coming into Being, Hidden by the Void, was generated by the power of heat. In the beginning this [One] evolved, became desire, first seed of mind. Wise seers, searching within their hearts, found the bond of being in Notbeing. . . . Casters of seed there were, and powers; beneath was energy, above was impulse. Who knows truly? Who can here declare it? Whence it was born, whence is this emanation. By the emanation of this the gods only later [came to be]. Who then knows whence it has arisen? Whence this emanation hath arisen, whether [God] disposed it, or whether he did not — only he who is its overseer in highest heaven knows. [He only knows,] or perhaps he does not know![73]

Many writers consider this cosmogony to be monotheistic and creationist, but it is not. In the beginning there was only darkness and "unmanifested water," not God. Furthermore, the author — whoever it may have been — says he does not know whether his cosmogony is true or not and doubts whether even God knows!

The early Aryan immigrants into India came by way of Iran, where Zoroastrianism would eventually become the religion of the Medo-Persian Empire. However, this religion built on earlier cosmogonic myths and modified them in the direction of monotheism. In addition to its basic dualism (as opposed to true monotheism) it also deified Time and Light as the eternal "gods" from which the world was created. Sproul elaborates:

---

72. Sproul, *Primal Myths*, p. 179; bracketed material supplied by present writer.
73. *Hindu Scriptures*, translated by R.C. Zaehner (London: J.M. Dent, 1966), p. 11–12. Bracketed sections are inserted by the translator. Cited in Sproul, *Primal Myths*, p. 184.

The *Avesta* depicts creation in abstract physical terms as a kind of birth of matter out of pure "form." In the beginning, only endless light existed. Without external boundaries, it is the One, pure and without other. But within it is twofold: an ideal creation containing the Spirit of the Power of the Word and a material creation with its nucleus of the Spirit of the Power of Nature. After the two spirits were united by the will of the creator (the Light conceived as a whole and personalized?), the material world evolved.[74]

Whatever this system is, it is certainly not true creationism.

As far as Buddhism and Jainism are concerned (both originating in the sixth century B.C. in India), neither had a cosmogonic myth, for neither believed there had ever been a creation:

> The Buddha . . . rejected any idea of a personal creator god, claiming that the world goes through successive periods of expansion and contraction, unaffected by the activities of the gods.[75]

> The Jains hold that no god created the universe, that it is in fact uncreated and indestructible, maintained and changing according to natural principles.[76]

These concepts would fit perfectly in the modern "oscillating universe" theory!

The evolutionary myths of China, transmitted long before the rise of Confucianism and Taoism there, have already been mentioned briefly. Although the ancient Chinese believed in a high God, Shang Ti, they explained creation itself in terms of natural evolutionary processes, regarding them as established by Shang Ti. The Chinese never developed an elaborate pantheon of gods and goddesses, as did the Greeks and Indians and others, except that Shang Ti soon became identified essentially as heaven, or the sun. Early in their history, they were monotheistic and still worshiped the true God of creation, but this knowledge soon deteriorated into theistic evolution. By the time of Confucius, it had become little better than atheism combined with ancestor worship and spiritism.

The religious myths of Japan were in part derived from China, and those of Rome from Greece. These, as we have seen, also were evolutionistic and pantheistic.

---

74. Sproul, *Primal Myths*, p. 135.
75. Ibid., p. 194.
76. Ibid., p. 192.

What about the early nations of northern Europe? These were considered barbarian by the Mediterranean peoples, but their creation myths were also evolutionary:

> Even some primitive mythologies express the idea that life in all its diverse manifestations is not the creation of the gods but a purely natural phenomenon, being the result of normal flux of the world. The ancient Norse, for example, held that the first living beings, the giant Ymir and the primordial cow Audumla, were formed gradually from the ice melted by the action of a warm wind which blew from a southern land Muspellsheim, the land of fire.[77]

The myths of the Scandinavians are now contained in collections called the Eddas, but these were compiled in their present form in only the 12th century A.D. They are believed to be much older, of course. Their cosmogony as handed down is somewhat as follows:

> According to the Eddas there was once no heaven above nor earth beneath, but only a bottomless deep, and a world of mist in which flowed a fountain. . . . Southward from the world of mist was the world of light. From this flowed a warm wind upon the ice and melted it. The vapors rose in the air and formed clouds, from which sprang Ymir, the Frost giant and his progeny, and the cow Audhumbla.[78]

From this cow the Norse gods were formed, especially Odin, their chief. Odin was then able to form the earth from the body of the slain Ymir, and the first humans from the trees. This is crude mythology, but again it is fundamentally evolutionistic.

There are also the numerous origins myths of the Africans, the Native Americans, and other animists to be considered, but only a few examples will indicate their usual characteristics. Consider an Apache myth: "In the beginning nothing was here where the world now stands; there was no ground, no earth — nothing but Darkness, Water, and Cyclone. . . . Only the Hactcin [personifications of the powers of objects and natural forces] existed. . . . All the Hactcin were here from the beginning."[79] These personified natural

---

77. Michael Denton, *Evolution — A Theory in Crisis* (London: Burnett Books, 1985), p. 37.

78. Thomas Bullfinch, *Bullfinch's Mythology* (New York: The Modern Library, n.d.), p. 262. This standard reference work was first published about 1840.

79. Morris Edward Opler, *Myths and Tales of the Jicarilla Apache Indians* (New York: American Folklore Society, 1938), p. 1.

forces, the so-called Hactcin, proceeded then to form animals and humans, one by one, out of clay and other materials. Before these, heaven and earth evolved, as father and mother of all:

> All the Hactcin were here from the beginning. They had the material out of which everything was created. They made the world first, the underworld, and then they made the sky. They made the Earth in the form of a living woman and called her Mother. They made sky in the form of a man and called him Father.[80]

Mother Earth and Father Sky — evolutionary pantheism again! First, however, as in so many other cosmogonies, there was only eternal darkness, water, and wind.

Other Indian myths more nearly approached monotheism, though with pantheistic and spiritistic incrustations. Here is one from one of the Mayan tribes of Central America, as described by B. Sproul:

> In the beginning, only Tepcu and Gucumatz existed as sun-fire powers in the middle of the dark waters of the void. They thought and spoke together and then, joined in agreement, created the world by command: "Let the emptiness be filled!" and it was. The earth rose out of the water and the gods made all the animals and birds to live on it. But these creatures were flawed in that they could not speak to praise their creators, so the gods set out to make people.[81]

Made out of clay, the first people melted in the waters. The second race of people devolved into monkeys. The third attempt succeeded.

The greatest of the South American cultures was that of the Incas. Their famous historian Garcilaso de la Vega, son of an Incan princess and a Spanish conquistador, writing in approximately 1556, said that their religion was centered in sun worship. They considered themselves, in fact, to be direct descendants of the sun. "But the sun was only the outward manifestation of the divinity for the sake of the common people. One is able dimly to perceive as in the Old World, that for the more sophisticated, the sun was a symbol of the intelligence that runs through the universe."[82]

The Incas' religion came close to monotheism, even though sun worship is basically pantheistic. They believed in a future resurrection, as well

---

80. Ibid. Cited in Sproul, *Primal Myths*, p. 263.
81. Sproul, *Primal Myths*, p. 287.
82. Bailey, *The God-Kings and the Titans*, p. 269.

as heaven and hell, and were a highly moral people. Not even de la Vega, however, says much about their original cosmogony.

Among the islanders of the South Pacific, the Maori of New Zealand are perhaps most significant. Sproul writes:

> The Maori envision a gradual evolution of Being-Itself, described as pure thought, first into not-being (the void, chaos, darkness) and then into being (sky and earth, order, light). Like the early Vedic thinkers, they argue that gods evolved with the specific forms of being: Being-itself, on the other side of nothingness, is neither deified nor anthropomorphized. . . . Maori creation myths . . . continued through the evolution of various forms of being to the creation of man.[83]

In Africa, there exists a great variety of origins myths, most of them highly animistic and anthropomorphic. One of the more sophisticated myths is that of the Dogon people of Mali and Upper Volta.

> The Dogon envisage creation in several stages, each culminating in a sacred "word" or revelation. The first is nature, a simple but eloquent language expressed in the sounds of grasses covering the nakedness of the earth. The second, an attempt to redeem mankind, concerns the social order and is symbolized by weaving. This word caused men to leave their caves and live with each other in community.[84]

Most of the African myths have little to say about ultimate origins, the tacit assumption being that the world was originally caused by the "high God" of their dim tribal memories, but about whom they had retained little knowledge after several millennia of animistic practice.

While there are scores of other "creation myths" that could be discussed,[85] the above examples are certainly sufficient to make the point. Except for the biblical record and those directly based on it, all such accounts of origins are essentially *evolution myths,* not creation myths at all. All begin with the universe of space, time, and matter already in existence, commonly in some formless, watery, empty state. Then the forces of nature, usually personified as gods and goddesses, act upon it to bring it into its present form with all its animal, human, and super-human inhabitants. Although many of these

---

83. Sproul, *Primal Myths*, p. 337, 339.
84. Ibid., p. 49.
85. Sproul (*Primal Myths*) gives over 120 such myths, some from each continent.

stories do contain overtones of a high God who was ultimate Creator, such notes are dim and confused, if present at all. Nowhere in all the world do we encounter the clear concept of a transcendent, personal, omnipotent Creator God who brought the cosmos itself into existence out of nothing but His own Word of power. Nowhere, that is, except in the Bible!

This is a remarkable situation. For one thing, it proves that modern "scientific" evolutionism is not new at all, but merely an updated and somewhat more sophisticated version of ancient cosmogonic myths. Second, it strongly suggests an ultimate common origin of all such myths. There are too many points of commonality among them for each to have risen indigenously. Modern evolutionary anthropologists agree with creationists on at least one important fact — namely, that all the different nations and tribes have a common origin. The old polyphyletic idea of the origin of races and nations has been universally rejected. The Bible, of course, teaches a monophyletic origin of all mankind, and so do all present-day anthropologists, so this suggestion — a common origin for all these ancient origins fables — should not be too controversial.

The question is, *where* is that common origin? To explore this question, we need to look closely at the records in the most ancient nations of all. Particularly significant are the great nations of Egypt and Babylonia/Assyria/Sumeria. There are others, of course — the Hittites, Syrians, Eblaites, Phoenicians, Scythians, Minoans, and various others. All are important, but the Egyptians and Sumerians are surely the most significant, because theirs were the first important civilizations. The Greeks, in particular, acknowledged that their religious philosophies were largely derived from these two ancient peoples. Many scholars, of course, have noted that the Greek and Roman pantheons bore an essentially one-to-one correspondence not only with each other, but also with those of the Babylonians and Egyptians.

How, then, did the Egyptians and the first Babylonians (the Sumerians) explain the origin of the universe? One of the greatest of all Egyptologists, E.A. Wallis Budge, has a discussion of one of the Egyptian papyri that sets this forth:

> Be this as it may, our present interest in the papyrus centers in the fact that it contains two copies of the story of the Creation which are of the greatest interest. . . . Each copy is entitled *The Book of Knowing the Evolutions of Ra, and of Overthrowing Apepi*. The word here rendered by "Evolutions" is *kheperu,* being derived from the

root *khper*, which means "to make, to fashion, to produce, to form, to become," and in a derived sense "to roll." . . . In the text, the words are placed in the mouth of the god Neb-er-tcher, the lord of the universe and a form of the Sun-god Ra, who says, "I am he who came into being in the form of the god Khepera, and I was the creator of that which came into being. . . ."[86]

It is interesting that the very word *evolution* appears in the title of this ancient document, used in the same sense as it is today. But the more important information is in relation to the subjects of the primordial evolutionary process:

> Returning to our narrative we find that the god continues. "I came into being from primordial matter, and I appeared under the form of multitudes of things from the beginning. Nothing existed at that time, and it was I who made whatsoever was made. . . . I made all the forms under which I appeared by means (or out of) the god-soul which I raised up out of Nu (i.e., the primeval inactive abyss of water)."[87]

This strange boast of the sun-god — Ra, Khepera, Nebertcher, or whatever name he would assume — is noteworthy in that he claims to have *created himself* (!) as well as everything else. This is obviously a false claim, for, in the very same context, he admits that he came into being from primordial matter and raised himself up out of the primeval watery deep. What are we to make of the anomalous claim of this most ancient "god"? There are several other Egyptian cosmogonies, most variants of the above, but they all begin with the primeval watery chaos, rather than with Ra or any other god.

Finally, consider the Babylonian cosmogony, which is probably even older than that of Egypt. Several such cosmogonies have been discovered by archaeologists, but by far the most important in the famous *Enuma Elish*. Although this account was found in Nineveh, the capital of the Assyrians, internal and external evidences both indicate that its origin dates back to the Sumerians. Most of it deals with the exploits of Marduk and his elevation to supremacy among the Babylonian gods, but it begins with the account of origins.

---

86. E.A. Wallis Budge, *The Gods of the Egyptians*, Vol. 1 (New York: Dover, 1969), p. 293–294.

87. Ibid., p. 302. This book by Wallis Budge actually was first published in 1904. It was later made available as a Dover reprint.

Specifically, *Enuma Elish* assumes that all things have evolved out of water. This description presents the earliest stage of the universe as one of watery chaos. The chaos consisted of three intermingled elements: Apsu, who represents the sweet waters; Ti'amat, who represents the sea; and Mumnu, who cannot as yet be identified with certainty but may represent cloud banks and mist. These three types of water were mingled in a large undefined mass. . . . Then, in the midst of this watery chaos, two gods came into existence — Lahau and Lahamu.[88]

Soon after these first two gods, various other "gods" also evolved out of the primeval waters. Only then did the earth begin to take shape. "Together, so the myth tells us, these waters existed before land or sky or even the gods came into existence."[89]

Once again, the primeval watery void is the eternally existing universe before even the gods evolved. Furthermore, this cosmogony, apparently the oldest of all, is the one that the later Greek philosophers adapted to their own systems, first by Hesiod, then by Thales and Anaximander. In fact, it is probable that the *Enuma Elish* may reflect the original evolutionary cosmogony that served as the source and model for all the rest.

Mother of Harlots

We have now traced evolutionism, in its age-long, worldwide conflict with God, back to its roots in Sumeria, the first Babylonia. All the different religions and philosophies of the world have been shown to be merely different varieties of evolutionism. With all their differences, they are alike in one essential — namely, rejection of the Creator and his purpose in creation. That in itself is the one essential that marks them all as false and deadly.

To confirm that Sumeria was indeed the most ancient civilization, consider the testimony of the leading modern authority on the Sumerians. Dr. Samuel Kramer, curator of tablet collection at the world-famous archaeological museum of the University of Pennsylvania, has written a book with the striking title of *History Begins at Sumer*. In his later book, *The Sumerians*, Dr. Kramer says:

> Sumer, the land which came to be known in classical times as Babylonia, consists of the lower half of Mesopotamia, roughly identical with modern Iraq from north of Baghdad to the Persian Gulf.

88. Thorkild Jacobsen, "Enuma Elish — the Babylonian Genesis," in Munitz, *Theories of the Universe*, p. 9.

89. Munitz, *Space, Time and Creation*, p. 10–11.

. . . But the people that inhabited it, the Sumerians . . . turned Sumer into a veritable Garden of Eden and developed what was probably the first high civilization in the history of man.[90]

Dr. William F. Albright, acclaimed by many as the greatest archaeologist of the 20th century, said that Dr. Kramer's works had made the most important contributions to Sumerology of any scholar of our time. Reviewing Kramer's book, Albright said: "Virtually every printed synthesis of Sumerian civilization is completely antiquated by *The Sumerians*."[91] With such a recommendation, we do well to take Kramer seriously. For example, he attributes to these ancient Babylonians the invention of true writing:

> They originated a system of writing on clay, which was borrowed and used all over the Near East for some two thousand years. Almost all that we know of the early history of western Asia comes from the thousands of clay documents inscribed in the cuneiform script developed by the Sumerians and excavated by archaeologists in the past hundred and twenty-five years.[92]

Kramer also stressed that most of the important aspects of later civilizations originated here:

> But the fact is that the land of Sumer witnessed the origin of more than one significant feature of present-day civilization. Be he philosopher or teacher, historian or poet, lawyer or reformer, statesman or politician, architect or sculptor, it is likely that modern man will find his prototype and counterpart in ancient Sumer.[93]

And, as we have seen, the modern evolutionist certainly had his "prototype and counterpart" in ancient Sumer. From there evolutionism spread to every nation and every age.

From the thousands of tablets excavated in Sumer and at least partially deciphered, it is clear that polytheism and all its accoutrements were already well established among the Sumerians before any of their tablets were written. The complex mythology of their numerous gods and goddesses, angels and demons suggests a long preliterate history, and it also strongly indicates

---

90. Samuel N. Kramer, *The Sumerians: Their History, Culture and Character* (Chicago, IL: University of Chicago Press, 1963), p. 3.
91. William F. Albright, "Sumerian Civilization" (review of Kramer's *The Sumerians*), *Science* 141 (Aug. 16, 1963): p. 624.
92. Kramer, *The Sumerians*, p. 4.
93. Ibid., p. 5.

that polytheistic idolatry (with its assumed pantheistic substrate) had its beginning in this first Babylonia. Says Kramer: "On the intellectual level Sumerian thinkers and sages . . . evolved a cosmology and theology which carried such high conviction that they became the basic creed and dogma of much of the ancient Near East.[94]

Kramer also noted that the Sumerian cosmogony involved primeval waters, out of which all things evolved: "First, they concluded, there was the primeval sea; the indications are that they looked upon the sea as a kind of first cause and prime mover, and they never asked themselves what preceded the sea in time and space."[95]

Another very important quasi-religious system that apparently originated in Sumeria was the practice of astrology, along with the other occult "sciences" that usually accompany it. This practice has always centered around the 12 groups of constellations known as the "signs of the zodiac," each with three "decans," or accompanying constellations, thus making a total of 48 key signs. The annual progress of these signs across the heavens, along the path of the sun (the "ecliptic"), is believed by astrologers to control human lives and destinies, particularly in relation to the concurrent paths of the planets (i.e., the "wandering stars"). This system has been believed and followed by people in many nations throughout the ages and is still believed by millions today. As absurd as it may seem on the surface, astrology has maintained an amazing hold over the minds of hosts of intelligent people. The ancients believed the stars were real beings, or at least the habitations thereof, who controlled events on the earth.

> Thus the revolving heavens gave the key, the events of our globe receding into insignificance. Attention was focused on the supernal presences, away from the phenomenal chaos around us. What moved in heaven of its own motion, the planets in their weeks and years, took on ever more awesome dignity. They were the Persons of True Becoming. The zodiac was where things really happened, for the planets, the true inhabitants, knew what they were doing, and mankind was only passive to their behest.[96]

---

94. Ibid., p. 112.
95. Ibid., p. 113.
96. Giorgio do Santillana and Hertha von Dechend, *Hamlet's Mille: An Essay on Myth and the Frame of Time* (Boston, MA: Gambit, 1969), p. 60. The authors were, respectively, professor of the history and philosophy of science at Massachusetts Institute of Technology and professor of the history of science at the University of Frankfort, both scholars of the highest rank.

Because of the personalities controlling these star motions, along with their pantheistic faith in the unified operation of all components of nature working deterministically together, the ancients invested these star movements with prophetic significance, with the astronomic conditions associated with each person's birth thus foretelling all the later events of his life.

The modern "scientific" mind may think such concepts are absurd — but it is even more absurd to think that these profoundly pervasive notions could have arisen by chance and that they are founded on nothing but wishful thinking and wild imagination. These star signs, with all their strange figures of beasts and giants and monsters in the sky, have been essentially the same in every nation since before the beginning of written history. Yet the star groupings themselves bear no resemblance whatever to the signs they are supposed to depict. Furthermore, before the star signs could be used for astrological forecasts, a high precision of astronomical observation and calculation must have been developed and established, involving even such subtleties as the precession of the equinox. That is, true astronomy must have preceded astrology or at least have developed simultaneously:

> It is now known that astrology has provided man with his continuing *lingua franca* through the centuries. But it is essential to recognize that, in the beginning, astrology presupposed an astronomy. Through the interplay of these two heavenly concepts, the common elements of preliterate knowledge were caught up in a bizarre bestiary whose taxonomy has disappeared.[97]

The learned authors of the treatise from which the above quotations were taken have developed in great detail an elaborate thesis uniting the myths from all parts of the world in one common source — namely these remarkable signs of the zodiac and their "bizarre bestiary." In the words of the promotional description on the dust jacket of their 505-page volume:

> The trail, pursued necessarily by induction, leads around the world through many lands. . . . It also recedes in time until the beginning is reached several millennia ago in Mesopotamia.
>
> As innumerable clues emerge and begin to interlock, several conclusions become inescapable. First, all the great myths of the world have a common origin. Next, the geography of myth is not that of the earth. The places referred to in myth are in the heavens and the actions

---

97. Ibid., p. 345. See the further discussion of primeval astrology in chapter 6 of this book.

are those of celestial bodies. Myth, in short, was a language for the perpetuation of a vast and complex body of astronomical knowledge.

This evaluation is justified in part, for the authors have certainly demonstrated the worldwide interconnection of myths from every nation and their intimate relationships with astronomy and astrology, especially the constellations and planets associated with the signs of the zodiac. Furthermore, they all had a common origin in Mesopotamia — indeed in Sumeria — before even the development of writing. These high-ranking scholars add: "In the same way, the strange hologram of archaic cosmology must have existed as a conceived plan, achieved at least in certain minds, even as late as the Sumerian period when writing was still a jealously guarded monopoly of the scribal class."[98]

This cannot tell the whole story, of course, for the authors recognize that the "taxonomy" of the "bizarre bestiary" has been lost to history. Where did these ancient astronomers ever get the strange idea of denoting certain star groupings as a great lion or scorpion or bull or virgin? And how could the mythological tales spun around these celestial beasts and heroes ever have been derived from any possible actions of the stars and planets in the heavens? Indeed, the whole system must somehow, as the authors admit, "have existed as a conceived plan" in certain minds before it was ever published and spread around the world. Another mystery is just when and how and why such multitudes in every age and clime were persuaded that professional astrologers could use this remarkable system to forecast the future and guide individual lives and the destinies of nations. And how was it all spread around the world? Finally, what has all this to do with the ubiquity of evolutionism, for both astrology and evolutionism are, as we have seen, closely integrated with pantheism and polytheism?

To answer such questions, however, we have to get back to the origins of Sumeria itself, for all this monstrous system of evolutionary pantheism, idolatry and polytheism, astrology and demonism began there — all in deadly rebellion against the true God of creation. But how can we do this, since archaeologists say they don't know where and how these first Babylonians originated, and since there are no written records earlier than the cuneiform tablets with their fanciful and immoral mythologies inscribed on the most ancient of them?

Despite all these presumably scientific opinions, however, there is *one* document that does antedate all these Sumerian tablets and does answer these questions. That document, of course, is the Bible's Genesis record, though evolutionists commonly either reject or ignore it. Since this is the

---

98. Ibid., p. 346.

written Word of the Creator Himself, their own evolutionary presuppositions require them to use every possible device to escape its clear teachings.

The fact that *they* reject it, however, is the very reason why *we* must not do so. It is always perilous for a Christian believer to try to accommodate any portion of God's Word to any form of evolutionary theory. We are confident, with an abundance of sound evidence, that the Bible is divinely inspired, inerrantly true, perspicuous, and authoritative in all matters that it treats, including matters of science and history.[99]

It is no accident that the writer of the final book of the Bible, looking back at its earliest records, ties the end-time conditions of the world to its beginnings, speaking of "MYSTERY, BABYLON THE GREAT, THE MOTHER OF HARLOTS AND ABOMINATIONS OF THE EARTH" (Rev. 17:5). This is an awesome ascription to apply to Mother Babylon, but it is well justified, for she did indeed give birth to every form of spiritual adultery known to history, as well as every form of idolatry (the implication of "abominations").

The key record of these vital events is written in the 10th and 11th chapters of Genesis. Although secular archaeology has not been able to decipher the origins of Sumeria, that earliest Babylon, the Bible tells about it quite clearly:

> And Cush begat Nimrod: he began to be a mighty one in the earth. He was a mighty hunter before the LORD: wherefore it was said, even as Nimrod the mighty hunter before the LORD. And the beginning of his kingdom was Babel, and Erech, and Accad, and Calneh, in the land of Shinar. Out of that land went forth Asshur, and builded Nineveh, and the city Rehoboth, and Calah, and Resen between Nineveh and Calah: the same is a great city (Gen. 10:8–12).

This important passage is in the chapter known as the Table of Nations, the unique document that tabulates the early descendants of the three sons of Noah — Shem, Ham, and Japheth — in the early generations after the Great Flood. Nimrod was the grandson of Noah's youngest son, Ham, and he soon became the first great king of the post-Flood world. The *beginning* of Nimrod's kingdom was Babel — undoubtedly the same or essentially the same as later Babylon — but he also gained control of several other cities, all of them in the land known now to archaeologists as Sumeria, including part of Assyria and the ancient capital, Nineveh. There is some disagreement about

---

99. For readers who question this fact, many volumes defending it are available. One by the present author is *Many Infallible Proofs* (Green Forest, AR: Master Books, 1974).

whether "Shinar" is the same as "Sumer," but the evidence strongly favors this identification.

As to whether or not this passage really gives reliable data about the origin of Sumeria and its capital, Babel, one should note the informed opinion of that greatest of archaeologists, William F. Albright, who said, concerning this remarkable tenth chapter of Genesis: "It stands absolutely alone in ancient literature, without a remote parallel, even among the Greeks, where we find the closest approach to a distribution of peoples in genealogical framework. . . . The Table of Nations remains an astonishingly accurate document."[100]

Many writers have discussed the 70 names recorded in this chapter, tracing thereby the origin of most of the key nations of ancient history.[101] The one of greatest interest to our own discussion, however, is Nimrod, for it was he who was evidently founder and first king of Sumeria and therefore of Babylon (or Babel). Nimrod's exploits as an indomitable hunter were notorious, perhaps as a conqueror of the mighty beasts that proliferated for some centuries after the Flood (possibly even dinosaurs, or dragons, as well as others now extinct). More importantly, he was probably a tyrannical hunter of men and lands, and all of this grasping for power was "before" (in the sense of "against" or "in the face of") the Lord, rebelling against God and His plans for the post-Flood world.

The name of Nimrod (probably meaning "Rebel") persisted in various forms long after he was gone. It is more than possible that he was eventually deified, with his name being gradually changed to Merod-ach, or Marduk, the chief god of the later Babylonians. On a more mundane level, his name persists to this day in the town Nimrud, near Nineveh, where many of the most important archaeological finds relating to the Sumerians (as well as the Akkadians and Assyrians) have been found, and also in the name Birs-Nimrud (or "Tower of Nimrod"), the name of the remains of a mighty tower in Borsippa, about ten miles south of Babylon.

This brings us to a critical event in history — the building of the Tower of Babel and the resulting divine judgment of the confusion of tongues, as described in Genesis 11:1–9. We need to have that whole record before us:

> And the whole earth was of one language, and of one speech [that is, probably, of one phonology and one vocabulary]. And it came to pass, as they journeyed from the east, that they found a plain in the land of Shinar [that is, presumably the Mesopotamian plain around

---

100. William F. Albright, "Recent Discoveries in Bible Lands," appended to *Young's Analytical Concordance to the Bible* (New York: Funk & Wagnalls, 1936), p. 25.

101. For one summary of these data, see Henry M. Morris, *The Genesis Record* (Grand Rapids, MI: Baker, 1976), p. 245–290.

the Tigris and Euphrates Rivers, or the land of Sumer]; and they dwelt there. And they said one to another, Go to, let us make brick, and burn them thoroughly. And they had brick for stone, and slime had they for mortar. And they said, Go to, let us build us a city and a tower, whose top may reach [the words *may reach* are not in the original] unto heaven; and let us make us a name, lest we be scattered abroad upon the face of the whole earth [thus deliberately rejecting God's command in Genesis 9:1, 7 to multiply and fill the earth]. And the LORD came down to see the city and the tower, which the children of men builded. And the LORD said, Behold, the people is one, and they have all one language; and this they begin to do: and now nothing will be restrained from them, which they have imagined to do. Go to, let us go down, and there confound their language, that they may not understand one another's speech. So the LORD scattered them abroad from thence upon the face of all the earth: and they left off to build the city. Therefore is the name of it called Babel; because the LORD did there confound the language of all the earth: and from thence did the LORD scatter them abroad upon the face of all the earth.

This amazing story may sound like a fable to the naturalistic skeptic, but it is a true event of history. No other explanation can even begin to account for the multitude of different languages on the earth, especially in view of the now universally accepted monophyletic origin of the human race. It also accounts for the relatively recent origin of writing and civilization, for the confusion of tongues would have left all tribes without any knowledge of the previous script and vocabulary, and it would take a long time to develop a new one, even for those who might have been highly literate scholars before this judgment. Furthermore, the subsequent dispersion of each small family group to fend for themselves in a strange environment would necessarily result in a long period of hand-to-mouth survival methods, at least until they could multiply sufficiently and find suitable lands and resources to allow them to begin to develop a real civilized culture.

Even though modern linguists and ethnologists tend to scoff at the biblical explanation, they are forced again and again at least to resort to its terminology in trying to explain the different languages. It is common for them to refer to Semitic, Japhetic, and Hamitic language types for example, using the same threefold division of the nations given in Genesis 10. Three times (once for each group) this account says that the descendants of Noah were divided "in their lands; every one after his tongue, after their families, in their nations" (Gen. 10:5; cf. v. 20 and 31). Thus, each of the 70 "families" was given its own tongue and its own land or country, and became a distinct nation: "These are the families of the sons of Noah, after their generations, in their nations: and by these were the nations divided in the earth after the flood" (Gen. 10:32). That this scattering was eventually to apply to the whole earth (though this would take time and further multiplication into still other nations) is evident from Genesis 9:18–19: "And the sons of Noah, that went forth of the ark, were Shem, and Ham, and Japheth. . . . And of them was the whole earth overspread."

Even the name *Babel* has been used ever since the dispersion to represent confusion and incoherent "babble." Linguistic scholars have also used the concept in developing their own theories. A standard text/reference book says, for example:

> Leibnitz, at the dawn of the eighteenth century, first advanced the theory that all languages come not from a historically recorded source but from a proto speech. In some respects he was a precursor of the Italian twentieth century linguist Trombetti, who boldly asserted that the Biblical account of the Tower of Babel is at least figuratively true, and that all languages have a common origin.[102]

Although the world's many thousands of languages and dialects today are vastly different from each other, they are all still *human* languages. Since even those most diverse from the European languages (e.g., the tonal and agglutinative languages) still have many points of commonality, it is quite possible, with enough effort, for a person of one language to learn to read and speak any other. The "deep structure" or "semantic component" of all languages is still the same, even though the "surface structure" and "phonological component" of one may be quite different from the others. As one scholar explains:

> Hence, it is merely the phonological component that has become greatly differentiated during the course of human history, or at least since the construction of the Tower of Babel. The semantic component has remained invariant and is, therefore, the "universal" aspect of the universal grammar, which all natural languages embody. And this presumed constancy through time of the universal grammar cannot be attributable to any cause other than an innate, hereditary aspect of the mind.[103]

---

102. Mario Pei, *The Story of Language* (New York: Lippincott, 1965), p. 22.
103. Gunther S. Stent, "Limits to the Scientific Understanding of Man," *Science* 187 (March 21, 1975): p. 1054. Dr. Stent is referring to the linguistics terminology of MIT's famed linguist, Dr. Noam Chomsky.

The very existence of human language is itself inexplicable except on the basis of special creation, so it may well be impossible also to explain the confusion of tongues on any but a miraculous basis.

> We know a lot about the structure and function of the cells and fibers of the human brain but we haven't the ghost of an idea about how this extraordinary organ works to produce awareness; the nature of consciousness is a scientific problem, but still an unapproachable one. . . . We do not understand language itself. Indeed, language is so incomprehensible a problem that the language we use for discussing the matter is itself becoming incomprehensible.[104]

There is no clue to be gained by studying the languages of supposedly "primitive" tribes, nor by attempting to decipher the language of extinct tribes.

> The so-called primitive languages can throw no light on language origins, since most of them are actually more complicated in grammar than the tongues spoken by civilized peoples.[105]

> Human language is absolutely distinct from any system of communication in other animals. . . . It is unlikely that we will ever know just when and how our ancestors began to speak.[106]

In short, there is no better explanation for the very existence of human language, nor for the existence of so many different languages in a humanity of common origin, than that both are miraculous gifts of God, for the accomplishment of His purpose in creation. The confusion of tongues, along with the dispersion of the nations, certainly accounts for the remarkable evidence that all the mythologies of the nations have a common origin, and that all the ancient nations had an essentially one-to-one correspondence in their pantheon of gods and goddesses. It accounts also for the universal practice of astrology and animistic spiritism. Finally, it alone

---

104. Lewis Thomas, "On Science and Uncertainty," *Discover* 1 (Oct. 1980): p. 59. Dr. Thomas is chancellor of the Sloan Kettering Memorial Cancer Center in New York City. He is a very eminent and respected scientist, and has become a proponent of the Gaia Hypothesis that the earth is a living organism.
105. Ralph Linton, *The Tree of Culture* (New York: Alfred A. Knopf, 1955), p. 9. Dr. Linton was one of the nation's outstanding cultural anthropologists.
106. George Gaylord Simpson, "The Biological Nature of Man," *Science* 152 (April 22, 1966): p. 476. Dr. Simpson was one of the world's leading developers of neo-Darwinism, and a top paleontologist.

explains the universal prevalence of evolutionary pantheism and/or evolutionary atheism, along with the age-long warfare between true creationism and evolutionism.

The Tower of Babel, along with the city of Babel, was built by Nimrod or perhaps by his father, Cush, or perhaps by both, essentially in rebellion against God. Whether or not the Birs-Nimrud represents the ruins of the original Tower — or perhaps the Tower of Babylon described by Herodotus[107] when he visited great Babylon during the heyday of its later empire — it seems likely that all the Mesopotamian ziggurats, as well as the pyramids, towers, and high places all over the world, were patterned after it.

The rebellion at Babel consisted not only of the people's refusal to scatter around the world, as God had instructed, but also of their instituting the new world "religion" in the temple at the top of the Tower. The Tower had not been designed to "reach unto heaven" in the physical sense (this would have been an absurd thing to attempt, as Nimrod and his colleagues well knew), but to reach heaven spiritually, there worshiping and communing with the "host of heaven," and to "make us a name" rather than honoring the name of the true Creator.

This host of heaven consisted of the sun-god, the moon-god, and the "gods" represented by the various planets (Saturn, Mars, Venus, etc.), as well as the other stars. They actually involved the great hosts of rebel spirits that have fought against God and His saints all through the ages. As Paul said, "For we wrestle not against flesh and blood, but against principalities, against powers, against the rulers of the darkness of this world, against spiritual wickedness in high places" (Eph. 6:12).

It was almost certainly here that the Sumerian priests were instructed in the secrets of astrology and the other occult sciences, as well as the religion of evolutionary pantheism, whereby the initiates soon "changed the truth of God into a lie, and worshipped and served the creature more than the Creator" (Rom. 1:25). It is no wonder that God finally had to intervene — this time not with a world-destroying Flood, as in the days of Noah, but with the confusion of tongues and the necessary dispersion that followed.

In somewhat corrupt form, this event has been preserved in the annals of the later Babylonians. The archaeologist George Smith found an inscription

---

107. Herodotus, the Greek historian, visited Babylon during the reign of Nebuchadnezzar, and described the Tower as consisting then of eight stages, totaling over 300 feet in height, with a spiraling ascent on the outside. It had been restored at the time, with the original structure considered very ancient. As with almost all such structures, there was a shrine at the apex, dedicated to the worship of the sun-god and the host of heaven.

in Babylon that read in part as follows: "The building of the illustrious tower offended the gods. In a night they threw down what they had built. They scattered them abroad, and made strange their speech."[108]

Although there are other traditions of the confusion of tongues found around the world, for some reason such traditions are not nearly so numerous as the traditions of the Great Flood. Possibly the different family groups leaving Babel did not really understand what had happened. They did retain the tradition of the Flood but otherwise tended to begin their own records with the foundation of their particular settlements. It should also be remembered that they had no ability to record these events at Babel, for an unknown but lengthy period of time. They had lost whatever written language they once may have had and were without it until such time as they could eventually develop their own new system.

One thing these ancient peoples did carry with them, however, was the religious system they had been taught at Babel. The stars were still unchanged in the heavens, so their astrological knowledge was intact. The names of the stars and their associated deities had to be changed to correspond to their new language, but the stories and their meanings were still the same in all essentials. Most importantly, the religious mythologies and their pantheistic evolutionary framework were still unchanged and so were carried around the world to every nation. "Mystery Babylon" is the rebellious system of religious adultery that originated at ancient Babel and has since permeated every nation. Its modern face is seen in the pseudo-science of evolutionary humanism.

Father of Lies

The question remains: If Babel, in ancient Sumeria, was the original mother of spiritual harlotry and idolatrous abominations, then who was the father? To anyone who believes the Bible, the solution must be obvious. The answer given by Jesus to the Pharisees makes it plain: "Ye are of your father the devil, and the lusts of your father ye will do. He was a murderer from the beginning, and abode not in the truth, because there is no truth in him. When he speaketh a lie, he speaketh of his own: for he is a liar, and the father of it" (John 8:44).

Satan was the original rebel against the Creator and has been attempting to deceive all mankind into following him in that same rebellion ever since. He is "the great dragon . . . that old serpent, called the Devil, and Satan, which deceiveth the whole world" (Rev. 12:9). Modern-day naturalistic

---

108. As cited in *Halley's Bible Handbook* (Grand Rapids, MI: Zondervan, 1965), p. 84.

evolutionists ridicule the idea that the devil might have anything to do with the worldwide prevalence of evolutionism. They do not believe in God, so obviously they would not believe in the devil.

Nevertheless, the devil — Satan — is a very real being, and one of his deceptive devices is to persuade a certain class of intellectuals that the natural world is all there is. It is significant that, despite these skeptics and even in this supposed scientific age, occultism and Satanism are probably followed by more people today than ever before in history. In fact, according to the prophetic Scriptures, there is a time soon coming when essentially the whole world will be worshiping Satan (Rev. 13:4).

However, the plain assertion by Jesus Christ, who is Himself the Creator, the creating Word made flesh (John 1:1–3, 14), is that Satan is the father of lies. And there has never been a greater deception in all history than the lie of evolution! The very notion that this mighty and infinitely complex cosmos, with its amazing array of living creatures and spiritual realities, could some-how create itself out of primeval chaos (or even out of nothing, as modern cosmogonists are suggesting) is nonsense of the highest order.

Yet that is what both ancient pantheism and modern scientism have insisted, with great popular success. Evolutionism has deceived the whole world, and there can really be no other explanation for such a phenomenon than the supernatural deceptions of the great Deceiver. Especially must this be the case in the modern world, where evolution is proclaimed everywhere as a basic and sure fact of science, yet without one iota of scientific proof. No one in all human history has ever observed one species evolve into a more complex and better adapted species by natural selection or any other mechanism. No one has seen evidence of any mechanism that would make evolution work. In the fossil record of the past, with billions of fossils preserved in the earth's sedimentary crust, no one has ever found any fossils showing incipient or transitional structures leading to the evolution of more complex species. The same applies in greater degree to the evolution of higher genera, families, or any other classification.

Yet large numbers of examples are known of deterioration and extinction, both in the present and in the records of the past. It is estimated by modern ecologists that several species of plants or animals are becoming extinct each day,[109] yet no one has ever seen a truly new species evolve! All

---

109. "Today's rate can be estimated through various analytical techniques to be a mini-mum of 1,000, and possibly several thousand, species per year," according to Nor-man Myers in a recent study entitled "Extinction Rates Past and present," *Bioscience* 39 (Jan. 1989): p. 39.

of this is perfectly in accord with the universal scientific law of increasing entropy (that is, decreasing complexity) in the world, but is directly contrary to the supposed law of evolution.

Can there be any other explanation but the biblical one? "In whom the god of this world [that is, the devil] hath blinded the minds of them which believe not, lest the light of the glorious gospel of Christ, who is the image of God, should shine unto them" (2 Cor. 4:4). Therefore, it is not at all farfetched to infer that the ancient universal "world religion" of evolutionary pantheism was first introduced at Babel by Satan and his fallen host of heaven, to Nimrod and his followers, then carried around the world by the dispersed emigrants from that wicked city.

The remarkable complex of astrology, spiritism, mythology, polytheistic idolatry, and evolutionary pantheism has been variously masked in pseudo-scientific verbiage and humanistic speculation (something for every taste!), which marked the ancient religions as well as modern evolutionary scientism. This worldview could never have been devised by men alone, not even such powerful men as Nimrod and his followers. The supernatural hold that this system has maintained over multitudes through the ages surely implies nothing less than a supernatural origin.

Somehow, in connection with the building of that first pagan temple at the peak of Babel's Tower, Satan and his powers of darkness must have communicated these occultic revelations to Nimrod, setting the first great post-Flood rebellion against God under way. That rebellion was interrupted for a time by the Babel judgment, but it continues today worldwide, stronger than ever in history.

There is an important twofold question remaining. Assuming this analysis to be correct, as all the evidence seems to suggest, Satan and his principalities and powers of darkness have been actively promoting anti-creationism behind the scenes all through the ages. Depending on times and places and circumstances, this can sometimes take the form of overt Satanism, for the ultimate goal of Satan is to usurp the throne of God himself (e.g., Isa. 14:12–14) and win the obedient worship of all God's creatures. More commonly, his anti-creationism takes the form of pantheism or humanism or atheism, all of which dethrone God as Creator but do not immediately enthrone Satan as the high God he aspires to be. Certain forms of applied pantheism (e.g., polytheism, animism, idolatry, demonism) involve obedience to invisible spirits other than the true God and thus come close to Satanism.

So the question is: *Why?* Why did Lucifer desire to take the place of God? Even more to the point, why did he possibly think he could succeed in such an impossible adventure as rebelling against his own Maker?

The Bible teaches that the reason why he wants to do this is simply pride. Lucifer/Satan was created as the highest of all angels, the "covering cherub" (Ezek. 28:16) — "full of wisdom, and perfect in beauty" and "perfect in thy ways from the day that thou wast created" (v. 12, 15). Except for God Himself, no being in all the universe was wiser, more powerful, more exalted, and more beautiful than Lucifer. But that was not enough!

Pride is defined in the New Testament as "the condemnation of the devil" (1 Tim. 3:6), for he was the first sinner and his sin was pride. God said to him, "Thine heart was lifted up because of thy beauty, thou hast corrupted thy wisdom by reason of thy brightness: I will cast thee to the ground [same word as "earth"]" (Ezek. 28:17).[110]

One element of that satanic pride may have been resentment against God's plan for men and women. They had been created in God's own image (Gen. 1:26–28). On the other hand, the angels were created specifically to be "ministering spirits, sent forth to minister for them who shall be heirs of salvation" (Heb. 1:14). In any case, Lucifer's pride led to his fall, and has served as a warning ever since: "Pride goeth before destruction, and an haughty spirit before a fall" (Prov. 16:18).

The more difficult "why" deals not with Lucifer's motive but with his rationale. Why and how could he possibly think that he, as one of God's created beings, could ever manage to vanquish his Creator? He was "full of wisdom," so surely he was intelligent enough to realize he could not possibly defeat his Creator.

Unless, that is, he did not believe that God really was his Creator! After all, the only evidence he had was God's word, and he evidently chose not to believe what God had told him. There seems no other possible way to rationalize what seems otherwise to have been an incredibly foolish decision on Satan's part.

But if God had not created him, then who did? And who made God? What could Lucifer have been thinking?

It would seem that the only possible alternate solution that Lucifer could imagine would be *evolution*! Perhaps — just perhaps — both he and God had somehow evolved out of the primeval chaos, with God just happening to precede him chronologically. If so, they were both really the same kind

---

110. The passages commonly cited to describe the sin and fall of Satan, or Lucifer, are Isaiah 14:12–15 and Ezekiel 28:11–19. These are ostensibly addressed to the wicked kings of Babylon and Tyre, respectively. In both cases, however, the words can only be applied literally to the evil spirit that possessed the human kings. Evidently, these were not ordinary cases of demon possession, but possession by Lucifer himself.

of being, as were the other angels. Therefore, a well-planned rebellion just might be successful!

This seems like an absurd proposition, but Lucifer was both proud and desperate, and there was evidently no other possible way to account for their mutual existence. Anyway, how can it be so "absurd," when this is essentially what all anti-creationists have always believed? The ancient pantheists believed that the gods created themselves out of the primeval chaos, and modern scientific evolutionists believe that human beings have evolved out of the chaos of the primeval big bang. So far as Lucifer knew, all the angels could have evolved along with himself and God, either slowly over long ages or very rapidly. Since they were not able to observe the process, who could know?

Lucifer's first moment of awareness (and the same would apply to all the angels) after God created him was one of waters all around him. The angels were probably created on the first day of creation week, immediately after the creation of the space/matter/time cosmos itself. This is the implication of the remarkable introduction to Psalm 104.

> Bless the LORD, O my soul. O LORD my God, thou art very great; thou art clothed with honour and majesty. Who coverest thyself with light as with a garment; who stretchest out the heavens like a curtain: who layeth the beams of his chambers in the waters: who maketh the clouds his chariot: who walketh upon the wings of the wind: who maketh his angels spirits; his ministers a flaming fire: who laid the foundation of the earth, that it should not be removed for ever (Ps. 104:1–5).

That is, God made His angels immediately after He had stretched out the vast space of the heavens and established His own presence in the primeval created waters. This correlates with the revelation at the very beginning of the Bible: "In the beginning God created the heaven and the earth. And the earth was without form, and void; and darkness was upon the face of the deep. And the Spirit of God moved upon the face of the waters" (Gen. 1:1–2).

Without embarking on an exposition[111] of this passage, it is clear that the first experience of God's newly created angels would be one of vast watery, cloudy expanses everywhere. The earth itself was still "without form;" its "foundations" were not "laid" until after the angelic creation. All of this suggests that if Lucifer (soon to become Satan — "the Adversary") desired to

---

111. See *The Genesis Record* (Grand Rapids, MI: Baker, 1976, p. 37–82) for the author's exposition.

find some explanation other than God for his existence, he would be forced to think that he was somehow derived from the vast presence (literal meaning of "on the face" in Gen. 1:2) of waters, which he encountered with his first awakening.

This explains the fact that not only the Sumerian cosmogony (the *Enuma Elish*), but also that of the Egyptians and most of the others that have been handed down by the various tribes and nations, all began with an eternal watery chaos from which the gods eventually evolved by some unknown process. This was Lucifer's best guess as to his own origin, and so this is what he would have to use to persuade men to join with him in opposing the God of creation.

Since much of this scenario is inferential, it is not presented dogmatically. If there is some better and more realistic way of accounting for Satan's long war with his Creator, we should be open to it, but something like the above is surely strongly implied.

This means, finally, that the very first evolutionist was not Charles Darwin or Lucretius of Thales or Nimrod but Satan himself! He has not only deceived the whole world with the monstrous lie of evolution but has deceived himself most of all. He still thinks he can defeat God because, like modern "scientific" evolutionists, he refuses to believe that God is really God.

6

The Everlasting Gospel

This book has been written to delineate the long, long war against God — the conflict of the ages. To this point, however, we have concentrated mostly on the history of just one side of that conflict. We have surveyed the history and pervasive influence of evolutionism from the present on back into the remotest antiquity, coming out finally at the primeval rebellion of Satan against God, soon after the beginning of time. And evolutionism seems to have been winning the war all through history, especially in this present age.

But there is another side of the conflict, and age after age the truth of theistic creationism has continued to fight the battle, despite all odds. The prophetic Scriptures indicate, of course, that the Creator must eventually triumph and put down all of Satan's rebellion and deception, but because Satan and his hosts (both human and demonic) refuse to believe the Word of God, the conflict goes on.

In fact, the prophecies of Scripture indicate that there will soon be established a global, humanistic, and totalitarian government, under the control of "the great dragon . . . that old serpent, called the Devil, and Satan" (Rev. 12:9; cf. 20:2). This regime will forbid the preaching of the gospel and require all to worship the Satan-empowered man on the throne, under pain of death (Rev. 13).

God therefore will then send His angel to proclaim His gospel to the whole world. John says:

And I saw another angel fly in the midst of heaven, having the everlasting gospel to preach unto them that dwell on the earth, and to every nation, and kindred, and tongue, and people, saying with a loud voice, Fear God, and give glory to him; for the hour of his judgment is come: and worship him that made heaven, and earth, and the sea, and the fountains of waters (Rev. 14:6–7).

The "gospel" that the angel will preach is the *everlasting* gospel — the same gospel preached by God in the Garden of Eden (called the "prot-evangel," or, literally, the "first gospel") when He promised that the coming "seed" of the woman would eventually crush the old serpent (Gen. 3:15). It is the saving gospel preached by Paul — stressing the substitutionary death, burial, and Resurrection of Jesus Christ (1 Cor. 15:1–4). It is "the gospel of the kingdom" (Matt. 4:23) and "the gospel of the grace of God" (Acts 20:24). It is the gospel preached before "unto Abraham" (Gal. 3:8). The everlasting gospel is the *good tidings* of the wonderful work of God through Christ on behalf of the redeemed, from creation to consummation.

Here in this final occurrence of the word *gospel*, John calls it "everlasting," stressing its timeless nature, embracing all God's purposes from eternity to eternity. In view of the nature of the long conflict, intensifying as the end of the age approaches, it is appropriate to stress the gospel's creation component. "*Worship the One who is the Creator of all things,*" the angel cries, speaking of the Lord Jesus Christ, of course. "For by him were all things created" (Col. 1:16).

This gospel of creation *is* everlasting. Despite the prevalence of evolutionary hilosophy age after age, the evidences of creation have always borne their witness, and there has always been a remnant witnessing to the ungodly world concerning the Creator and His great promises of redemption and salvation.

"When They Knew God . . ."

The Apostle Paul mentions a very brief time in world history "when they knew God" (Rom. 1:21), meaning that all mankind at that time knew and believed the true God of creation. Such a condition has existed only twice in history thus far. Once was in the primeval world of Adam and Eve before their son Cain sinned and slew Abel. Cain proceeded thereafter to establish his ungodly Cainitic civilization, which God eventually destroyed by the Great Flood.

The second time was after the Flood, when Noah and his family started the post-Flood population. Then came the sin of Noah's son Ham, the resulting curse on Canaan, and eventually the great rebellion at Babel led by Ham's grandson Nimrod.

These developments in the ancient world are described in Genesis 1–11, a section of the Bible that most modern intellectuals dismiss as either myth or allegory. The fact is, however, that the writers of the New Testament quote from, or clearly refer to, these first 11 chapters of Genesis no less than a hundred times in their own divinely inspired writings, always accepting them as real history. If we accept the New Testament as coming from God, then we are logically bound to accept the New Testament evaluation of these Genesis chapters.

Accordingly, we are on solid ground when we adopt Genesis 1–11 as the true framework of ancient history. When we take our stand on this fundamental premise, we find that all the phenomena of mythology and all the discoveries of archaeology and geology correlate with each other *and* with the Bible in a most satisfying way. These data, when carefully examined, all point to a world where the people first knew the true God, then rapidly corrupted that knowledge into pantheism, polytheism, occultism, and idolatry, with all the evil practices these encourage. This was true in the primeval world and then again in the postdiluvian world.

All of this is graphically portrayed by the Apostle Paul in the burning words of his introductory section in the epistle to the Romans. As these words are read, we should see in our mind's eye the events accompanying and following Nimrod's rebellion at Babel.

> When they knew God, they glorified him not as God, neither were thankful; but became vain in their imaginations, and their foolish heart was darkened. Professing themselves to be wise, they became fools, and changed the glory of the uncorruptible God into an image made like to corruptible man, and to birds, and fourfooted beasts, and creeping things. Wherefore God also gave them up to uncleanness through the lusts of their own hearts, to dishonour their own bodies between themselves: who changed the truth of God into a lie, and worshipped and served the creature more than the Creator, who is blessed for ever. Amen (Rom. 1:21–25).

Nevertheless, even though most people — both before and after the Flood — quickly capitulated to one of these ancient anti-God, evolutionary religions, there has always been a genuine witness in the world for the true God and His gospel. This is evident not only in the Bible but also from many extra-biblical sources.

In the antediluvian world, as the Cainitic civilization departed further and further from God, it evidently also carried along most of the other descendants of Adam and Eve. According to Jewish tradition, Adam had 33 sons and 23 daughters during his 930-year life span. The line from Seth, leading through Enoch and finally to Noah, maintained the true faith and a sound testimony all through this period (see Gen. 5).

So far as we know, there were no written Scriptures to guide them, except for the first few chapters of Genesis. And in these chapters the only statement of the gospel was God's promise when sin first came into the world: "And I will put enmity between thee [that is, Satan, that old serpent] and the woman, and between thy seed and her seed; it [or "he"] shall bruise thy head, and thou shalt bruise his heel" (Gen. 3:15). This protevangel (or "first gospel," as it has been called by both ancient and modern theologians) left the "good news" that — despite Satan's victory over Adam and Eve in the garden — he and his spiritual posterity would eventually be mortally wounded by a coming Seed of the Woman, who would Himself be seriously wounded in the conflict but would finally emerge triumphant.

In addition to this, there was the implied promise of personal salvation when God clothed Adam and Eve with coats of skins (Gen. 3:21). This taught them that innocent blood of sacrificial animals must be shed in order to provide a temporary atonement (or "covering") for sinful men and women, to fit them for the presence of God, which they had lost by their disobedience to His word. This divine object lesson evidently introduced the regular custom of substitutionary sacrifice, as evidenced by the accepted sacrifice of Abel and the rejected sacrifice of Cain (Gen. 4:3–5).

God may well have provided additional special revelation to Adam and his posterity, especially to Seth, Enoch, and Noah, but we have no specific record of any of this now, with one exception. There are three ancient books attributed to Enoch ("the seventh from Adam" [Jude 14]), and some of the early Church fathers thought these should be part of the canon of Scripture. However, since most scholars, both Jewish and Christian, believe these were actually compiled during the period between the Old and New Testaments, they have rejected them as part of the inspired Scriptures. Nevertheless, portions of them possibly do represent Enochian traditions, and one particular segment has actually been given canonical sanction by its inclusion in the epistle of Jude. This fragment is as follows: "And Enoch also, the seventh from Adam, prophesied of these, saying, Behold, the Lord cometh with ten thousands of his saints, to execute judgment upon all, and to convince all that are ungodly among them of all their ungodly deeds which they have ungodly committed, and of all their hard speeches which ungodly sinners have spoken against him" (Jude 14–15).

This fragment does indicate the terrible extent to which human rebellion against God had progressed in Enoch's time. Noah was Enoch's great-grandson and, by his time, "the wickedness of man was great in the earth, and . . . every imagination of the thoughts of his heart was only evil continually" (Gen. 6:5). Satan had so corrupted man's knowledge of God that the only remedy was the universal Flood and a new beginning for only Noah and his family.

In any case, the antediluvian world did know *about* God, even though most of its inhabitants chose Satan and his rebellious ways instead. When the Flood came, it "destroyed them all" (Luke 17:27), according to Christ Himself. "All in whose nostrils was the breath of life, of all that was in the dry land, died" (Gen. 7:22), and "the world that then was, being overflowed with water, perished" (2 Pet. 3:6).

This was obviously not a mere local flood or a "tranquil" one, as many modern compromising Christians have proposed, but a vast hydro-tectonic cataclysm that literally overturned the earth (Job 12:15). Except for those in the ark, and whatever records of the early earth they could salvage, all vestiges of the antediluvian civilization were either destroyed or else buried so deeply in the Flood sediments that they have never been found.[1]

There is one other intriguing possibility, however. In connection with the creation of the stars and other heavenly bodies on day 4 of creation week, God said that one of their purposes was to "be for signs" (Gen. 1:14). God also asked, in His remarkable monologue in the very ancient Book of Job (probably the oldest book of the Bible except for these early chapters of Genesis that we have been discussing):

> Canst thou bind the sweet influences of Pleiades, or loose the bands of Orion? Canst thou bring forth Mazzaroth in his season? Or canst thou guide Arcturus with his sons? Knowest thou the ordinances of heaven? Canst thou set the dominion thereof in the earth? (Job 38:31–33).

These rhetorical questions all refer to familiar constellations, and identify their regular circuits as "ordinances of heaven" that somehow exercise a kind of "dominion" in the earth.

---

1. There are several books available describing the tremendous geological activities of the Flood and the resultant worldwide "geological column" of fossiliferous sedimentary rocks. One example is *The Genesis Flood* by Henry M. Morris and John C. Whitcomb (Philadelphia, PA: Presbyterian and Reformed, 1961), 518 p.

The term *Mazzaroth* (coming "in his season") is agreed by all scholars to refer to the famous zodiac, with its season-by-season procession of 12 great key signs in the heavens. These signs are certain constellations of stars, with each constellation appearing to an observer on earth to be a number of stars grouped together in an association bearing the name of a certain object. Strangely, however, not one of these 12 signs of the zodiac bears the remotest resemblance to the object it is supposed to depict. Yet the signs go back to the beginning of history and are essentially the same in all ancient nations.

The evidence seems compelling (as discussed in chapter 5) that the astrological meaning of these signs dates from the rebellion at Babel and its association with the "host of heaven." On the other hand, this system could hardly have sprung full-blown from Nimrod or the fallen angels, and then been so quickly accepted and permanently preserved by people who still had a nominal belief in God and His purposes. It much more likely represents a gradual corruption from its true and original message. After all, Satan is a counterfeiter and a corrupter and a deceiver, rather than a creator. Astrology has, ever since Babel, been associated with pantheism and occultism, and therefore firmly condemned by God, but it was *God* who established these stars in the first place to "be for signs"!

What, then, was the intended original message of the signs, before Satan (through Nimrod and his followers) twisted it into astrology, with all its baggage of pagan mythology? While it is impossible at this late date to be certain about such a reconstruction, the most reasonable inference would be that the signs were originally a prophetic representation of God's everlasting gospel, an expanded exposition of the great protevangelic promise of Genesis 3:15–21.

Some such concept was held by the ancient Jewish scribes. Josephus, the famous first-century Jewish historian who is agreed by all to have been one of the most gifted and reliable of ancient historians, held that its interpretation, as well as the astronomical knowledge on which it necessarily was based, was originally developed by Seth, the son of Adam, and his own sons, perhaps referring to his posterity for seven generations. Specifically with respect to the sun, moon, and stars, Josephus wrote:

> On the fourth day [God] adorned the heaven with the sun, the moon, and the other stars; and appointed their motions and courses, that the vicissitudes of the seasons might be clearly signified.[2]

---

2. Flavius Josephus, *The Antiquities of the Jews*, book 1, chapter 1, section 1, in *The Works of Josephus*, translated by William Whiston (Lynn, MA: Hendrickson Publishers, 1984), p. 25. The original Whiston translation of Josephus was published in England in 1737.

Now this Seth, when he was brought up, and came to those years in which he could discern what was good, became a virtuous man; and he was of an excellent character, so did he leave children behind him who imitated his virtues. . . . They also were the inventors of that peculiar sort of wisdom which is concerned with the heavenly bodies, and their order.[3]

The writings of Josephus are not divinely inspired, of course, but they do represent the beliefs of the Jews at the time of Christ, as well as the research of a competent historian familiar with the writings and traditions of his people. Other ancient Hebrew writings (e.g., the Books of Enoch, the Book of Jubilees), probably written one or two centuries before Christ, reflect similar traditions.

Many of the star pictures do seem to reflect the crushing of the serpent's head and the wounding of the Redeemer's heel (cf. Gen. 3:15), as well as other biblical concepts expressed in later Scriptures. One British astronomer prominent around the turn of the century was impressed with this evidence. E.W. Maunder, who was in charge of the Solar Division of the Greenwich Observatory, as well as a fellow of the Royal Astronomical Society, wrote the following discussion:

> As we have just shown, the constellations evidently were designed long before the earliest books of the Old Testament received their present form. . . . When the constellations are compared with [the first nine] chapters, several correspondences appear between the two."[4]

Maunder goes on to say, in summary of these correspondences, "More than one-third of the constellation figures appear to have a close connection with some of the chief incidents recorded in the first ten chapters of Genesis as having taken place in the earliest stages of the world's history."[5]

Many older writers[6] believed that these 12 zodiacal constellations and their 36 side constellations accomplished much more than memorializing key events in the early chapters of Genesis. They have been able also to show

---

3. Ibid., book 1, chapter 2, section 3, p. 27.
4. E.W. Maunder, *Astronomy of the Bible* (London: T.S. Clark, 1908), p. 162.
5. Ibid., p. 168.
6. For example, *The Witness of the Stars* by E.W. Bullinger and *The Gospel in the Stars* by Joseph A. Seiss, both republished by Kregel (Grand Rapids, MI) in 1967 and 1972, respectively. For a summary of this evidence, see the writer's *The Biblical Basis for Modern Science* (Grand Rapids, MI: Baker, 1984), p. 176–182, 476.

correlations in some detail with the main prophetic promises of God, destined to be fulfilled at the first and second comings of Christ. These and others have shown that the various signs, beginning with Virgo and concluding with Leo, tell the whole story of God's creation, judgment, redemption, and consummation, and correlate perfectly with the written Scriptures that would be given to men later through inspiration by the Holy Spirit. Some of these suggested correlations appear arbitrary and tenuous, but they are still too strong to be dismissed as coincidence.

The evidence does seem to indicate that an outline of the everlasting gospel was impressed on the unchanging heavens in the earliest stages of human history, there to give its silent but eloquent testimony all over the world through every generation. God probably revealed His future program to Seth or to one of the other patriarchs in the godly line. If this revelation was put down in writing, as seems likely, it has somehow been lost. But it was also being recorded in the sky, where it could never be lost, not even in the waters and upheavals of the Great Flood.

First, of course, these antediluvian astronomers had to observe the stars long enough to chart their courses and to select and record the various constellations they would use to tell the gospel story. Josephus, in fact, says that the very reason God allowed the antediluvian patriarchs to live so long was to give them many centuries to identify and understand all the astronomical motions.[7]

That gospel in the stars has been there ever since, and presumably was well understood by those on Noah's ark, from whom all postdiluvian nations would eventually descend. In any case, it took only a few generations for most of Noah's descendants to forget God again, just as their ancestors had done before the Flood. This time Satan used the events at Babel to his great advantage.

As noted in the preceding chapter, the great Tower of Babel, symbolizing mankind's united rebellion against God's command to fill the earth, almost certainly had a great shrine on its apex, emblazoned on its circumference with the signs of the zodiac. It was there that Nimrod and his associates, presumably guided by the fallen "host of heaven," were able to lead their generation — that of Noah's great-grandchildren — into astrology and pantheism, thereby rejecting the word and authority of their Creator.

This could hardly have been accomplished overnight with a population still acquainted with the teachings of father Noah and nominally believing in God. We can surmise that they were gradually seduced by their prior

---

7. Josephus, *Antiquities,* book 1, chapter 3, section 9, p. 29.

association of the star signs with the gospel promises. Nimrod gradually persuaded them to shift their faith from the spiritual message represented by the signs to the stars themselves and then to the rebellious angels associated with the stars. Then proceeded the tragic apostasy so eloquently outlined by Paul in Romans 1:21–25, already cited.

The people had known God, but they soon became pantheists, identifying Him more and more with sinful men and birds and beasts and creeping things and all the other systems of nature. Then, with the dispersion and confusion of tongues, they carried this occultic, evolutionary religion with them all around the world.

The Inescapable Witness

As the emigrants from the judgment at Babel scattered around the world — each group now with its own distinctive language and developing its own distinctive tribal (eventually national) culture — the pantheistic evolutionistic, occultist religion established at Babel under Nimrod was carried with them. In effect, the whole world was being gradually converted to evolutionary pantheism from its original monotheistic creationist faith in the true God.

Since the world at large again had failed spiritually, just as it had before the Flood, God would no longer deal with mankind as a whole in pursuing His plan of redemption. Instead He chose one particular nation — founded by Abraham and developed by Jacob and Moses — through which to reveal His Word and bring His Redeemer into the world.

At the same time, the Creator God by no means had forgotten the other nations. He was as concerned as ever for their salvation, for He is "LORD of all the earth" (Josh. 3:11), and "the eyes of the LORD run to and fro throughout the whole earth, to shew himself strong in the behalf of them whose heart is perfect toward him" (2 Chron. 16:9).

Consequently, even though God chose Israel for a special purpose, "he left not himself without witness" (Acts 14:17) to the other nations. That witness — in the testimony of conscience, in the light remaining in their ancient traditions, in the structure and processes of the creation, in the very logic of thought itself, and in many other forms — is so pervasive as to be inescapable. If a person in any culture fails to believe and obey the true God, he or she is "without excuse" (Rom. 1:20). Jesus Christ, especially, who is both the Creator and Savior of the world, is Himself "the true Light, which lighteth every man that cometh into the world" (John 1:9).

In this section, we will survey the various ways in which God continues to testify to all His creatures, even though the nations as a whole long ago rejected Him as Creator. His "everlasting gospel" has always been there, freely offered to all "whose heart is perfect toward him."

In the first place, Israel herself, with her divinely given Scriptures and theocratic system, has always served as a witness to the other nations, and many have been the proselytes from these nations to the God of Israel. A prime example was the preaching of the prophet Jonah to the people of the wicked city of Nineveh, capital of the great nation of Assyria, as a result of which "the people of Nineveh believed God" and "turned from their evil way" (Jon. 3:5, 10). One thinks also of the testimony of Daniel in Babylon and of Esther in Persia. Then, too, there were Ruth the Moabitess, Uriah the Hittite, Rahab of Jericho, the Queen of Sheba, and many others. There also are numerous admonitions and prophecies in the Old Testament to the effect that the Jews and their Messiah are to be "a light to the Gentiles" (e.g., Isa. 49:6).

Even before God gave the written law to Israel, the earlier nations had somehow received an extra-biblical knowledge of God's commandments. For example, God told Isaac, "Abraham obeyed my voice, and kept my charge, my commandments, my statutes, and my laws" (Gen. 26:5). The patriarch Job, who lived in the land of Uz sometime before Moses and possibly even before Abraham, testified: "Neither have I gone back from the commandment of his lips: I have esteemed the words of his mouth more than my necessary food" (Job 23:12).

Whatever these primitive revelations may have been, they have all been replaced by the eternal Scriptures of the Old and New Testaments and have since disappeared. However, each nation or tribe does have its own traditions or religious writings, and these all reflect to some faint degree the primeval events of history and certain aspects of the eternal gospel. They have been grossly corrupted with the satanic doctrines of evolutionary pantheism, but the truth is never completely destroyed.

For example, the Great Flood that terminated the antediluvian world has been retained in some form in the traditions of almost every nation and tribe in the world. As noted in the preceding chapter, most nations and tribes also possess a record of the creation, although it has been largely corrupted in most cases into the evolutionary perspective invented by Satan in his attempt to displace God. As we shall see in the following section, these religious cosmogonies all retain a dim concept of the true God of creation, even though their beliefs and practices have long reflected the corrupt influence of evolutionary pantheism. In any case, there is hidden deep within all such traditions the faint knowledge that there is a Creator God, and that He judges sin.

Then, as a consequence of their primal beliefs, there also have been transmitted the almost universal concept of religious worship and prayer to a higher power or powers. This in itself is highly significant, for no animal — not even the chimpanzee, which modern evolutionists are currently proclaiming to be genetically almost identical to man — can have any concept whatever of religion or prayer.

Surely, if human tribes have ever evolved from tribes of animals, there should be some primitive tribes — past or present — with no religion at all, living like animals. But this is not the case. As Professor Zwemer of Princeton said, in his classic work on the origin of religion:

> Again, man always has been, and is, incurably religious. This is the verdict of archaeology and anthropology. The rude art on the walls of caves in which the folk of the Stone Age took shelter has religious significance. The graves of the dead testify to their faith in a hereafter. Religion is as old as the oldest record and is universal among the most primitive tribes today.[8]

Zwemer cited authority after authority, including the greatest scholars (most of them evolutionists) in support of this assertion. There is really no question that all known tribes (even the Neanderthals!) believed in some kind of higher power and some form of immortality. The only creatures who do not are animals and atheists!

Some of the ethnic religions (e.g., Buddhism, Confucianism) seem superficially to be atheistic, but they are really pantheistic and polytheistic in practice. They both involve much praying, and their belief in immortality involves reincarnation in one case and ancestral spirits in the other. Only creationist religions (Christianity, Judaism, Islam) believe in bodily resurrection, but all others believe in other forms of immortality.

Religion, prayer, belief in immortality — all are present in some degree in every known tribe, ancient or modern, but they are completely absent and even unthinkable in animal societies. Naturalistic (atheistic) evolution is completely impossible as an explanation for this dimension of human life.

On the other hand, these elements are all compatible with the evolutionary pantheism that, as we have seen, is really the world's religion — developed in opposition to the true faith that is centered in creation and redemption.

---

8. Samuel M. Zwemer, *The Origin of Religion* (New York: Loiseaux Brothers, 1945), p. 26. Dr. Zwemer was professor of the history of religion and Christian missions at Princeton Theological Seminary.

However, the prayers and concepts of immortality in pantheistic religions are merely deceptive counterfeits to true worship, true prayer, and true life eternal in Christ.

More to the point is the equally universal belief in substitutionary and propitiatory sacrifice. Although this concept has also been grossly corrupted in the world's pantheistic religions, its universal practice does indicate a common awareness that forgiveness of sin requires the death of an innocent substitute. E.O. James, not a creationist but formerly president of the Folklore Society of Great Britain, said in an authoritative work on the ubiquitous ritual of sacrifice:

> The author believes, with Dr. Westermarck, that the idea of substitution is vital in blood sacrifices. In this practice of offering life to preserve life may be discerned the beginning of the idea of substitution and propitiation, which in many of the higher religions have taken over a lofty ethical significance.[9]

Dr. James, while recognizing the substitutionary meaning in the offering of sacrificial animals, was still seeking an evolutionary explanation for the origin of this practice, but was unsuccessful. The only reasonable and true explanation is the record of the first sacrifice (see Gen. 3:21), when God had to slay an innocent animal, probably a sheep, to prepare coats to cover the nakedness of Adam and Eve. Thereafter, Abel offered such a bloody sacrifice before he dared enter God's presence. The first thing Noah did after the Flood was to offer sacrifices (Gen. 8:20), and the practice continued with all his descendants, even though many soon forgot its original meaning, as well as its ultimate prophetic meaning (in the "bruising" of the coming Seed of the Woman, the Lamb of God).

In addition to the testimony of Israel to other nations, which reached only a relatively small (though significant) number, the testimony of sacrifice, the gospel in the stars, and other primeval traditions, which soon lost much though not all of their original meaning, there is the universal witness of God and His law in each human soul. This is what Paul stressed in his message to the evolutionary philosophers at Mars Hill in Athens:

> [God] hath made of one blood all nations of men . . . that they should seek the Lord, if haply they might feel after him, and find him, though he be not far from every one of us: for in him we live,

---

9. E.O. James, *Origins of Sacrifice* (London: 1935), p. 47. Cited in Zwemer, *The Origin of Religion*, p. 143.

and move, and have our being; as certain also of your own poets have said, For we are also his offspring (Acts 17:26–28).

That is, God has so made man that he intuitively recognizes God's existence, at least until his training or religious traditions have educated it out of him. It has been said that there is a "God-shaped vacuum" in the heart of every person and one can never be whole until it is filled.

During World War II, a common cliché was that "there are no atheists in foxholes." And it is common experience that skeptics and ungodly sinners almost inadvertently tend to call on God for help when they get into sudden danger or encounter an overwhelming loss. The very fact that people so commonly use one of the names of God or of Christ in their profanity indicates a subconscious awareness that He exists and that they are rebelling against Him. Whoever heard of a Buddhist using Buddha's name as a profane expletive? Or Confucius, or Mohammed? It is only God, or Christ, whose names are so blasphemed.

Furthermore, every person has a moral nature, able to differentiate between right and wrong. The most depraved sinner and the most hardened atheist are no different in this respect from the holiest of men. Although standards as to the rightness or wrongness of certain actions may differ widely among different people, all are aware that there is a difference between right and wrong and that somewhere, sometime, somehow, an accounting has to be made. Animals have no such awareness.

Notably, although there are many differences in the various moral codes, there are far more similarities among them. The ancient Hittite legal code is similar in many details to the Mosaic laws in Scripture, and so are the unwritten codes of so-called savages in the jungle. All of these, distorted though they may have become over the ages, still bear a deep-down testimony to the responsibility of men and women to their Maker.

The Apostle Paul, writing to people in the greatest world capital of his day, expressed it thus:

(For not the hearers of the law are just before God, but the doers of the law shall be justified. For when the Gentiles, which have not the law, do by nature the things contained in the law, these, having not the law, are a law unto themselves: which shew the work of the law written in their hearts, their conscience also bearing witness, and their thoughts the mean while accusing or else excusing one another;) in the day when God shall judge the secrets of men by Jesus Christ according to my gospel (Rom. 2:13–16).

It is clear from this and other passages that all men are to be judged by Christ according to His everlasting gospel, and that at least one basis of His judgment will be the law of God as written intuitively in their hearts and consciences.

Beyond all this, of course, there is abundant evidence of God in His creation itself. In fact, this assertion is set over against Paul's searing exposition of the decline of the ancient world into evolutionary pantheism (Rom. 1:21–25). Just before this, Paul had said: "For the invisible things of him from the creation of the world are clearly seen, being understood by the things that are made, even his eternal power and Godhead; so that they are without excuse" (v. 20).

The essence of the everlasting gospel, as proclaimed by the angel of Revelation 14:6–7, is that God must be worshiped first of all as Creator of all things. That is not *all* the gospel, of course, for He must also be received as Savior and Lord, but it is the very *foundation* of the gospel, and the whole structure collapses without it. This is why Satan has attacked it so vigorously and consistently through the ages, and this is also why it is increasingly important to emphasize it as the end approaches. The extremely powerful testimony of God in His creation has been corrupted and undermined and almost obliterated in the minds of men by the evolutionary reinterpretation of that testimony.

Nevertheless, the evidence is still *there*, clear and powerful for all whose hearts and minds are willing to see it. Only an omnipotent, omniscient, personal God could possibly account in any rational sense for the evidences of limitless power in the processes of the universe or the infinite complexities of design in the organized systems of the universe (especially living systems!) or the attributes of personality in human beings (self-consciousness, will, emotion, abstract reasoning, etc.). This is only logical, cause-and-effect reasoning, which is supposed to be the basic approach to any scientific study of the universe.

But evolutionists — both ancient and modern — ignore logic when it comes to origins. In order to avoid having to recognize God, "professing themselves to be wise, they became fools" (Rom. 1:22). They have imagined that all these things could somehow be generated by the forces of nature and properties of matter, either personified as various gods and goddesses and then energized by invisible spirits (in the ancient religion) or else all produced by some primordial explosion of primeval nothingness (in the modern cosmogony).

The fact is, however, that true science, seeking to describe things in the universe as they really are, is no less an enemy of evolutionism than is God's revelation in Scripture. True science actually supports Scripture at every point of contact between the two. For example, the two most basic and universal laws of science that have been recognized by scientists to date are the two laws of thermodynamics (or "heat power"), and these testify clearly to the "eternal power" of the Creator, as noted in Romans 1:20. The first law (conservation of energy) recognizes that the total power of the universe is not still being created, but always stays at the same magnitude. The second law (decay of energy) recognizes that this power is always becoming less and less available to maintain the systems and processes of the universe. Thus, the universe must eventually die if the second law continues to function. Since the universe is not yet dead, it must have been created at some point of time in the past, with its tremendous power imparted to it then by its eternal Creator. Otherwise it would already be dead.

Furthermore, the basic structure of the physical universe is actually that of a tri-universe, consisting of space, time, and matter — no more, no less. This is not a *trio* (three entities combined together to make a whole) but a true *trinity* (three distinct entities, each of which *is* the whole). The universe is not part space, part time, and part matter. All of it is space, all is time, and all is matter, permeating all space-time.

This system is clearly the same type of system as the divine Trinity of the godhead — Father, Son, and Spirit — each of whom is equally and always the one God who created all things, sustains all things, and will reconcile all things. And this is not all. The Bible reveals that the Father is the invisible, omnipresent foundation of the godhead; the Son is the manifestation of the godhead, eternally proceeding from the Father; the invisible, omnipresent Spirit comes from the Father through the Son, to interpret the godhead in human experience.

In similar fashion, space is the omnipresent basis of all physical reality, manifested in the phenomena of matter, interpreted and experienced through time. In the foregoing sentence, one can substitute *Father, Son,* and *Spirit* for *space, matter,* and *time,* and the sentence is equally true. Thus the tri-universe is a remarkable model of the triune godhead.

This is still not all. Each of the three dimensions of the physical universe is also a triunity. Space is three-dimensional, with each dimension comprising the whole of space. Space is always identified in terms of one dimension, seen only in two dimensions, experienced in three dimensions. Similarly, time is future, present, and past, with each comprising the whole of time. The future is the unseen source of time, the present is time manifested, the past is time experienced.

The phenomena of matter occur in many different forms. In general, any event that occurs in space during time can be considered a phenomenon of matter or energy and is manifested by its motion, which is expressed as space traveled per unit of time. Motion can only be generated by energy, however, and experienced in the phenomenon it produces. For example, light energy generates light waves moving rapidly through space and then experienced in the seeing of light. Sound energy generates sound waves, experienced in the hearing of sound. Always, it is thus. Unseen, omnipresent energy perpetually generates motion through space during time, which we experience in various phenomena. These relationships again are those of a triunity, fully analogous to the triunity of the godhead.

We see, therefore, the remarkable fact that the physical universe is a marvelous trinity of trinities, each a specific model of the godhead. Whatever the explanation of this fact, it *is* a fact, fully confirmed by modern science but also known to ancient philosophy and indeed substantiated by everyday logic and experience. This is bound to be more than coincidence. Such a remarkable effect requires an adequate cause to explain it. Furthermore, one can find many other such trinities in the world and in human life.[10]

A very adequate "cause," of course, would be that our tri-universe was designed to reflect the triune nature of its Creator, as a perpetual testimony to the people of all times and places. Thus everyone could come to understand, if he or she truly sought such understanding, that the universe has a Creator who is both infinite and eternal, like space and time, but also manifest in human life and experience by caring for His creation.

This also is the testimony of Romans 1:20. Not only is God's eternal power seen in all the processes of His creation, but His godhead is seen in the basic nature and structure of His creation. The invisible things of God have been visible to the eye of faith from the very creation of the world, and those who do not try to see are without excuse. This witness of creation is inescapable, for it surrounds and affects us always and everywhere.

In the same way, the internal witness of the law of God in our hearts and the convicting testimony of the Spirit of God in our consciences are inescapable. The external creation and the internal conviction of God's reality are both there — always there. Men and women should seek God, for He "now commandeth all men every where to repent" (Acts 17:30).

---

10. See Nathan R. Wood, *The Trinity in the Universe* (Grand Rapids, MI: Kregel, 1978), 220 p. For a summary of the evidence from both the laws of thermodynamics and the tri-universe, see Henry M. Morris, *The Biblical Basis for Modern Science* (Grand Rapids, MI: Baker, 1984), p. 50–70, 185–215.

Some may object that these evidences are too subtle and tenuous to expect ordinary people to see and understand them. Nevertheless, they *are there,* and they are certainly not too subtle and tenuous for their leaders and teachers to understand. In any case, the evidences of intelligent design and special creation abound everywhere in nature, and there is no real excuse for anyone to believe in naturalistic evolution, for which there is no legitimate scientific or historical evidence whatever. The probability that even the simplest imaginary form of life — say a replicating protein molecule, if there were such a thing — could ever, by chance, arise from nonliving chemicals in some primeval soup is so infinitesimally small as to amount to zero. Michael Denton, a distinguished Australian molecular geneticist, recently wrote:

> It is the sheer universality of perfection, the fact that everywhere we look, to whatever depth we look, we find an elegance and ingenuity of an absolutely transcendent quality, which so mitigates against the idea of chance. Is it really credible that random processes could have constructed a reality, the smallest element of which — a functional protein or gene — is complex beyond our own creative capacities, a reality which is the very antithesis of chance, which excel in every sense anything produced by the intelligence of man? Alongside the level of ingenuity and complexity exhibited by the molecular machinery of life, even our most advanced artifacts appear clumsy.[11]

Life could never begin by any combination of natural processes. The very existence of living organisms testifies to a living God, for life can only come from life, as far as all knowledge, observation, and history testify.

Neither can one kind of organism evolve into a more complex organism, as far as all knowledge, observation, and history testify. The history of life is supposedly preserved in the fossil record from past geological ages, but the basic kinds of creatures are as clearly distinct from one another in the fossils as they are in the present world. Geologists J.W. Valentine and D.H. Erwin write:

> If ever we were to expect to find ancestors to or intermediates between higher taxa, it would be in the rocks of late Precambrian to Ordovician times, when the bulk of the world's higher animal taxa evolved. Yet transitional alliances are unknown or unconfirmed for any of the phyla or classes appearing then.[12]

---

11. Michael Denton, *Evolution — A Theory in Crisis* (London: Burnett Books, 1985), p. 342.
12. James W. Valentine and Douglas H. Erwin, *Development as an Evolutionary Process,* "Interpreting Great Developmental Experiments: The Fossil Record" (New York: Alan R. Lias, 1987), p. 84.

The fact that there are no transitional forms documented out of the billions of known fossils preserved in the rocks has, ever since Darwin, been an unsolved mystery to evolutionists. It is currently being explained *ad hoc* on the assumption that, when evolution does take place, it takes place so rapidly that it leaves no record. Leading paleontologist Steven Stanley, of Johns Hopkins University, summarizes this view: "Evolution happens rapidly in small, localized populations, so we're not likely to see it in the fossil record."[13]

That "explanation" may accord with the magical theories of evolution encountered in the New Age pantheism (turning frogs into princes, reincarnating an Egyptian slave into a Wall Street banker), but it has no support in observational science. Say Valentine and Erwin, "We conclude that . . . neither of the contending theories of evolutionary change at the species level, phyletic gradualism or punctuated equilibrium, seem applicable to the origin of new body plans."[14]

The ubiquitous absence of transitional structures in the fossil record is no mystery to creationists, of course. No transitional forms can be found because they never existed! Each kind reproduces only after its own kind, as the Bible says in its very first chapter. This is a clear, inescapable witness to special creation.

If, however, evolution happens rapidly in small populations, as Dr. Stanley and many others allege today, then it seems that we should occasionally be able to see it happening. After all, genuine science deals with facts, and evolution is continually being trumpeted as a proved fact of science. The word *science* means "knowledge," so somewhere we should be able to see evolution in action, with some kind of plant or animal evolving rapidly into a more complex kind of plant or animal.

But, of course, no one has ever seen such a thing in all human history. In fact, Dr. Pierre Grasse, one of the greatest modern zoologists, has written the following: "Today, our duty is to destroy the myth of evolution, considered as a simple, understood and explained phenomenon which keeps rapidly unfolding before us."[15]

---

13. Steven M. Stanley, "Resetting the Evolutionary Timetable," interview by Neil A. Campbell, *Bioscience* 36 (Dec. 1986): p. 725.

14. Valentine and Erwin, *Development as an Evolutionary Process*, p. 96. Dr. Valentine is a professor of geology at the University of California (Santa Barbara), and Dr. Erwin at Michigan State University.

15. Pierre P. Grassè, *Evolution of Living Organisms* (New York: Academic, 1977), p. 8. Dr. Grassè held the Chair of Evolution at the Sorbonne University in Paris for 30 years.

Instead of evolution rapidly unfolding before us, what we really see taking place everywhere is deterioration and extinction: "As in the past, new life forms will arise, but not at a fraction of the rate they are going to be lost in the coming decades and centuries. We are surely losing one or more species a day right now out of the five million (minimum figure) on Earth."[16] During recorded history (say, 6,000 years) and at this rate, over two million species have become extinct, but not one has ever been observed to evolve from something lower. Evolution is going in the wrong direction!

The fact is that there is no scientific evidence whatever for evolution. All the actual scientific evidence is exactly what would be predicted if God had created each kind of creature in the beginning, just as described in the Bible. Says mathematician-physicist Wolfgang Smith: "We are told dogmatically that evolution is an established fact; but we are never told who established it, and by what means. We are told, often enough, that the doctrine is founded upon evidence . . . but we are left entirely in the dark on the crucial question wherein, precisely, this evidence consists."[17]

As we have shown, modern evolutionary "science" is nothing but ancient philosophy or even more ancient mythology, revived and dressed up in modern garb. According to Smith:

> The point, however, is that the doctrine of evolution has swept the world, not on the strength of its scientific merits, but precisely in its capacity as a Gnostic myth. It affirms, in effect, that living beings create themselves, which is, in essence, a metaphysical claim. This in itself implies, however, that the theory is scientifically unverifiable (a fact, incidentally, which has often enough been pointed out by philosophers of science). Thus, in the final analysis, evolutionism is in truth a metaphysical doctrine decked out in scientific garb.[18]

People believe in evolution because they want to, not because of the evidence, for the evidence unequivocally speaks of creation.

The above discussion is, of course, only the barest outline of the testimony of the real *facts* of science (as distinguished from the *speculations* of evolutionary scientists) to the original creation of all the basic systems of the

---

16. Norman Myers, "The End of the Lines," *Natural History* 94 (Feb. 1985): p. 2.
17. Wolfgang Smith, *Teilhardism and the New Religion* (Rockford, IL: Tan Books, 1988), p. 2. Smith is a Catholic mathematician and physicist with an MIT doctorate, now a professor at Oregon State University.
18. Ibid., p. 242.

cosmos by God. Much more complete discussions of the relevant scientific evidence can be found in the many creationist books that are available today.[19]

The evidence can never be strong enough, however, to compel people to believe when they refuse to. Though Satan himself was "full of wisdom, and perfect in beauty" (Ezek. 28:12), even in the very presence of the glorious Almighty God he refused to believe that God was really the omnipotent Creator. And so Satan instigated his age-long war against God. Adam knew God yet disregarded His word; Cain knew all about God yet deliberately refused to bring an acceptable sacrifice.

And so it has been through the ages: "When they knew God, they glorified him not as God, neither were thankful: but became vain in their imaginations, and their foolish heart was darkened" (Rom. 1:21).

In today's America, churches and Bibles and Christian testimonies abound, yet most people reject God. We should therefore not be surprised to learn that most people have also rejected the evidence of conscience and tradition, the evidence of triunity in nature, the testimony of the gospel preserved in the star signs, even the tremendous scientific evidence of God in the systems and processes of nature. These are less compelling evidences than those in the Holy Scriptures, and they reject *them*.

Yet these evidences *are there*! And they do provide adequate evidence of at least the creation component of the everlasting gospel for those who are *willing* to believe God, even if they do not yet have access to God's written Word. This must be so, because God has said they are "without excuse" if they do not believe what is "clearly seen" (Rom. 1:20).

Furthermore, if one comes to believe (as he should) that there is a God who created all things, then he must also know that sin has somehow separated him from God's presence. This very intuition is confirmed by the accusations of his own conscience, for he knows that he has failed to live even by the light he still has. The tragedy is that most "men loved darkness rather than light, because their deeds were evil" (John 3:19).

Nevertheless, this universal awareness of separation from God did cause people of all nations to maintain the universal practice of some form of religion, of prayer, and of substitutionary sacrifice. All people have agreed that death is the ultimate and apparently invincible enemy — that "the sting of death is sin" and that "the last enemy that shall be destroyed is death" (1 Cor. 15:56, 26).

---

19. For example, see *Scientific Creationism*, edited by Henry M. Morris (Green Forest, AR: Master Books, 1985). This book also contains an extensive bibliography (p. 257–264) of other books on both biblical and scientific creationism.

Thus, all people in all religions and in all times, as the Bible puts it, "through fear of death were all their lifetime subject to bondage" (Heb. 2:15). Yet they also sought life beyond death, and all peoples have consequently retained belief in some form of immortality.

This also is a remnant of God's testimony to all the nations. As Paul and Barnabas told the pagan worshipers at Lystra, when they wanted to honor them as miracle-working gods:

> We also are men of like passions with you, and preach unto you that ye should turn from these vanities unto the living God, which made heaven, and earth, and the sea, and all things that are therein: who in times past suffered all nations to walk in their own ways. Nevertheless he left not himself without witness, in that he did good, and gave us rain from heaven, and fruitful seasons, filling our hearts with food and gladness (Acts 14:15–17).

The testimony of God's providence — His care and love for His creatures — has always been everywhere evident for those whose hearts are willing to hear and see. He provides even for the animals (note His beautiful message to Job on this theme in Job 38 and 39; also the beautiful psalm of creation and providence, Psalm 104).

This very goodness of God should convince all people to believe and trust their Creator. Although they know that sin has separated them from God and that death is the result of sin, they also know that He has not abandoned them, for He sends the sun and the rain. They can still experience hope and happiness, at least to some degree. Even though night comes, the morning always follows. Winter comes, but so does spring. Individuals may die, but children are born, and life goes on. Men and women should always have known that there is a God of creation and that He is also a God of holiness who must punish sin. But they should also have realized that He is a loving God who will somehow provide salvation. The God of creation must also be the God of redemption.

The creation component of the everlasting gospel, therefore, has always been indissolubly intertwined with its redemption and consummation components. The evidence of creation abounds, but this also implies redemption and fulfillment. Similarly, evidence of God's redemptive love abounds, and this implies that He is also Creator and coming King. With or without the Scriptures, men are "without excuse" if they are without God. "Or despisest thou the riches of his goodness and forbearance and longsuffering: not knowing that the goodness of God leadeth thee to repentance?" (Rom. 2:4).

We have no way of knowing whether any individuals in other nations and times may have responded to this universal and inescapable complex of witnesses. Most of them certainly did not. And most people still reject God, even today, when there is so much more light — not only the Scriptures but the testimony of Christ and all Christian history.

With any who did respond, God was surely pleased, "for the Father seeketh such to worship him" (John 4:23). Whatever additional light may have been needed for them to understand and believe unto salvation, we can have confidence that God somehow provided. "For the eyes of the LORD run to and fro throughout the whole earth, to shew himself strong in the behalf of them whose heart is perfect toward him" (2 Chron. 16:9).

Despite the universal drift into evolutionary pantheism or atheism after Babel, most or all of the nations managed to retain at least a dim recollection of the true God. This we shall discuss in the next section.

Into All the World

There have been two great worldwide commissions given by God to His people. The second is much better known than the first. After His Resurrection, the Lord Jesus commanded His disciples: "Go ye into all the world, and preach the gospel to every creature" (Mark 16:15). This is the so-called Great Commission, according to which each one who has believed on Christ for salvation should seek to spread through all the world His everlasting gospel — acknowledging Him as Creator, Redeemer, and Lord of all.

Long before this, however, another commission had been given to all mankind — first to Adam as God's very first commandment, then renewed to Noah at the world's new beginning after the Flood. To Adam and Eve, He said, "Be fruitful, and multiply, and replenish [the Hebrew verb, *male*, simply means "fill"] the earth, and subdue it: and have dominion over the fish of the sea, and over the fowl of the air, and over every living thing that moveth upon the earth" (Gen. 1:28). Then, to Noah and his sons, God said, "Be fruitful, and multiply, and replenish the earth" (Gen. 9:1), repeating the same command given to Adam and Eve. He expanded it this time, however, giving mankind dominion over not only the animal creation but also over his own society, even authorizing capital punishment for murder (Gen. 9:2–6).

This "dominion mandate," as it has been called, is still in effect, for all mankind. It indirectly authorizes all honorable human occupations — science, technology, commerce, government, education, arts — if performed to benefit mankind and to honor God. It implies the sanctity of the home and family (especially as expanded in Gen. 2:18–24 and 9:9) and of the creation as a whole, with men and women assigned stewardship over it, under God who created it. The three sons of Noah, the Bible tells us, "were Shem, and Ham, and Japheth" and eventually "of them was the whole earth overspread" (Gen. 9:18–19), as God had commanded.

Before this was done, however, the great rebellion at Babel was instigated by Nimrod, Ham's grandson. Instead of implementing God's command to go into all the world, the people said, "Let us make us a name, lest we be scattered abroad upon the face of the whole earth" (Gen. 11:4). So they built the great Tower of Babel, dedicated "unto heaven," and there, as we have already shown, were planted the seeds of the satanic religion of evolutionary pantheism that later spread around the world.

> So the LORD scattered them abroad from thence upon the face of all the earth: and they left off to build the city. Therefore is the name of it called Babel; because the LORD did there confound the language of all the earth: and from thence did the LORD scatter them abroad upon the face of all the earth (Gen. 11:8–9).

The people thus obeyed God's first commission, under duress as it were, but they did soon fill the earth. They also began to "subdue it" by developing science and technology and all the other activities that this implied. But instead of doing this to God's glory and man's good, they carried it out in the context of the pantheistic philosophy they had learned at Babel. Instead of gently developing the creation as God's stewards, they plundered it. Instead of cooperating with each other in the optimum use of their individual talents and nature's resources as God had desired, they fought each other in endless aggressions and tribal conflicts, which eventually grew into national wars and finally world wars. And all of this was the natural accompaniment to the pagan cosmogony and evolutionary philosophy learned by their ancestors at Babel.

It is fascinating to retrace these developments in the context of biblical history. All the evidences in archaeological discoveries, tribal traditions, the writings of ancient historians, and the ancient myths support the biblical outline when properly correlated. The record in the first chapter of Romans is all too true. They "changed the truth of God into a lie, and worshiped and served the creature more than the Creator," and therefore "God gave them up unto vile affections" (Rom. 1:25–26). Furthermore, because "they did not like to retain God in their knowledge, God gave them over to a reprobate mind," and soon their societies were "filled with all unrighteousness, fornication, wickedness, covetousness, maliciousness; full of envy, murder . . . covenant breakers, without natural affection, implacable, unmerciful" and other such ungodly characteristics (v. 28–31). As documented in earlier chapters, the rejection of creation and the Creator has led to these very evils.

There is also ample documentation of this dismal description in the Bible, insofar as those nations coming into contact with Israel were concerned. There were, for example, the Sodomites of Abraham's day, whose "filthy conversation" (or "lascivious behavior") and "unlawful deeds" (2 Peter 2:7–8) led to God's fire from heaven. The Egyptians and their pharaoh lost their firstborn sons and then drowned in the Red Sea because of their fierce persecution of God's people (Exod. 12:29, 14:27–28, cf. 15:9–10).

God warned the children of Israel against compromising with the sins of the Canaanites in the Promised Land with these words:

> Thou shalt not learn to do after the abominations of those nations. There shall not be found among you any one that maketh his son or his daughter to pass through the fire, or that useth divination, or an observer of times, or an enchanter or a witch. Or a charmer, or a consulter with familiar spirits, or a wizard, or a necromancer. For all that do these things are an abomination unto the LORD: and because of these abominations the LORD thy God doth drive them out from before thee (Deut. 18:9–12).

In addition to these occult practices with their ritualistic child sacrifices, the Canaanites were practitioners of the vilest forms of sexual sins, a fact abundantly confirmed by archaeology.

Then there were the fearful Assyrians, against whom Nahum prophesied: "Woe to the bloody city! It is all full of lies and robbery; the prey departeth not. . . . Because of the multitude of the whoredoms of the well-favoured harlot, the mistress of witchcrafts, that selleth nations through her whoredoms, and families through her witchcrafts" (Nah. 3:1, 4). Nebuchadnezzar, the greatest of the kings of the mighty Babylonian Empire, cast all who would not worship his image into a fiery furnace (Dan. 3:6), and the Median king decreed that all who prayed to any god except himself would be cast into a den of lions (Dan. 6:7–9). The later king of the Persians even decreed genocide for all the Jews in his empire (Esther 3:12–13). The cruelty and licentiousness of the Syrians, Greeks, Romans, and other nations mentioned in the Bible is also well documented. The same is true of the Oriental and African nations, the Teutonic and Scandinavian tribes of ancient Europe, the Mongol and Turkish hordes, the Islamic armies, even the American Indians. In more modern times, one quickly thinks of the

Nazis and the Communists, both slaughterers of millions. Almost every nation and tribe throughout history not only has embraced some form of evolutionary pantheism or atheism as its religious philosophy but has also been bitterly cruel and immoral, in comparison to God's standards. In some measure, the nation of Israel and the Christian nations have been exceptions, but these have also been contaminated to a great extent by pagan philosophies and practices. No wonder the Scriptures condemn ancient Babel, the source of it all, as "the mother of harlots and abominations of the earth" (Rev. 17:5). "For all nations have drunk of the wine of the wrath of her fornication, and the kings of the earth have committed fornication with her, and the merchants of the earth are waxed rich through the abundance of her delicacies" Rev. 18:3).

The confusion of tongues at Babel resulted in a rapid worldwide dispersion. In that vein, it is noteworthy that a fascinating corpus of literature has been accumulating during the past century that documents the impressive evidence for the development of complex civilizations and worldwide navigation and commerce for thousands of years before Columbus and the 14th-century European explorers. This literature has been largely ignored by establishment historians, archaeologists, and anthropologists, who are still largely mind-bound by Darwinian concepts of human evolution.

We are not speaking here of creationist writers but of non-Darwinian evolutionist writers, the number of whom is growing rapidly these days. We have already noted that the 19th-century evolutionary concepts of Tylor and Frazer have been largely abandoned by modern cultural anthropologists, even though they still accept the evolutionary worldview. Physical anthropologists still believe in human evolution from uncertain "hominid" ancestors, but the evidence is so fragmentary and equivocal that there is no consensus on the particular line of descent, with some even favoring the notion that the apes have descended from men, instead of vice versa.

In any case, there is today much evidence that confirms the biblical record of the dispersion. The arts of metallurgy, construction, agriculture, animal husbandry, and even writing were known to the antediluvians (note Genesis 4:2, 17, 20, 22, etc.). This knowledge, along with shipbuilding skills, was undoubtedly transmitted by Noah's sons to their descendants. However, after the confusion of tongues at Babel, they lost the art of writing, except perhaps for Shem's immediate family (since these probably did not participate in the rebellion). Other skills were not forgotten, but they could not be employed until each small family group scattering from Babel could find a new home and new resources and also develop a population large enough to permit some specialization. Until then they would have to live in caves or crude huts, surviving by a hunting-and-gathering culture, although this situation needed to last for only a few generations at most. This type of evidence, of course, is exactly what archaeologists find at ancient occupation sites all over the world.

Again and again, all over the world are found evidences of complex societies that achieved a relatively high status after an apparently brief "Stone Age" foundation (brief, at least, as measured by the quantity of evidence found at the sites), followed by a long period of moral and spiritual and (often) technological deterioration. After a remarkable survey of the artifacts of ancient intercontinental and transoceanic trade and navigation, James Bailey gives the following summary:

> I suggest that human history can now hesitantly be traced back as an unbroken narrative to 4000 B.C. The facts must not, however, be twisted to suit the fallacy of necessary human progress. For the picture emerging from the gloom cast by two Dark Ages is one of the Fall of Man in historic terms as well as of his rise: it is a picture in our period more of degradation than of success; it is also a picture of monotheism breaking down into polytheism and of the struggle to return to monotheism. The establishment view of the history of religion gradually progressing from animism to polytheism, from polytheism to monotheism is the reverse of the facts.[20]

Despite the biblical terminology in this summary, the above author was not a Christian. He argues, in fact, that Christianity is a continuation of the ancient sun worship. Nevertheless, Bailey compiled a remarkable mass of evidence indicating high civilizations in remote antiquity all over the world. In fact, the foreword that strongly commended his book was written by one of the world's most distinguished anthropologists, Raymond Dart, discoverer of the first *Australopithecine* fossil and recipient of many honors.

Indirect and unrecognized confirmations of the Genesis record are found in many other unexpected places. For example, "ley lines" have been receiving attention in recent years. First noticed extensively in England, they have since been found in Peru, Bolivia, and many other places. These are long, straight lines apparently laid out across the landscape by pre-historic surveyors whose identity has been long forgotten. It is at least possible, however, that they represent ancient landmarks, laid out when the scattering tribes

---

20. James Bailey, *The God-Kings and the Titans: The New World Ascendance in Ancient Times* (New York: St. Martin's, 1973), p. 296.

first attempted to survey and divide up the lands of the post-Flood world. They were given the name "ley lines" by Alfred Watkins in 1921, the term being an old dialectical term for "lines laid down." The Table of Nations in Genesis 10 may be relevant here when it concludes: "These are the families of the sons of Noah, after their generations, in their nations: and by these were the nations divided in the earth after the flood" (Gen. 10:32).

But what *are* the criticisms of the ley concept? When Watkins put forward his observations regarding remnants of prehistoric alignments in Britain he ran head-on into official archaeological thinking which still believed in the Piltdown Man. The orthodox view was that the megalith builders were just savages quite incapable of surveying or having any finer thoughts than grubbing for food and feuding with other tribes. The whole idea of leys was an unprecedented absurdity — "damned nonsense" as one archaeologist put it.

Modern archaeology shows that prehistoric societies were complex. . . . And the prominent prehistorian Professor R.J.C. Atkinson has clearly demonstrated that the laying out of an accurate straight landscape line would have been well within the means of the megalithic builders.[21]

Such megalithic monuments as Stonehenge, other "henges," and stone monuments of various types — apparently having both astronomical and religious uses — have been found in many places. The giant stone faces on Easter Island, isolated in the middle of the Pacific, constitute another well-known case in point. There should be no doubt that ancient people were highly intelligent and capable.

With reference to the possible significance of "ley lines," it is noteworthy that the Bible speaks of "the ancient landmark, which thy fathers have set" (Prov. 22:28). The same word is more commonly translated "border" or "bound" and is first used in the Table of Nations, referring to "the border of the Canaanites" (Gen. 10:19). That the original boundaries of the nations were providential was affirmed by Moses: "Remember the days of old, consider the years of many generations. . . . When the Most High divided to the nations their inheritance, when he separated the sons of Adam, he set the bounds of the people according to the number of the children of Israel" (Deut. 32:7–8). The 70 nations of Genesis 10 thus corresponded in number to the 70 original Israelites (Gen. 46:27).

---

21. Paul Devereux and Robert Forrest, "Straight Lines on an Ancient Landscape," *New Scientist* 96 (Dec. 23/30, 1982): p. 822.

However, the spreading tribes were not merely carrying civilization with them around the world. They were also carrying their Babel-derived evolutionary religion, astrology, occultism, and pantheism — along with warfare, plundering, and general destruction of the world that God had given them. On the other hand, almost every tribe and nation carried the vague tradition with them of a "golden age" at the beginning of their history. But their current and known past histories are filled with tales of lust and greed and fighting, and in many cases physical and social deterioration.

In every part of the world are found evidences of man's destruction of his environment and of the creatures over which he had been given dominion. Consider the recent history of the Americas, for example: "When Europeans began to settle America, the air and rivers were pure, the landscape green, the great Plains teeming with bison. Today we breathe smog, worry about toxic chemicals in our water, pave over the landscape, and rarely see any large animal."[22]

But modern peoples in the Western world are not the only ones who have despoiled their environments. The Pleistocene Epoch has been notable for its many extinctions of large animals such as the mastodon and saber-tooth tiger. Much evidence has accumulated in recent years that these great animals of the distant past — like the American bison in the 19th century — were simply hunted to extinction by ancient hunters. More recently the giant moa birds met a similar fate at the hands of the Maori in New Zealand. Similar happenings abounded in other islands of the Pacific and among ancient tribes in the Americas. Great deserts in the Sahara and other regions, once well watered and sustaining large populations, have now been rendered useless.

> The damage is likely to occur when people suddenly colonize an unfamiliar environment (like the first Maori and Easter Islanders); or when they advance along a new frontier (like the first Indians to reach America) and can simply move beyond when they've damaged the region behind. . . . And some habitats and species are more susceptible to damage than others — such as a dry, unforgiving desert environment, or flightless birds that have never seen humans.[23]

The ancient migrations from Babel quickly filled the earth, but they also defiled it. The story of the rise and fall of these early civilizations is fascinating, though they are now largely covered by jungles or buried in desert sands and thus have been largely lost and forgotten. But they all carried their Babel

---

22. Jared Diamond, "The Golden Age that Never Was," *Discover* 9 (Dec. 1988): p. 71.
23. Ibid., p. 79.

religion with them, along with some remnants of the true faith and history inherited from Noah.

Another fascinating evidence of these primeval migrations is the occurrence of equivalent ancient place names and object names all over the world. These often correlate with common mythological figures around the world. Many authors have noted the existence of this kind of data. Cohane, for example, has compiled many hundreds of such correlations. After evaluating all these names, he concluded: "Within a relatively short time, it became apparent that, for better or worse, all of them figure prominently in ancient Semitic legends and mythology. Most of them are to be found in the Old Testament, notably in Genesis."[24] Cohane also commented in some detail on the similarity of myths and legends in the Old and New Worlds:

> Alfred Maury commented in regard to some of them: "There is scarcely a prominent fact in the opening chapters of the Book of Genesis that cannot be duplicated from the legends of the American nations. . . . It is a very remarkable fact that we find in America traditions of the deluge coming nearer to that of the Bible and the Chaldean religion than among any people of the Old World."[25]

> Of another native myth Kingsborough stated that it was "a clearly established legend which singularly resembles the Bible record of the Tower of Babel."[26]

As noted earlier (see chapter 5), two leading historians of science have shown the commonality of the world's mythologies from a still different line of evidence, tying them all back in to the widespread ancient knowledge of astronomy and astrology, combined also with mathematics and number theory. In the process of a remarkably scholarly and insightful analysis, these authors — G. de Santillana and H. von Dechind — also decry the baleful influence of evolutionary theory on the study of ancient cultures:

> The simple idea of evolution, which it is no longer thought necessary to examine, spreads like a tent over all those ages that lead

---

24. John Philip Cohane, *The Key* (New York: Crown, 1969), p. 19. The approving foreword to this book was written by Cyrus H. Gordon, one of the world's greatest authorities on the languages of the ancient world.
25. Ibid., p. 24. Alfred Maury authored the article "Deluge," in *The Encyclopidie Moderne* (Paris, 1860), from which Cohane quotes here.
26. Ibid., p. 25, citing Edward King, Viscount Kingsborough, the 18th-century explorer who authored the monumental ten-volume *Antiquities of Mexico* (London: 1830–1848).

from primitivism into civilization. Gradually, we are told, step by step, men produced the arts and crafts, this and that, until they emerged into the light of history.

Those soporific words "gradually" and "step by step," repeated incessantly, are aimed at covering an ignorance which is both vast and surprising. One should like to inquire: which steps? But then one is lulled, overwhelmed, and stupefied by the gradualness of it all, which is at best a platitude, only good for pacifying the mind, since no one is willing to imagine that civilization appeared in a thunderclap.[27]

As these and other scholars have shown, however, civilization *did* appear suddenly, all over the world at about the same time. The evidence for the supposed million-year history of slow evolution from an unknown apelike ancestor is trivial and confusing at best, but the evidence for worldwide high civilization before even the beginning of written historical records is clear and abundant.

The mythologies of all these ancient cultures were both similar to each other and also astronomically based, tied in also with the actual, though legendary, exploits of ancient heroes. As pointed out in chapter 5, de Santillana and Dechind have asserted:

> It is now known that astrology has provided man with his continuing *lingua franca* through the centuries. But it is essential to recognize that, in the beginning, astrology presupposed an astronomy. Through the interplay of these two heavenly concepts, the common elements of preliterate knowledge were caught up in a bizarre bestiary whose taxonomy has disappeared.[28]

These learned authors tried to decipher the possible original meaning of this "bizarre bestiary," this "Star Menagerie of profoundly meaningful animal characters,"[29] but they finally acknowledged that "there is nothing left of the ancient knowledge except the relics, fragments, and allusions that have

---

27. Giorgio de Santillana and Hertha von Dechind, *Hamlet's Mill: An Essay on Myth and the Frame of Time* (Boston, MA: Gambit, 1969), p. 68. As previously noted, the first author was professor of the history and philosophy of science at MIT; the second was professor of the history of science at the University of Frankfort.
28. Ibid., p. 345. David Hughes, who is on the faculty in astronomy at the University of Sheffield, notes that "the originators of the constellations must have lived somewhere on the longitude line 36°N . . . around 2500 B.C.," following the studies of Professor Archie Roy of Glasgow University. See "Draughtsmen of the Constellations," *Nature* 312 (Dec. 20/27, 1984): p. 697. This corresponds closely to the time and place of Nimrod.
29. Ibid., p. 347.

survived the deep attrition of the ages. . . . The system as a whole may lie beyond all conjecture, because the creating, ordering minds that made it have vanished forever."[30]

These and the other brilliant investigators we have been quoting in this section have uncovered striking evidences of the brilliant — though destructive and aggressive — capabilities of ancient peoples all over the world. With their naturalistic presuppositions, however, such writers are at a loss how to correlate all the evidence, not realizing that it all fits perfectly into the framework of the early chapters of Genesis.

The High God

Much of the above helps to explain why it is that almost all nations and tribes, ancient or modern, cultured or savage, still seem to retain a vague awareness of God in their tribal memories. The Darwinian generation thought that people had advanced from savagery to animism to polytheism to monotheism, but modern archaeologists now admit that religions in every case have degenerated from primitive monotheism down into pantheism and polytheism, and from thence either to animism or occultism or even atheism in some cases.

The fact is that all these old evolutionary ideas about the origin of religion have come up against the essential universality of the concept of a high God. Archaeologists have uncovered this testimony in the tablets of ancient civilizations; ethnologists have discerned it in the earliest myths of the classical civilization; anthropologists have discovered it in the religions of the animistic tribes all over the world today. In fact, the evidences already noted — the universality of prayer, sacrifice, a standard of righteousness, and belief in immortality — are commonly associated with the belief that these practices all originated with that high God.

The latter is called by many different names, of course, varying from tribe to tribe. In most cases, the prominence of the high God was greatest in the very earliest stages of the history of the tribe. He eventually became almost forgotten among the host of lesser gods and goddesses that crept into each particular religion, or else among the host of spirits that seemed to need placation. His memory was never completely expunged, however. Somehow, the awareness of God's existence continued indelibly, though faintly, in each soul everywhere.

---

30. Ibid., p. 348. These authors overlook the strong possibility that astrology represents a satanic corruption of an original "gospel in the stars," impressed upon the heavens by Seth or other antediluvian patriarchs (see discussion earlier in this chapter).

The teaching that religion — especially monotheism — had arisen by evolution was widely promoted in the mid-19th century by such ardent Darwinists as Auguste Comte, Herbert Spencer, James Frazer, and Edward Tylor. These and others each had their pet theories of the origin of religion — whether henotheism (nature worship), animism, fetishism, totemism, magic, or whatever — but all were evolutionary concepts related to the gradual rise of man from some ape-like ancestor.

Soon, however, as more and more data came in from those actually working with the various "primitive" tribes around the world, as well as from archaeologists and ethnologists studying ancient languages and cultures, it became obvious that these old evolutionary ideas were wrong. Languages and social systems were all highly complex in the very earliest records of the ancients and among the most "primitive" of all existing tribes. Furthermore, it became obvious that the pantheism, polytheism, or animism characterizing their religions (all various forms of evolutionism, as we have seen) actually had degenerated in every case from primitive monotheism and recognition of God as supernatural Creator.

This is a large and complex subject, and we can only give here a few testimonies from leading authorities in the field, beginning with the scholars of the late 19th century. Andrew Lang, for example, wrote, "Of the existence of a belief in the Supreme Being among primitive tribes there is as good evidence as we possess for any fact in the ethnographic region."[31]

Speaking with reference to the original religion of India, where Hinduism is probably now the most pantheistic and polytheistic of all present-day religions, the great Oriental scholar Max Muller said, "There is a monotheism that precedes the polytheism of the Veda; and even in the invocations of the innumerable gods, the remembrance of a God, one and infinite, breaks through the mist of idolatrous phraseology like the blue sky that is hidden by passing clouds."[32]

With respect to the equally ancient and polytheistic religion of the Egyptians, the noted archaeologist Sir Flinders Petrie commented: "Wherever we

---

31. Andrew Lang, *The Making of Religion* (London: Longmans & Green, 1898), p. 18. Lang, a famous Scottish author, was one of the first post-Darwinian scholars to argue for extrabiblical primeval monotheism.

32. Max Muller, *History of Sanskrit Literature* (London: 1859), p. 559. Professor Muller is considered the founder of the science of the history of religions. Born in Germany and educated in Paris, he was a professor at Oxford University in England. He wrote many authoritative volumes on Eastern religions but believed that religion had evolved from nature worship.

can trace back polytheism to its earliest stages, we find that it results from combinations of monotheism."[33]

The Bible's account of Abraham and Sarah also indicates that the Egyptian pharaoh at that time (about 1900 B.C.) knew about the true God (see Gen. 12:17), as did the king of the Philistines, in the land of Canaan (Gen. 20:3–4).

The ancient religion of Sumeria, as well as the Semitic religions of Assyria, Babylonia, and other related peoples, were thoroughly analyzed by Stephen Langdon, who wrote, "In my opinion the history of the oldest civilization of man is a rapid decline from monotheism to extreme polytheism and widespread belief in evil spirits. It is in a very true sense the history of the fall of man."[34] He added: "All Semitic tribes appear to have started with a single tribal deity whom they regarded as the Divine Creator of his people."[35]

With regard to the primitive tribes of the present day, Catholic scholar Pere Wilhelm Schmidt of the University of Vienna, who is probably the most knowledgeable of all writers on the subject, has said, "A belief in a Supreme Being is to be found among *all* the peoples of the primitive culture, not indeed everywhere in the same form or the same vigor, but still everywhere prominent enough to make his dominant position indubitable."[36]

China is the world's largest nation, as well as one of the most ancient. Although its chief religions have long been evolutionistic and even atheistic to a degree, its original religion was, as in all the rest of the nations, monotheistic. Many years ago, Professor Legge of Oxford University wrote a masterful work on the Chinese religions, in which he concluded, "Five thousand years ago the Chinese were Monotheists, but even then there was a struggle with nature-worship and divination."[37]

---

33. Flinders Petrie, *The Religion of Ancient Egypt* (London: Constable, 1908), p. 4. Petrie was considered one of the greatest of all Egyptologists.
34. Stephen Langdon, *Semitic Mythology*, Vol. 5 in *Mythology of All Races* (Boston, MA: Archaeological Institute of America, 1931), p. xviii. Langdon was a professor at Oxford University and universally recognized as one of the greatest scholars in his field. By "oldest civilization" in this quote, Langdon meant the Sumerians.
35. Ibid., p. 93.
36. Wilhelm Schmidt, *Origin of the Idea of God*, translated from his German work *Der Ursprung der Gottesidee* (Munster: 1926–1934) and quoted by Samuel Zwemer in his *Origin of Religion* (New York: Loisseaux Brothers, 1945), p. 14–15. Dr. Schmidt published over 150 books and pamphlets, founded and edited by the journal *Anthropos*, and is, by any realistic measure, the greatest modern authority on the origin of religions. His conclusions are ignored by evolutionists, but they have never been refuted.
37. James Legge, *The Religions of China*, as quoted in A.C. Gaebelein, *Christianity or Religion?* (New York: Our Hope Publishing, 1927), p. 44.

A remarkable new study has emerged in recent years on the religious origins of the Chinese language. The subject is too complex to discuss here, but abundant evidence has been given to show the characters of the most ancient Chinese script (largely preserved in the present written languages of China) are composed primarily of pictographic and ideographic symbols, which in turn tie back in a remarkable way to the events described in the first 11 chapters of Genesis. For those who are interested in this subject, two volumes of exposition are now available.[38]

This surprising discovery has received considerable support from competent Christian linguists and is being further extended by a number of Chinese Christian scholars. This adds a unique new line of documentation to the already strong list of evidences that all nations and tribes originally believed in one high God, whom their ancestors had worshiped in the beginnings of their respective histories. As already stated, this primeval monotheistic faith was later gradually corrupted and eventually almost banished from their memories by the deceptions of some form of evolutionary pantheism, polytheism, or occultism.

An excellent summary statement of the situation has been given by the great philologist and ethnologist Wilhelm Schmidt:

> As external civilization increased in splendor and wealth, so religion came to be expressed in forms of ever-increasing magnificence and opulence. Images of gods and demons multiplied to an extent which defies all classification. . . . But all this cannot blind us to the fact that despite the glory and wealth of the outward forms, the inner kernel of religion often disappeared and its essential strength was weakened. The results of this, both moral and social, were anything but desirable, leading to extreme degradation and even to the deification of the immoral and antisocial. The principal cause of this corruption was that the figure of the Supreme Being was sinking further and further into the background, hidden behind the impenetrable phalanx of the thousand new gods and demons. . . .
>
> But all the while, the ancient primitive religion still continued among the few remainders of the primitive culture, preserved by

---

38. C.H. Kang and Ethel R. Nelson, *The Discovery of Genesis* (St. Louis, MO: Concordia, 1979), p. 139. Dr. Kang originally published much of this material in a small book, *Genesis and the Chinese* (printed independently in Hong Kong in 1950), while serving as a missionary and hospital chaplain. Dr. Nelson is a former medical missionary working with the Chinese in Thailand. Ethel R. Nelson and Richard E. Broadberry, *Mysteries Confucius Couldn't Solve* (South Lancaster, MA: Read Books, 1986), p. 182. Mr. Broadberry is a medical laboratory specialist in Taiwan.

fragmentary peoples driven into the most distant regions. Yet in their condition of stagnation, poverty, and insignificance, even there it must necessarily have lost much of its power and greatness, so that even among such peoples it is much too late to find a true image of the faith of really primitive men. It remains for us, by dint of laborious research, to put gradually together from many faded fragments a lifelike picture of this religion.[39]

This lengthy quotation from Dr. Schmidt describes a situation very much like that described by the Apostle Paul in his discourse on the origin of paganism in Romans 1:20–25, as discussed previously. Since Schmidt, in his voluminous writings, never gives biblical references or makes appeal to the Scriptures in his argumentation, we do not know whether or not this remarkable parallel was intentional. In any case, the copious global documentation incorporated by Schmidt makes it certain that the Pauline analysis precisely fits the facts of history.

A more recent Christian scholar, Dr. Arthur Custance, has written many books supporting the Genesis record of the dispersion from Babel, with the nations carrying with them around the world both the remnants of the true religion and the false religion of Nimrod. Summarizing the evidence for primitive monotheism, he wrote:

From high cultures and low cultures the same picture emerges. It is a picture of a remarkably pure concept of the nature of God and His relation to man being gradually corrupted on the one hand by rationalizations which resulted from the gradual substitution of man's own thinking in place of revelation and on the other hand by superstition which stemmed from ignorance and forgetfulness of the original revelation.[40]

Nevertheless, despite the sad picture of rebellion and spiritual deterioration throughout the world after the Babel dispersion, God has not left Himself without witness. In one way or another, God's everlasting gospel has always been available in every time and place to any who would truly seek Him. Therefore, they are "without excuse" when they do not.

39. Wilhelm Schmidt, *The Origin and Growth of Religion: Facts and Theories,* translated by H.J. Rose (London: Methuen, 1931), p. 289–290. This one-volume English translation summarizes the monumental seven volumes of Schmidt's *Der Ursprung der Gottesidee* (see note 36), in which he shows conclusively that monotheism was the primeval faith of all nations and tribes in every part of the world.

40. Arthur C. Custance, *Evolution or Creation?* (Grand Rapids, MI: Zondervan, 1976), p. 131. Dr. Custance held an MA in Oriental languages and a PhD in anthropology.

As we have seen, all nations and tribes still have at least a dim tradition of the true God who created them, even though the concept is now largely hidden by corrupt religion. The witness of God in creation itself is always there. Even pagan astrology and mythology still contain some distorted fragments of the creation, the Fall, the Flood, the dispersion, and God's primeval promise of a coming Redeemer.

Furthermore, there were the primeval (pre-Sinai) divine laws and ordinances, now lost but still partly preserved in the legal codes of the various nations and tribes. These, along with a condemning conscience in each man and woman, perpetually testify to them of their separation from God and their need for a Savior. The ancient tradition of substitutionary sacrifice is further indication that innocent animal blood must be shed to cover and cleanse their sins before a holy God. Yet, since such sacrifices obviously provide only temporary relief, they must be offered again and again.

The goodness of God (life and breath, sunshine and rain, food and gladness) provides continual evidence of His love, but pain and death are perpetual reminders of His holy judgment on an alienated world. God has also given His written revelation through Israel. And even before their captivity in Assyria and Babylon, there were many Israelites who carried it to other lands via caravan and sea lane, as well as transmitting it to people who visited Israel.

There has always been a witness, sometimes clear but more often dim, of the true God and His eternal gospel. It has always been opposed where given, because Satan and his hosts are subtle and powerful. Evolutionism has dominated the world in one form or another ever since Babel, as we have already seen, but there has always been a creationist movement that testified against this dominant system.

Creation is "only" the foundation of the eternal gospel, of course, but we can hope that there have been those in all nations who trusted in God not only as Creator but also as Savior and Lord. The world is in darkness, but the light of the glorious gospel shines in the darkness (2 Cor. 4:4, 6; John 1:4–5). If men and women have a heart that is toward God and will respond to such light as they have (through such witnesses as in the various types of testimony outlined in this chapter), then God will see that they receive whatever additional light may be needed for salvation. The Word of God assures us that

> God is no respecter of persons: but in every nation he that feareth him, and worketh righteousness, is accepted with him (Acts 10:34–35).

But the hour cometh, and now is, when the true worshippers shall worship the Father in spirit and in truth: for the Father seeketh such to worship him (John 4:23).

The eyes of the LORD run to and fro throughout the whole earth, to shew himself strong in the behalf of them whose heart is perfect toward him (2 Chron. 16:9).

The long, long war has continued age after age, as the everlasting gospel struggles against the forces of darkness in an apparently losing battle. The war is not yet over, however, and the great victory will come eventually, a victory assured by the accomplished fact that God in Christ "spoiled principalities and powers" in his death on the Cross, "triumphing over them in it" (Col. 2:15).

Resurrection of the Creator

Before Christ came into the world, God's promises of redemption and reconciliation of that lost world were seen only in type and prophecy and tradition. These promises were valid and were sufficient unto salvation for all who would respond in faith to the dim light that transmitted them. They could only be fully implemented, however, when God the Creator became man the creature, taking on Himself the sin of the whole world and dying as man's substitute, thus paying the penalty for the guilt of that sin.

The dim light became a very bright light when God became man, for "In him was life; and the life was the light of men. . . . That was the true Light, which lighteth every man that cometh into the world" (John 1:4, 9). No longer could people excuse themselves for not having sufficient evidence of God to come to His light. God Himself was now with them in the world, just as He had walked with Adam in the garden when the world began.

Yes, "He was in the world, and the world was made by him, [but] the world knew him not" (John 1:10, emphasis added). Men could finally see God and hear God and marvel at His miraculous works of creation, demonstrating clearly that He was indeed their Creator. But instead of believing and receiving Him, they "crucified the LORD of glory" (1 Cor. 2:8). This teaches us plainly that no one can be persuaded to believe in creation if he chooses *not* to believe, for men rejected the Creator even when they saw Him face to face!

There is an important principle here. No matter how dim the light, men who want to see it *can* see. No matter how bright the light, men who do *not* want to see it will never see.

And this is the condemnation, that light is come into the world, and men loved darkness rather than light, because their deeds were evil. For every one that doeth evil hateth the light, neither cometh to the light, lest his deeds should be reproved. But he that doeth truth cometh to the light, that his deeds may be made manifest, that they are wrought in God (John 3:19–21).

We trust and hope that there were some in those ancient times who responded in faith to the faint light of the everlasting gospel that they could see. But no doubt most remained in the darkness of their humanistic reasonings and God-dishonoring behavior to the light of salvation. This is bound to be true, because the vast majority of even those who saw God in person, when He became the God-man, still rejected the brilliant Light of His presence, and joined in spirit with those who nailed Him to the Cross.

Yet even this was part of God's plan of redemption, proving beyond all measure that He is not only the omnipotent Creator, the God of infinite holiness and perfect justice, but also the God of infinite grace and perfect love. "For he hath made him to be sin for us, who knew no sin; that we might be made the righteousness of God in him" (2 Cor. 5:21). All men and women, by both nature and practice, are sinners and therefore alienated from their Creator, deserving nothing but death and eternal separation from Him. "But God commendeth his love toward us, in that, while we were yet sinners, Christ died for us" (Rom. 5:8). We deserve eternal separation from Him, but He offers us eternal life with Him, as a free gift: "For the wages of sin is death; but the gift of God is eternal life through Jesus Christ our Lord" (Rom. 6:23).

Although the Creator suffered infinitely as He bore the sins of all the world on the Cross, shedding His blood and dying the cruelest of deaths, He could not die eternally. If God were to die forever, the universe itself would vanish away, for He is "upholding all things by the word of his power" (Heb. 1:3), and it is "in him we live, and move, and have our being" (Acts 17:28).

God's human body died and was buried, but three days later He conquered death and hell and Satan, and He rose again, alive forevermore. Herein is the infinite power of His everlasting gospel. Because He is the Creator, He — and He alone — could conquer death. "I declare unto you the gospel," wrote Paul, ". . . how that Christ died for our sins according to the scriptures; and that he was buried, and that he rose again the third day according to the scriptures" (1 Cor. 15:1, 3–4).

All the pagan gods and goddesses, all the great religionists of the past (Buddha, Mohammed, et al.), all the great modern evolutionists (Darwin, Marx, Hitler, Freud, and so on) who have so greatly impacted the modern world — all are dead, though their influence lives on.

But Jesus Christ is alive! God is not dead! The great Creator is now our resurrected Redeemer and living Savior. In His glorified resurrection body (still truly a physical body but no longer limited by the constraints of physical forces), He will live forever (Rev. 1:18). And, "because I live," He said, "ye shall live also" (John 14:19).

It is important that we understand the vital connection between the creation of the world and the Resurrection of its Creator. These are the two greatest miracles of all the ages, and each one implies the other. It is remarkable and disturbing how many professing Christians observe Easter and apparently believe in Christ's Resurrection and yet either ignore the creation or even try to combine it with evolution.

The Creator has imposed the law of decay and death on His whole creation because of the rebellion of its human stewards. Therefore only *He* can defeat death, and this only by paying the redemption price Himself, dying for sin and then rising victoriously from the dead. Thus the great miracle of Resurrection requires the great prior miracle of supernatural creation.

By the same token, the omnipotent, omniscient Creator cannot fail in His creative purposes, even though man's sin has brought the universal reign of death into the world. Therefore, He *must* conquer death and redeem His creation. This He can only do by His incarnation, His dying for sin, and His Resurrection. Thus it is that creation demands resurrection, and resurrection requires creation. Neither is truly meaningful without the other.

It is significant that the greatest resurrection chapter in the Bible, 1 Corinthians 15, ties in the gospel (v. 1–4) so definitely with not only the substitutionary death of Christ (v. 3–4, 8, 22) and his bodily Resurrection (v. 5–8, 12–20), but also with the creation (v. 38–41), 45–47) and the subsequent curse of death (v. 21–22), as well as the second coming (v. 23–28, 51–55). The creation, the Cross with the empty tomb, and the ultimate kingdom of God are all included in Christ's everlasting gospel, embracing as it does all His purposes and works from eternity to eternity.

It is also significant, as noted before, that only those religions that postulate special creation (orthodox Christianity, Judaism, and Islam) teach a future bodily resurrection. Conversely, even though all religions (except raw atheism) teach some form of soul immortality, only those that postulate a future bodily Resurrection teach the doctrine of primeval special creation.

And of the three creationist/resurrectionist religions, only Christianity accepts the death and Resurrection of the Creator. Islam and Judaism, although incorporating the creation record of Genesis in their tenets, teach an emasculated gospel that still requires human works for salvation, denying the identity of Jesus Christ as the redeeming Creator and thus also rejecting His bodily Resurrection.

Therefore, of all the world's religions and philosophies, only orthodox biblical Christianity teaches both the supernatural creation of all things by the transcendent yet personal Creator God, and also the substitutionary death and bodily Resurrection of the Creator, the Lord Jesus Christ. The everlasting gospel is still preached implicitly by the data of creation and the various other faint witnesses described in this chapter, but it is only formulated and proclaimed *explicitly* through the New Testament Scriptures and orthodox Christian doctrine.

The classic sermon of the Apostle Paul to the Athenian philosophers provides an ideal case in point. The atheistic Epicureans and the pantheistic Stoics — both firmly committed to an evolutionary philosophy — heard Paul preaching about the Resurrection, and their curiosity impelled them to listen to this man they called a religious "babbler." Although both groups adhered to sophisticated philosophical systems, both also had easily adapted to the idolatrous cults of the many popular gods and goddesses whose images adorned the streets and temples of Athens. Whether these merely represented the forces of nature or were actually energized by the "spirits" of the gods they honored mattered little to their devotees.

Paul, however, knew that these people still remembered an "unknown God," who to them represented the high God honored by their ancestors as the Creator and Ruler of all things. Therefore, he appealed to their instinctive and traditional knowledge of the Creator by first calling attention to this unknown God:

> Him declare I unto you. God that made the world and all things
> therein, seeing that he is Lord of heaven and earth, dwelleth not in
> temples made with hands; neither is worshipped with men's hands,
> as though he needed any thing, seeing he giveth to all life, and
> breath, and all things; and hath made of one blood all nations of
> men for to dwell on all the face of the earth, and hath determined
> the times before appointed, and the bounds of their habitation; that
> they should seek the Lord, if haply they might feel after him, and find
> him, though he be not far from every one of us: for in him we live,
> and move, and have our being (Acts 17:23–28).

Note how Paul began his message — not by quoting Scripture but by talking about the Creator and His purposes in creation. These people, unlike the Jews to whom he always witnessed first, neither knew nor believed the Scriptures, so he must appeal first to what they knew. Note also that God's reason for assigning each nation its own time in history and place in geography was so that its people could seek the Lord and find Him.

This can only mean that the Athenians really *could* have found their "unknown God" if they had sought Him. Instead, like those in other nations, they had gone their own way. "But now," said Paul, "[God] commandeth all men every where to repent: because he hath appointed a day, in the which he will judge the world in righteousness by that man whom he hath ordained; whereof he hath given assurance unto all men, in that he hath raised him from the dead" (Acts 17:30–31).

Men were already "without excuse" if they rejected God as Creator, but their guilt would be magnified manyfold if they continued in their rebellion. God has demonstrated — not just in the complex designs of the natural world but in the very world of human experience — that He is the living and true God. For He has conquered death itself, and only God the Creator can raise the dead. He is fully justified in commanding all men everywhere to repent (that is, "change their minds") about God and His right to rule and judge the world. Those who still reject God as both Creator and Savior will indeed encounter Him on that appointed day as righteous Judge.

The fact of special creation is surely the most certain truth of science, and the truth of Christ's Resurrection is surely the best-proved fact of history.[41] The dim light of antiquity has become the "marvellous light" (1 Pet. 2:9) of the finished work of God in Christ, "the light of the glorious gospel of Christ" (2 Cor. 4:4). Men are "without excuse" if they reject God as Creator. They are "condemned already" if they now reject His Resurrection and have "not believed in the name of the only begotten Son of God" (John 3:18). God's plan of redemption is no longer merely an ancient promise but a glorious accomplishment, so there is no longer the slightest justification for doubting Him or His Word.

The death and Resurrection of Christ marked the beginning of the so-called Christian Era. Indeed, many from every nation have come into the redeemed family of God through trusting Christ as Son of God and personal Savior. After His Resurrection, He gave His small initial band of followers

---

41. For a brief summary of the evidences of the Resurrection (a full recital of which could take volumes) see Henry M. Morris, *Many Infallible Proofs* (Green Forest, AR: Master Books, 1974), p. 97–105.

God's second Great Commission: "Go ye into all the world, and preach the gospel to every creature" (Mark 16:15). As previously mentioned, the first worldwide commission, given to all mankind and still in effect, was the "dominion mandate," given to Adam and Eve in Eden and renewed to Noah after the Flood. The second mandate was given only to Christian believers, who now have the responsibility of implementing *both* the second in the context of the first, and the first in support of the second.

For example, a Bible-believing scientist can (indeed, should) do his research both with the purpose of "thinking God's thought after him" in carrying out God's mandate to subdue the earth for the good of mankind and the glory of God, and also with the goal of using the testimony of science to support God's Word and to win people to faith in Christ as Creator and Savior. A Christian teacher should both transmit knowledge of God's created world to his or her pupils and also teach them by practice and precept the saving grace of God in Christ, insofar as the law and opportunity allow. Similarly, Christians in every honorable profession should seek to both bring individuals to personal knowledge of our Creator/Redeemer and also win to Christ their own professions (science, teaching, business, etc.), so to speak, by redeeming the goals and practices of their respective vocations to a God-honoring status.

At Babel, God had forced the people of an unwilling generation to go out into all the world with the "dominion mandate." Much later, at Jerusalem, He forced the first generation of reluctant disciples to scatter around the world with their Great Commission by allowing "a great persecution against the church" to arise, so that "they that were scattered abroad went every where preaching the word" (Acts 8:1, 4).

That this statement could well be taken literally is suggested by the fact that, in the great conversion wave at Jerusalem beginning on the Day of Pentecost, 50 days after Christ's Resurrection, "there were dwelling at Jerusalem Jews, devout men, out of every nation under heaven," and through the miraculous power of the Holy Spirit, "every man heard them speak in his own language" (Acts 2:5–6). These included both Jews of the dispersion and Jewish proselytes, all of whom were devout enough in their creationist, messianic, biblical faith to make the long journey to Jerusalem from their homelands for the great festival of Pentecost. There they were converted, returning later to their own countries to proclaim the everlasting gospel with a new dimension, that of God's primeval promise now fulfilled.

The Apostle Paul, who himself preached the gospel all over the Graeco-Roman world, could later write to the Christians in Colosse of "the hope of the gospel, which ye have heard, and which was preached to every creature which is under heaven" (Col. 1:23).

In this verse the phrase "to every creature" could also be translated "*in every creature*," meaning that nature itself (in the manner suggested in Rom. 1:20), is always silently witnessing to God's creative power and redemptive purpose. In any case, it is certain that the first generation of Christian believers did travel far and wide preaching the Word. The Apostle Thomas, for example, is said to have founded the Mar Thoma Church in India, and tradition says that Matthew preached in both Persia and Ethiopia. All of Europe and North Africa had heard the gospel by the end of the first century, and there are at least traditions to the effect that Christ was preached in other more distant lands as well.

Much of the fruits of this first wave of evangelism, however, lasted only a short while. The Roman persecutions — and later the Mohammedan scourge — destroyed multitudes of churches and Christian schools. Even more seriously, the tendency of church leaders to compromise Christian doctrine with Graeco-Roman philosophies soon led to serious heresy and even apostasy in great segments of the Christian community.

In one way, the Resurrection of Christ was the seal of Satan's doom, with all his deceptions exposed and disarmed. Nevertheless, the latter continued to prevail in most of the world and eventually regained most of their influence, even in Christendom.

Creation — the Foundation of All Truth

I have tried to show in previous chapters that evolutionism has been made the foundation of all disciplines of study, as well as the pseudo-scientific rationale for all the belligerent politico-economic systems (communism, fascism, imperialism, etc.) and the harmful social practices (abortionism, racism, promiscuity, etc.) that have so tormented the world in recent generations. Worst of all, evolutionism has been the chief opponent of the saving gospel of Christ, undermining the faith of multitudes in the Bible and its promises. It is not too much to say that evolutionary theory, in one form or another, has provided the pseudo-rationale for all that is false and harmful in the world (the real *cause*, of course, is the innate sinfulness of the human heart, with its rebellion against the Word of God). Furthermore, it has been shown that this has been true all through history. All who oppose the true God must always resort to some kind of evolution, for this is the only possible alternative to special creation by a transcendent God. Both modern ethnic religions and ancient pagan belief systems are essentially variant forms of evolutionism, and this is true of every variety of human-oriented philosophy. In the last analysis, Satan's long war against God is founded upon the premise of evolution and is implemented through a wide-ranging variety of applications of evolutionism in every area of human thought and life.

What all of this means is that, as evolutionism is the foundation of all that is false and harmful, so creationism must be the foundation of everything true and good. This *must* be the case if indeed God *did* create the world as He said. God recorded the account of creation first of all in the Bible because it is the foundation of His revelation about all other things. In an important sense, Genesis 1:1 is the most fundamental affirmation ever written. If a person *really* believes that God created the universe and all things therein, then he or she should have no difficulty believing anything else in the Bible, nor have any reservation about the importance of obeying all God's commands and trusting His promises.

In this section, I want to show that the doctrine of creation is indeed the foundation of every other doctrine or precept of Christianity. Furthermore, it is the foundation of true science, true government, true education, and every area of effective, happy, and productive relationships in human society. To cover this subject adequately would require a large volume,[42] but a brief survey here should at least make the point.

For example, evolutionists commonly claim that the development of modern science was hindered by biblical Christianity, and that science could make little progress until Darwinism defeated the Bible and drove religion out of the schools and colleges. But nothing could be further from the truth! It is significant that the "scientific revolution" did not take place until the way for it was prepared by the Reformation and the Great Awakening in Western Europe and North America, with the great upsurge in Bible study and evangelical Christianity that followed. The biblical world outlook *is* the scientific world outlook — namely, that the universe had a beginning and that its processes and systems are reliable and intelligible, operating in accordance with fixed laws that can be discovered and used.

It is no coincidence that most of the founding fathers of modern science, those still regarded as the greatest scientists of all (men such as Newton, Boyle, Ray, Steno, Faraday, Maxwell, and a host of others[43]) were men who believed the Bible and its account of creation. In their science, they believed

---

42. For a more detailed (though still only introductory) exposition of the foundational importance of creationism, see Henry M. Morris, *Creation and the Modern Christian* (San Diego, CA: Master Books, 1985), p. 1–142.

43. For 101 brief biographies of such scientists, see Henry M. Morris, *Men of Science — Men of God*, 2nd edition (Green Forest, AR: Master Books, 1988).

they were thinking God's thoughts after Him, carrying out His "dominion mandate."

Some of the most incisive modern thinkers have recognized that science could only have arisen in a creationist context. Alfred North Whitehead, the distinguished English mathematical physicist and philosopher of science, has said:

> Without this belief [that is, the "inexpugnable belief that every detailed occurrence can be correlated with its antecedents in a perfectly definite manner, exemplifying general principles"] the incredible labors of scientists would be without hope. . . . Every detail [of creation] was supervised and ordered; the search into nature could only result in the vindication of the faith in rationality.[44]

The pagan philosophies of the Greek and other ancient nations all involved belief in eternal cycles and a more or less idiosyncratic view of nature as a living entity and therefore subject to unpredictable behavior. The founders of modern science, however, adopted the biblical linear view of time, with a beginning and a pre-ordained goal, obeying rational and predictable laws established and maintained by the Creator.

Similarly, Stanley Jaki, a Hungarian-born Benedictine priest, after quoting Psalm 136:4–9 as illustrative of God's creative design and control of heaven and earth, says, "It should not be surprising that this unconditional and firm trust in Yahweh produced a warm, confident, optimistic appraisal of nature which once more sets apart the realm of the Covenant from the surrounding cultures."[45] Professor Jaki has written extensively and compellingly in proof that modern science had its genesis in the Christian, creationist view of the world. Elsewhere Jaki has written:

> How did the West acquire in the first place its astonishing scientific lead? It did so by rejecting what was distinctly and fundamentally pagan in Greek science. . . .
>
> The newly established universities taught everything that could be known (that is why they were called universities) but they taught it from the Christian perspective, the cardinal and essential point of which is the dogma of creation in time. This dogma means that the

---

44. A.N. Whitehead, *Science and the Modern World* (New York: The Free Press, 1953), p. 12.
45. Stanley L. Jaki, *Science and Creation* (New York: Science History Publications, 1974), p. 149. Jaki is distinguished professor of history of science at Seton Hall University.

past history of the world is finite, that there is a point back in history where all motion had to start. This perspective was inconceivable, or at least repugnant to the Greeks, but was most natural for Christians.[46]

Many other scientists have agreed that science arose out of a Christian worldview. For example:

It is widely accepted on all sides that, far from undermining it, science is deeply indebted to Christianity and has been so from at least the scientific revolution. Recent historical research has uncovered many unexpected links between scientific enterprise and Biblical theology.[47]

These scientific premises define and limit the scientific mode of thought. It should be pointed out, however, that each of these postulates had its origin in, or was consistent with, Christian theology.[48]

Evolutionism, on the other hand, has contributed nothing whatever to the advance of true science. Says H.F. Judson,

Evolutionary theory has not bred a single new species of animal or vegetable, let alone improved the intensity of our pleasures or the intelligence or docility of our children.[49]

If any evolutionist questions this evaluation, let him present one example of any real advance in medicine or agriculture or engineering or any other technology benefiting mankind that was brought about by evolutionary "science" (in the sense of macroevolution, of course, not ordinary variations or mutations or breeding experiments, since these fit the creation model better than they fit evolution).

As another example, consider the field of government and law. Most Americans — certainly most Christian Americans — believe strongly that their system of representative government within a legal framework of checks and balances based on the United States Constitution and the traditional common law of England (which, in turn, was based essentially on the Bible, especially the Ten Commandments) is the best ever devised by human minds. The only one surpassing it would be the theocracy outlined in the

---

46. Stanley L. Jaki, "On Whose Side Is History?" *National Review* 37 (Aug. 28, 1985): p. 42.

47. Colin Russell, "Whigs and Professionals," *Nature* 308 (April 26, 1984): p. 777.

48. Stanley D. Beck, "Natural Science and Creationist Theology," *Bioscience* 32 (Oct. 1982): p. 739.

49. Horace F. Judson, "Century of the Sciences," *Science* 84 (Nov. 1984): p. 42.

laws of Moses, which was actually given by God Himself but never really implemented in Israel or anywhere else.

The American system was based on creationism (note the words "Nature's God" and "Creator" in the opening sentences of the Declaration of Independence) and the laws of "Divine Providence." Even modern humanists admit this. Fred Edwords, executive director of the American Humanist Association, writes:

> As early as 1749, Benjamin Franklin pointed to "the Necessity of a Publick Religion" that would promote good citizenship and ethical standards. Later in his *Autobiography,* he laid out "the essentials of every religion," limiting them to the following four items:
>
>> The existence of the Deity; that he made the world and govern'd it by his Providence; that the most acceptable service of God was the doing good to men; that our souls are immortal; and that all crime will be punished, and virtue rewarded, either here or hereafter.[50]

Ben Franklin was not a fundamentalist Christian, and neither was Thomas Jefferson. Both may have been deists, but both believed in God and special creation. So did practically all the founding fathers of our country, including Tom Paine. According to Edwords, "Conspicuously absent from the writings of many of the nation's founders and first presidents are indications of belief in Christ, hell, and Original Sin. But they all mentioned God — and not merely the clockwork God of deism but a god actively involved in history."[51] For example, note especially the testimony of George Washington:

> It is impossible to account for the creation of the universe, without the agency of a Supreme Being.[52]

> It is impossible to govern the universe without the aid of a Supreme Being. It is impossible to reason without arriving at a Supreme Being. . . . Well has it been said, that if there had been no God, mankind would have been obliged to imagine one.[53]

---

50. Frederick Edwords, "The Religious Character of American Patriotism," *The Humanist* 47 (Nov./Dec. 1987): p. 21.
51. Ibid.
52. George Washington, quoted in *Maxims of Washington,* John F. Schroeder, editor (Mt. Vernon, VA: Mt. Vernon Ladies Assoc., 1942), p. 275.
53. James L. Paulding, *Life of Washington* (New York: Associated Faculty Press, 1970), p. 209.

Sad to say, the governmental and legal systems of the United States have departed far away from their Christian and creationist foundations. Today's lawyers, jurists, political scientists, and similar professionals largely view the law and government as evolving entities, changing with time and society's flexible mores. Even the Constitution is no longer considered an absolute; it also must evolve in accordance with the changing times. Dr. John Eidsmoe, who is both an attorney and a theologian, as well as a student of legal history, has evaluated all this as follows: "Underlying the disagreement over interpretation of the Constitution is a major confrontation between the two world views — the creationist, absolutist, Newtonian views of the Framers, versus the evolutionist, relativist, Darwinian views of most legal scholars today."[54]

This new view of law and the Constitution is attributed mainly to the Darwinian jurist Christopher Columbus Langdell, who became dean of the Harvard Law School in 1870, participating in the "Darwinization" of Harvard under President Charles Eliot, whose influence was discussed in an earlier chapter. Langdell introduced the dismal practice of case study and legal precedent in the law. This approach allowed the judges to become the lawgivers, instead of relying on the time-honored dependence on absolute principles of law — as defined by nature and nature's God and codified principally in William Blackstone's famous *Commentaries on the Laws of England* (first published in 1765). Langdell was followed by Roscoe Pound, both of whom became known as "legal positivists." Their most prominent disciple was probably Justice Oliver Wendell Holmes, the man chiefly responsible for undermining the longstanding absolutes of the Constitution in Supreme Court decisions.

Comments L.E. Robbins, "Why was Dean Langdell so anxious to divert the attention of his students from Blackstone? The answer is that Langdell was an evolutionist."[55]

The result has been the free-wheeling interpretations of constitutional law in recent generations, which have so devastated American morals and public safety. Dr. Eidsmoe comments:

> Thus the debate over constitutional interpretation is no mere academic or legal matter. Rather it is a major battle between two conflicting philosophies, two conflicting religions, and two conflicting world views. Justice Brennan openly acknowledged this in his Georgetown address ["The Constitution of the United States: Con-

---

54. John Eidsmoe, "Creation, Evolution and Constitutional Interpretation," *Concerned Women* 9 (Sept. 1987): p. 7.
55. L. Edward Robbins, "Evolution and the Law," *The Constitution* (May/June 1988): p. 17.

temporary Ratification," Teaching Symposium, Georgetown University, Washington, DC, October 12, 1985, p. 51], declaring that our society must continue its upward progress unbounded by the fetters of original intent or the literal words of the Constitution, through an *"evolutionary process (that) is inevitable and, indeed, it is the true interpretative genius of the text"* [emphasis supplied].[56]

Just as creationism was the original foundation of American law and government, so it was the original teaching in America's schools and colleges, the foundational principle implicit in every field of study. The famous McGuffey Readers, which were so effective in teaching many generations of children in earlier days in this country, were based on presuppositions of creationism and biblical authority.

Biblical creationism is also the basis of family life. God himself set the standard:

So God created man in his own image, in the image of God created he him; male and female created he them. And God blessed them, and God said unto them, Be fruitful, and multiply. . . . Therefore shall a man leave his father and his mother, and shall cleave unto his wife: and they shall be one flesh (Gen. 1:27–28, 2:24).

The Christian standards of family life, beautifully set forth in the Epistles of the New Testament (e.g., Eph. 5:22–6:4, 1 Pet. 3:1–7, and many other such passages) are based on the teachings of Christ, which in turn come specifically from the creation account (note, for example, how Christ quotes [Matt. 19:3–9] from the above passages in Genesis).

For a long time, evolutionary anthropologists fostered the myths about cavemen dragging captured women into their caves, tribal promiscuity among savage tribes, communal marriage, and other such notions as evolutionary stages among early peoples. More careful and detailed study, however, has shown that the biblical norm of the family (father, mother, children) has been established everywhere from the most ancient times. Marxists and Freudians have argued otherwise, but the great weight of evidence proves that monogamy and the nuclear family have always been the standard. When polygamy and/or promiscuity appear, they come in as abnormalities and inevitably lead to social disorder and personal unhappiness. Brunislaw Malinowski, who was professor of anthropology at the University of London from 1927 through 1942, concluded after a thorough review of the evidence:

---

56. Eidsmoe, "Creation, Evolution and Constitutional Interpretation," p. 8.

> Monogamy is not only the most important form of marriage, not only that which predominates in most communities, and which occurs, statistically speaking, in an overwhelming majority of instances, but it is also the pattern and prototype of marriage. . . . Monogamy is, has been, and will remain the only true type of marriage.[57]

True creationism is even the foundation of true chronology. When God created the sun, moon, and stars, He said, "And let them be for signs, and for seasons, and for days, and years" (Gen. 1:14). And so they have been, ever since. If it were not for the regularity of the earth's rotation on its axis and its orbital revolution about the sun, calendars and dates would have been meaningless. The Jewish people still use a calendar with all dates referred to A.M. (*anno mundi*: "year of the world"), as based on their calculated date of the creation, approximately 3761 B.C.

It is interesting that the standard nomenclature of Western chronology, based on years before and after the incarnation of the Creator (B.C. and A.D. — "before Christ" and "*anno Domini*: year of our Lord"), is becoming increasingly unpopular today, with many intellectuals, especially liberal theologians, preferring B.C.E. and C.E. ("before the common era" and "common era").

The most fascinating aspect of chronology is the history of the "week," which has no astronomical basis. The "day" is measured by the regular appearance of the sun as the earth rotates; the "year" is measured by the annual rotation of the heavens as the earth orbits the sun; the "month" is measured approximately by the moon's lunations, or intervals between new moons, caused by the revolution of the moon around the earth.

The week, however, has no astronomical basis at all, yet people everywhere have always observed a weekly cycle: six days of work and a day of rest. The rest day may be Friday among the Muslims, Saturday among the Jews, and Sunday among Christians, but the concept of the weekly cycle is the same. There is no better explanation for this remarkable phenomenon than the one given by God Himself:

> Remember the sabbath [literally "rest"] day, to keep it holy. Six days shalt thou labour, and do all thy work: but the seventh day is the sabbath of the LORD thy God: in it thou shalt not do any work. . . . For in six days the LORD made heaven and earth, the sea, and all that in them is, and rested the seventh day: wherefore the LORD blessed the sabbath day, and hallowed it (Exod. 20:8–11).

---

57. Brunislaw Malinowski, "Marriage," article in *Encyclopedia Britannica*, 17th edition (1949), Vol. 14, p. 950.

The basis of the six-day work week is nothing else than the six-day work week of God in creation! There is no other satisfactory explanation. Even evolutionists who deny the creation commemorate it once a week — they take their weekly day off from work just as though they believed the Bible!

Incidentally, this fact is also a rebuke to those professedly Bible-believing Christians who accept the geological ages as their "creation" period and call themselves "progressive creationists." They accept man's literal work week, but not God's. The fact is, however, that these days of God were literal days just like man's days: "Six days may work be done; but in the seventh is the sabbath of rest, holy to the LORD. . . . It is a sign between me and the children of Israel for ever: for in six days the LORD made heaven and earth, and on the seventh day he rested, and was refreshed" (Exod. 31:15–17). Note that these verbs are in the past tense. God is not still "resting," as some claim — "he rested, and was refreshed." The work of creation is not still going on, for "the heavens and the earth were finished, and all the host of them. And on the seventh day God ended his work which he had made . . ." (Gen. 2:1–2) — theistic evolutionists to the contrary notwithstanding!

Some cultures have tried a "week" of slightly more or less than seven days for a while, having forgotten their beginnings, but all have continued throughout history to follow a weekly cycle that was at least close to the biblical one. Even secular scholars have recognized this fact. While reluctant to acknowledge God's work week as the original source, it is obvious to them that the Jewish week is the most ancient and venerable of all. The "astrological week," based on the sun, moon, and five visible planets, is the most favored alternate explanation, but it does not suffice. E. Zerubavel explains that "the Sabbath observance had been established long before the astrological week even came into being."[58]

It is noteworthy that the two greatest atheistic regimes in history — the revolutionary governments of France in 1792 and Russia in 1929 — tried to change the traditional week, hoping thereby to destroy Christianity. The French set up a ten-day week and the Soviets a five-day week, and both were rigidly enforced, but each lasted only a few years. Says Zerubavel: "The complete failure of the eleven-year Soviet calendrical experiment, just like that of its French predecessor 140 year earlier, attests to the tremendous resilience of tradition in general and of religion

---

58. Eviatar Zerubavel, *The Seven Day Circle* (New York: Macmillan, 1985), p. 17, 19.

in particular."[59] The seven-day week stands as a unique and unanswered testimony to creation.

The Foundation of True Christianity

Most importantly of all, creationism is the foundational doctrine of genuine biblical Christianity. Whenever it is rejected or compromised by Christians and such a position is maintained long enough, either heresy or apostasy ultimately results. Even when it is merely neglected, there is real danger that such Christianity will become self-centered rather than God-centered, focused on human goals rather than God's purposes.

We tend too easily to forget that Jesus is God. "I and my Father are one," He told us (John 10:30). He is "God our Saviour," Paul declared (Titus 2:10). John said: "We are in him that is true, even in his Son Jesus Christ. This is the true God, and eternal life" (1 John 5:20).

One of the mountaintop passages of Scripture is the great Christological passage in the first chapter of Colossians:

> For by him were all things created, that are in heaven, and that are in earth, visible and invisible, whether they be thrones, or dominions, or principalities, or powers: all things were created by him, and for him: and he is before all things, and by him all things consist [that is, "are sustained"]. . . . And, having made peace through the blood of his cross, by him to reconcile all things unto himself; by him, I say, whether they be things in earth, or things in heaven (Col. 1:16–17, 20).

These verses beautifully summarize the person and work of the Lord Jesus Christ — past, present, and future. As Creator, He created all things in heaven and earth. As Savior, He sustains and redeems all things. As coming King, He will reconcile all things to Himself, having already paid the price by shedding His blood on the Cross to make peace for man with God.

This is Christ as He really is — Creator, Conservator, and Consummator. There are many Christians who preach the saving work of Christ and a fair number who preach His coming kingdom, but few preach about His work of creation. Yet He was Creator first of all. In fact, the reason He had to become Savior was because men and women had rebelled against him as Creator by rejecting His Word and breaking His commandments. Further, the only way the lost creation could ever eventually be reconciled to its Creator would

---

59. Ibid., p. 43. This book is written from a naturalistic perspective but is probably the most complete treatment of the history and influence of the weekly cycle.

be for the Creator Himself to redeem it. Paul said, "For since by man came death, by man came also the resurrection of the dead" (1 Cor. 15:21). Or, putting it another way, if Adam's sin did not bring death, then Christ did not bring life! The work of creation is therefore essential to both the saving work and the reconciling work of Christ, and one does not really preach the person and work of Christ without it.

The same is true of the gospel. In fact, the Christological exposition from Colossians cited above is itself called "the gospel," by Paul both before (in Col. 1:5) and after (v. 23) this passage. The gospel is the "good news" concerning Christ and the great work He has accomplished. The first time the word is recorded in the New Testament is in Matthew 4:23, where Christ is seen "preaching the gospel of the Kingdom," anticipating the coming reconciliation and consummation of all things. The last time has already been noted, where "the everlasting gospel," through the voice of the angel, is calling the world of the last days back to acknowledge Him as Creator of all things (Rev. 14:6–7). The central occurrence of the word is in 1 Corinthians 15:1, where "the gospel" is defined in terms of the substitutionary death of Christ, plus his bodily burial and resurrection (v. 3–4).

Thus the gospel includes the *creation* of the world, the *redemption* of the world, and the *reconciliation* of the world — all by and through Jesus Christ. Once again, creation is the foundation, and one cannot really "preach the gospel" without incorporating the basic truth of divine special creation somewhere in the message.

It follows that the great doctrines of salvation are based upon creation, for Christ could only be our Savior because He Himself was our offended Creator. The doctrine of the unmerited grace of God in Christ is wrapped up in this truth. No man, dead in trespasses and sins, could ever save himself, but "the grace of God that bringeth salvation hath appeared to all men" — so that it is "not by works of righteousness which we have done, but according to his mercy he saved us" (Titus 2:11, 3:5).

Then, since it is "by grace are ye saved through faith" (Eph. 2:8), the faith that appropriates His gracious gift of salvation must also be founded first of all upon the fact of creation. This is made especially clear in the great "faith chapter," Hebrews 11. This wonderful chapter, which outlines so beautifully the evidences and works of true faith in the lives of the Old Testament saints, is introduced by the last two verses of Hebrews 10, where such faith is defined as both *living* and *saving*: "Now the just shall live by faith" for we are "of them that believe [literally, "have faith"] to the saving of the soul" (Heb. 10:38–39).

Now faith is not merely some vague sentimentality. Everyone has some kind of faith — whether it is faith in himself, in evolution, in the future, in some political or religious or intellectual guru. It is vitally and eternally important exactly *where* one's faith is placed. It should be a faith that brings salvation and a faith by which one can live now and forever, as stressed in these verses.

And this kind of faith, with its proper object, is defined first of all in the third verse of the faith chapter: "Through faith we understand that the worlds were framed by the word of God, so that things which are seen were not made of things which do appear" (Heb. 11:3). This faith is not only a living, saving faith but also an *understanding* faith — the only kind of faith that makes sense — because its object is the omnipotent Creator and His *special* creation. It is faith not in some kind of emergence from pre-existing materials in the eternal universe (as in all forms of evolutionary pantheism), but in *creation ex nihilo*. By God's omnipotent word, all things were simply called into being, and from the beginning all were "very good" (Gen. 1:31).

The great "faith chapter" ends by recognizing the Lord Jesus as not only Creator but also Savior and coming King: "Looking unto Jesus the author and finisher of our faith; who for the joy that was set before him endured the cross, despising the shame, and is set down at the right hand of the throne of God" (Heb. 12:2).

When a person is saved by grace through faith, it requires a new miracle of creation by God to cleanse his sins, create for him a new nature, and implant in him God's own eternal life: "Therefore if any man be in Christ, he is a new creature: old things are passed away; behold, all things are become new" (2 Cor. 5:17).

Thenceforth the person has two natures, the two struggling against each other. The first is the old nature that was dead in sin and inherited from Adam, who first rebelled against his Creator and thus marred the image of God in which he had been created. The second is the redeemed, newly created nature, "the new man, which is renewed in knowledge after the image of him that created him" (Col. 3:10). Again we note how vitally important is the concept of special creation, right at the very beginning of each Christian life.

This emphasis continues to be true throughout the Christian life. Our common bond of fellowship with other believers is that we all have the same Creator/Savior, Jesus Christ, who created us in spirit before the foundation of the world, "to make all men see what is the fellowship of the mystery, which from the beginning of the world hath been hid in God, who created all things by Jesus Christ" (Eph, 3:9). Throughout our Christian life, we should be "zealous of good works" (Titus 2:14), for the compelling reason that "we are his workmanship, created in Christ Jesus unto good works, which God hath before ordained that we should walk in them" (Eph. 2:10).

Even when we are called on to suffer for Christ (as we almost certainly shall be if we faithfully proclaim Him as Creator and Savior), it is the truth of creation that sustains us, for we know He created all things and therefore controls all things. Consequently, "let them that suffer according to the will of God commit the keeping of their souls to him in well doing, as unto a faithful Creator" (1 Pet. 4:19).

And what about witnessing and leading people to Christ? Some would say that the duty of a Christian is simply to win others to Christ, not to preach creation. But the creation, of course, is exactly the point. We must lead them to believe in the *real* Christ, not a false Christ, or "another Jesus, whom we have not preached" (2 Cor. 11:4). As repeatedly stressed in this book, Jesus Christ is Creator, and the everlasting gospel that we must preach is founded on creation. Paul warned, "But though we, or an angel from heaven, preach any other gospel unto you than that which we have preached unto you, let him be accursed" (Gal. 1:8).

The Gospel of John is the one book of the Bible written specifically to lead people to Christ. "But these are written," said John near its conclusion, "that ye might believe that Jesus is the Christ, the Son of God; and that believing ye might have life through his name" (John 20:31). That being the case, it is very significant that John began his Gospel with these tremendous words:

> In the beginning was the Word, and the Word was with God, and the Word was God. The same was in the beginning with God. All things were made by him; and without him was not any thing made that was made. . . . He was in the world, and the world was made by him, and the world knew him not. . . . And the Word was made flesh, and dwelt among us, (and we beheld his glory, the glory as of the only begotten of the Father,) full of grace and truth (John 1:1–3, 10, 14).

If John, the great Apostle and evangelist, thought it well to begin his soul-winning message with an assertion of the deity of Christ and His great work of creation, then we would be well advised to do the same!

We have already noted that this was the approach used by the Apostles as they went forth preaching the gospel to a pagan world in the first century. Recall that when addressing the Greek evolutionists at Athens (Epicurean atheists and Stoic pantheists), Paul began by reminding them of their al-most-forgotten high God, who had created them and who would therefore someday judge them, conclusively demonstrating His omnipotent deity by defeating sin and death (Acts 17:23–31).

Similarly at Lystra in Asia Minor, where the priests of Jupiter tried to incorporate their preaching and healing testimony into the system of Roman paganism, Paul and Barnabas strenuously refused, crying out:

> We also are men of like passions with you, and preach unto you
> that ye should turn from these vanities unto the living God, which
> made heaven, and earth, and the sea, and all things that are therein:
> who in times past suffered all nations to walk in their own ways.
> Nevertheless he left not himself without witness, in that he did good,
> and gave us rain from heaven, and fruitful seasons, filling our hearts
> with food and gladness (Acts 14:15–17).

Neither at Lystra nor at Athens did the Apostles preach from the Scriptures, for the obvious reason that their hearers neither believed nor even knew the Scriptures. Paul began with what they *did* know, namely their intuitive knowledge (from their consciences, their dim traditions, and the evidence in nature), that there was somewhere a great Creator God, who had made them, provided for them, and would someday judge them.

On the other hand, when the Apostles preached to the Jews, they could begin with the Scriptures, knowing that their listeners already believed in the God of creation and in His Old Testament revelation. At the synagogue at Thessalonica, for example: "Paul, as his manner was, went in unto them, and three Sabbath days reasoned with them out of the scriptures" (Acts 17:2).

The Lord Jesus Christ had commanded them to "preach the gospel to every creature" (Mark 16:15), and this they set out to do. And they did so with the greatest effectiveness any generation of Christians ever experienced. We would do well to follow their example, which was to preach from the Bible when their audiences already believed in biblical authority and in God as Creator. On the mission field, however, or to Bible-rejecting evolutionistic audiences anywhere, we (like those Apostles) should undertake to lead our listeners to accept these foundational truths: first through the evidence of creation, next through Christ's Resurrection, and finally through God's revelation in the Old and New Testaments.

That such an approach does indeed work more effectively than any other is the testimony of those missionaries who have tried it.[60] Similarly, the

---

60. Don Richardson, *Eternity in Their Hearts* (Ventura, CA: Regal, 1981), 176 p.

creationist testimony has proved highly effective among university students saturated with evolutionary teachings on their campuses.[61] Creationism is surely the foundation of true evangelism and missions, just as it is for all the basic doctrines of the Bible.

Creationism is even foundational in the application of the gospel to modern social problems. There is no biblical warrant for a "social gospel," of course, but the true gospel (creation-redemption-reconciliation, through Christ) does have vital application to every problem.

Consider, for example, the modern concern with ecology and the environment. Evolutionists argue for conservation measures in terms of our "relatedness" to all other creatures and the supposed millions of years it took for them to evolve in their respective environments. Since such arguments are not realistic, they seem to have minimal influence. Man is *not* "related" to the animals or plants, but rather was given dominion over them by God, who created each kind of creature with its own unique design and function. The true motivation for taking care of God's creatures is that they *are* His creatures, and even one sparrow "shall not fall on the ground without your Father" (Matt. 10:29). However, only humans are eternal, for they alone have the image of God in them. It is proper for people to use animals for food in the present world (Gen. 9:3; 1 Tim. 4:4; etc.), and thus also for other purposes beneficial to human beings (e.g., transportation, medical research). But this must be done with as much care and consideration as reasonably possible, for they are God's creatures, and He cares for them. The same is true of our natural environments. Mankind has been placed in stewardship over the world by God's Edenic "dominion mandate" at creation, and those who "destroy the earth" will be held accountable (see Rev. 11:18).

The same approach should be followed in dealing with specific social problems. Racism, for example, can best be combated by helping all men to realize that "all men were created equal," as the Declaration of Independence asserts, and that God "hath made of one blood all nations of men for to dwell on all the face of the earth" (Acts 17:26).

Since evolutionism is not only the pseudo-scientific rationale of racism but also of communism, fascism, imperialism, and other such deadly socio-economic systems, the best way to deal with these threats is to restore our national faith in divine creation and in the authority of Scripture. The tragic reality, however, is that the universal dominance of evolutionary

---

61. Henry M. Morris, *King of Creation* (San Diego, CA: Creation-Life, 1980), p. 185–220; Henry M. Morris, *Creation and the Modern Christian* (San Diego, CA: Creation-Life, 1985), p. 23–39.

teaching in our schools and colleges provides fertile soil for the growth of such philosophies. Marxism in particular seems to be rapidly growing in influence.

Obviously, the same is true for the conglomeration of New Age cults and practices that are growing like weeds today. All of them, but especially the various occult and pantheistic systems, are based squarely on evolutionism. It is interesting that these are being vigorously opposed by atheistic and humanistic groups, whose beliefs are also based on evolutionism. Both factions unite whenever necessary to oppose creationists, just as did the Epicureans and Stoics in ancient times! By the same token, the only real answer to either set of these systems and all their dangerous tenets is a return to the creationist faith of America's founding fathers.

This is also the only true answer to the problems of drugs, crime, abortionism, homosexuality, and all the other anti-God practices that are plaguing the nation and the world today. Concerned Christian and secular groups quite properly are doing much to fight these evil practices, but such efforts in the long run will prove futile unless focus is directed toward the root problem that is the basis and supposed rationale for all the rest. Plucking and discarding bad fruit from a bad tree is not the answer; the diseased tree itself must be uprooted and destroyed. Until evolutionism is replaced once again by creationism in our schools and media and government, these evil conditions can only grow worse. The embryonic creationist revival that has been gathering strength for the past quarter-century needs to be aided and encouraged by Christians everywhere, if there is ever to be any hope of solving these problems. After all, these are all simply modern expressions of the age-long war against God, evolution versus creation, Satan opposing the true Creator.

Finally, in concluding this section, we should note God's own testimony concerning the vital importance of the doctrine and truth of creation. This is found in the final chapters of the ancient Book of Job. The basic theme of Job is the satanic testing of godly Job, seeking to demonstrate before God and all the host of heaven that even the most righteous and godly of men will renounce God if put to the test. The first 37 chapters of the book describe the incomparable trials to which Job was subjected by Satan, along with extensive discussions between Job and his friends as to why he was being subjected to such severe tribulation.

Most commentators suppose that the purpose of the Book of Job is to answer the age-long question as to why the righteous encounter suffering. It is true that Job and his friends argue at great length about this problem. But Job admits he doesn't know the answer, and the friends have the wrong answer, according to God's own testimony (Job 42:7).

One would expect, then, to hear God's answer to this most difficult and vexing of all human problems, the problem that appears to give the greatest support to atheism, humanism, pantheism, and all forms of evolutionism. That is, if there really is an omnipotent, righteous God who cares for His creatures, why does He allow the ungodly to prosper and the righteous to suffer? Surely God would provide the answer when He finally comes down to interrupt the long dialogue between Job and his critics! In chapters 38 through 41, we do find a long and beautiful monologue by God, but the most amazing thing in this divine testimony is that there is not a single word about Job's sufferings, or even about the sufferings of the righteous or of mankind in general.

All four chapters deal exclusively with God's primeval creation of the world and His providential care of that creation! Here God had the unique opportunity of speaking at great length to His most faithful servant in all the world, at the time, a man undergoing the greatest sufferings ever experienced by anyone save Christ Himself when he died on the Cross. Yet not a word of comfort or explanation is given!

All God talked about was creation! This surely tells us something about the supreme importance of this truth, in God's own judgment. It also tells us indirectly that, when any believer is called upon to undergo privations or ill-ness or sufferings of any sort (and we all must face these, in greater or lesser degree), the basic answer of God is simply to remind us that He is the Creator and that He cares for his own, perhaps in ways we shall never understand in this life.

All of this is discussed more fully in the writer's small commentary on the Book of Job.[62] I mention this problem here merely to point out God's great concern that we understand and appreciate His creation, and also to stress again that every problem of the world at large or of the individual Christian in particular is always best resolved in the context of creation. We do not have to understand *why* God works in certain ways. We just need to know by reasoned faith that He is the Creator. Therefore, by definition, what He does is always right and always best. Our duty and deliverance is simply to believe and obey His Word.

In Job 40 and 41, God also adumbrates His final victory over Satan by as-suring Job that He, God, can and will prevail over the greatest of all animals,

---

62. Henry M. Morris, *The Remarkable Record of Job* (Green Forest, AR: Master Books, 1988), 144 p.

"behemoth" and "leviathan," both of which, as great dragons (actually, probably dinosaurs), are symbolic of that "old serpent," the devil — and all who oppose God. The conflict and the testings have been long and bitter, but we know that one day "the Lamb shall overcome them: for he is Lord of lords, and King of kings: and they that are with him are called, and chosen, and faithful" (Rev. 17:14).

He Shall Overcome

In the meantime, the long war continues and is heating up. As shown earlier, evolutionism today controls the schools, the media, and almost all segments of society in every country. Every discipline of academic study in the secular universities is structured around an evolutionary premise. Creationists, both faculty and students, are subjected to gross discrimination and sometimes even dismissal if they are outspoken about their beliefs. Even Christian churches, all of which should be in the front lines against evolution, have for the most part either surrendered or retreated on this key issue. The liberal churches, including most of the so-called mainline denominations, have long since capitulated to theistic evolution or worse. Meanwhile, the evangelical churches have mostly either compromised with the enemy (via some accommodationist concept such as "progressive creationism") or else are trying to ignore the battle, even while their young people are being subverted and taken captive. Only a small minority of churches are willing today to take an aggressive stand on behalf of genuine biblical creationism and absolute biblical inerrant authority. Nothing less than this, however, stands a chance against such a powerful yet subtle enemy.

The Darwinian century, beginning in 1859 with Darwin's *Origin of Species*, has been heavily influenced by evolutionary scientists who proclaim at every opportunity the falsehood that "evolution is a proven fact of science." In a technological civilization reveling in the material products of science (automobiles, telephones, etc.), most people have come to accept as truth any evolutionary pronouncement by a so-called scientist, especially since our sinful natures tend to make us desire to escape God anyhow. Today, evolutionism dominates the social sciences and humanities even more than the natural sciences, but the rationale offered for this is always the premise that evolution is a law of nature, so proven by the natural scientists.

On the other hand, there has been a dramatic resurgence of creationism during the past quarter-century, largely spearheaded by Bible-believing scientists. Considering that evolutionary scientists led the world to capitulate to evolutionism, it seems appropriate that creationist scientists attempt to win it back, by refuting the so-called scientific arguments that won it over in the first place.

Since the history of the modern creationist movement has been discussed elsewhere,[63] it will not be repeated here. Suffice it to say that there are now thousands of scientists who have become creationists, plus many times more in other fields, particularly among young people. Creationist books, stressing both scientific and biblical creationism, have played a major role in this movement, as have the hundreds of creation-evolution debates and lectures on university campuses that involve creationist scientists. Seminars, Back-to-Genesis conferences, church meetings, radio programs, and other media presentations have also been effective. Creationist thought today is more widespread, more scientific, more biblical, and more influential than at any time since Darwin.

More than a hundred creationist organizations and associations have sprung up all over the world. In this country, attempts have been made in several states to get creationism legislated back into the public schools, but these have been unsuccessful except in generating more public awareness of the issue.

A very influential creationist membership association has been the Creation Research Society (CRS), organized in 1963 and with a current regular membership roster of about 700 (scientists with post-graduate degrees in science).[64] The society publishes a quarterly journal of peer-reviewed research papers on all aspects of scientific creationism.

Probably the most effective creationist organization (as distinct from a membership association) has been the Institute for Creation Research (ICR), with a full-time staff of PhD scientists, an active research and publications division, an extensive ministry of speaking and debating all over the world, and a unique creationist graduate school that offers MS degrees in several key fields of science. The institute was formed in 1970 and its graduate school started in 1980.[65]

As might be expected, this revival of creationism, particularly as led by scientists with respectable professional credentials, soon produced an

---

63. Henry M. Morris, *The History of Modern Creationism* (San Diego, CA: Master Books, 1984), 382 p.

64. The Creation Research Society currently has its membership office at P.O. Box 14016, Terre Haute, IN 47803.

65. For an ICR publications catalog, graduate school catalog, or other information, write to Institute for Creation Research, 1806 Royal Lane, Dallas, TX 75229.

explosive reaction by establishment scientists, who had long been trumpeting to the world that evolution was a "scientific fact." For example, in his famous keynote address at the Darwin Centennial, held in 1959 at the University of Chicago, Sir Julian Huxley arrogantly proclaimed the following blasphemous opinions:

> The first point to make about Darwin's theory is that it is no longer a theory, but a fact. No serious scientists would deny the fact that evolution has occurred, just as he would not deny the fact that the earth goes around the sun.[66]

> In the evolutionary pattern of thought there is no longer either need or room for the supernatural. . . . Evolutionary man can no longer take refuge from his loneliness in the arms of a divinized father figure whom he himself has created.[67]

Naturally, when quite a number of "serious scientists" began presenting evidence in print and in public debate that evolution was *not* a scientific fact — and that there really *was need for the supernatural* if scientists are ever really going to explain the created world — there quickly developed an emotionally charged anti-creationist reaction. Most of these attacks have consisted of bombast, ridicule, and *ad hominem* diatribes, with almost no reference to scientific "evidence" favoring evolution. At least 40 anti-creationist books have been published in the past decade, plus hundreds of such articles in just about every magazine and newspaper in the country. "Committees of Correspondence" (actually committees of anti-creationists) have been formed all over the country, ready to go into action whenever and wherever creationism surfaces. A number of anti-creationist journals are being published, and such organizations as the American Humanist Association, the American Civil Liberties Union, and the American Atheist Association belabor creationists almost constantly. Court decisions have everywhere gone against allowing any creationist influence in public schools, on the absurd pretext that this would be an unconstitutional establishment of religion.

Not content with controlling the public schools, the secular educators seek ultimately to control the teaching in Christian schools as well. The strategy in California will probably later be a pilot model for other states, since

---

66. Sol Tax, editor, *Issues in Evolution* (Chicago, IL: University of Chicago Press, 1960), p. 41.
67. Ibid., p. 252–253.

California has the largest population and thus the largest influence on textbook publishers and other spheres of influence. In 1989, under the leadership of Superintendent of Public Instruction Bill Honig, the California Department of Education imposed on all public schools a Science Framework that states evolution to be as sure a scientific fact as gravity or electricity, and therefore to be taken as the basic premise in all courses of instruction — all subjects at all levels. Creation is to be eschewed as strictly a religious belief of an insignificant fundamentalist fringe. This framework requires all textbooks and course syllabi to conform to this premise.

It is bad enough to impose such an exclusivist indoctrination on public schools,but Honig is also trying to extend it to Christian schools, over which state law also gives him jurisdiction. The first object of attack on this front has been the ICR Graduate School, where he has attempted to eliminate its M.S. degree programs in science. The basis of this attempt has been that these are "religious" degrees rather than science, since the coursework is taught in a creationist context. At this writing, the ultimate outcome is uncertain, but ICR plans to go to court, if necessary, to be able to continue teaching science in a creationist framework.

Despite all the difficulties, however, the creationist movement continues to grow. Creationist books are being purchased in record quantities, and creationist meetings are being held in more and more places and with greater interest and larger audiences than ever. All polls indicate that, in spite of unfavorable court rulings and intensive negative media propaganda, the great majority of Americans would like to see scientific creationism back in our public schools[68] — and certainly in Christian schools.

What the immediate future holds in relation to the creation-evolution conflict one cannot say, except to predict that the situation will never revert to the situation existing between the Scopes trial (1925) and the Darwinian Centennial (1959), when there was almost no creationist voice in science or education. There is now a great army of sharp young people who have become convinced creationists in recent years, in spite of evolutionary indoctrination in their classes. They can be expected to continue the fight in days to come, unless Christ returns first.

This brings us finally to consider the ultimate future, as revealed in biblical prophecy. We cannot know when Christ will come back to His creation (though the prophetic signs indicate that His coming is near), but return He

---

68. For example, a nationwide poll by Associated Press and NBC news (October 25–26, 1981) found that 76 percent of the people wanted creation to be taught along with evolution. An additional 10 percent wanted only creation to be taught.

will. As God, He cannot fail in His purposes in creation. Even though the various forms of evolutionism seem now to dominate the world, preparing it for an eventual reign by Satan, God's age-long adversary and pretender to the throne, Satan's apparent victory will be very superficial and brief.

We can read about the eventual outcome in the Book of Revelation, God's infallible record of the future. Though one should not be dogmatic about it, the present world situation could easily merge into the world situation of the end-times, as described in Revelation. There we read of a global government (shades of the globalism now being vigorously promoted by the schools, by international communism, and by the various New Age cults), ruled by a powerful person who will demand worship as the representative "Man," personifying all the achievements of mankind through the ages. As an evolutionary pantheist, he will not honor the God of creation, "he shall magnify himself above all. But in his estate shall he honor the God of forces" (Dan. 11:37–38).

> And he opened his mouth in blasphemy against God, to blas-
> pheme his name, and his tabernacle, and them that dwell in heaven.
> And it was given unto him to make war with the saints, and to over-
> come them: and power was given him over all kindreds and tongues,
> and nations. And all that dwell upon the earth shall worship him,
> whose names are not written in the book of life of the Lamb slain
> from the foundation of the world (Rev.13:6–8).

The condition of the world during the coming reign of this humanistic, totalitarian system will be much like that of the world today. It will be a time of high technology, great scientific insights, and lucrative world commerce: for it is "the time of the end: many shall run to and fro, and knowledge shall be increased" (Dan. 12:4 — and "the merchants of the earth are waxed rich" (Rev. 18:3). There will be worldwide television networks: "And they of the people and kindreds and tongues and nations shall see . . ." certain great events taking place in Jerusalem before their eyes (Rev. 11:9–12).

But it will also be a time of great famines and pestilences (AIDS?) and earthquakes and murders and destructive "beasts" (perhaps poisonous insects, or serpents, or rabid animals, or possibly even drug-crazed men):

> . . . to take peace from the earth, and that they should kill one
> another. . . . And power was given unto them over the fourth part of
> the earth, to kill with sword, and with hunger, and with death, and
> with the beasts of the earth. . . . And, lo, there was a great earthquake.

... and every mountain and island were moved out of their places (Rev. 6:4, 8, 12, 14).

It will furthermore be a time of widespread occult religion and the full flowering of the New Age movement, including the restoration of the worship of ancient gods, along with widespread promiscuous sex, use of drugs, especially in occult rites, and thievery:

> And the rest of the men which were not killed by these plagues yet repented not of the works of their hands, that they should not worship devils, and idols of gold, and silver, and brass, and stone, and of wood ... neither repented they of their murders, nor of their sorceries [incantations using drugs], nor of their fornication, nor of their thefts (Rev. 9:20–21).

The greatest of these idolatries will be to worship the "man of sin . . . the son of perdition: who . . . exalteth himself . . . so that he as God sitteth in the temple of God, shewing himself that he is God" (2 Thess. 2:3–4). This is humanism in its ugliest aspect — that a mere man could claim deity. That such a claim is within the range of human conceit and deceit, however, is obvious when one thinks not only of the ancient Roman emperors but of Hirohito, Lenin, Hitler, Mao Tze-tung, or various other modern "gods." Or even the rock-and-roll idols that many practically worship today (Elvis Presley, John Lennon, and the rest).

The future "god" will be extremely charismatic and successful, as well as expert in the occult sciences: "And his power shall be mighty, but not by his own power. . . . And through his policy also he shall cause craft to prosper in his hand; and he shall magnify himself in his heart, and by peace shall destroy many" (Dan. 8:24–25). "He shall come in peaceably, and obtain the kingdom by flatteries" (Dan. 11:21). This man will soon gain absolute world power, as all the leaders of nations "have one mind, and shall give their power and strength" over to his leadership (Rev. 17:13).

A magnificent statue will be erected in the "god's" honor, to be worshiped by all, under pain of death. Modern technology will enable him and his "minister of religion" (the Bible calls this minister "the false prophet") to convey an image of this dictator into every community and, by complex circuitry and programming, to know who is worshiping him at the proper time. All persons will be required to receive some kind of "mark in their right hand, or in their foreheads," without which "no man might buy or sell" (Rev. 13:16–17). Somehow, perhaps through this mark and an intricate tracking computer network, he will also "cause that as many as would not worship the image of the beast should be killed" (Rev. 13:15).

This idolatry, however, will be more than worship of a powerful man who calls himself God. The man whom God calls "the beast" will not have attained his position or his abilities by his own power. Revelation tells us that the world will recognize that "the dragon gave him his power, and his seat, and great authority. . . . And they worshipped the dragon which gave power unto the beast" (Rev. 13:2–4).

And who is this "dragon" whom the world will be worshiping? This is none other, of course, than "the great dragon . . . that old serpent, called the Devil, and Satan, which deceiveth the whole world" (Rev. 12:9).

Satan has been seeking to be worshiped as God since the beginning of time, and he has employed many devices (all involving some form of evolutionism, as we have seen) to seduce men and women to rebel against the true God of creation and ultimately to worship Satan instead. There have been satanic cults all through history, and Satanism is acquiring a large following today. In this day to come, however, the devil will finally attain his goal, and almost all people on earth will worship him. Evolutionary humanism, occult pantheism, idolatrous demonism, and finally overt Satanism will finally become the one world "religion" for which many have been striving.

But it will not last long. This will be the climactic confrontation of the age-long conflict. This will be the time when the angel flies back and forth across the sky preaching the "everlasting gospel," calling men and women back to worship the true Creator (Rev. 14:6–7). Finally, that Creator will come back in great power, as "KING OF KINGS, AND LORD OF LORDS" (Rev. 19:16), and the beast and his false prophet will be "cast alive into a lake of fire" (v. 20). A mighty angel will then lay "hold on the dragon, that old serpent, which is the Devil, and Satan . . . and cast him into the bottomless pit . . . that he should deceive the nations no more" (Rev. 20:2–3). Eventually he will also be "cast into the lake of fire . . . and shall be tormented day and night for ever and ever" (v. 10). This will end Satan's rebellion, the long war of the ages, and will obliterate every vestige of evolutionism and human skepticism concerning our great Creator God and Savior, Jesus Christ.

This is, of course, only the sketchiest outline of these great future events.[69] The main purpose of this book has been to place the present world and its problems in proper perspective with respect to past history and true causes. As we have seen, evolutionism is the proximate cause of the world's evils, for

---

69. For those wanting to study further along these lines, see the writer's commentary, *The Revelation Record* (Wheaton, IL: Tyndale, 1983), 521 p.

it is the basic belief and deceptive tool of Satan, who is himself the ultimate cause, in his role as the Deceiver.

Nevertheless, Jesus has said: "Be of good cheer; I have overcome the world" (John 16:33). Although today "the whole world lieth in wickedness [or "the wicked one]" (1 John 5:19), Satan's doom is sure, whether or not he believes it. Our responsibility is simply to believe, obey, and proclaim the inerrant, authoritative, and plainly revealed Word of our Creator/Redeemer, the Lord Jesus Christ. "To him that overcometh," Jesus said, "will I grant to sit with me in my throne, even as I also overcame, and am set down with my Father in his throne" (Rev. 3:21).

Henry Morris constructed the index entries for this book drawing on his vast experience and knowledge of the subjects. In the years since the original printing in 1989, due to changes in printing processes some of the content of the book has shifted in regard to applicable page numbers. We hope that the information listed here will still be a valuable help in finding topics of interest.

Subject Index

Name Index

Scripture Index

Other books by Henry Morris

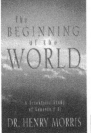

The Beginning of the World
Dr. Henry Morris gives a thorough explanation of the first 11 chapters of Genesis, the most contested chapters in the Bible. He shares his scientific insight and understanding in a format that can also be used for Bible studies.
Science and Faith • 184 pages • Paperback • $10.99
ISBN: 978-0-89051-162-6

The Bible Has the Answer
Dr. Henry M. Morris & Martin E. Clark
How do we know the Bible is true? How will we spend eternity? Here is a complete resource to these and other tough questions facing every individual today.
Apologetics • 394 pages • Paperback • $13.99
ISBN: 978-0-89051-018-6

Biblical Basis for Modern Science
Here is the most detailed analysis of all aspects of creation/evolution in one volume for the layperson. Includes illustrations, charts, tables, and appendixes and contains expositions of 12 major scientific disciplines, with all important Bible passages dealing with each.
Science & Faith • 475 pages • Paperback • $16.99
ISBN: 978-0-89051-369-9

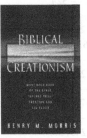

Biblical Creationism
This unique book discusses every passage in the Bible that deals with creation or the Flood. Dr. Morris shows that creation is taught not only in Genesis, but also throughout the whole Bible. Easy to understand and invaluable for all serious Bible students.
Science & Faith • 280 pages • Paperback • $14.99
ISBN: 978-0-89051-293-7

Christian Education for the Real World
Dr. Henry Morris has developed a thoroughly biblical approach to education in the world today, based on over 50 years of experience in teaching and educational administration.
Education • 296 pages • Paperback • $10.99
ISBN: 978-0-89051-160-2

Creation and the Second Coming
In this book, renowned creation scientist and theologian Dr. Henry Morris goes back to the beginning to unveil the details and events of our future. He begins the prophetic countdown at creation and reveals many fresh insights into Scripture.
Theology • 194 pages • Paperback • $10.99
ISBN: 978-0-89051-163-3

Available at Christian bookstores nationwide

Other books by Henry Morris

Days to Remember
This devotional, the final book from a great champion of the faith, gives fascinating background to Judeo-Christian holidays. Learn the purpose and context of Christmas, Easter, and other holidays.
Inspiration / Motivation / Devotional • 224 pages • Paperback • $12.99
ISBN: 978-0-89051-472-6

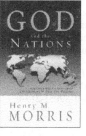

Defending the Faith
Dr. Henry Morris shows Christians the danger in compromising with a philosophy like evolution, so contrary to the love of God. This insightful work offers a fresh look at Satan's age-old war against God and the harmful effects it has had on society.
Apologetics • 224 pages • Paperback • $12.99
ISBN: 978-0-89051-324-8

For Time and Forever
Another classic from the "father of the modern creationism movement," this book explores the fallible, atheistic view of the universe, contrasted with the divine plan God set in motion. • 224 pages • Paperback • $12.99
Christian Living / Practical Life / Science, Faith, Evolution
ISBN: 978-0-89051-427-6

God and the Nations
A very interesting topic: how does God view individual nations, and what is His plan for each nation? Dr. Morris examines the history of nations in light of biblical history, and looks at the future of the nations in biblical prophecy. • 176 pages • Paperback • $10.99
Science & Faith / Prophecy
ISBN: 978-0-89051-389-7

The God Who Is Real
The perfect evangelistic tool, this quick-read helps Christians with some of the philosophical objections seekers have when confronted with the gospel. Morris contrasts other faiths with the true path to serenity, and does so by unabashedly pointing to the God of special creation.
Apologetics • 126 pages • Paperback • $9.99
ISBN: 978-0-89051-299-9

Many Infallible Proofs
Dr. Henry M. Morris & Henry M. Morris III
Widely used as a textbook, many consider this to be the most useful book available on the whole scope of Christian evidences and practical apologetics. *Christianity Today* calls it a "very valuable handbook in defense of biblical inerrancy."
Science & Faith • 400 pages • Paperback • $13.99
ISBN: 978-0-89051-005-6

Available at Christian bookstores nationwide

Other books by Henry Morris

Men of Science, Men of God

The *Baptist Bulletin* says, ". . . Should be required reading for teachers and students." Here are 101 mini-biographies of great Bible-believing scientists of the past, many of whom were the "founding fathers" of modern science.
Education 8-HS • 107 pages • Paperback • $8.99
ISBN: 978-0-89051-080-3

Miracles

Do miracles still occur today as they did in the Bible? Can we believe in miracles? Dr. Henry Morris covers all the bases in a fascinating study of these phenomena, looking at miracles from both a scientific and a scriptural viewpoint.
Apologetics • 128 pages • Paperback • $9.99
ISBN: 978-0-89051-413-9

The Modern Creation Trilogy

Dr. Henry M. Morris & John D. Morris
Produced by father and son, Drs. Henry and John Morris, this is the definitive work on the study of origins from a creationist perspective. This three-volume set looks at the creation/evolution issue from three main aspects: Scripture, science, and society. A masterpiece. • Includes CD-ROM
• Free Study Guide at www.masterbooks.net

Volume 1 - Scripture & Creation • 232 pages
Volume 2 - Science & Creation • 343 pages
Volume 3 - Society & Creation • 208 pages

Science & Faith
Gift-boxed set • Paperback • $34.99
ISBN: 978-0-89051-216-6

The Remarkable Journey of Jonah

Did Jonah really exist? Was he really swallowed by a whale? Contained in this book are some rich insights into the biblical account of Jonah from one of the world's foremost Bible commentators.
Commentary • 144 pages • Paperback • $9.99
ISBN: 978-0-89051-407-8

The Remarkable Record of Job

With its extensive treatment of behemoth and leviathan, the Book of Job is a revelation of God and His creation. Dr. Henry Morris presents it here as an amazing scientific record that provides clues to the great flood of Noah and the dinosaurs.
Commentary • 146 pages • Paperback • $8.99
ISBN: 978-0-89051-292-0

Available at Christian bookstores nationwide

Other books by Henry Morris

The Remarkable Wisdom of Solomon
This verse-by-verse commentary on the books of Proverbs, Ecclesiastes, and Song of Solomon is a must for the library of any pastor or Bible student. Much research and detail about the life of Solomon is also included.
Commentary • 240 pages • Paperback • $12.99
ISBN: 978-0-89051-356-9

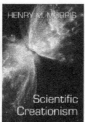

Scientific Creationism
This book is an excellent reference handbook for students and teachers with answers on important creationist viewpoints of history and science, easily understood by readers with non-scientific backgrounds.
Science & Faith • 284 pages • Paperback• $13.99
ISBN: 978-0-89051-003-2

What Is Creation Science?
Dr. Henry M. Morris & Gary Parker
This is the best introduction available to the science of creation. Perfect for pastors, parents, and instructors as well as the science student, great evidence is shown for design in both physical and biological sciences.
Science & Faith • 336 pages • Paperback • $12.99
ISBN: 978-0-89051-081-0

Available at Christian bookstores nationwide

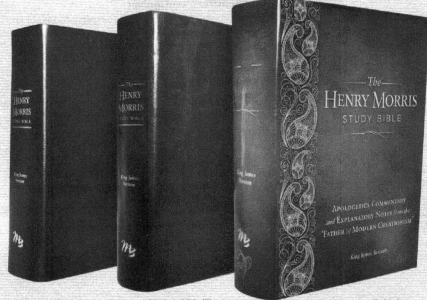